Harry Scherman

The Promises Men Live By

THE
PROMISES
MEN
LIVE BY

A New Approach to Economics

BY HARRY SCHERMAN

RANDOM HOUSE · NEW YORK
1938

PRINTED IN U. S. A. BY H. WOLFF, NEW YORK

To K. and T.

—and to all young people like them who are eager to learn the truth, whatever it may be, about the world they must live in, so that they may not make it worse than it is in trying to make it better—

this book is dedicated.

CONTENTS

INTRODUCTORY:

In Which Some Peculiarities of Economics as a Science Are Considered and the Intention of This Inquiry Is Set Forth

ANYONE who becomes seriously interested in economics ought to bear in mind at all times that he is concerning himself with the activities of about two billion human beings. We are all inclined to conceive, somewhat sketchily, of these multitudinous individuals *en masse*. Yet, of course, every single one of them is as sentient as you and I, and it is fatal, both to observation and reasoning, not to be forever conscious that it is the genuine living actions of all of them that we must study, and not some bloodless patterns of action called economic laws.

Perhaps the most interesting aspect of these activities of men is their diversity. Anyone who will stop long enough, in his own little orbit of busyness, to reflect upon what other men are doing, must marvel —and then be humble—before the strange skills they display. "O, brave new world!" a modern Miranda might exclaim, that has—not such people, but so many occupations, in it. These countless and finely variegated activities of human beings, and the spidery intricacy with which they hang upon one another, is what economics studies. Carlyle once referred to it as "the dismal science," and, ever since, this appellation has been popular. Yet, obviously, its subject matter embraces "the most interesting objects to be met with in life, human beings." There is something a little ironic, then, in the popularity of Carlyle's sour phrase. At any rate, it appears to be a condition that economists themselves might profitably do a little worrying about.

There are a certain few peculiarities of this study which it is helpful to be sharply aware of.

In the first place, it does not deal with bodies and forces, animate or inanimate, which can be seen, handled, measured, and, if necessary, isolated from their environment and taken into the laboratory for leisurely observation. The actions of human beings are incorporeal. Even as we look at them they cease to be, and are succeeded by new ones. Yet it would be the grossest mistake to assume that thereupon these actions become part of a dead past, which may be ignored. They determine the nature of the acts which follow them. Some of these are made necessary, and others are only possible, because of the specific actions which have preceded them. Less perceptibly than this, these past acts *endure*—as Bergson would put it—in the changes they have made, sometimes slight, sometimes profound, in the lives and minds of individuals. Because both the memory and the record of them is preserved, it is far from a passive economic role our past actions play, as we shall see.

Now, this set of facts has more than a speculative philosophic interest. For it largely accounts for a second peculiarity of economics. Since human actions are so short-lived, but still endure in their effects; since what this science attempts to study is our *complete living society*, in which multitudinous millions of actions are interrelated one with another and are then succeeded by new ones, in a ceaseless round of change—it follows that the principal intellectual faculty the study demands is imagination; and it must be of a high order.

This truth has such far-ranging consequences that it seems desirable to demonstrate at once, by a simple illustration, how completely the study must rely upon the imagination of those who pursue it.

Picture, for example, a group of important-looking gentlemen sitting around a mahogany table in the board of directors' room of a Detroit automobile factory. The car they manufacture is in the low-price field. They determine to lower its retail price by $75 a car. The economic consequences of this simple act (their decision) would soon extend in ten thousand directions. Its object, and no doubt its effect, would be to "increase the demand" for the car. But now, what

x

actually do we mean by that phrase? It means that literally tens of thousands of families will proceed to exchange their money for this car, instead of for some other car, or for some other type of goods. Still other persons may be induced to exchange a used car for this new cheap one—an action they might not otherwise have taken. Obviously, this would affect both the quantity and the price of used automobiles on the market; that in turn would influence tens of thousands of other individuals and families to purchases they might not otherwise have made. Now, of course, it is impossible to follow in one's imagination the consequences of these purchases on the lives of the hundreds of thousands of persons who make them. So let us block out this entire aspect of the picture. For, in the meantime, by reason of this "increased demand" for the new car, the plant machinery is certainly pounding as it never has done before. More laboring men must be employed, or the already employed men receive more money. A greatly increased total of money is received by men in wages. With more means at their disposal, the recipients of this money in turn buy from retail merchants a great variety *of other goods* they would not otherwise have obtained—at any rate, not quite so soon. This development radiates other economic consequences (each one slight, but in their totality impressive) to the many hundreds of firms which supply these retail merchants. Of equal, perhaps of even more importance, the automobile plant itself—because of the highly diverse components which go into the structure of its car—must make increased demands upon *its* suppliers—mines, factories and business houses of every variety.* These, in turn, with *their* employees, become involved in activities different from what they would have been, had it not been for the original decision from which we started; and each one of these suppliers has relations with other enterprises and innumerable individuals, who thus likewise become involved.

Is this all? It is hardly more than a beginning. The car's competitors, their wage-earners and suppliers, the workmen of these suppliers, the tradesmen catering to the additional workmen, all become drawn

* The Ford Motor Company, for example, states that there are over 5,000 concerns from which it orders goods used in the making of its products.

into the tangle. All are involved, for good or ill, in these spreading waves of consequence. In the meantime, also, the owners of shares in every automobile company—and in a great many other enterprises—take careful note of these developments. On a score of exchanges, in financial centers over the world, ownership of bonds and shares, measured possibly in tens of millions of dollars—changes hands. All through these developments literally thousands of banks are involved, through the deposit and withdrawal of money, and the extension of loans. Also tens of thousands of men, on ships and trains and lorries and camels and donkeys, move things long distances which they would not otherwise have moved. For not only are the new automobiles probably sold in almost every part of the civilized world, but the raw materials of which they are composed are even more widely international in their origin. Thus, somehow, the most remote individuals, in every conceivable character of occupation—strange, foreign men and women of whose existence the staid gentlemen, who made the portentous original decision, never even dreamed—become drawn, and cannot avoid being drawn, into the world-wide vortex of its consequences.

Now, the economist in studying even such a comparatively simple economic incident as this, must of course take into account all the strictly economic phenomena connected with it, such as those we have mentioned. But how can he "take them into account"? He can utilize none of his senses, nor any mechanical aid to his senses, in appraising them. He must, perforce, *imagine them as they take place*. He can see them only in the mind's eye. If he sets out to collect all the endless detail, to follow every trivial consequence—and yet, theoretically, it might be dangerous for him to count any consequence a trivial one—it would take him a lifetime and then would be but fragmentary. Actually, although with a great deal more minuteness and care, he must in principle do precisely what we have done here. He must rely, finally, upon his imaginative faculty to give him anything that approaches a full economic picture of even such an isolated simple incident as this.

When we consider, instead of something so simple, the sort of complex, inconceivable in its detail, that is involved in such a concept as "the business cycle"—those baffling alternations in the volume and nature of human activities which cover long periods and involve almost the whole two billion members of the race—the necessity of a broad and trained imaginative faculty in this field of study is apparent.

Yet, curiously, this is a quality not popularly associated with the economist, who is supposed to be a dull, pedestrian fellow with his nose always buried in something dry-as-dust. In truth, he must be forever on wings. Sometimes, when he is a person not over-imbued with scientific caution, they may be the butterfly wings of fancy. His imaginings may be so bright, they may fit in so neatly with the perpetual tendency of human nature to blind itself to the disagreeable, that millions may be misled over long periods of time. This happens only because very few men realize how utterly this study relies upon the imagination.

Now, the great dependence of this study upon the imaginative faculty is, almost certainly, the chief source of both the real and the apparent disagreements which exist among economists; and, indeed, it lies at the root of most of the difficulties the study must contend with.

There is one clear result of it, which everybody—I feel—should be conscious of. There have been intellectual giants among economists who have exhibited extraordinary imaginative powers. The task they set themselves was to reduce this vast mass of continuing human action to comprehensibility; to give an account of what order, if any, could be observed and verified in it. No one can read the masters of this science—Smith, Mill, Ricardo, Marx, George, and a host of others of little less stature—without being conscious, if he is at all reflective, of the almost Shakespearean range of the imagination displayed—in a wholly realistic field. But even in the most titanic intellect the imaginative processes, after a time, must flag, must falter, in the presence of such a vast body of ever-changing phenomena, which must both be studied and reported upon as a living and ever-changing whole. The imagination has a fatal weakness in that it tends—for relief, shall we say?—to abstraction and generalization, from which a great part of the acid reality of existence has been pressed, like a squeezed lemon. Almost every statement, historical or theoretical, which one reads upon economic matters is, in fact, a generalization in which are embraced countless real actions of unknown and unknowable human beings, sometimes extending over long periods of time. The obvious danger is that, in dealing with these abstractions, one forgets to keep in mind the multiform realities *of genuine action* which underlie them.

Accordingly, it has been almost inevitable that the material which economists have come to represent in their so-called laws has, very often, not been full-blooded human existence itself. Frequently, one can see, these "laws" do not arise from original observation of human living, but consist rather of reasoning from human motives. Often they outline what appear to be mere *patterns of action*, a sort of desiccated life. There has even appeared in economic literature the concept of an "economic man," who has never had a counterpart in a living being, and never will. This perhaps may provide one explanation for the popularity of Carlyle's damning "dismal science." The average alert-minded person, meeting this study for the first time in classrooms and in books, feels instinctively that its material is, somehow, remote from his real experience. He is uncomfortable with its abstractions. He cannot understand them; and then, finally, in a sort of self-defense—like Carlyle—he becomes contemptuous of them. He counts them dismal because he is finally worn out mentally, trying in some way to identify these cold abstractions with his own warm daily experiences.

In its more modern developments, economists have sought a greater degree of verifiability than personal observation and experience could provide. They try to find it in the recorded events of history, in the annals of business, and during recent decades, in the records of current history—that is, in statistics. But both history and statistics, discerning economists themselves always recognize, *are never anything but records*. They are not the actions of human beings themselves, not the living actuality. Of course, they have their revelations to offer. They are necessary stepping-stones to anything like a comprehensive understanding of this great earth-wide complex that is human society in action. But, notoriously, they are dangerous stepping-stones, which may loosen and plunge the unwary, at any moment, into swampy reasoning. Both history and statistics can necessarily present only a fragmentary picturization of human life. They may be and often are erroneous, in spite of the most honest intention. Since they must be incomplete, they are also open to varying interpretations; and they can always be made to rationalize and even deliberately to lie—both by those who set down the records and by those who interpret them.

We are here, it seems to me, at the very heart of this subject. No one who is impelled to this study, with an honest desire to resolve its seeming complexities, may ever forget this fact; its raw material is genuine human action, even though great masses of men are involved; and in the necessity we are under—to use the imagination to observe whatever order there is in it—we must be forever conscious of the weakness of that mental tool. We must not abstract life from the actuality, and then proceed to reason with the abstractions. We must check up on the reasoning, time and time again, unwearyingly, by reference to real experience. Equally important is it to be aware that economics does not deal, except secondarily, with material things. It deals with living people alone and with things at all, only as they are used by and affect living beings.

In short, those "blind economic forces," which we are so accustomed to hear editors and politicians invoke, are entirely psychological. If we are to identify and understand them, we must seek their ultimate explanation in the nature of human existence itself; in human needs and desires, which are quite as often unconscious as conscious; in inherited instincts, tied in with our very physiology; in traditions that have persisted in some cases a few hundred years and in others that clearly extend beyond recorded history; in strange customs and institutions, widely varying among localities and peoples; in the ambition and ability of exceptional individuals, and in the curiosity and inventiveness of others; in passions and prejudices, the sources of which are often all but unaccountable; in habit which has become ossified; and not the least—and this particularly must be observed—in pure economic error which has become widely prevalent, but which, no less than reason and intelligence, may be at the springs of action.

Looked at as a whole, these ceaseless and ever-changing activities of tens of millions of human beings—what they consist of, why they are what they are, how they fit in with one another, and how, for example, they sometimes result in such deep-going disturbances as the great Depression of the thirties—make up a complex that seems, for all practical purposes, to defy analysis into any sort of order.

So most of us look at the matter. Even confronted as we have been, in the past troublesome years, with the imperious need of a more precise understanding of how human society functions, most of us long ago have all but given up the riddle. The inclination, even of intelligent citizens, has been to retreat into a sort of defeatist bewilderment. The problems that have beset us one after the other in the past quarter-century have indeed been staggering: world-wide war, with all its ramifying disorder; the emergence of a so-called communist state in which the initiation of enterprise by individuals has been all but obliterated among a population covering a sixth of the earth's surface; the rise of dictatorships, parading under mouthy philosophies, in a dozen other states; enormous rises, and then precipitate drops, in the exchange-value of things we own; agricultural populations harassed and industrial millions beggared; our very money changing in value, most of us know not how nor why; the total volume of human activity diminished by a proportion that formerly would have been inconceivable; and many of the peoples of the world as blindly engaged in bitter economic warfare as they were in military warfare two decades ago. This whole record of continuous disturbance has been looked upon by most of us as simply a hopeless tangle of events, which it is vain to try wholly to comprehend. Sometimes it has seemed possible, under good guidance, to trace the clear connection between specific events. But the tracing has seldom gone far. Our tendency has been to ignore this endless trouble—whenever it seems not too immediately disagreeable. As best we can, we endure it.

xvi

Can this bewildering complex of events ever be disentangled into order and comprehension by an ordinary citizen? *Yes, in large part it can be.* Such is the apparently brash position from which this inquiry begins. In large part, I say: not entirely. No doubt there will always be some mystery to remain. However, it need only be the mystery which arises from incomplete information, not that much more perplexing sort which comes from fallacious observation and reasoning.

But the real point I wish to make here is that it requires no extraordinary intelligence, as many persons think, to grasp—*in its principal essentials*—the way in which human society functions. These matters, as I hope to demonstrate in this inquiry, are well within the capacity of anyone with a little will to understand them. What is chiefly necessary—besides that first indispensable will, of course—is to cease being so ready to accept surface appearances for the deeper actualities. This involves, principally, being on guard against the worst kind of confusion, that which arises from the unthinking acceptance of words. We should keep our eyes upon our experiences, and not let the seeing be obscured by what is *said* about them. "We must survey that form of economic organization which has come to prevail in all 'advanced' communities," says one of our own foremost economists, "as if it were a curiosity instead of our familiar environment." * Wisdom as well as Charity begins at home. There is enough raw material in the daily life of every one of us, if we will only look with a seeing eye upon it, to build up a picture of our society in action that may be nearer to the actuality than that which a good many economists acquire, who allow themselves to be blindered by their dialectics.

It may be a little reassuring to modest laymen to identify two factors which, to a considerable degree, are responsible for the bewilderment in which they generally find themselves.

The first is that fine-spun diversity in occupation which is the principal economic characteristic of men in the modern world. The way in which human society functions, in its entirety, has always been regarded by the average person—in good short words—as none of his

* Wesley C. Mitchell, in *Business Cycles: The Problem and Its Setting.*

business. We have all been quite content to leave it to those few who seem quixotic enough to choose it as their business. Each one of us is wholly engrossed in his own little round of activities. We are thus inclined to indulge only in the most occasional speculation as to how we fit into the whole, how our own actions determine those of others, and how the whole world of human actions largely determines our own. Of course, this deep-dyed specialization is hardly conducive to that state of detachment and disinterest in which alone truth may be tracked down. But quite aside from this, it is clear that the very organization of the society we are born into as our environment, and become unthinking units in, has militated against any individual concern, and therefore any general understanding, about economics. The world, after all, does wag on, and until we become aware of the fact that the way in which it is doing its wagging affects our own activities, and *uncomfortably* changes our settled manner of life, the matter is in the realm of the academic; and until recent years, when that awareness has begun to penetrate through the society by a sort of osmosis, we have been content to leave economics to those whom we consider, for all practical purposes, academicians.

The second factor principally responsible for our ignorance grows out of this state of affairs. Our specialized experience rarely gives us information about many other occupations. Now, other pursuits than our own always partake of the deep, dark and mysterious. We attribute special casts of mind and uncommon intellectual capacities to those who perform them. This sheer unfamiliarity with the nature of other important occupations—in particular, with certain key occupations of men, like banking, international commerce and certain aspects of government—and the aura of mystery which surrounds the unfamiliar, have certainly tended to enhance the apparent difficulties of economics. In short, most of us approach the subject under a curious and groundless mental hazard.

But, after all, economics is a special field of knowledge. Is there any particular reason, one may well ask, why all men, or even many men, should be fully informed in it? We cannot in this hard world hope to be omniscient. Why not leave this branch of inquiry, as other branches are left, to the experts? There is no practical need discernible for any wide diffusion of understanding—shall we say?—about Professor Einstein's theories of relativity. No disastrous consequences seem to arise from the almost universal absence of understanding of the simplest aspects of chemistry, physics, astronomy, geology, archaeology, philology, botany, and a hundred other fields of inquiry that might be cited. The rest of us can go about our own pursuits, safe in the confidence that the discovery of truth in these fields will slowly seep into the general body of wisdom the race inherits and will change our lives, if at all, in that slow way. Certainly, the common ignorance that prevails about such sciences seems to have no immediate harmful social consequences.

The reverse is true of economics. It differs indeed, in this respect, from almost every other pursuit of knowledge that one can think of. With the world constituted as it now is, the well-nigh universal ignorance among men as to how their society functions—*since it determines the nature of their actions*—is itself a governing factor, which can be seen operating in a thousand positive ways, in what currently happens to the human race. This universal ignorance has the most direct effect upon the fortunes of every single one of us—upon how we live and what we are compelled to do every day. What we are compelled to do—that is the point!—whether or not we are conscious of the compulsion. What the great masses of men, for example, do *not* know about the processes of trade and even the very nature of trade; what they do *not* know about what they call their money; about banking; about tariffs and the more modern restrictions upon international enterprises; about taxation; about the very institutions— let alone the current policies—of the nations in which they are units; indeed, about almost anything with an economic implication—all this ignorance has a far more profound influence upon the daily welfare of each one of us than what a few men *do* know!

The disasters, which proceed from this ignorance, come first from those who have acquired the position of leadership in our states. Their policies and their acts, when misguided in an economic sense —as we have seen only too unhappily in the past quarter-century—

may engulf literally tens of millions of human beings in the most tragic circumstances. It is a bitter truth that the masses of men have had to pay, through their suffering, for the education of their leaders in economics; in spite of which, too often, no education seems to result.

Nevertheless, these persons, whom we allow to rule us, are only partly to blame. They acquire whatever power they have from our acquiescence. Their ignorance is really but a segment of our own, and rests finally upon our own. No doubt there have been demagogues among them who will never hesitate to make full use of the general ignorance, if it is necessary for the retention of the power they crave to feed their vanity. But rulers of men, honest as well as dishonest, are compelled to deal with the mental states they find in their citizens. Their supremacy rests completely upon those notions which represent so-called "public opinion" among the millions whom they govern. These notions—so far as they relate to economic matters—would almost be dignified by being called befuddled.

I refer here not merely to uneducated and unlettered masses of people. Time and again one comes upon men and women who are highly cultivated in other directions, but in this regard their current turns awry. They feel no shame over an economic illiteracy, such as they would feel over ignorance manifested in any other direction. They seem to have only the haziest idea as to their real relations, as close as blood and tissue, with other individuals and groups. Rarely, if ever, does their economic understanding extend beyond the point where they are aware that they may lose some possession or perquisite they are enjoying; or may fail to gain one they covet. Is there anything else which constitutes the play and interplay of politics?

It must be apparent, indeed, to any person of reflection, that the universal ignorance which prevails about how human society functions is the first and perhaps the most impervious of all the obstacles which stand in the way of orderly human progress.

From the long-range point of view, the program which this state of affairs demands almost seems to map itself out. It is a program of the widest possible economic education. The human race has now acquired a control over Nature which—so we have been told a thousand times in recent years—promises us an Elysian existence, from a material point of view. This vision has too many indications of actuality in it to be considered, in these days, a mirage. The natural sciences have been the tools of knowledge by means of which this development has gone on. It seems now, clearly, to be true that the next broad line of advance the human race will make—indeed, must make—will be in the direction of control of its own organization; that is, in self-understanding. And, manifestly, economics is the principal tool of knowledge by which that eventuality may be attained. But it must—this is equally clear—be a knowledge very widely diffused.

There has been a fashion in late years to decry democracy; to believe that human beings in the millions, for their best good, must be managed something like sheep. This is a myopic philosophy, in my own belief, which seems to issue direct from personal vanity. For it is a fact that those who advance it never fail to show traces of an assumption that they themselves are somehow superior to the common breed. But it seems inconceivable that any form of orderly human society can ever evolve that is not based upon an acquiescence in leadership which proceeds from intelligence, operating in complete freedom, and not from stupidity and submission. As the *sine qua non* of such an orderly society, in time there must prevail among men a comprehension of how this world-wide organism, of which they are cells, really functions.

Not that all men must ultimately think alike, heaven forfend! But this in turn is not to say that *the measure of agreement* as to what constitutes the truth about human society cannot be enormously widened. Popularly it has been regarded as a sort of scandal among economists that they seem to disagree so widely. Actually their differences have, so to speak, been on the frontiers of the subject, where they are an inevitable and healthy manifestation in any growing body of knowledge. This is the way Science has always advanced its conquests over the unknown. The fact remains that there are now clear a few basic certainties about human society which are inestimably important to recognize. Moreover, they are phenomena which economists of even the most divergent schools would agree upon as being indisputable. The trouble is that fighting zealots concentrate upon their differences, and seem wholly unaware of the common ground they must occupy. In the meanwhile, there these basic certainties stand; but they are far—very far—from being common property. Yet they must become so, if there is to be an orderly progress of civilization—that can be consolidated! Otherwise mankind, in such advances as it may make, can have its flanks turned at any time by general ignorance, and rout ensues—such rout as we have seen many times in human history. Certainly we have witnessed one in the past quarter-century, and it is clearly, also, a rout not yet ended.

If any valid criticism may be made at all of the work of economists, it is upon this ground: they have not sufficiently recognized that widespread economic illiteracy itself is perhaps the most obdurate and active of all the so-called economic "forces" which determine what the changing pattern of human affairs is to be. The economist, that is, has failed to realize that his function, in a vital respect, is different from that demanded of almost every other specialized seeker after knowledge. He cannot remain on the Sinai of inquiry all the time. He must come down like Moses and impart currently to the people, so that it becomes as much a part of all lives as his, such verifiable truth as he can be sure of. But the effectual dissemination of truth on a wide scale, as poor Moses found, is quite another matter from its discovery; and perhaps, interestingly, the experience of Moses may be taken as the first recorded demonstration in history of that stubborn and eternal fact. It is on this sector of effort, distinct from that of analysis and research, but of equal practical importance to society, that economists have been most deficient.

This is to say, quite obviously, that the economist must, more than any other scientist, be an educator as well as a seeker after knowledge. And surely, the word does not mean that haphazard system by which anyone impelled to seek our knowledge may have it. The word implies a public, and a wide one. It means, if it means anything, an active, organized, unwearying effort at the dissemination of all economic truth which—at the moment, anyway—seems to be always

xxii

verifiable. It is hard to see what the world of men needs more at the present time.

No reflective person can have any illusion as to the difficulties in the way of this development. To have human affairs determined by rational decisions rather than by the anarchic interplay of ignorance and special interest, seems almost in the realm of fancy. The educational processes, by which this might be brought about, could occupy centuries. But who, looking at the past, can question at least its attainability? A simple parallel will throw some light upon this matter. Economic illiteracy, as we have called it, can be no more stubborn to change than simple illiteracy. The very cement of our present intricate civilization is communication of thought by the written word. Yet only a few hundred years ago—a moment in the history of the race—the ability either to write or to read was an accomplishment of but a tiny fraction of the earth's inhabitants. Were the masses of men then, unable even to read, innately less intelligent than their present descendants? Of course not. It is highly doubtful whether the inherent mental powers of human beings have changed greatly, if at all, over long eons of time. And is the comprehension of the elementary processes of our society a more difficult mental task to cope with than to learn how to read and write and figure?

The real difference, one may reasonably assume, is that a few hundred years ago it became more and more widely recognized that, in order to participate in the material benefits an advancing civilization began to provide, *it was highly advantageous for the individual* to acquire the ability to read, to write, and to number. As this realization spread, the organized efforts of society—in educating the young— were directed to endowing every individual with this accomplishment. We have at last come to count it as the principal test of what we call the "enlightenment" of a nation. Throughout this process there was never any question as to the *educability* of individuals in this direction. It seems apparent that the seed of the development lay in the recognition of the necessity. A recognized necessity is the mother of social invention, as it is of the material variety. Just so, there can be little doubt that the almost universal state of economic illiteracy that prevails today, as simple illiteracy did yesterday, finds its explanation in the fact that the deep-lying need of a more universal understanding of our functioning society, *has not as yet been generally recognized*. In the past twenty-five years, it has begun to be. As that recognition becomes more acute and more general, it is something less than prophecy to foresee the time when our educational efforts will be as intelligently directed to make men and women understand how they keep one another alive, as they are organized now in teaching us the present elementary subjects of education. This surely will be a future measure of the "enlightenment" of a people; and a man or woman who does not understand all that his fellowmen can teach him about how his society functions will be as deeply ashamed, in his own eyes, of such ignorance, as now he ought to be.

The analysis which follows in these pages I myself regard as a mere reconnoiterment in this educational direction. No lone individual, in such an effort, can help but be aware of the limitations in his imaginative capacity; or, if not that, in the accuracy of his observation; or, if not that, in the range of his information; or, if not that, in the caution of his reasoning; and—after everything else—in his skill at exposition. This inquiry, clearly, is a pedagogical venture. That is a great art—it strikes me—that almost requires invention of different method for every separate important subject; and in this particular subject pedagogical invention seems to be still in a primitive stage. It is for these reasons I call this study, necessarily, a mere "approach" to economics.

Obviously there can be other avenues of approach to the subject; and the approach is all-important. The first few steps inevitably determine how far one shall get in understanding. The mere approach may lead one quickly to a bog, in which one wanders, weighted down, forever after. The approaches to this study that now exist, that have long been used, are certainly, in common esteem, dismal ones; and at least they have not allowed many of us to proceed very far forward in a comprehension of the phenomena. In time—when awakened educators jointly have put their minds upon this problem—certainly there will be far better approaches than any we now have, including, of course, the one presented here. Perhaps they may not have to rely so greatly, as we all now do, upon the printed word and will-o'-the-wisp attention to it, for the effectual communication of the portentous truths this study embraces.

I present this particular approach because I myself have found it an easy and an especially absorbing one to travel. It seems like a good old basic Roman road, from which it is actually difficult to stray, and with a broad view open all the time, so that the observer can see where he is going. It is clarifying chiefly, I think, because it *unifies* a very large part of the phenomena to be observed. It does not, however, presume to give any pat answers to the controversies over social programs, about which earnest men and women differ so violently today. These are differences, in my own belief, which proceed more from present incomplete knowledge than from anything else. In this connection, Ambrose Bierce's aphorism is a good one never to forget, that the positive person is usually he who is being "wrong at the top of his voice"; and this may not be a wholly unfair description of a good many so-called economic convictions. Dogmatism has no more place in economics than in any other science; it is the reverse of the scientific temperament, and blocks truth-seeking and understanding here, as it does wherever it is manifested.

But does the study provide any basis for what might be called informed convictions? As I have said above, at present it can disclose at least a few basic certainties about human existence. It is necessary to grasp these, and they cannot be ignored, if any rational conclusions are to be arrived at, to provide a basis for intelligent social action. Unfortunately, at present, these certainties about our society are the intellectual property of the few. The society as a whole can progress nowhere, except into further anarchy, until they are very much more widely shared.

The simple—and the restricted—purpose of the analysis that follows in these pages is to lay bare some of these certainties for the average intelligent person, young or old, who up to now has done little thinking about the matter.

Let us imagine that you were confronted with a badly tangled ball of twine, and that you were determined to unravel it. What would be your procedure? The first thing you would do, as a sensible person, would be to examine the tangle with the greatest care, and see if you could find a loose end. Having found one, patiently you would pull it through knot after knot. The unraveled string would become longer and longer, the knotted center smaller and smaller. Such shall be the method of this analysis. For it is possible—as we shall soon see—to take hold of such a loose end of truth, a simple and incontrovertible fact, in this tangle of human problems which we are all eager to understand better. It is possible to observe it, beautifully and clearly, as it reveals itself, a golden thread, winding its way through the mesh of human relationships. Slowly and carefully we can dissect this bright truth from the great tangle of affairs, and thus in the end a very large part of the apparent disorder and mystification in human events can be dissipated.

The Promises Men Live By

I

We Take Hold of a Loose End of Truth in
the Tangle of Human Affairs

WISDOM, so we have said, begins at home. There can be no better point at which to begin an analysis of human society than by examining perhaps the commonest experience in that enormous complex of activities men and women are daily engaged in the world over. From the time we are a few years old—and can lisp, "Gimme a penny's worth of candy"—almost to the moment we die, there is hardly one of us who does not daily buy or sell something. We begin this experience so young, and we soon come to accept it so entirely as part of our environment, that few of us ever make an analysis of what happens in these transactions. Were we asked what we mean by the words, we should say at once that when we "buy" we *give money* for some thing we wish to own or to enjoy, and when we "sell" we *receive money* for a possession we already own. They thus appear at first glance to be separate actions, entirely different in nature. But of course the most cursory reflection reveals that every purchase is at the same time a sale. Whenever we buy, somebody else sells, and vice versa. They are not two separate actions, but a *single action regarded from a different angle*—like two faces of the same coin. To call any occurrence of this kind, then, either a purchase or a sale is to tell only half the story about it.

This seems almost too elementary to mention, but the sad fact is that many of us have one-way minds. We are unconsciously inclined, not merely to call such transactions either a purchase or a sale, but *to think and reason* about them only from the standpoint from which

3

we personally approach them. Inherent in an astonishingly large amount of discussion over current economic problems is the tendency of one or the other of the disputants (or both) to regard these common and universal transactions with the mental attitude of either a buyer or a seller. Political programs, for example, always reveal this tendency. Less excusable, some intricately reasoned economic philosophies are vitiated at their source by not paying meticulous attention to this elementary mental disposition to a partial view. For example, it is apparent that the none-too-clear notions that are involved in the word "profit" are inextricably associated with every purchase-and-sale transaction. This is no place to analyze what is involved in the notion of profit. Certainly there is far more assumed in the notion, once it is examined, than most people are ever aware of. It is enough here to point out that the very word is tied up in a preoccupation with, a concentration upon, the *seller's* side of the purchase-and-sale transaction; and economic notions galore can be found, seriously advanced and highly respected, where the reasoner clearly is quite unaware of this preoccupation, and where, therefore, he is only partially, and not wholly, assaying these common purchase-and-sale transactions.

For ourselves it seems wise, at this opening of our inquiry, merely to take note of the tendency to this universal failing, so natural a one and so difficult to avoid, and to skirt for the time being the marshes of discussion in which common words like "buy" and "sell" and "profit" and "loss" would soon lead us. It is better, instead, merely to examine one such simple transaction, and see whether there is anything about it *which is not open to dispute or controversy*, from any school of thought.

Assume that you are a slightly grizzled middle-aged gentleman on his way home from work on a late Saturday afternoon. At the corner of your home street, as you pass a bakeshop with which you have had some pleasant experiences in the past, your eye happens to fall upon a large and tempting cake displayed in the window. It occurs to you at once, unselfishly, that it would be a delightful surprise to the rest of the family if you bought that cake and took it

4

home as a crowning end to the evening meal. You go within and ask the price. The white-capped baker tells you one dollar. You hand him a dollar bill, he carefully wraps up and hands you the cake, both of you murmur something like "Thank you," and out you go.

What has happened? At the least, a simple exchange—a swap of a dollar bill for a cake. Or, to be slightly more sociological, what may be called *an exchange in ownership*. A moment before you owned the dollar bill, which means pragmatically you could have done whatever you pleased with it; the baker owned the cake and could have done what he pleased with it. Now the baker owns the dollar bill and you the cake. Observe, also, that the transaction is over and done with. This exchange can fairly be called *a completed exchange*.

Let us assume now a slight change in the circumstances.

At the moment the baker tells you the price of the cake is one dollar, you suddenly recollect something: you had been paid by check that afternoon and have only a few coins in your pocket. "Gracious!" you exclaim, "I have no money with me. I'm sorry"—and you proceed to walk out. "That's all right," says the baker, hurriedly. "You can pay me when you come around this way again. You are certainly good for a dollar and a great deal more." Accordingly, he wraps up and hands you the cake, you thank him with real appreciation for his courtesy, and out you go.

In this case, what has happened? An exchange in ownership, also —that is clear; but plainly, up to the point described, a *one-sided* exchange. A moment before the baker owned the cake; now you own it and within a few hours it will cease to exist. On the other hand, you have not as yet transferred ownership of anything to the baker. With no reflection upon your integrity, it is within the bounds of possibility *that you never will*. You may be stricken with amnesia before you get home, or be killed by a taxicab. All that remains with the baker—is it not true?—is his mere recollection, perhaps enforced for reminder by a scribbled notation somewhere, that you promised to give him one dollar within a day or so. One might say, then, he has exchanged his cake for a promise. But this is hardly an inclusive description of the incident. The whole transaction is better described, it seems, as an exchange of ownership *which has not yet been completed.* One half of it, by mutual understanding, has been *deferred* to an indefinite moment when you again pass by and—if you are not forgetful—hand over a dollar bill to the baker. At that moment the exchange will indeed be closed and completed, like the first one.

This may, therefore, properly be called *a deferred exchange in ownership.*

We have arrived here, thus simply, at the most salient fact about the modern world.

It can be stated as an incontrovertible truth that incompleted, deferred exchanges, of this second type, *make up by far the larger part* of that immense volume of transactions by which the two billion human beings on the planet now manage to keep themselves alive.

More than this: in this simple distinction—between fully completed and temporarily incompleted exchanges—there lies the first key to unlocking a thousand economic mysteries which currently bewilder the average citizen. Unless all the implications of this simple distinction are fully grasped it is impossible to arrive at any satisfactory comprehension, first, of how our so-called advanced civilization has developed into its present forms; and, second, how it *continues* in all its complexity to function.

These are large-scale generalizations, obviously; but it is one of the purposes of this entire study to demonstrate the truth of them. Assuming for the moment they are well-founded, it seems desirable to examine more closely this little transaction of yours with the baker. For, as we shall soon see, it holds another truth quite as basically important as this difference between completed and temporarily incompleted exchanges.

The first obvious thing to be noticed is that when the baker handed you the cake—himself at the moment receiving a mere promise—he did so with no apparent worry. You, also, took the transaction as quite a matter of course. One might say, then, that this "confidence," on both sides, was the principal motivating factor in the transaction.

The word, however, reveals little. Indeed, it is an excellent illustration of what was referred to in our Introduction, of the way in which words that are commonly used obscure rather than reveal the actualities they ought to convey. The incident cries out for a much fuller explanation than the mere word "confidence" carries. How, for example, did the baker happen to be so sure your promised action would be performed? Your certainty on this point might need no explanation. His most assuredly does.

Perhaps he had dealt with you many times before. Possibly, even, at other times you had shown a similar thoughtlessness, had come in without a penny and had unfailingly paid him afterward. At any rate it is certain he had picked up considerable information about you, and was thoroughly satisfied in his mind about two things: first, that it was quite within your means at any time to pay him one dollar; and, second, that you were not the type of person likely to cheat him out of a dollar. Your *beaux yeux* alone would not have inspired him to such a quick and unhesitating offer. Would he have so readily relinquished ownership of the cake had he never seen or heard of you before? The question answers itself.

It will be observed, therefore, that the all-important economic question as to *whether or not the transaction should take place* depended upon the baker's certainty about two matters: first, your available resources; and, second, your probable intention to complete the exchange. That is, it was no mere vague, good-natured, mental predisposition in the baker, called "confidence," but *certainty about your very particular solvency and honesty*, that was responsible for the transaction taking place.

While this seems to be getting nearer the actualities in the incident, we still have but a circumscribed picture of it. The baker's state of mind was, of course, a *sine qua non* of the transaction. But, after all, that state of mind had you as its object. His unquestioning faith that you would carry out this simple economic promise demands a little further examination. We have seen it must have arisen either from previous experience with you, or through information he had acquired about you. His faith in your integrity, which was necessary for the transaction to take place at all, could only have been the result of past demonstrations of your integrity.

In other words, the ultimate core of fact to observe about this entire incident is not so much that the baker had an unhesitating "confidence" in you, but that he had reason to have confidence: *that in fact you always did carry out such promises.*

That this distinction is not mere quibbling, but is indeed like a peephole in a black curtain through which a vast lighted scene may be beheld, appears immediately when its implications are considered. For there is involved here an explanation of the greater part of the transactions that go on in modern life—what we have called deferred exchanges in ownership. It would be a narrow, almost an unmeaning, picture of our society to say that it is the confidence of men in one another's dependability which is responsible for their taking place. For, as we have seen in your own simple incident, analysis reveals a fact of the most profound social significance: *that this faith arises only because men in their dealings with one another actually do carry out by action the greater part of the economic promises they make.* It is the exception for them to fail to do so.

Here is our loose end of indisputable truth, with which to begin to unravel the tangle of human affairs.

Let us be doubly certain what it is, by summarizing, and that we have hold of it firmly.

There are without question two categories of exchanges of ownership which go on among men: those that are completed forthwith, mere swaps, and those where one half is deferred, to be completed after a lapse of time, either short or long. The latter category (as we shall have to demonstrate) constitutes by far the larger part of the economic activities that go on among men and make up the total phenomena, on its economic side, of what we mean by civilization. This second and largest category, of *temporarily incompleted* exchanges of ownership, finds its prime explanation in the fact that men ordinarily can be relied upon to carry out, with scrupulous fi-

8

delity, what they promise to do. There can be no other explanation. For we have seen that deferred exchanges of ownership *would not take place* unless the person on one side who relinquishes his property, or who gives his service, is convinced that the exchange will infallibly be completed. But this conviction arises—not from the mere promise, which is nothing—*but from the past record of performance of the promisor*. It is thus performance—real action—which counts, and not the mere promise of action. This is our simple loose end of truth: *that men can on the whole be relied upon to do what they say they will do.*

This truth will turn out to be revealing in two directions. We shall be able to see, as we unravel it in the mesh of human relationships to be studied, what results proceed when men do fulfill their economic promises, and—equally important—what happens when they do not.

Before proceeding to this fascinating detail, it may be helpful to take note of certain simple but important generalities that have been uncovered by our analysis, even up to this point. This distinction we have made—between immediately completed and deferred exchanges —permits at last a clarifying definition of two words that are more widely used, and perhaps with less insight, than almost any others in the economic dictionary: *debt* and *credit*. The absence, even among the theorists, of a precise understanding of these terms is responsible, in my own opinion, for as much confusion about the nature of modern society as any other single factor.

From our foregoing analysis, it is now clear that *credit constitutes the first half of every deferred exchange*. The creditor is simply he who relinquishes his property in the first half, relying upon the debtor for some benefit in the second half.

Debt is best understood as constituting the second half of every deferred exchange. The debtor, obviously, is he who first benefits in such an exchange. When he completes the promised second half, the

9

creditor benefits, and the deferred exchange becomes a completed one. Both the "debt" and "credit" then cease to exist.*

Thus, the nature of neither "debt" nor "credit" can ever be properly comprehended unless the more basic fact is observed: *that an exchange has actually taken place*, where either debt or credit are being considered, but that a lapse of time intervenes between the first and second half of it. But far more important than this, *a promise intervenes!* Now, all the considerations which govern the giving and acceptance of the promise—and, later on, the performance of it—constitute that detail by which alone the continuous functioning of human society can be properly comprehended. The words "debt" and "credit" have become far too static in their connotation —if, indeed, they have ever been anything else—even to suggest that rich and living detail.

In short, the almost incomprehensible "credit system," by which all-inclusive term our modern economy is so often described, would be more exactly called a "promise system," if we may use a single descriptive term at all. The word "credit" attached to the word "system" is not only unilateral, but even so far as it goes, sadly undescriptive. It concentrates far too much, for comprehension of all the phenomena, upon the relinquishment of property *in the first half* of the exchange. Certainly an equally important portion of the total phenomena is the necessary relinquishment of property in the second half—debt! But perhaps the most important portion of the

* I once asked H. G. Wells how it happened that he could write almost a thousand pages about economics in *Work, Wealth and Happiness of Mankind* —and a highly clarifying book it is, too!—and devote only perhaps a dozen pages of it to credit, and none at all to a discussion of debt. "Ah!" he laughed, "nobody knows anything about debt, and what I wrote concerning credit is about all anybody understands." But if justification is needed for the statement that debt and credit have seldom been properly analyzed in economic theory, it will be found by searching through the textbooks. For all the ages debtor and creditor have worried about debt—their own debt—but seldom the educator, at least effectually; else how could this illuminating identification above—of credit as the first half and debt as the second half of an exchange which has been deferred in completion—have failed to become a commonplace in economic theory? Its supreme usefulness, in unifying most of the phenomena of modern society, will become clear as we later examine the *consequences*, in every economic area, of this deference of the second half of any exchange. The economic theorist will notice that this is really what constitutes that "new approach" to an elucidation of society, which this particular study undertakes.

transaction obscured by this unilateral term, "credit system," is *the necessary psychological background* of the transaction: namely, the reason why these common and universal deferred exchanges come to take place at all! "Debt" always has to be wiped out before new "credit" can come into existence in the same quarter. But, as they are commonly used, these are mere words befogging the actuality. What we really mean, in actual human existence, by such a generalized statement, is that *no half exchange is ever entered into unless it is virtually certain the second half will be completed.* It is not the promise that counts, but action only—justifying the promise. Promises to be believed must be fulfilled! *Past performance*, accordingly, is the ultimate explanation of all the multitudinous deferred exchanges which go on among men; of all the "credit" extended and all the "debt" incurred.

Ultimately, then, *it is economic promises and their performance* which we must study, if we wish to understand the mechanism of our dynamic society, in its modern detail. The best way, it will be found, to disentangle the complexity of that detail into some sort of comprehensible order is to keep our eyes unfailingly upon the fundamental fact: that, *on the whole, human beings can now be relied upon to do what they promise to do.*

This simple fact, then, must be our loose end of truth.

2

Some Basic Psychological Aspects of Labor to
Which Long Habit Has Blinded Men

WITH this simple loose end of truth disentangled, the general direction our inquiry must take is clearly indicated. We must investigate carefully two matters: first, how large a part deferred exchanges of ownership play in the sum total of human activities; and, second, precisely how they play their part.

This will involve, of course, *identifying* the various types of deferred exchanges, a highly revealing business in itself. They assume many forms, and some of them, by reason of their very commonness and universality, *are never recognized by us as deferred exchanges.* One of the principal certain causes of the confusion which prevails about human affairs is the fact that long habit blinds us to certain important types of deferred exchanges.

Since we are totally unaware that promises are involved, we are unable to discern clearly the consequences that arise, both from fulfilling the promises and breaking them.

This sheer failure to observe the existence of certain types of deferred exchanges, with their attendant promises, is particularly true of an experience which today is as universal as buying and selling: namely, working for money.

There are few of us nowadays who have not had this experience, and most of us have it the greater part of our lives. If we were asked to describe the experience for an economic textbook nobody should have any difficulty in doing so. On one side always there is an employer. He may be a single individual; or a great many, as in the case of a corporation; or the comparatively small community, of which we are citizens; or even the entire State, as in Russia. When we "work for" this employer, we mean that by agreement we perform more or less definitely specified tasks which do not *directly* benefit ourselves, and we receive money from the employer for doing so.* This is the almost unvarying nature of the employer-employee relationship.

Universal as this experience is, and hoary with age as one of the basic folkways of the race, there is no area in economics where more disputatious nor more questionable reasoning goes on. This is hardly strange. The liveliest emotions are involved on both sides, and emotions are jungle soil, in economics or in any science. In this compost fallacious ideas can sprout swiftly, flourish luxuriously, and are almost impossible to extirpate from one's reasoning. This rich emotional content of almost all ideas pertaining to labor vitiates many economic philosophies, and it is surely responsible—through leading men into unreasoning political policy—for a great deal of trouble in the modern world. There are many of these emotionally colored notions about labor that can be traced out, as they lead men astray in their economic reasoning. But to present them (like bacteria) with the emotion carefully colored for easy observation, and to show how they influence the actions of men, and therefore the sequence of economic events, would involve a long digression; and would, no doubt, end up by altering nobody's ideas.

Better, at this point, to keep carefully to the narrower program we first mapped out: to try to discover what little there is that is indisputable about human affairs. And there are at least two facts, in this polemic region of labor relations, which can fairly be put in the category of certainty, and which at the same time are entangled with our own particular loose end of truth.

* In ancient times, the material benefit the laborer received from his employment was direct and not indirect, as almost invariably it is today. He was paid in kind, not in money; that is, the product of his labor was *divided between* himself and his employer. This is not an entirely extinct relationship, even in the most advanced industrial nations. It survives, for example, in domestic service and sometimes in farm labor; in both cases the laborer, as a part of the household, may receive smaller money wages because of the food and shelter given.

13

In the first place, the slightest reflection upon the human scene reveals that working for others and receiving money for the labor, whatever our emotional state may be about it and whatever our ideas as to how it might be altered, is a basic relationship to which all of us must now conform. It is an inexorable necessity, arising from that worldwide system of specialization of activity which has come to prevail. For untold millennia the human race has been organizing itself into this refined diversity of occupation; and that evolution has now reached the stage—one need only open one's eyes to see it—where all but a very few of us are under a clear compulsion, merely in order to remain alive, to work for others than ourselves. Such work as each one of us is personally able to do seldom has any direct value in keeping the breath within our bodies. The truth seems to be apparent that only in a comparatively primitive state of society may human beings, singly or in families, enjoy the privilege, if it be one, of "working for" themselves alone—that is, by their personal and unaided efforts provide themselves with the food and shelter they need, and the rough luxuries they hope to enjoy. Rousseau's natural man, therefore, and Thoreau's completely self-reliant one, seem to be nothing but philosophic anachronisms. The best to be said of them is that they no doubt flower from an independence that is one of the most admirable manifestations of the human spirit; but is there not, in the ideas, a clear dream-element of "escape"— from the more unpleasant aspects of current existence—which is not so acute as it might be in either a Latin or a Yankee?

True enough, in little economic pockets, so to speak—as vestiges of past economic conditions from which the main body of human society has long since evolved—there can be found groups of families which still approach this state of complete self-sustainment.* It gave color and character and adventure to pioneer life in the United States, and still exists in areas which we consider economically backward—

* Ralph Borsodi, the author of *Distribution Age*, has worked out an economic philosophy, with some challenging ideas in it, the general purport of which is that human society has gone too far in the direction of specialization of labor; that even in this machine age, we could—and would, if we were wise—all be more or less self-sustaining units.

14

among poor farmers, peasants and primitive peoples in remote sections, who grow what they eat, do little trading, and live in what we now consider poverty. But although these individuals may perhaps still be counted in millions, they are certainly outside the vast and turbulent tides of modern human activity. The clear state of affairs is that we are all obliged to do work for others, to obtain sums of money, with which in turn (by exchange) we may obtain the necessities to keep ourselves alive and the little luxuries to make us somewhat happy. In short, this employer-employee relationship *is now an ineradicable part of modern society*. This is true, obviously, quite as much when the State is the employer in the relationship as when the employer is an individual. It would be true if all the world were Soviet Russias, and equally true, if by some strange development, all States were to withdraw wholly from interference with economic enterprise.

A second truth about this employer-employee relationship is equally indisputable.

It is at the least, clearly and always, *an exchange*—like the swap of your dollar bill for the baker's cake. It is an exchange, not of a material thing for money, but of something incorporeal—labor, manual or mental, for money. There is no gainsaying so much. It is the ineradicable feature of every one of the multitudinous transactions of this type which go on in the modern world. It is true, no matter whether one be employed as a cook in a household, or in a factory "owned" by the 170,000,000 people of Russia.

Possibly, for the reason that what is exchanged is on one side corporeal and on the other incorporeal, few of us realize that the relationship is primarily an exchange. Far less do we observe *that necessarily it is a deferred exchange*, which one of the parties is trusted by the other to complete at a later date. This is so habitually overlooked that it seems desirable to examine with some care one simple such transaction—in order to disclose the underlying phenomena which nobody ever bothers to notice. They are particularly worthy of notice, if only to discover the reasons why these large facts go unnoticed by almost everybody.

15

Imagine yourself, for example, in that humming Detroit automobile plant which we looked at a short way back. You are now, let us assume, a grease-streaked common laborer on the so-called belt, over which endless machines being fabricated are carried past thousands of stationary men, each one of whom does something to it. Your employer in this case is a society of thousands of persons called a corporation, a very interesting modern institution which we shall analyze more closely later on. Recall carefully what happened before you went to work. You first saw one of its representatives (himself, of course, an employee) who had been empowered by this society of persons to make wage agreements in its behalf. You asked him for a job, going through whatever red-tape the corporation required for its records. At the end of this process, he told you that you were hired, he specified what work you were to do, and—what you considered the most important part of the deal—the wages you were to receive. You agreed. And what was the essence of the agreement? Obviously, that in exchange for certain specified work to be done by you, this vast society of unnamed and unknowable persons (it is called in France, interestingly enough, a *société anonyme*) would hand you, at agreed intervals of time, an agreed sum of money.

From the point of view of the economics student, much the most significant element in this agreement—although neither you nor the impassive agent of the corporation gave the slightest attention to the matter—was *when* you were to receive this money. It was to be at the end of each week.

That is, before receiving any money, *you were always to do a week's work!* *

* I develop later in this chapter one particularly significant fact which is commonly overlooked, by reason of the oversight of this simple and self-evident fact about the labor relationship. But its oversight has had other damaging consequences, which at least call for attention here. It set economic theory on a fallacious path for quite a period. Until the time of Henry George, most respected economists held that "wages were paid out of capital." In his usual turgid style Karl Marx had some unsparing comment to make about those who held this "labor-fund theory." (See Pages 667-670, in the Modern Library edition of *Capital*.) The notion at bottom, as Henry George observed, was that "wages are fixed by the ratio between the number of laborers and the amount of capital devoted to the employment of labor." The obvious importance of this idea lay

Accordingly, you go to work. You stand day after day turning a single bolt on the partly finished automobiles as they go by you on the belt. You work all day Monday—and get nothing; all day Tuesday—nothing; all day the succeeding days—nothing; until Saturday. Then you go to the pay-window, and, *mirabile dictu*—though you yourself do not seem surprised by it—you are handed the precise sum of money you expected to receive.

Of course, what has been going on all this time is a simple deferred exchange, like the one analyzed in the preceding chapter. You have been doing nothing *but trusting your employer for one week*. On your part you provided the week's work as you agreed. This was the first half of the exchange. The second—the deferred, half—called for the handing over of money to you by the corporation. On Saturday, as agreed upon, that half was indeed completed. On the following Monday a new deferred exchange is begun. And so on, as long as you are employed.

Every single one of the multitudinous wage and salary relation-

in the fact that if it were true, the amount of the "labor fund" in existence was what determined the amount of employment going on in the society. Time was when pretty nearly everybody held this notion.

Now, in reading the classical economists, it can be seen that the reason for the fallacy, with all its pernicious consequences in political policy and business action, lay clearly in sheer oversight—on the part of economists, business men and politicians—of this simplest fact about the modern world: that the laborer performs his work *before being paid for it*. Since he does so he is creating new forms of wealth by his labor, sometimes indirectly and imperceptibly, but most often directly and observably. Accordingly, as Henry George pointed out, the sum he receives in wages comes to him, in a sense, *in exchange for* the new wealth created by his labor. Whether or not one regards the relation as a mere exchange, it is clear that he creates new wealth by his labor, and that his "wages" constitute the money received in exchange for the new and added values produced. "Wages" are labor's share in the new wealth, and statistical records now show that it constitutes by far the greater share. In any case, the "wages" do not have to be *deducted from* some store of previously accumulated wealth in the society, available for distribution among the laboring population. Accordingly, the total amount of such available "capital" in existence at any one moment *is not what determines* the total amount distributed in wages. It is not, therefore, the principal governing factor—as older economists thought, and some unthinking business men still do—*in determining the amount of labor* that can go on, and does go on, in the society.

What almost certainly is the principal governing factor in this crucial matter (perhaps the most important phenomenon for men to reeognize about their world) will appear clearly, I hope, from the later analysis made in this book.

17

ships that go on among men throughout the world is a simple deferred exchange like this, of labor for money.

Now, what are the basic psychological elements in this type of transaction? Are they the same, or are they in any respect different from those which prevailed in the transaction between you and the baker, analyzed in the preceding chapter? They involve—if you are reflective and not unseeing—a somewhat curious unquestioning faith in that anonymous society of persons, the corporation. In the beginning you accepted the suggested agreement, that you work first and be paid later, without a tinge of misgiving. So, throughout the first week, you contributed your work without thought,-utterly confident the corporation would carry out its promise to complete the exchange. But looked at more critically than you regarded it, how remarkable this faith of yours might be considered!

How could you be so sure the corporation would perform what it promised—through an individual of whose identity its directors were probably totally unaware? Corporations! Notoriously, they have no souls nor morals. The persons who compose them, whose money you were to receive, it was impossible for you to know, and they in turn certainly did not know you. Your work in the meantime is incorporeal. Once done, it is irrecoverable. If it is manual, what does it prove to be, upon analysis, but a change either in the form or location of the material things being worked upon? These material things, usually, are the property of the employer, as in the case of the partly finished automobiles going by you on the belt. Each one, as it left you, became slightly different from what it was a moment before. It had an *added value*, however infinitesimal. It had a new form, the result of your work and nothing else; and you could never recover that particular bit of labor and offer it to someone else for money, nor could you personally get any benefit from it whatsoever. Your employer once and for all received all the benefit there was to be received. And while this was going on, what did you get?

But let us imagine now—as we did with you and the baker—a slight change in the circumstances. Suppose, after contributing these innumerable bits of irrecoverable work to your employer for a full

18

week, that you went to the pay-window and found a sign announcing: "No pay this week; men will be paid next Saturday."

Well! At least you would then be shocked into realizing, if only vaguely, that the relationship between you and your employer is, basically, one of *promise and performance*. There is the immense social fact of which you are so blithely unaware. In seeing such a sign, perhaps you would cease to accept the payment of wages as a phenomenon infallible as the sunrise. During the second week of freely contributed work on your part, what would be your thoughts? They would center darkly upon whether or not the firm was actually going to complete the incompleted exchange. If, at the end of the second week, the same sign appeared again, then indeed your fear, either of the corporation's solvency or its integrity, would become acute. And pretty soon, unless it actually completed *all* the deferred exchanges—that is, paid your past wages in full—such exchanges of labor for money between it and you *would cease to go on*. You would promptly look for another job.

Thus, it is clear that the animating reason—more than that, the *only* reason—why you were willing to enter into such an agreement with your employer, necessarily one-sided, was because you were completely certain both of its ability and of its intention to carry out the promises made to you. Now these, of course, were the precise considerations that were uppermost in the mind of the baker, when he allowed you to walk out of his shop with a cake, upon your mere promise to give him a dollar bill the next time you happened along. The same pattern fits.

Just as in that case, the reason for this state of mind cries out for more explanation. It would explain nothing to say that when you were told you were employed, you accepted this one-sided relationship because that is the customary way labor is paid. Such a statement simply avers that all wage-earners trust their employers in such one-sided agreements, which is what we want to explain. Upon reflection, it would surely appear that this state of complete confidence in which you went to work arose from facts which you had learned, not only about this firm, but about others like it. You first assumed it always *had* faithfully fulfilled such promises to give agreed sums of money for labor performed. Had you heard anything to the contrary in its past record, you would have been—to say the least—worried. You might not even have applied for the job.

Aside from the past, obviously at the moment it was fulfilling such promises, or otherwise the thousands of men you knew to be working in the plant would not be there.

Moreover, at the end of the first week and each succeeding week, as you found each half-exchange infallibly completed by the corporation at the pay-window, *your own personal experience* confirmed your original faith in the reliability of the corporation's promises—at least insofar as they concerned you.

The basic fact, then, about the transaction—without which, it is clear, it would not take place—is that your complete confidence in your employer rested not upon the promise, but *upon actual past performance*. Your employer in actuality had never failed—certainly not within your knowledge—to fulfill its promises, renewed each week, to complete these deferred exchanges of money for labor.

If and when an employer does fail in this respect, neither you nor anyone will do work for him without being paid in advance. In other words, you compel *him* to trust *you*. Of course, among the millions upon tens of millions of these wage and salary transactions that go on among men over the world, occasionally the employer does welch on his deferred half of the exchange. When cases of this kind do occur, they are usually in small irregular enterprises, where the employer is more or less unknown in the community and can move his enterprise quickly, if necessary; and his Lares and Penates, if he has any. A good example would be the adventurous theatrical entrepreneur who in our palmy days would take a troupe of actors on the road, and, usually during an evening when his unsuspecting Thespians were deep in their tragedy, would decamp on a night freight with all the available cash. Cases of this kind, where both the laborer and the enterprise are more or less peripatetic, still occur. But it is perfectly clear that no man, and no group of men, *can remain permanently* in any community and hope to be able to employ laboring men, if they fail to meet their wage and salary agreements. The very first necessity of any economic enterprise, no matter how small —*if it wishes to remain in existence*—is that it must scrupulously and infallibly complete this particular type of economic promise. This would be true, it must be observed, even of an all-powerful employer like the Soviet Government. States can welch on any promise —and they do, as we shall see—but not these. They must never fail to be fulfilled, if they are to be continued.

An obvious characteristic of the wage and salary agreement is that the exchanges of money for labor are continuous, each exchange being completed at a regular interval. There is another common employer-employee relationship, where the work is neither continuous nor is the settlement—the completion of the exchange—made at fixed intervals. They might be called, without in any way disparaging their importance, the odd jobs of the world. The worker is paid for each job as he does it. Almost all so-called professional services are in this category. Instances outside of professional services are equally plentiful. A tailor making a suit for a customer, whether or not he supplies the goods; a barber shaving every Tom, Dick and Harry who presents himself; a carpenter called in for special work—all provide simple examples of a host of like situations. These *irregularly recurring* deferred exchanges of labor for money often call for a greater degree of confidence in one of the parties than most wage and salary agreements. For, very often, the date when the exchange shall be completed by the handing over of money is left undetermined, and as physicians, dentists, tailors and lawyers have reason to know, is often long delayed. Obviously, too, these exchanges involve precisely the same psychological elements as in the more regularized relationship, where the worker receives a wage. Trust of one of the parties in the other, *a trust arising only from known past performance*, is the *sine qua non* of the transaction.

Now, of course, it is the *infallibility of performance* in this great area of human relations that renders all of us blind to the fact that the labor relationship is really a deferred exchange, where a lapse of time and promise and performance are all very much involved. This infallibility also, most certainly, is responsible for another remarkable phenomenon, peculiar to this economic region. Almost all such agreements, all over the world, *are oral,* not written. Only when the element of distrust enters is the agreement recorded in writing. Of course, that mere recording, when it occurs, does not alter the fact that one of the parties trusts the other to fulfill a promise. The recording is nothing but a cautionary memorandum, so that in case of dispute later—in case one of the parties finds it necessary to call in the State to compel completion—the memorandum may help to govern the decision. It has no other value. Almost all wage and salary agreements are by word of mouth. The mere pronunciamento of the employer suffices for both sides. "I will pay you so much a day, a week or a month," he may say. But, in effect, what he says is: "Give me your work for a day, a week, a month, and when you have done so, I will give you in exchange for it so much money. On this mere verbal assurance, informal and unrecorded, you proceed to do your part; and, as we have seen, it is the exceptional event among men for promises of this particular kind not to be fulfilled.

Later we shall acquire, wherever it is possible in this study, an arithmetical measure of the dependability demonstrated by men, in their various economic relations. In the labor relationship this is particularly easy. For whenever a wage is paid, the second half of a deferred exchange is completed, *an economic promise is fulfilled.* None of us may regard the matter in that light, but this common thoughtlessness of course does not alter the fact. Total wages and salaries paid, therefore, must certainly represent *total promises fulfilled* in this particular economic relation.

Now, take the seventeen-year period from 1919 to 1935, inclusive. In this period, the best available computation * estimates that $741,-114,000,000 was received, *in the United States alone,* in wages and salaries. Immense as it is, of course this is only a portion of the total sum received in wages and salaries over the entire world. The individuals who got this money were each interested only in the tiny

* *National Income, 1919–1935,* by Simon Kuznets, Bulletin 66, September, 1937, National Bureau of Economic Research.

driblet of it received, and what this immediately meant to him. There are other economic points of view from which this vast sum may be regarded. But the viewpoint which would reveal most about our society is to look at this, not as an inconceivable sum of money, *but as a vast sum of men's promises merely measured by money.* These promises were all fulfilled!

Now, to get an exact arithmetical measure of men's dependability in this field of action, there would have to be compared with it the total sums which were *not paid* to laborers, after they had done work they were employed to do. No such figures are available. And, fortunately here, none seems necessary. Common experience, most certainly, would confirm the fact that *the failures to fulfill such promises,* if totaled, would perhaps not amount to a thousandth of a per cent of this astronomical total of promises which, as the records show, *were* fulfilled.

In short, the measure of promise-fulfillment here would be so close to pure perfection that the difference, for practical purposes, is indiscernible.

What this signifies, socially, can best be understood when we compare it, as we shall do later, with the records of promise-performance that can be gathered in other fields of human relations.

3

The Role of Promises in Production—Revealing How Almost All Modern Wealth Is Given Away as Soon as Possible after It Is Produced

MEN work, and from their labor there issues a never-ending stream of goods. We are in the midst of that ceaseless activity which economists call Production.

Let us ignore for the moment those goods which men acquire from the earth, in the form of crops and minerals. Consider only fabricated goods. One might picture, in piecemeal imaginings, literally hundreds of thousands of structures dotted here and there over our planet. Some are tiny, others sprawl over square miles. Each one of them is a unit specializing upon a particular variety of commodity. Out of them all there comes forth an endless flow of all those tangible forms of wealth with which we are familiar in the modern world. Here is one, with comparatively slow birth-pangs, bringing forth into the world huge locomotives; and there another producing billions of pins. Here are some that are turning forth endless rolls of cotton cloth, or silk, or other fabrics, that could enwrap the planet itself till it was hidden; and there is another, after years, producing triumphantly a single telescope lens.

All the thousands of finished things, which we so commonly see about us that we never notice them—railroad cars and steel rails, automobiles and gasoline, the pavements on our roads, the brick and cement and paint and metal and glass in our homes, the variegated furnishings in these homes, the common tools we buy, the many kinds of things we wear, the books and periodicals we read, the paper and ink which make them, the ingredients and chemicals of which all these things are composed, the thousands of different machines and tools in the factories themselves—one could go on, in a volume that would become as thick as an encyclopedia, merely to list them.

Try, if you can, to imagine at this moment the source-point of each one of these myriad things, and then realize that while you are reading these lines a steady stream of all these finished commodities is issuing forth out of the factories of the world. The totality is beyond imagination, of course. We can do no more than flickeringly to see bare segments of it, as it goes on. But this is the rich and vibrant reality that the dismal word, Production, describes! It is the consummation in achievement of Man's millions of years upon the planet. It is both the manifestation, and the measure, of the control he has attained over inanimate nature.

What role do deferred exchanges play in this vast field of human activity?

They are wholly responsible for it! It would cease to exist without them.

This so-called mass-production of goods, by machine and human organization, has evolved *only because of the gradual widening among men of the giving and acceptance of economic promises.*

To disclose in what way economic promises play this paramount role in Production, again the simplest personal experience will end up by revealing the most. Let us imagine, therefore, that you are now a mere office boy, in the mill responsible for making the paper in this book. Assume that one of the duties assigned to you is to open the incoming mail and distribute it where it belongs. One of the first things you observed in this job was that the most important category among the pieces of mail the postman hands you are orders. To lose one, or to destroy one, might cost you your job. And what are these sacred pieces of paper? Manifestly, they are nothing but written agreements—that is, recorded, instead of oral promises—which in effect say the following: "Let us have the quality of paper specified here, under the conditions outlined here, and when it is received, we will then send you the sum of money specified here."

What happens to these orders? In the first place, you soon find that immediately they come under the scrutiny of the High Mogul in your factory. He seems, in fact, to be more interested in them than in anything else which goes on upon the premises. Aside from this, however, they go through a prescribed routine, and very soon —just as speedily as possible, indeed—the paper specified goes forth by truck or railroad. Day after day whole carloads of paper go forth in this way. It is shipped out; it is gone. Has anything come in to the firm in place of this valuable property? Not a thing. You open the mail, and you know. Your firm holds nothing but the original bits of paper which came in, the orders—promises!

How astonishing! For, if you transcend your habitual state of unreflectiveness, it appears that upon the strength of these mere promises, your firm *has completely relinquished any claim to ownership* in the thousands of reams of paper which, so short a time before, it owned. Once this is received by the consignees, or even turned over to a carrier which represents them, they have complete say as to what may be done with it. Now, that complete say as to its disposition represents "ownership." In short, *the paper no longer belongs to your firm,* any more than the cake belonged to the baker when he allowed you to step out of his shop without giving him the dollar bill.

Here, of course, is our former acquaintance, the deferred exchange of ownership. By express agreement, which was stated in the order, the exchange of the reams of paper for some money will be completed *later*—the exact date of completion being specified in the order.

You may let your imagination range as wide as it will. Consider yourself the mail-clerk in any kind of organized production enterprise in the world. Precisely this procedure is what you would invariably see. Perhaps ninety-nine one hundredths of your firm's transactions, whatever goods the firm fabricated, would be transactions, like this one, where your employer *voluntarily relinquished*

26

possession of valuable property which it owned, upon the mere promise of the customer *later* to complete the exchange by handing over an agreed sum of money. A few transactions would occur which might appear to be different. Occasionally, accompanying these sacred orders, which as the mail-clerk you open, a bank check would also be in the envelope. This, of course, is payment of the money in advance. But what is it, manifestly, other than a mere reverse in the order of the incompleted exchange? The firm giving the money first has merely divested itself of *its* property, trusting your firm to complete the exchange later by delivering the paper specified in the order.

One can do worse at this point than sit back and reflect at length upon this indisputable set of facts—in a mounting wonder, as the veils of habit drop from before our eyes and the implications of these phenomena unfold. The economists have a word for it: they call it "book credit"—another excellent example of words which, by thoughtless acceptance, utterly blinder us in our observation of life.

Offhand it would seem inconceivable, against all common sense, were we to state baldly that this ceaseless stream of fabricated things, continuously being produced all over the earth, *is given away by those who own it*, as soon as possible after it is produced.

Yet that is what happens in this field of Production. No more precise description of the actuality could be given. When we relinquish ownership of something, and put it into the possession of someone else who may do with it what he pleases, we certainly "give it away." True, under the system that prevails we receive a promise in return for the property of which we divest ourselves. But what is a promise? Is it a thing? Can it be used? Can it be enjoyed in and of itself? Is it a form of wealth? Absurd! In actuality it is only a careless manner of speaking, which means little and hides far too much, to say that we exchange a ship or a locomotive, or an automobile, or our bales of cotton, or any of the other myriad forms of real wealth which circulate in modern commerce—for mere promises. *The promise is a promise to perform a specific action.* It is a promise to complete the half-exchange by giving us some other specified property. In reality, *only when that action is performed*, only when that property is received by us, may we, as clear-eyed realists, say that an exchange has been consummated. In short, a lapse of time is an essential part of the understanding, and during that period, short or long, we ourselves have *dispossessed ourselves* of something of value. We have given it to the other fellow, for his sole delectation or use. We ourselves have nothing to replace it, until the promise is fulfilled. *And the promise may not be fulfilled!*

It is far from quibbling, then; on the contrary, it is the only exact and true vision of what goes on in our society, to say that those who own these inconceivably abundant and variegated forms of tangible wealth, that are being ceaselessly produced the world over, *for the most part give them to others as quickly as they can;* and that they do so in the expectation that they will subsequently be recompensed.

Faith alone can be the explanation of this indisputable set of facts. But faith in that most wanton and selfish of all living creatures, the human being! And, of all things, in that trickiest variety of human being, the business man! We are all born misanthropes enough to say that, as a principle of action, no possible course would seem more inadvisable. Yet here is the truth laid open before us—that such acts of faith are literally numberless among men. This utter and continuous trusting of one another is the ineradicable and ultimate bedrock of the very system by which modern human society manages to produce that vast abundance of goods, of which in late years we have become so conscious. Our new wise young economists seem sometimes dizzy in their pride over this abundance; but they are often a trifle cavalier, for sound reasoning, in their oversight of the basic human relationships which alone make the abundance possible. Perhaps, in spite of its many undeniable blacknesses, the human race is not wholly unregenerate.

For true faith, among men, can be born of nothing but experience. Here again, as in our previous analysis, we strike the same hard core in the set of facts we are considering. Faith proceeds, not from

28

promises, but from performance alone. Old promises must be infallibly carried out before new ones will be believed. And it is particularly interesting, in this large and important area of human action which we term Production, to trace out, clear as they can be, the same elementary psychological factors—it is our loose end of truth becoming longer.

They are the more fascinating because here they manifest themselves in a highly organized form. This complete relinquishment of property by production enterprises—without immediately receiving anything tangible for it—is not arbitrary, and still less irrational. Its social explanation and significance appear at once when we examine more carefully the course which an order takes, when it is received by any enterprise engaged in the production of goods.

Every such enterprise employs as one of its main functionaries a so-called credit man. Sometimes, in small enterprises, he is not a separate individual. The autocrat of the enterprise, the boss, often performs this function, in addition to others. But separated or not from other duties, in the end his is the most vital function in every modern business. For to the credit man first comes every order, and he must subject it to analysis to see whether it should be accepted. Acceptance means fulfilling, and fulfilling means—as we have demonstrated—*relinquishing the firm's property to somebody else, temporarily receiving nothing in exchange.* If the credit man is either careless or incompetent in judgment, he is in a position, literally and actually, to hand out the firm's property as largesse—here, there and everywhere, like a Timon of Athens; until pretty soon the firm has nothing left with which to complete the half-exchanges it has itself entered into with its suppliers and its laboring people; and then, obviously, it must cease all operations.

Nor is this so insane a procedure as to be uncommon. Frequently, in small enterprises where the boss acts as his own credit man and is inexperienced, precisely this unthinking relinquishment of most of the firm's property occurs. The firm then, as it is called, "fails." Fails to do what? Fails to complete the half-exchanges it has itself entered into. It acknowledges publicly that it cannot do so, and leaves it to the State to distribute what is left of its property proportionately among those who relied upon its promises.*

But this injudicious relinquishment of property is far from being ordinary. The reverse is the case. The very function of the credit man is to be supersensitively cautious—that is, he must scrutinize with the utmost care every economic promise his firm accepts. He must be as certain as it is possible in business matters to be, that every such half-exchange will be completed. But how is it possible for him to be certain? What can create in him the mental state we call certainty, which must be precedent to any action on his part in this respect?

Some of the orders are from firms with which his own has dealt for a long period. He need go no further in any such case. *His own experience* not merely suffices, but is of much more importance to him than anything that can be told to him by others. Time and again he has relinquished his own firm's property to these concerns in half-exchanges, and infallibly he has found that this half-exchange was later scrupulously completed by the date agreed upon.

But frequently, another type of order comes to him from firms with which his own has had no previous dealings. He knows noth-

---

* Some interesting things might be revealed if some day psychological research was directed at the psychological reasons for business failures, as distinct from economic ones. My own belief is that the conclusion would be that the causes of failures are more often psychologic than economic in character. The sequence of psychological causes would, in most cases, be as follows: The business man who fails, very often, is even more unanalytic about his own activities than the common run. He has a particularly bad case of this form of business-blindness: the inability to observe that "credit" means nothing but giving away one's property in half-exchanges. He becomes, then, completely unthinking in this economic procedure. He himself, and possibly his father, has always carried on business by means of these half-exchanges; everybody has and everybody does. So in the end habit does its petrifying job. At one moment he gives away so much of his own property in half-exchanges that he finds he cannot complete his own economic promises, if even a small portion of the promises made to him are unfulfilled. These latter turn out not to be fulfilled, and he fails. In short, my notion is that habit forming—bad-habit forming—might be found the principal cause of business failures, and the bad habit involved would be based on inability to observe this simple fact—that what we call "credit" is merely the first half of a deferred exchange, and means nothing but giving away one's property, relying upon a mere promise of recompense.

ing, from his own past experience, about either their integrity or their resources. Clearly, he must become assured that it is safe to involve his firm in this risk. In doing so he turns for reliance upon one of the most fascinating developments of our modern society—when it is looked upon from this angle—the mercantile reporting agency. These are highly organized enterprises which collect and keep up-to-date the record in business of every individual and group of individuals. They do not ignore even the tiniest unit of enterprise.

Precisely how, now, does our credit man make use of the mercantile reporting agency? He looks up the name of the unknown solicitant for his firm's property in an enormous volume, which is usually reprinted once a year. There, indeed, as in Saint Peter's Golden Book, is inscribed the cold record of his good and evil deeds in business. The record appears as a symbol; a "rating" in the form of a letter and a figure—the two together indicating what? Simply the extent to which the firm can be relied upon to complete any half-exchanges it may enter into.

Here, in a highly formal and organized system, is that information *about the past performance* of every unit of enterprise in the business world.

In finding one of these symbols alongside his own customer's name, obviously the information obtained by the credit man is of the most general character. He may want to know more. He will certainly want to know more if an appreciable portion of his own firm's property is to be relinquished. In that case he asks his agency for a "special report." Within a few days he receives a mimeographed statement giving the up-to-the-minute information available. This statement outlines in detail all the data the agency has been able to obtain, bearing upon both the resources and the integrity of the firm. But how does the reporting agency obtain this information? First, by going directly to the firm and asking for it. "Tell us—nay, show us—why you think you are entitled to ask for somebody else's property without immediate recompense," its ubiquitous reporters in effect inquire. "Give us all the figures about your business. Give us the names of firms and persons who have trusted you in the past, so that we may inquire of them how you complete your half-exchanges." Inquire they do; nor are their questions notable for delicacy.

"How much do you allow So-and-So to owe you regularly?"

"What has been your experience with him?"

"Does he carry out his promises infallibly, or is he slow or contentious about them?"

They go to his bank without fail, and ask how much money he ordinarily keeps on deposit, and whether the bank ever lends him money—and how much! They search court records. A "judgment" may have been entered against him—that is, on some occasion the State may have compelled him, against his will, to complete a half-exchange he has entered into. There may have been a justifiable excuse for his unwillingness. He may indeed have been quite right in refusing to complete the exchange. Nevertheless, apparently the judge or jury did not think so, and the mere fact that he had failed in a single case to complete a half-exchange *willingly* looks suspicious. The reporters will want to know all about it. So will the credit man. Thus, all the good that can be told about you in your business, and all the evil, is collected, unsentimentally, in your record.

All this, it will be seen in contemplation, sums up into a simple thing: Not having himself experienced any past demonstrations of your integrity and solvency, the credit man, by every means within the power of a highly organized society, attempts to learn *how you have demonstrated your reliability in these respects in the past with other persons*. It is the record alone that counts. If not the credit man's own record, then that which others have had with you. *Past performance*, not present promise, is the sole criterion that governs. Only if he is certain of the past will the credit man risk entering into a half-exchange with you, which involves the future.

Thus, it can be seen, it is practically impossible in our society for an individual to be wholly dishonest and remain in an established business, just as we saw it was impossible for an employer, for even a short period, to welch on his wage and salary deferred exchanges.

32

The reason for this is that it is practically impossible, in a modern production enterprise, to keep the fact of such dishonesty hidden. The business man may, at his risk, be slow in completing these half-exchanges, but completed they must be. Once he fails to do so in a single case, his deferred exchanges with that firm abruptly end. If he tries the same practice with another firm, they end in that quarter. One of them hales him into court to compel him to complete the exchange. The information about him spreads. Soon or late, but inevitably, it becomes known to anyone, even slightly cautious, with whom he may seek to enter into half-exchanges. And since, as we have seen, modern production enterprise consists almost wholly of these half-exchanges, the only way in which he can acquire the raw materials or the finished goods he needs continuously for his own enterprise, is by paying money in advance. But this is merely saying that he must enter into deferred exchanges in which he trusts other firms, for nobody will trust him. Seldom, if ever, has such a person sufficient money to carry on an enterprise in this way.

Thus, it is somewhat obtuse to say that honesty is the "best" policy in business; *it is the only possible policy* under which modern economic enterprise can be conducted. Dishonesty, it clearly appears, is the suicide of economic enterprise in the modern world.

It will have been seen from this survey, sketchy as it has been, that deferred exchanges in this vast field of human activity, Production, are in every respect similar to those which take place in employment. The psychological factors that both animate the transaction, and explain it, are precisely the same: they arise only *from past demonstrations of reliability on the part of the trusted person*, only from infallible performance.

But there is one slight difference that is clear: that the deferred exchanges here take place under a highly organized system. Instead of being oral and unrecorded, every detail about them is scrupulously set down in writing. The order itself, almost always, is a formal agreement, specifying in full detail all the items of understanding between the parties. The record of the shipment is kept, and of receipt by all parties, down to the final delivery. There is an obvious reason for this formality and caution. Far more often than in the case of labor agreements, the State is called in to compel one of the parties to complete these exchanges of property for money. This proves to be so because the difficulties which may at any moment beset production enterprises are not as predictable as entrepreneurs would like to have them. Accordingly, the losing party in such deferred exchanges must be in a position, if necessary, to prove that the other *did* make the promise. He must prove likewise that he himself actually *did* relinquish his property and that the other in actuality received it. Thus, records of the entire transaction are vital, until the exchange is completed. Even then they are necessary for other purposes.

Incidentally, it may be of sociological interest to note here, that the greater proportion of the activities of judges and lawyers in civilized nations have come to be concerned with controversies over this simple matter: whether or not half-exchanges of property shall be completed.

But no grosser mistake could be made than to conclude, from all this careful preparation for the eventuality of *in*completion, that such compulsion by the State is an ordinary procedure in deferred exchanges of ownership. The truth is that unwilling compulsion is the very rare exception. And it is possible, interestingly enough, to obtain a fairly accurate arithmetical measure of the degree of reliability men manifest, as illustrated in this field of Production.

Every firm keeps a record of its total sales. We have seen that these consist, in the field of Production, almost entirely of deferred exchanges. They also keep a record of what their accountants call "losses from bad debt." These latter, when analyzed, are simply the sums which they *failed* to receive in the latter half of a deferred exchange. A comparison of the two, if obtainable, would provide rough, but illuminating testimony, *as to the degree of reliability* which men display in deferred exchanges of property for money—in this particular field.

34

Now, both of these records, in the United States, are included in the Federal income tax reports every year. For example, let us take the seven years from 1927 to 1933 inclusive. This, rather roughly, covers the period of the last great business cycle, in all its phases of rise and fall. The total sales reported by American corporations in this period was over $623,000,000,000. These were *almost all* half-exchanges. The "losses from bad debt" reported by the same concerns in the same period was about $7,250,000,000. This latter is slightly over 1.1 per cent of the first total. In other words, almost 99 per cent of the promises to complete deferred exchanges represented by these astronomical figures were fulfilled by those who were being trusted.*

But, of course, even this tiny lapse of 1 per cent from pure perfection is not a true picture *of the degree of integrity alone* which men display in their dealings with one another in this field. For most of the "losses from bad debt," included in the above total, represent uncollected sums from firms which had gone bankrupt. But most bankruptcies occur, not as the result of dishonesty, but of mismanagement. In other words, most of the persons who failed to complete the particular deferred exchanges, represented by the total figure of "losses" above, did not do so from deliberation, but simply because they had not the resources to do so. Now, the strain upon available resources of all economic enterprises was particularly heavy during the period covered by the above figures. Over 9,000 banks in the United States failed in this particular period of seven years,† and there were over 176,000 bankruptcies reported,‡ more than in any like period of our history. Obviously these abnormal figures of bank failures and bankruptcies tend unduly to swell the total loss represented by the figures above, even though it is only 1 per cent.

Incidentally, the causes of bankruptcies themselves have been stud-

* *Statistics of Income*, Bureau of Internal Revenue. It must be observed by the reader that these figures are for *all* corporations, not only for production enterprises. The published data are not broken down for the various categories of enterprise.

† *U. S. Statistical Abstract*, 1936, Page 252.

‡ *Ibid.*, Page 249.

ied and analyzed; and fewer than 9 per cent of them appear to have fraud and dishonesty as either their prime or contributory cause.* Accordingly, it is not an unfair conclusion to make that something less than $650,000,000 (9 per cent of $7¼ billions) of the losses above, can fairly be laid to dishonesty. This represents *about one one-thousandth* of the total sales of the corporate enterprises reporting over the seven-year period covered. It is about one dollar lost for each thousand dollars of business done.

* This figure of 9 per cent is taken from a study made by John G. Cover, in *Business and Personal Failure in Chicago,* one of the most thorough of the few analyses that have been made in this field. Professor Cover's analysis of bankruptcies indicated that about one-half of the bankruptcies studied were due to discernible errors in management; about one-quarter of them were due to environmental factors such as competition with nearby enterprises; about one-tenth to family troubles such as illness; and about one-fourteenth to speculation. Fraud and dishonesty are apparently so unimportant that he includes them among "miscellaneous causes," and in 3 per cent of the cases "miscellaneous causes" are put down as the *principal* factor in the failure, and in 6 per cent of the cases as a *contributory* factor. I add them together to make the 9 per cent, and assume that fraud and dishonesty appeared in all of them. This is both a generous and gratuitous assumption, from Professor Cover's own figures, and is done only in order not to be a tiny bit rosy in this respect, and because the percentages for this one cause are not separately broken down in the data published.

Another interesting set of figures, covering this matter of integrity in business, may be found in *Bradstreet's* (weekly), of January 28, 1933. From 1923 to 1932, inclusive, the number of bankruptcies reported was 217,289. Of these, 5,189 were analyzed as being due to fraud and dishonesty. This is less than 2½ per cent, and compares, interestingly enough, with the 3 per cent, which Professor Cover reported, where a "miscellaneous cause" was the principal factor in the failure. There is no indication of how many cases the Bradstreet figures would include, where dishonesty was clearly not the principal, but a contributory factor in the failure. However, it is very interesting to note that of the 217,289 bankruptcies over this period, in only about 4½ per cent of the cases—9,767—does Bradstreet's count the bankrupt as being "culpable"—for dishonesty, or any other reason. In over 95 per cent of the cases, in short, the failures were due, according to Bradstreet, to causes beyond the bankrupt's control; he could be counted culpable only in that he did not have the economic intelligence to foresee them.

4

To Market! To Market! The Only Economic Area
Where Swaps Now Take Place as They Did at
the Dawn of Human Society

THE myriad forms of wealth which men produce are divided by economists into two main categories. One they call consumers' goods. They are those which go out of existence, soon or late, after giving some sort of enjoyment to individuals. The other are called production goods. As the name implies, these latter are not enjoyed in and of themselves. They are those which are utilized, directly or indirectly, in the fabrication of consumers' goods. They are but tools; they are like numberless additional hands, which humankind has created to help tame and train the more or less tractable forces of Nature.

As it streams forth endlessly from the farms and factories of the world, what happens to all this wealth that men produce? By far the greater part, we all know, goes first into the hands of individuals and groups who have no more interest in consuming it than the original producers. It goes to persons whom we variously call traders, jobbers, retailers—or as one broad classification—middlemen.

The function of these distributors, in general, is to locate the particular ultimate consumers who need and want the goods sufficiently to exchange money for them, to transport the goods to them, and then to act, in a sense, as storers of goods—*to hold them* until such time as each ultimate consumer chooses to exchange his money for them. This large field of human activity, which occupies the physical labor, thought, ingenuity, and—it should be observed—wealth, of

37

about two-fifths as many individuals as are engaged in Production is termed by some economists Distribution.*

It is a theater of human activity in which there has been, and no doubt always will be, great "argument about it and about." There are not a few persons, indeed, who regard this economic service as something which should descend upon us like a blessing from on high, and cost nothing. Certainly it is no uncommon notion that this intermediary, between those who originally produce wealth and those who consume it, uses his strategic position, like the robber baron of old at a pass, to "exploit" either the producer or consumer, or both. The middleman has long been regarded, by the unanalytic, as an Old Man of the Sea on the back of primary producers. He is accounted, essentially, an economic parasite who, under hazily imagined "ideal" conditions, would probably be eradicated from our midst. At any rate, there are few primary producers of goods whose economic views are not suffused, to a greater or less degree, with this notion.

It is a notion which frequently gets translated, more or less consciously, into political action. Perhaps the most striking exemplification of this action occurred during the first years of the Russian Revolution. The distributors of goods, the retailer and jobber, came quite as promptly under the economic guillotine in Russia as capitalists who owned "the means of production." It seemed perfectly clear, to rough-and-ready theorists, that the middleman battened on other people's labor. The degree of his exploitation could be precisely measured, in the case of any product, by the difference in money between what the peasant or the manufacturer received and the sums later paid by consumers for the same product. Who got the difference? Obviously, the middlemen—the jobber and the retailer. Thumbs were down on them from the beginning; they had to

* According to the 1930 U. S. Census, 12.5 per cent of our gainful workers were engaged in "trade." To this, perhaps, should be added the 7.9 per cent engaged in "transportation and communication," and the two together then compared with 21.4 per cent engaged in agriculture, .5 per cent in forestry and fishing, 2 per cent in extraction of minerals, and 28.9 in manufacturing and mechanical industries. The balance were engaged in various forms of service, public and private, and in clerical occupations.

38

go. Complete chaos swiftly ensued, as their enterprises were progressively destroyed, until the canny Lenin inaugurated the New Economic Policy, which in reality was the old one. It allowed the former distributors of goods to perform their time-hallowed function. This policy remained in effect until the Russian State was able to improvise *its own equally elaborate system* for the distribution of goods. After which event—without any question, if the figures were obtainable—the full economic cost of distributing the goods to consumers, *which would finally be measured by the cost of supporting the total number of individuals who were engaged in the service,* was probably quite as great, if not greater than before.

Now, what is the reason for this common notion that the economic service of distributing goods should be in a sense, free—or at any rate, very nominal in cost? It is not far to seek. We can all find it in our own mental attitude—there, right on top of the heap of our prejudices. Very quickly its psychological ingredients appear. First, it is clear that the distributor has obtained the goods for less money than we are giving; occasionally, it is a great deal less. At the same time *we remain unconscious* of the service that has been performed in making the goods available to us when we want them, and which we should otherwise have had to perform ourselves. If each one of us did perform this service ourselves—presuming we were able to—it would certainly cost us, in the expenditure of time and in the actual outlay of money, perhaps scores of times more than the extra amount we are so conscious of giving the middleman.

What this amounts to is that we are not so clearly aware as we should be of *what* we are giving our own money for. If we were asked the simple question, we should say at once that we are giving our money to the middleman for the goods we obtain. Not at all. We are paying him for the goods, but we are *also* paying for the labor of transporting them to us, and of holding them at a place where it is convenient for us at any moment to obtain them. Ordinarily, large outlays of money have been made, and often thousands of persons have been working together in organized units, in order to perform this service. But, unfortunately, *there is no indi-*

cation on the goods themselves—nor anywhere else available to us—to inform us accurately as to how much actual money has been spent, how many hundreds of people have been working, and what precisely these unknown persons have been doing, for our own anonymous convenience. The goods remain in every respect the same as when they left the original producer. It is this fact, chiefly, I believe, which leads us unthinkingly into the often mischievous notion that rightly *they should cost the same* as when they left the producer; or, at any rate, very little more.

It is clear enough, in short, that this ineradicable and beautifully organized system of men working together, operating like djinns of the Arabian Nights to meet the instant whim of the humblest citizen of our modern world, has become the victim (so far as appreciation is concerned) of its own infallible efficiency. We become so habituated from childhood *to its complete dependability*, in providing us immediately with what we want, that we finally take it for granted, as part of our natural environment. For all the world, our attitude is that of spoiled little princes. We clap our hands, and at once our minions bring us what we ask for. How it gets there, who must slave *and pay* to get it there for us—what business is that of ours, since we are all now kings? It requires an effort—indeed, it calls for some real hard work of the imagination—to become properly aware of all this labor, and money laid out, on our behalf. This is the simple explanation of the notion that, ideally, the service of distribution should be free, or, at the most, should cost very little. Of course, our statesmen and other intelligent gentry, never, never trip upon this simple fallacy. Never, never? Well, hardly ever.

In general economic terms, the fallacy can be presented in this form: *that produced wealth has the same value when and where it is produced as when and where it is finally exchanged for consumption.* But the absurdity of this, as an account of the facts, is apparent when it is applied to the commonest circumstances of production in the modern world. The truth clearly is that produced goods have very little value at all, *unless they are moved from where they are produced.* If they had to stay there, they would ordinarily be of

40

trifling value. It is their availability, actual or potential, at the place of demand, the market, which alone gives them any exchange value.

What can a farmer, for instance, do with ten thousand bushels of wheat, were it not that a widely organized system, in which thousands of persons unknown to him are involved, stood ready to transport it and then deliver it at the hundred thousand widely separated spots where women are ready to give money for it, not as wheat, but transformed into flour or bread or cake? These thousands of women cannot, if they would, come to him. The wheat has very little exchange-value unless, like Mahomet, it goes to the mountain. The farmer can, of course, feed it to pigs, if he has them. Surely, it might be argued, all the wheat has "value" in this respect. But then what will he do with his pigs, if still another well-organized army of distributors did not stand ready to get them somehow—when they have been transformed into ham and pork and bacon—to the thousands of persons who will exchange money for them? Thus his pigs also are practically valueless, if they remain at the source-point of production. True, he can himself eat them, if most of them did not die before he were well along in the consumption; or if he himself did not pass out, surfeited with the one diet.

But to get to the crux of the matter: it is apparent that the very reason why he produced his wheat or his pigs in such quantity (instead of producing only things which he and his family alone would consume) was because he knew that thousands of other persons than himself were organized into a system, all contributing their labor and quite a few large sums of money, in order to deliver his product to those who wanted it, at the moment and in the form they wanted it. He knows this so well that he takes it for granted as part of his human environment. He bases all his actions upon it. But then he proceeds to forget it in his reasoning. Now, is it not a fair part of the entire truth to say that the distributors of his goods *are as much responsible for their existence as he*? For first, without these distributors, the goods would not have been produced. Second, without the distributors, even if produced, they are ordinarily valueless to the producer himself.

41

The truth is that throughout history it has been largely the distributor of goods, the trader, the widely despised middleman, who has lifted the producer himself, with all the rest of us, out of a primitive and poverty-stricken economy in which each family produced pretty much for itself. It was first he, with his endless adventuring, carrying goods hither and thither over the world, who both spread and cultivated the seeds that have now flowered into this world-wide system of diversified occupation that we call civilization.

From the most ancient times we can see the trader carrying forward this process; hugging the shores closely in his perilous cockleshell boats, on voyages which often stretched remarkably to thousands of miles. Or on land we see him faring boldly into unknown paths, his footsteps finally deepening into caravan routes. We see him killed, as often as not, by those who found this the only way to acquire the precious goods he carried. He it was who first enabled the more stolid home-staying primary producer to grow or fabricate *an excess of goods which could be exchanged*. The most romantic book in the world remains to be written; it will be the History of Peddlers, and how they lifted the human race out of barbarism. For these prehistoric merchants were essentially what we now call peddlers; they were the *mercatores*, whom Caesar casually mentions, saying nothing more about them, save that they gave him all the information he needed about the barbarian tribes. Several thousand years before the Romans marched over the known world, these individual adventurers had penetrated on their own little private business to wherever they could make their way. And what was their business? They were swapping the few goods they could carry. They were middlemen. Obscure and unnamed, no one can read history intelligently without being aware of them as the constant leaven in the economic development of the human race. The modern middleman is the direct economic descendant without break of the prehistoric peddler, the first foreign merchant, who then and since, throughout all history, has done so much to originate and support specialization on the part of producers.

There is the salient point! The distributor always has, and still does, *both originate and support excess production*. Without him it would be, as it originally was, accidental and sporadic. But now, considering this fact, would it not be a fair picture of our modern society to present a caricature of the distributor, the middleman, carrying the primary producer on his back as an Old Man of the Sea? Would it not be as fair as the reverse picture? The full truth, of course, would be no caricature. The relationship, if one must put it in a figure of speech, is like a marriage, and no more certain to be idyllic. A mutual understanding and continuous adjustment is necessary for peace and happiness in the relationship. The distributors constitute more the adventurous masculine element in the relation, the producers the feminine element. It is the latter who bring forth the economic progeny, the goods. They thus *seem* to be wholly responsible for this, and many of them so regard themselves, just as some women curiously count themselves the sole parent of their children. But to say that the distributor, because he has nothing to do with the actual parturition of the goods, so to speak, is an economic parasite upon those who do, is quite comparable (with our society constituted as it now is) to saying that men have nothing to do with the birth of children.

What part does the half-exchange play in Distribution? So far as consumers' goods are concerned, it is the one great field of human activity where deferred exchanges play a slightly lesser role than immediately completed exchanges. It is hardly necessary to cite chapter and verse for this statement. The average person, in buying consumers' goods, more frequently "pays cash" for them than otherwise. That is, he completes the exchange then and there. No promises intervene. Why is this true? Here is the ultimate end of the entire modern economic process. It seems, at the least, curious that men will rely upon one another's honesty so generously in other fields, and balk here. Is there reason for any greater distrust?

The reason why immediately completed exchanges are found abundantly here, but seldom elsewhere in modern economic relations, is due primarily to the conditions under which these particular con-

43

sumer exchanges must take place. An analysis of these conditions quickly throws an additional illumination upon those simple factors which we have found to be essential before any deferred exchange can occur. What we have to examine is perhaps the most basic of modern human institutions, the Market.

The Market is any and every place to which men bring their excess of wealth, to exchange for something they want more. For untold centuries the greater part of the activities of the human race has centered about its markets. The lives of every one of the numberless billions of human beings who have passed through the ages have been largely conditioned by their markets; and that cross-grained sequence of events we call History has been determined principally, without any doubt, by what has gone on in men's marketplaces. Moreover, a very interesting fact emerges upon the briefest examination: the complexity of our modern markets is only an appearance, and skin-deep. The truth is that in all the many thousands of years men have lived by trading with one another, the markets to which they have brought their precious little things, to exchange for other precious little things, have altered but slightly. During the past two or three hundred years, there has indeed been a change in the direction of *increased specialization* of markets. But still, in every city, every village, every tiny aggregation of men on the planet, markets exist which, in no respect that can be considered essential, differ from those in which our earliest ancestors chaffered with one another in bygone ages. The goods themselves now are different. The means by which they are brought to the market are different. The distances from which they come to the market are now far extended. The exchanges, particularly in so-called wholesale markets, are now deferred in their completion, instead of being immediately completed. But the market itself—as a localized center, where exchanges of property can most advantageously take place— has remained practically unchanged throughout the ages. Moreover, all the simpler forms through which markets have progressively evolved *still exist and flourish vigorously*, alongside the more intricate forms of the modern market.

44

Because of the revelations it provides about our modern life, we must trace that evolution—even if briefly. Men live by exchanging, says Adam Smith. This was not always true; and never, at any age, has it been true *of all men*. But as the centuries have passed, it has become ever more and more to be the prevailing condition. Yet even today, enough millions of human beings can be found who depend principally for their existence on the efforts they themselves make to obtain food and shelter. This, in the dimmest past of the race, was of course the way in which all men lived. Nobody can know with exactitude how and when men began *swapping their possessions with one another* as a way of improving their conditions of life. One widely accepted theory is that the formal and organized swapping—which we call trading—originated as an exchange of gifts. Speculation here, obviously, is unavoidable; yet desultory trading, occasional swapping of excess for excess, may have gone on thirty thousand years ago or more, when men owned nothing but the rudest stone implements and, naked savages that they were, lived in caves. For in some of these caves materials have been discovered not indigenous to the locality, but only found far afield. How could they have been obtained? Only through trading, or by forcible seizure, in warfare. Both are equally fair presumptions.

Another speculation is less venturesome: that, after many thousands of years, wherever a nomadic existence became unnecessary for particular groups of men, and they were able to establish themselves *with some degree of permanence* close by one another, soon or late a market must have sprung up. The market would be a convenient meeting-place. It was the spot where members of a clan, a group of related families clustered together for protection, found they could most easily and advantageously meet representatives of another clan. Here they would come, to exchange possessions which they owned and did not need, for other things which they preferred. The habitual meeting-place may have been here at a ford, there at the end of a mountain pass; at a juncture of valleys or a confluence of streams; or merely a pleasant grassy place, with water nigh, where cattle could graze while they were being swapped for something else.

The earliest records of history reveal these natural meeting-places to us as markets, and needless to say they must have existed long millennia before there were any records. For example, tourists today stroll about in the very spot where some of the earliest trading among men certainly went on. It is at Assuan, in Egypt. The old Egyptians at least seven thousand years ago, and no doubt unknown thousands before then, would row up the Nile to the Cataracts. Their boats could go no farther. The blacks from the Soudan would come down to the Cataracts. It was a natural meeting-place. There they traded possessions—and there men trade today! The word "suan," preserved in the modern name, means market.

So likewise a guide today may casually tell you, as you wander open-eyed through the ruins of the Roman Forum, that this nub of the ancient world was first a mere convenient meeting-place. Here, at this spot by the muddy Tiber, the inlanders would come, probably to exchange cattle or grain for salt—obtained nearby at Ostia, by a primitive evaporation process from the blue Mediterranean. Out of this simple meeting-place great Rome and its Empire burgeoned. Incidentally, the physiological necessity for salt—among agriculturists living largely on cereal foods—was certainly one of the impulsions driving men into this practice of swapping possessions. The Via Saleria—salt road—is unquestionably older than Rome itself. It was the prehistoric way (similar to the Indian trails worn down by passing feet for a thousand years, which can still be seen in the Canadian wilds) by which salt was carried inland from the Mediterranean to be swapped for grain, cattle or slaves.*

It is pretty certain that this settlement of people, not too far from an habitual meeting-place, on the whole represented a clustering of families; and the families were not tiny units, such as the family we know, but large and numerous, including remote relatives and in-laws and retainers and slaves. It constituted a clan. The clans traded with one another, and frequently had to move long distances, as distance was then measured, to do so. That is, the first trading *was*

---

* Salt was so commonly exchanged for slaves, says Zimmern in *The Greek Commonwealth,* that a certain kind of cheap slave became known as a "saltling."

46

comparable to our international commerce of today. It did not first arise from division of labor within an organized unit of society. The objects traded in were those which could not be got within the family group, no matter how large it had become. They were not indigenous to its territory, or its members had not yet acquired the skills to produce them. Within each clan-family itself, without doubt, specialization had crudely begun. Some individuals would be more expert than others in making useful things. Whether they remained attached to their larger group, or were more or less free in smaller units, it was obviously far more advantageous for these makers of articles to station themselves permanently at the marketplace. Right on the spot they could then fashion the things which they discovered other men sought eagerly. *So the first handicraftsmen must have tended to center* about the spot which was the habitual meeting-place—the potter, the worker in metals, the weaver of cloth, the maker of footgear, and so forth. This must, indeed, have been the first vital variation from the simplest form of the market. In its first phase, the swappers came to the meeting-place and then left, after having done their swapping. At this next stage, *settlement* begins about the customary meeting-place. An appreciable portion of the exchangers —handicraftsmen—are now permanent fixtures there.

But another necessity, another condition, must coincidentally have been responsible for a second important change. Frequently individuals must have come to the meeting-place with things to exchange, and found nobody there who *at the moment* cared for the things they had to swap. If they were farmers, hunters, herdsmen, fishermen, their very occupations called and kept them afield. They could not remain, like handicraftsmen, in one spot. Very early they must have found it to their advantage, instead of waiting around the marketplace until their excess was gone, to exchange it entirely with one or a few persons who stood ready to perform two economic services for them: first, to *wait* until exchangers appeared in the marketplace who wanted their goods, and second, to assume the risk of there being any exchangers at all. Thus, the middleman developed. In effect, he worked for the primary producer. He assumed, for the pro-

47

ducer, the *time*, the *labor*, and the *risk* which otherwise the producer would have been obliged to contribute himself. Of course, the trader, like the artisan, could stay permanently at the meeting-place, and it was obviously advantageous for him to do so. Here then is the middleman established at the market. The bazaar, as well as the artisan's shop, develops. Cities slowly accrue around the marketplaces, and empires blossom from them.

This striding through long eras on phrases is, of course, the vice of History. The truth is that historical research, in this absorbing field of the early evolutionary stages in the growth of markets, is of the most fragmentary character. It hardly exists, indeed. This sketch is presented, not as a history, whose very life is detail, but more *as a pattern*, in very broad strokes, of what must have happened. It is the logical, if not the chronological development, in the phrase of one careful historian. That it is well-grounded and broadly true appears not only from the fragmentary bits we can garner about markets in the days before recorded history, but from something more definite which we can put our fingers upon. For all of the stages, which have been roughly delineated in this pattern, are equally observable, still flourishing about us today.

Let us ignore nothing because it seems too simple. A good present example of the marketplace in its amoebic form are the frail roadside stands which now dot our every automobile highway. Here is *the original producer* offering to exchange the little excess of goods, fruit, vegetables, honey, jams and whatever he can spare, for something he prefers—money. So, precisely, might a prehistoric family group, at an advantageous defile in a valley, have offered its little excess to adventurers who had to pass by, in exchange for something of value the strangers carried. The only difference is that our ancestors would not so boldly have displayed their excess wares, because trading was certainly not, to them, the second nature it is to us.

Somewhat similar to the roadside stand, but beginning to approach *the grouping of exchangers* at a fixed spot, are the peasant women and children, whom one can see at every Russian railroad station, tempting with their little supply of foodstuffs the travelers who get

48

off to stretch their legs. The Soviet officials control them. They may not step beyond a specified line. But the communists are far too wise in their judgment of mass opinion, much as it contradicts their theories as to the proper way in which goods should be distributed, to try wholly to control the basic human behavior-patterns which bring these primitive peddlers together. These again—observe!—are the original producers, who have come from afield to this odd but natural meeting-place. There they stand, in long uneven rows beside the roadbed, each one holding up hopefully for sale a few cucumbers; a tomato or two; three or four hardboiled eggs; a few pads of cheese on a lettuce leaf; even occasionally a thin cooked chicken. The reflective traveler gasps. Land of the future this may be. But here is the past alive, as it has been for ten thousand years or more!

One of the most unspoiled manifestations of the early form of marketplace, as it has come quite unchanged down through history, can be seen today in picturesque Haiti. The whole land of two million blacks seems intent, most of the time, upon getting to market. Before the faintest streak of day is in the sky, one will see the lines of men, women and children marching in long graceful steps by the side of the roads, or down winding mountain paths. Their arms swing free, their wares are balanced on their heads; foods of every description, handiwork of every character. To market, to market! In the few cities and villages that exist the marketplace consists of a simple structure, about which are scores of squatting groups, with their goods in order about them. Outside the villages, more often than not, *the marketplace has no structure*. It is simply the habitual meeting-place. Bright-eyed with the excitement of exchange, women squat before their little piles of goods. Children run about in high-voiced play. All day long the exchanges go on, in a riot of endless noise and moving color. Then comes night—and all are gone. The meeting-place is silent and deserted. Not a thing now remains to distinguish it from any other place, nothing to show why the meeting is always there, and not elsewhere.

Here, in these daily Haitian scenes, is the organized marketplace, well out of its amoebic stage. It is in the same form as markets must

49

have existed from those earliest times, when aggregations of men settled near one another. The actual producers of foods, or of little articles of handicraft, flock to a central place, exchange their goods for other goods, and then depart for home—to produce a new small excess.

Can this be considered a mere freakish survival of primitive custom in a modern world? Hardly. Under less picturesque conditions the precise counterpart of the Haitian markets—particularly insofar as foods are concerned—will be found at this present moment not merely in lands that are not industrialized, like Haiti, but in the most highly organized centers of population all over the earth.

The truth is that, so far as perishable foods are concerned, it has only been within the last few decades that their collection *for distant distribution* has been organized. Until then, it was the established rule for the original producer of perishable foods himself to bring them to the nearest central meeting-place for direct exchange with the consumers. Or, if he did not do it himself, a special kind of middleman did it for him. Do you remember, for example, the huckster of your childhood, as his bony nag straggled slowly down the alleys? No one could imitate his halloo. One had to be a huckster to acquire it. In parts of the world which are not highly industrialized, this method of personal transportation and distribution of perishable goods is still largely the procedure. It is probably safe to venture that there is not a village or city on the earth—and the most "advanced" may be included, London, New York, Paris, Berlin, Moscow, Peiping, Yokohama—where nearby original producers do not *themselves* still bring their foods for direct exchange with consumers in a marketplace. As Egyptian fellahs did to the first important clustering communities on the Nile; as the Chinese peasants did long millennia before Confucius; as the Sumerian wheatgrowers to Nippur; the Cretan shepherds to Cnossus; the Doric herdsmen to Mycenae; the first Attic wine-growers to the Acropolis; and the Etruscan farmers to that town by the muddy Tiber which became Rome. Man's social behavior-patterns, no doubt, have changed greatly through the ages, but not so noticeably in this respect.

50

Our very towns and cities now are our markets, which cover square miles. The ancient meeting-place merely has proliferated. It has had to be broken up, for convenience—because of the abundance of modern forms of wealth. But let us try to imagine something magical here. Suppose it were possible to ride upon a radio wave, as easily as we do in an airplane, over the earth's surface. Suppose we could be, with practical simultaneity, within seeing distance over every group of habitations upon the planet, from the tiniest village to the greatest sprawling metropolis. We should witness an incredible spectacle of *similarity in movement*. As we went westward, with the break of day at each place, out from the dwellings which spread in every direction, with wisps of smoke rising from them, we should see little figures of men and women begin to emerge. With but few exceptions, on foot or in moving lines of vehicles, we should watch these little figures streaming, for the most part, pretty much toward the center of each aggregation of structures. What are they doing—all these people, in all the villages and cities of the world, converging all alike toward the center of their group of habitations? Like the Haitian women streaming down the mountainsides, *they are simply going to market!* In the center of the city itself, the converging streams from every direction would soon become a maze of movement, like thousands of little insects scurrying over the surface of a pool. Then, as the day wore on, there would be a movement, *again similar all over the planet*. These streams of tiny creatures would move outward as they had moved in, until in the end the cities' centers are deserted.

But, since we are being magical, why should we eliminate the element of time? Suppose we go back through time, and see this process going on. Conceive of this ebb and flow of individuals, to and from the center of every village and city on the planet, *taking place day after day, year after year, century after century!* Imagine, if you can, straggling groups of your ancestors, moving to and from their simple meeting-places—a ford at a river, or a juncture of mountain-pass and plain. If one reflects that all the billions upon billions of men and women who have lived between those distant ancestors and ourselves have gone through this almost daily round—in to their meeting-place, to exchange their excess for excess, and then out again—we should begin, perhaps, to have a faint glimmer of the role which the Market has played in human destiny.

The cord which links us with all the past is still straight and stout and unbroken. Because we do not squat on the earth while we buy and sell, like Haitian peasants, or haggle craftily in a bazaar like Orientals, it is not good for our souls to believe that we have advanced very far from them on some hazy road called Progress. We do precisely what they do, under slightly different conditions. If we think of the so-called business center of every city as its marketplace—as we must—what actually do we see? Hundreds of what we call "stores." For proper comprehension they cannot be looked at individually; they must be considered as an aggregation. Comparable to that Haitian woman sitting before the pile of palmetto hats she has fashioned, is this nobby hat store. To that other woman beside the mounds of sugar cane she has grown, is our grocery store. To that one beside her clucking hens, is our butcher store. To her who displays the simple herbs she has gathered in the fields, our drug store. To this one who has hammered out a few trinkets, the jewelry store. And so on! In what respect do they really differ? They are both marketplaces—that is obvious. But the women come and go, the stores remain; that is one difference. A second is that the producers themselves, both of articles and foods, *are now almost entirely out of our modern markets.*

In short, our modern cities have reached the last stage of that evolution we sketchily traced a moment ago. Our markets now are composed entirely of *specializing distributors.* Even the clustering artisans' shops, which were perhaps the first and have forever been a characteristic feature of the established marketplace, are disappearing. Nonetheless they still persist, not as the little manufacturers which they were in the beginning, but more as "service" occupations. We can still see a cobbler here, a milliner there, a carpenter, a locksmith, or handicraftsman of some kind, playing his ancient primitive role in the marketplace. He is straight in economic descent,

52

without the slightest change in function, from his counterpart seen to be plying his trade in pictures left by Egyptians of the Old Kingdom, about 3000 B.C.!

Now, actually this is a very recent change in our society—*this practically complete conquest of the market by distributors,* and the fine-drawn specialization of distribution which has accompanied it. It has come from two developments: first, the revolutionary advances that have been made within the past half-dozen generations in processes of machine production, which has resulted *in an infinitely wealthier variety of goods* for human beings to enjoy; and second, from the even more recent revolutionary improvements in communication and transport. It is simply stupid for the primary producer today to try to engage personally in the ultimate distribution of his product. For not merely a small nearby marketplace, but the marketplaces of all the earth have been made available to him. Highly trained bodies of men, with marvelous mechanical devices— railroads, ships, trucks and even airplanes—stand ready to carry his goods for him, not to a single nearby marketplace as of old, but to wherever on the earth's surface men may want them; and then other trained and organized bodies of men, each in the numberless local marketplaces that still exist, stand ready to assume the risk of finding the particular consumers who want the goods enough to exchange something valuable for them.

So, by this roundabout route, we return to our mutton. Just as it did of old, *the excess wealth of each producer* still comes to the marketplace; even if the producer himself no longer does. Those actual consumers who want it, step up and exchange money for it. Most of these exchanges are completed then and there. No trust and no promise is involved. You walk off with the goods which belong to the middleman. The middleman at once puts in his till the money that was yours. There is a full *quid pro quo*—no mere *quid,* nor no mere *quo,* as in the deferred exchange. Now, why is this the prevailing rule in the marketplace? Why does less trusting go on here than elsewhere?

Even the swift survey of consumers' goods markets which we have

53

made here supplies the answer. Every half-exchange, as we have seen in the preceding chapters, involves the total relinquishment of property by one of the parties, with nothing to show for it but a promise. But the very conditions under which most marketplace exchanges take place make it impracticable that their completion be deferred to a later date. How, for instance, can a roadside-stand woman, offering her yellow pumpkins for sale, hand them just-so to any motorist who slows up and stops? She has never seen him before, and a hundred-to-one she will never see him again.

Where the exchangers are not only unknown to one another, but in addition are unlikely ever to meet again, obviously any exchange they want to enter into must be immediately completed!

Now this, more or less, is the condition of affairs under which most exchanging in consumers' markets takes place. Markets are thronged. Most of those who are trading do not know one another, or if they do, only in a casual way. Moreover, the transactions are occasional; they may never recur. But, as we have seen, the prime prerequisite of any deferred exchange is *dependability demonstrated by past performance* on the part of the person who is being trusted. Where the transactions do not recur, there is no opportunity for continuous demonstrations of reliability.

This, surely, is the underlying reason why the ancient practice of swapping is still so noticeable in this field of human activity, and not elsewhere. It is not because men have been proved more often unreliable in this field, and that therefore distrust is more justified. It is simply because there is frequently neither chance nor occasion for men to prove themselves reliable. This proof, of course, is the vital consideration in the deferred exchange, *and it can only be by past performance.*

5

Are the Promises of Consumers Dangerous or Beneficial—A Common Fallacy about Instalment Contracts

ALTHOUGH the consumers' market is the only economic area where the old swap now goes on to any appreciable extent, it does not follow that the economic promises that do occur in this field are not of the most vital importance. As we all know, most modern merchants will "extend credit" to consumers; they will—to describe exactly what happens—allow certain favored people to walk off with their property, without immediately giving anything in exchange. Your baker did it with the cake in our first chapter. But observe closely: this only happens *where the trading regularly recurs;* where the trusted party is well known to the merchant who is relinquishing his property.

No comprehensive record exists as to the full extent of this promising on the part of consumers, but several reliable sampling studies have been made. One good one * shows that the total purchases of consumers, in the United States alone, during the eight years from 1929 to 1936, inclusive, were over $268,500,000,000. Of these, a little less than $191,000,000,000 were cash sales. The balance, about $78,-000,000,000, were half-exchanges—consumer promises. Quite a sum of promises, both to make and to complete! Of this $78,000,000,000, $52,000,000,000 consisted of so-called charge accounts. The balance,

* An unpublished study by Scudder, Stevens & Clark, Inc., New York, investment counsellors. A careful analysis principally of statistics published by the U. S. Census Bureau and the Department of Commerce.

55

about $26,000,000,000, consisted of so-called instalment purchases.

Percentages here may be a little revealing.

The total consumer promises constituted 29 per cent of the total consumer purchases in the eight years.

The "charges" constituted just about 20 per cent of the total purchases.

The instalment promises constituted about 9 per cent of the total purchases. The greater part of this 9 per cent consisted of purchases of automobiles on time payments.

When you promised the baker to give him a dollar for his cake—in our first chapter—it may have seemed a rather trivial matter. But here, you see these paltry transactions adding up to over *seventy-eight billion dollars in a few years.*

It need hardly be pointed out that those who owned these seventy-eight billion dollars' worth of goods would not have given them away, for mere promises, if the *past performance* of the persons, like yourself, who received the goods, did not justify such faith.

A great part of this trusting, as we all know, takes place in neighborhood stores. Here, obviously, actual *personal experience* of the shopkeeper with the buyer explains the relinquishment of ownership of the property and acceptance of the promise.

But an ever-increasing portion of these consumer economic promises are now accepted by department stores. This is one of the most interesting modern developments of the consumers' market—the last word in twentieth-century systematization, in this realm of Distribution. Of course, in these thronged modern markets, immediately completed exchanges predominate. Nevertheless, all but a very few department stores seek diligently *to increase their deferred exchanges;* that is, they are highly cordial in inviting "charge accounts." Yet dealing with tens of thousands of individuals, and ordinarily run by corporations, it is impossible for them to acquire the personal knowledge about their customers, which the neighborhood tradesman quickly collects. What happens? Like the credit man, whom we have seen operating in every production enterprise, they go *impersonally* about the business of acquiring the information that

56

is necessary before they can feel safe in relinquishing their valuable property for promises. What is that information? The same old thing: first, the resources and income of the prospective buyer, and second, the complete record of his integrity—how he has proved his honesty in completing deferred exchanges with other persons. If that record is unimpeachable, the department store says in effect: "Here are the riches of all the world to choose from. Come in and take away what you please; you can complete the exchange by giving us your money later."

There is one section of the consumers' market which seems comparatively unimportant. Yet, from a theoretical standpoint, it holds a specially valuable lesson. It consists of those little stores, where the country people are supposed to foregather and sit around on cracker barrels—the "general stores" which constitute the central marketplace of agricultural localities. The farmer receives the greater part of his money after harvest; only then can he exchange his own excess of goods for money. Frequently enough it happens that some time before that happy period of incoming cash, he must go to the general store, or to the hardware store, or lumber dealer, or feedmill—and ask for some needed property in return for a promise. Sometimes its completion is deferred far longer than intended. The crop may fail, or conditions outside the farmer's control may mow down prices as a tornado would a field of corn. The incoming cash depended upon by both the parties fails to materialize. The completion of the transaction then must be deferred another twelvemonth, and probably other economic promises added to them.

Now, the deferrence of these exchanges is clearly imperative. The *current exigency* of one of the parties necessarily throws half of the transaction into the future. There is no element of the philanthropic present. The storekeeper will benefit by the transaction, but *there can be no transaction*—that is evident—unless he is willing to let half of it be completed later. He therefore relinquishes his property in a deferred exchange, but he does so, in a sense, under compulsion. In short, the stream of exchanging here would diminish to a mere trickle, if the exchanges could not be deferred in their completion.

57

The economics student might well play Hamlet here, take out his tablets and set down this seemingly inconsequential point as something never to be forgot. If these exchanges would not—and could not, possibly—occur unless their completion were deferred, here is a positive contribution to the total number of exchanges. Now, this *increase in the total volume of exchanges,* through the mere deferrence of their completion, is of the most momentous import in human affairs. How incalculably important it is, in any sane economic theorizing, will have to be developed more fully, later on, when we come to consider those strange tides in the affairs of men, called Business Cycles.

In somewhat the same category as these half-exchanges carried on in agricultural communities is one of the new economic devices of our era, the "instalment contract" applied to consumers' goods. Here again the *current absence of means* of one of the parties—instead of an abundance of means—throws the second half of the exchange into the future.

The full-fledged appearance of the instalment contract in our civilization may be said to herald the curiously long-delayed discovery that the honesty of the poor man may be relied upon quite as much as that of the man of means; and this discovery may in time mark a definite epoch in economic life. Of course, for a long, long time, certain consumers' goods, like sets of books and pianos, have been sold on instalment payments. After the World War, when certain enterprisers in the United States felt the pressure *to find exchangers for the increased excess created by their mass-production methods,* the instalment plan of exchanging goods for money was applied to an ever-increasing variety of manufactured products. These were principally forms of what might be called "home capital," for they consisted almost entirely of automobiles and household goods. When the depression fell upon us in 1929, there was not wanting a new crop of economists who discovered that instalment-buying was the "cause of it all." It was the poor man pledging his little income in advance. This upset some mysterious "flow" of a mystifying abstraction called "purchasing power." But why the mystery? If we cease being fooled

58

by such abstract terms, and simply observe what plainly occurs and what can be proved to occur, most of the mystery is dissipated; it turns out to be nothing but foggy reasoning.

It is plain, in the first place, that the instalment transaction is a mere deferred exchange, like all the others we have been examining. The buyer gets the goods in the first half of the exchange; the seller gets a promise. But the second half of the exchange, instead of being completed all at one time, is completed in separate small sums at stipulated intervals. Moreover, in most cases, where property of any value is transferred in the first half, he who "relinquishes" his property only does so pragmatically, not legally. The property being used is, by agreement, put up as forfeit, in case the exchange is not fully completed.*

Whether or not these instalment purchases do constitute a new, unhealthful and dangerous economic procedure can best be judged by comparing them carefully with the deferred exchanges that go on endlessly in production enterprises. This comparison quickly shows that all the circumstances, and all the considerations involved, are precisely similar in both cases.

When a laborer buys a new cheap automobile on instalment payments, he gives his mere promise for it. But the same thing happens when the automobile manufacturer *buys the steel* from which the automobile is made. He too gives his mere promise for it—to the steel company. He receives it under a procedure called "book-credit"—a different name for a slightly different economic promise.

Perhaps there is a difference in the fact that the laborer is "pledging his future income" to pay for the automobile. *But does not the automobile manufacturer do the same thing with the steel company?* When he promises to pay for the steel, he also pledges his future incoming cash to the steel company, in order to complete this half-exchange. Moreover, if he does not use his incoming cash to fulfill that exchange, the State will compel him to.

Perhaps there is a difference in the fact that the income of the la-

---

* The proper significance and the consequences of this practice of forfeiture we shall examine carefully in Chapter Seven.

borer is precarious and may end suddenly. He may lose his job. This perhaps makes his half-exchange more dangerous than others. *But the future income of the automobile manufacturer is not one whit less precarious!* His income too may unexpectedly decrease—for many reasons—which we will analyze later. The steel company is taking as much of a risk with him as he is taking with the instalment buyer of his car.

But then perhaps the *available current resources* of the automobile manufacturer makes his half-exchange safer—therefore, more healthful in an economic sense—than the half-exchange of the laborer, who has nothing perhaps but a few household belongings and a small sum in the bank. Not in the least, when one analyzes the matter. If the manufacturer's resources are greater, *so are the economic promises he is obliged to complete!* The laborer certainly has fewer available resources, but then he has only a trivial promise, comparatively speaking, hanging over him.

Another reason sometimes given as to why instalment purchasing is unhealthful, in an economic sense, is that the poor man is thus likely to be led into promises that he cannot complete. Loss thus ensues—to somebody. It certainly does. The *over*-extension of economic promises, on the part of a poor man, is undoubtedly bad. *But is it any less damaging than the over-extension of promises which occurs in production enterprises?* Moreover, is this over-extension of promises *any less likely* to occur in production enterprises? The obvious truth is that unfulfillable economic promises are far more damaging and dangerous when they occur in a business enterprise than in the case of a few scattered individuals; they may affect many other enterprises and thousands of persons, directly and indirectly. The full effect of this sort of thing we shall get some notion about, when we come to examine Business Cycles. But it is clear enough that when the poor man makes a volume of promises he cannot possibly fulfill, after all, the damage is slight because the promise is small.

Perhaps it might be considered that a large automobile manufacturer can be depended upon to *manage his affairs better* than a simple laborer can manage his. But is this really so? The affairs of the manufacturer are extremely complex and difficult to manage; he must take into account matters of which the laborer never dreams. The latter's economic problems in the meantime are of the simplest character. Comparison, so far as success in management is revealed, can be found in the record of *final performance* of the two kinds of promises. We shall demonstrate later in this chapter, by some interesting figures, that the certainty of fulfillment is practically as good in one case as in the other. But this is revealed immediately, just as well, by a new development that has just occurred in this country: namely, that Federal Reserve Banks will now accept, for rediscount, from their member banks, the paper promises made by the laborer —just as it will accept the paper promise of the automobile manufacturer—if his past record shows he is as reliable in his promises as a common laborer has been found to be. This new financial development really signifies only that realization has finally penetrated even into our High Moguls of Finance, that the poor man's economic promises can be relied upon just as much as those of the man of means; indeed, just as much as those of the hugest corporation in the land.

There is a final apparent difference, between these two kinds of half-exchanges, which might be examined. Is it not true that because the laborer has engaged to pay for the automobile in the future, a portion of his labor-income each week must be used in paying for this dead horse, so to speak? This portion is then *diverted from the purchase of other goods*, and by so much the production-volume of society is *later* lessened. This combination of obtuse reasoning and faulty observation is merely another form of the objection to instalment purchases on the ground that they "pledge the poor man's income in advance." For how does the situation differ, in this respect, from what happens with the automobile manufacturer? He too has engaged to pay for the steel in the automobile. If he had not, the incoming money he receives *could later be used to buy other goods* than this steel. If we consider the automobile a dead horse to the laborer, we must consider the steel in it a similar dead horse to the manufacturer. His unfulfilled promise to the steel company, which he must use his incoming money to wipe out, *diverts him from the purchase of additional raw materials or other goods he could use,* just as the unpaid instalments on the automobile diverts the laborer from getting other consumers' goods. *Total* production of wealth is lessened no more in the one case than in the other.

In considering this particular point, we can look at what happens in these instalment transactions from another angle, which curiously enough is seldom taken. In our example the laborer gets the automobile, and gives his mere promise for it. *The automobile has already been produced.* Many laborers and owners of raw materials have already received money from the manufacturer for it, and with that money are buying other goods. Now, the manufacturer (for illustrative purposes, let us assume the transaction is immediate and direct) gives the automobile to the buyer, and momentarily accepts little for it; he will get most of his money later. But suppose the laborer preferred not to give this promise. Suppose he was just an old-fashioned Yankee, blindly opposed to debt of any kind, and particularly to instalment debt. Suppose he collected $50 a month, himself put it in a bureau drawer, and when he finally had collected $600 in this fashion, went to the manufacturer and laid down all this cash for the car. *Would not the money being collected in the bureau drawer also have been diverted from the purchase of other goods?* Thus, the purchase of *other goods* is no more affected—directly—in the one case than in the other. Therefore, the volume of production is no more lessened, directly, in the one case than in the other. The chief effect of the instalment transaction, seen from this angle, is merely to allow the production of the car to take place *twelve months sooner* than it would have occurred otherwise.

We are insensibly getting into a field here which we shall have to examine more exhaustively later—in our chapter on banks—but this point brings up still another close correspondence between these two kinds of deferred exchanges. We said that the manufacturer, when he gives the car to the buyer, gets nothing but the buyer's promise. Nothing but? What happens? He takes that paper-promise to his

62

bank, and gets money for it. Therefore, he really does immediately get money for his car. It comes not from the buyer, *but from the bank*. In this slightly roundabout way, the bank is "financing" the laborer—who usually knows nothing about it. But, now, compare this with what happens to the automobile manufacturer. He may give a note for the steel to the steel company—also a paper promise. The steel company is not in the banking business, any more than the automobile manufacturer. It takes the promise to its bank, *and also gets money for it*. In one case the automobile manufacturer is thus *indirectly* "financed" by a bank, and in the other the consumer is *indirectly* "financed"—perhaps even by the same bank. In both cases *it is the bank's money alone* which enables the transaction to take place *sooner* than it otherwise would.

Thus, examined from every angle, it seems difficult to discover any reason why instalment purchases are any more detrimental and unhealthy than any other deferred exchanges.

Particularly is this so, when one observes the tiny proportion they constitute of the whole multitudinous volume of half-exchanges that go on in our society. They are almost negligible in this vast flood of promises. In the eight years from 1929 to 1936, inclusive, the economic promises of consumers—in these instalment purchases—totaled, in this country, about $26,000,000,000. In Chapter Three we showed that the economic promises, not of all business enterprises but of corporations alone, totaled in the neighborhood of $623,000,-000,000; and this was for a period of seven, not eight years—from 1927 to 1933. Since the deferred exchanges are alike in every respect, in all the considerations involved and in all the consequences, why should this small volume of the poor man's deferred exchanges be considered dangerous to society when all others constitute the normal and healthful procedure? It would be hard to find a rational answer. If one wants to view with alarm these economic promises of poor men, he would, rationally, have to be in a perpetual state of palsied fear over the incalculably greater volume of similar economic promises that go on in all other economic fields. Whether or not there is ground for such fear, and if there is, where the fear might wisely be concentrated—instead of upon this field of instalment purchases—our loose end of truth will later reveal, sharply enough.

In the meantime, this examination can end in one clear conclusion about this modern development of instalment purchasing. *It is simply a new form of deferred exchange.* Testifying to its newness is the fact that little of it goes on outside the United States and Canada. It is *an addition* to the other older forms of half-exchange, some of which—as we shall see—are not nearly so old as we may imagine. For example, "charge accounts"—that other form of so-called consumer-credit, was as occasional and unimportant in men's economic life a *hundred* years ago as instalment-credit was *twenty* years ago. Oh, yes, it existed; but only the wealthy were thus allowed to walk off with valuable property by the giving of economic promises. Our examination of other forms of deferred exchanges will reveal that some of them, too, are not nearly so ancient as we think; for example, the vital half-exchanges involved in deposit-banking itself.

Thus, one of the most illuminating views to take of instalment purchasing is that it *merely represents a new method of increasing the volume of economic promises that go on in our society.* This promising (in the United States, principally) has now finally got around to the poor man, who has become involved in the system, like everybody else. Is this pernicious? It would be if his promises were not fulfilled. But we have seen that, in deferred exchanges, *new* promises are never believed unless *old* ones are fulfilled. Past performance, logically, should play the same role here that it does in every other economic field. Past performance must, under our theory, explain the *very existence* of this immense new volume of economic promises.

Let us examine, then—if it is possible—how reliable individuals are in this field of consumer purchases. How dependable are men and women —not when they are conducting an economic enterprise—but just going about the mundane business of keeping alive, and occasionally happy? While some measures of this reliability have been available

64

in late years, it is a field, curiously, in which little inquiry has been made. Accordingly, the figures are not so abundant as they might be. Nevertheless, they are sufficient to supply a conclusion that cannot be questioned.

For a number of years now the United States Department of Commerce has issued what it calls a Retail Credit Survey. It is one of the best—and most interesting—of our Government's statistical jobs. If you will dig through the one dated 1935, it will appear that the Department made a very careful analysis of the experience of 1,566 retail establishments in 88 cities. The total amount of sales done by these stores was over $1,250,000,000. Stores of every character were included, and among them no fewer than 161 department stores, ranging in sales from $100,000 to well over $20,000,000 each.

Not quite 47 per cent of all the business done by these 1,566 stores in 1935 consisted of simple deferred exchanges—that is, they were sales made on what is called "open credit." An additional 12 per cent of the sales consisted of instalment-payments.* Needless to say, hundreds of thousands of individuals were represented in the figures. No doubt you were among them, if you live in a city and have a "charge account" in a representative store. What was the result?

Those who had promised to pay on "open credit" fulfilled 99⁹⁄₁₀ per cent of their promises!

Those who had promised to pay on instalment fulfilled 98½ per cent of their promises!

A similar striking illustration of the responsibility shown by plain everyday individuals in keeping their economic promises is supplied by the automobile industry. In 1935, it is estimated, 8,391,000 new and used automobiles were sold in the United States. Of these no fewer than 5,103,000 were sold on instalments.† In other words, about five

* This 59 per cent of total credit sales in 1,566 stores would seem to contradict the figures quoted earlier in this chapter, showing a total of only 29 per cent credit sales for all retail stores in the United States over eight years. The difference is undoubtedly due to the fact that among the stores sampled by this Retail Credit Survey there was a greater proportion of the stores which extended credit than there was among all retail establishments, taken together.

† Source, *Time-Sales Financing*, July, 1936; published by National Association of Sales Finance Companies, Chicago.

million people in that single year were entering into this particular type of half-exchange. We all know the nature of it: you complete the half-exchange, or you lose the car. What was the record of these promisors in 1935? They can certainly be considered a sufficient sample of the genus homo, *for they represent one out of every five or six families in the United States.*

The figures for the whole five million are not available. Most automobile dealers, however, discount the notes they receive with special finance companies, which are formed for this very purpose. The records of these finance companies are published. In 1935 they lent money—through the dealers—to 1,333,600 individuals who bought new cars, and to an additional 1,791,900 individuals who bought used cars.

The amount of money they advanced to the buyers of *new* cars was $734,000,000. And *the million and a third persons who promised to pay this astronomical sum paid all but a tiny fraction of 1 per cent of it.* In fact, only 27 out of every thousand persons failed to complete their promises—in full! Moreover, even this handful completed the greater part of their promises. They had promised on the average to pay $551, and they averaged 88 per cent of that amount in each case—before the car was taken from them! The finance companies failed to receive, from those few who did not complete their promises, a little under $2,500,000. *This is one-third of 1 per cent of the $734,000,000 they had advanced!* But was this lost? The companies then owned the cars taken from those who failed to fulfill their promises, and unquestionably recouped a great part of this "loss," already infinitesimal as it stands.

This—be it noted—was the companies' experience with persons who bought *new* cars in 1935. These were, of course, individuals with a higher income rating than those who bought *used* cars. Anybody who bought a second- or third- or fourth-hand car, and paid for it in instalments, was certainly not rolling in wealth. In that year—as stated above—the companies financed the buying of 1,791,900 used automobiles. They lent on these cars a total of about $424,000,000. Out of every 1,000 persons included in the paying of these millions, 893 came

66

through and paid every cent! This is not so good a record, obviously, as that shown by the million and a third persons who bought new cars—but it is a pretty good showing for the persons of small means who were obliged to buy used cars. For again, the 107 out of every thousand persons who failed to complete the contracts did not by any means *wholly* fail. On the contrary, they did remarkably well. These approximately 10 per cent who fell by the wayside, before being put to the necessity of giving up their cars, succeeded in paying 78 per cent of what they had agreed to pay. The total loss to the companies on all the used cars, was about $10,160,000. This was about 2½ per cent of the $424,000,000 which they lent on used cars.*

In short, in one of the lowest income strata of our population, very close to being continuously in straitened circumstances, the measure of the reliability manifested was 97½ per cent! One astute observer has suggested that these figures, as to losses on automobile instalment purchases, may represent the silver lining to the cloud, in that the finance companies only accept good risks from the dealers. The poor risks the dealers must themselves carry. But turn now to the U. S. Retail Credit Survey, which was mentioned above. There you find the Department of Commerce reporting upon the experience of automobile dealers. There are only 109 in the survey, but there is no reason to regard them as not typical. Their losses on instalment sales in 1935 were only four-tenths of 1 per cent!

The fact is that all experience in instalment contracts gives the same ungrudging testimony to the responsibility of the man of small and moderate means in this, his special field of economic promises. The 1935 record of the automobile finance companies was very little different from what it was all through the years of the Depression. There was a per cent or two variation of loss—not more—even in the worst years. When one considers the unprecedented economic pressure to which these millions of unassuming people were exposed during that period—an economic cataclysm occurring, the like of which the world has never seen; their banks closing; their employment ceas-

* These data are also from publications of the National Association of Sales Finance Companies, Chicago.

ing; and all sorts of black and sudden circumstances arising, to throw difficulties in the way of meeting their promises—surely this record of the reliability of little people stands out as a social fact of the most remarkable character.

6

*A Brief Analysis of the Compulsions Behind Economic
Promises, and Why the Promises That Center
Around Rent Are Unique*

How much of this dependability of men, in the keeping of economic promises, can be accounted for by what might be called pure honesty? Men keep their economic promises because they are honest; they keep them, also, for other reasons. Moreover, it is clear that a man can be honest as daylight and may still be highly undependable in his economic promises.

What do we mean by "honesty"? To get anything approaching a meticulous understanding of all that is involved in this word we should have to follow the anthropologists and sociologists deep, deep into the pre-history of the race, and the psychologists even deeper into the dark caverns of the unconscious mind. In this particular inquiry we cannot follow these beckoning scientists, tempting as they are; nor is it necessary.

It is enough here to observe that man is a herd animal. He must adapt himself to the herd of which he is a part. His immediate companions have forever constituted his environment as much as Nature itself. One of the deepest human instincts, then, is to be and remain part of the herd. This shows, positively, in our inborn need for love and approbation. It shows, negatively, in shame, which is the individual's reaction to *disapprobation* by those around him, and also in the fear of being hated, for hate also casts us out from the enfolding warmth of the herd. Speculation from these common emotional states

69

can hardly be far wrong in indicating the origin of honesty in human beings. For what most of us mean by honesty today is merely this unthinking impulse, surely arising from the instinctive need of love and praise, to do what those immediately around us confidently expect us to do.

But this is impulsion, not compulsion. It is not something disagreeable; it is pleasant. The human being *wants* now to be honest—on the whole. There is a genuine sense of accomplishment in completing promises. "See!" he can shout to all the world, "I have done exactly what I promised you and you and you that I would do!" Pride—a pride felt to be deserved—is a definite ingredient in the consciousness of every man when he completes the second half of a deferred exchange, no matter how small it is. Is this not really what we have in mind when we say that we hate debt? The *unfulfilled* promise haunts us. We cannot abide having somebody else expect us to do something we have engaged to do, and not do it. We would feel shame before others in not doing so; that potential shame then makes our conscience wince. This clear impulse to a specific action, of which we are conscious enough—no matter what its origin may have been in racial history and no matter what unconscious considerations it may even now ultimately spring from—is what we ordinarily mean by the word "honesty." At any rate, it is the sense in which the word is used in this book.

Honesty, so defined, I myself consider to be the *principal factor* in that almost invariable dependability which (our thesis runs) is the basic explanation of modern economic processes. But no doubt there will be readers who will regard other factors as more responsible than plain honesty for that almost universal dependability. The truth is there is hardly any way of reliably judging how great a part *in the whole society* any factor plays in this human dependability. It is at least valuable, however, to identify the chief compulsions that do exist, *in order to see how they affect the various kinds of half-exchanges that go on*. For it soon appears they do affect the details of various exchanges differently.

Honesty might be called the social compulsion. Alongside of it,

70

one can identify an *economic compulsion*. Cold and calculating self-interest, with not a trace of responsibility to others, often makes men complete half-exchanges. We shall show later that this is particularly true of corporations. In our chapters on Labor and Production, also, it was demonstrated how the deliberate failure to fulfill economic promises was followed by swift economic punishment, and was tantamount to business suicide in the modern world. To say "it pays to be honest" is wrong emphasis. The clearer view is that it is highly dangerous, economically, to be *dis*honest.

A third compulsion is neither social nor economic; it consists of outside force; it is that compulsion which proceeds from the State. Now, the truth is that, comparatively, very seldom is this compulsion brought into play. There, however, it stands, a potentiality to be resorted to. I think, however, that this anticipated compulsion by the State plays a far more important role *in the making of deferred exchanges* than in bringing about the completion of them. Our later analyses will demonstrate this. That is, a confident reliance upon compulsion by the State *induces the seller* to relinquish his property in the first half of the exchange, much more often than fear of compulsion by the State drives the promisor to complete the exchange. Nevertheless, fear of this compulsion is sometimes very much present as a factor in completion, as we shall see.

It is a valuable thing for those who theorize hastily about modern life to know that time was when the State did not interfere at all in these vital half-exchanges of men. Time was when this compulsion by the State was wholly absent. As Sumner and Keller observe in *Science and Society*, there is weighty opinion among sociologists that the first State really to exist in the world of men was the Roman State. For long thousands of years before then, and in the early stages of the State itself, the records show that the grouped power, which we call the State, kept hands off in the matter of these half-exchanges.* The relationship was one of individuals, and it was a

* An article on *Contract*, by Roscoe Pound, in the *Encyclopedia of the Social Sciences*, gives a succinct but revealing survey of this early point of view among men with regard to the completion of half-exchanges.

matter then for individuals to settle between themselves, as best they could.

How could they settle it, without that final recourse to a super-power, which we have today? As an economic practice among men, deferred exchanges may well be scores of thousands of years old. Yet we may be sure of one thing, that in the dimmest past of the race the same consideration implacably governed each transaction as it does now: namely, that the man who relinquished his property in the first half of the exchange made himself as nearly certain as possible *that the second half would be completed.* But how—without ultimate reliance upon the grouped force of his community—could any man be finally sure of this? Unquestionably, men then had to rely *principally* as they do today—upon that same deep-set folkway that we now call honesty. Where, however, this proved not so effectual, the creditor could indeed bring force to bear; but it was his own force! He could personally seize something the defaulting debtor owned, or something his family-group owned, or even the person of the debtor or some member of his family. Debt-slavery, for example—which we shall examine in the next chapter—was one of the commonest features of ancient life. But this primitive use of force to compel the fulfillment of economic promises was obviously a precarious procedure. Men did, however, finally find a sanction to rely upon, one that was certainly even more efficacious than mere forceful compulsion by the State is today.

It was fear of the gods!

When a deferred exchange was entered into between two men in antiquity, ordinarily they repaired to the temple, went through the most solemn rites, and he who received the property in the first half of the exchange took an oath to the gods that he would complete the second half. Woe betide him, if he did not. The powers of super-natural beings, of gods and daemons and ghosts, were almost the realest thing in the lives of our distant ancestors. These forces perpetually had to be propitiated. Zeus was the "hurler of thunderbolts," and he was far from being the somewhat amusing and pleasant mythological fancy we now regard him. Few facts are better substantiated

72

than the deep belief among primitive peoples, all over the world, that being struck by lightning was never accident, but retribution for having in some way displeased the gods. But gods and daemons visited this displeasure upon men in other ways than by lightning. Almost everything that might be a calamity, indeed, *was thought to proceed from the supernatural.* If a man, then, promised the gods to complete a half-exchange—that was a real sanction! He might break his promise to a mere creditor and fear little, particularly if he were part of a stronger group; but break it to the gods, and a real penalty lay in wait for him; not only possibly in the Hereafter, but also in the Here-and-Now. We can get a vivid idea of the sort of direct punishment he expected by reading the Book of Job.*

This was the ultimate reliance, then, upon which the completion of deferred exchanges depended in the distant past of the human race. The State finally became involved as the guarantor of half-exchanges only as fear of the supernatural gradually weakened among men. As the State has since supplanted the Church in other ways, it first superseded it here.

These three main compulsions that make modern men fulfill their economic promises—the social, the economic and the governmental —are not always present *in the same degree* in each deferred exchange. In fact, *all of them are not present in every deferred exchange.* This vital fact makes a necessary and a marked difference in the details of the deferred exchanges, therefore in human institutions, and finally in the determination of economic events. It is always important, accordingly, to identify as clearly as possible *what compulsion is principally operating* in any particular form of deferred exchange.

Let us now apply this illuminating distinction to a vast economic territory where a type of exchange exists, different from those we have already studied—namely, rent.

* The use of the supernatural as a debt-collecting agency is not extinct. Sumner and Keller, in *Science and Society* (page 1206) tell of a "quaint custom" still surviving in Southern India where a goddess is regularly relied upon for this purpose with recalcitrant debtors.

In the opening of his book on Pragmatism, William James refers, to that shrewd *bon mot* of G. K. Chesterton, that while it is important for a landlady to know the income of a new boarder, it is much more important for her to know his philosophy. This bit has its economic as well as its philosophic application. How neatly it describes the underlying considerations of all deferred exchanges! But it can be used in another way Chesterton hardly intended—to throw a broad illumination over what occurs in rent.

It may not be so easy to identify rent as a deferred exchange, or indeed as any form of exchange at all. What is exchanged? True enough, money passes on one side, but what passes on the other? Merely the right to use something—land, a building, or occasionally a machine. It may seem stretching the meaning of the word a little to call such a transaction an exchange. But this also was true of the employer-employee relationship. There money passed on one side, and nothing corporeal on the other, only labor; and we saw how illuminating it was to regard the relationship as an exchange of money for labor.

What really occurs in rent, if we wish to be juridical about it, is that the owner relinquishes possession of his property for a stated period. It might be said that temporary ownership is relinquished. The relationship might therefore fairly be described as an exchange in which money passes from one side, and property from the other, with the understanding that the property is to be returned to the owner at the end of an agreed period. That is, if we distinguish between the hazy legal implications of the words "possession" and "ownership," the fact that some form of exchange does take place is clear enough.

But why wander in these juridical labyrinths? For practical purposes, it is allowable to conceive of the relationship as an exchange of money on one side for something incorporeal on the other: *the use and enjoyment* of land, a building, or a machine. That is what actually happens. For the purpose of understanding our society better, the essential thing is to become aware of the promises of men that are involved in the relationship, to observe how extensive these are, how

74

they are interdependent upon all other economic promises, and how the vital matter of completion or incompletion of the promises affects the fortunes of everybody involved in them. When we do this, it becomes immediately apparent that in every essential respect the relationship is four-square with the deferred exchanges we have already examined, and others still to be analyzed. But these particular deferred exchanges between landlord and tenant have some differentiated aspects which the speculative economist finds—shall we say?—charming.

The antiquity of the relationship is at least one of these charms. The payment of rent is among the oldest of social relationships. It is as hoary a practice as working for other people. The most ancient records we have show it, even by that time, deep-set in the mores of the race. As soon as individual possession of land became, anywhere, even precariously established as a system, we find the landlord and tenant. Moreover, the very relation which these primitive bargainers entered into survives, in all its aspects, to this hour. Among modern uncivilized natives? Yes. But also, right here among ourselves, a people who without any question represent the vanguard of civilization in its economic achievement. Just as we can find, wherever we care to look over the world, counterparts of the most primitive market-places, so we find abundantly *the precise relationship* between landlord and tenant that existed in the deepest past of the race. I refer to what we call, in this country, share-cropping.

In the United States the 1930 Census counted 2,175,155 farmers who are share-croppers.* The relationship they have with the owner is that, having no money with which to pay for the use of the land, they pay for it—in whole or in part—by giving him an agreed portion of the crops they grow. The ancient landless and moneyless farmer entered into the same kind of contract as this; only instead of sealing the bargain with a written document which an outside power, the State, could be called in finally to enforce, they sealed it with oaths (in most cases, probably) given under highly solemn circumstances in the temple. The gods would see, in their own unpredictable way,

* *U. S. Statistical Abstract*, 1936, Page 579.

that the second half of this ancient exchange would be completed.

Hammurabi indicates the nature of the system in his Code, showing that in Babylon around 2000 B. C. it must even at that time have been a long-established and ancient relationship. The tenants in Hammurabi's time apparently paid one-third to one-half of their produce for the land they rented. As much as fifteen hundred years later, the records show, it was clearly the prevailing system of tenantry in Attica and other Greek States. In Attica tenants went by the description of "sixth-parters"; one-sixth of the produce went to the owner for the use of the land.

The system is also referred to time and again in the Bible. For example, we find that interesting passage (whether wholly accurate or not) outlining the shrewd financial operations by which Joseph took advantage of famine conditions to acquire a good part of the land of Egypt for his master, Pharaoh. All but the priests' lands, incidentally. These he and his Pharaoh were very careful not to gobble up. These ancient operations, as a matter of curiosity, are worth identifying in detail. First, anticipating famine, probably merely because it frequently occurred, Joseph

> gathered up all the food of the seven years, which were in the land of Egypt, and laid up the food in the cities. . . . And Joseph gathered corn as the sand of the sea, very much, until he left numbering. . . .
>
> And the seven years of dearth began to come, according as Joseph had said: and the dearth was in all lands; but in all the land of Egypt there was bread. . . .
>
> And when all the land of Egypt was famished, the people cried to Pharaoh for bread: and Pharaoh said unto all the Egyptians, Go unto Joseph; what he saith to you, do.

And what saith Joseph? Was he a prime minister, or was he a philanthropist? The first reference to his subsequent action, loosely read, might indicate that his economic program was just charitable forethought for the people. "And Joseph opened up all the storehouses, and sold unto the Egyptians." Sold! Sold for what? There was an exchange here. Six chapters later there follow these pertinent passages, showing the final result of this first recorded monopolistic operation.

And Joseph gathered up all the money [no doubt copper and bronze ingots, principally, with a little gold and silver.—Ed.] that was found in the land of Egypt, and in the land of Canaan, for the corn which they bought, and Joseph brought the money into Pharaoh's house.

And when money failed in the land of Egypt and in the land of Canaan, all the Egyptians came unto Joseph and said, Give us bread: for why should we die in thy presence? for the money faileth.

And Joseph said, Give your cattle; and I will give you bread for your cattle, if money fail.

And they brought their cattle unto Joseph; and Joseph gave them bread in exchange for horses, and for the flocks, and for the cattle of the herds, and for the asses: and he fed them with bread for all their cattle for that year.

When that year was ended, they came to him the second year, and said unto him, We will not hide it from our lord, now that our money is spent; my lord also hath our herds of cattle; there is not aught left in the sight of my lord, but our bodies and our lands.

Wherefore shall we die before thine eyes, both we and our land? buy us and our land for bread [debt-slavery and tenantry —Ed.] and we and our land will be servants unto Pharaoh: and give us seed, that we may live, and not die, that the land be not desolate.

And Joseph *bought all the land of Egypt for Pharaoh* [italics mine]: for the Egyptians sold every man his field, because the famine prevailed over them: so the land became Pharaoh's.

And as for the people, he removed them to cities from one end of the borders of Egypt even to the other end thereof.

Only the land of the priests bought he not; for the priests had

77

a portion assigned them of Pharaoh, and did eat their portion which Pharaoh gave them: wherefore they sold not their lands.

Then Joseph said unto the people, Behold, I have bought you this day and your land for Pharaoh: lo, here is seed for you, and ye shall sow the land.

And it shall come to pass in the increase, *that ye shall give the fifth part* [italics mine] unto Pharaoh, and four parts shall be your own, for seed of the field and for your food, and for them of your households, and for food for your little ones.

And they said, Thou hast saved our lives. . . .

And Joseph made it a law over the land of Egypt unto this day, *that Pharaoh should have the fifth part.* [Italics mine.]

Unto this day! These financial operations took place in Egypt—or something like them no doubt did—around 3500 B. C. The process described, by which Pharaoh acquired the land (in addition to money, cattle and tens of thousands of debt-slaves) is merely different from the historical process by which landowners in this country acquired *their* land. But the relationship between the modern landlord and his share-cropper is precisely like that of Pharaoh and "all the people of Egypt." Rent now merely comes somewhat higher, in produce, than it did in Pharaoh's day. "Give us seed that we may live and not die," the ancient Egyptian fellah cried to Joseph. The share-cropper is not so dramatic. His landlord frequently gives him seed, provides a mule or a cow or simple tools, and takes his pay in a fixed share of the crop (varying according to locality and with what the landlord provides), just as Pharaoh took his rent in wheat.

The clear fact is that our Southern and Western share-cropper could be transported back into the most ancient days of Babylon, of Egypt, of Attica and Rome, or indeed to any part of the world of antiquity, and find the economic scenery the same, and the economic atmosphere perfectly livable.

Just because the payment of rent—in produce or money—is among the very oldest economic relationships, and one of the commonest,

78

few of us ever become aware of how it rests entirely—now, as it always has—upon the dependability of human beings; just as we have seen that we are habitually unconscious of the predominant role of promises in labor relations, merely because the promise is invariably performed.

Now, how large a part do these obvious promises which we call "rent"—the necessary completion of which is not so obvious—play in our everyday life?

In the year 1930, when the last census was taken, no fewer than 15,300,000 families in the United States had entered into this kind of continuous relation with landlords. In addition, in the year 1935, our statisticians counted 2,865,000 farmers who had rented the farmland they were cultivating. Nor, of course, may we overlook the premises in our cities occupied by economic enterprises. The amount of money currently passing in these promises, centering around land and buildings, represents one of the major income items of our economy. Precisely how much, strangely enough, the government has never thought to measure. Estimates by reliable statisticians have been made, but—because of the lack of complete data—they include an element of guesswork and necessary error, which is the sort of thing statisticians most abhor. The most reliable estimate * covers a period of sixteen years, from 1919 to 1934, inclusive. It shows that something like $129,000,000,000 was paid on one side, and received on the other, in so-called rent. In this country alone!

Now, this is a sum about 3½ times the long-time promises—at the moment unfulfilled—of our national government, which stood at about $36,500,000,000 on June 30, 1937. The sum of $129,000,000,000 paid in rent in the last sixteen years represented a far greater volume of promises than any nation has ever had outstanding unfulfilled at one time—if we except those few governments which, after the war, recklessly plunged themselves into an "inflation" by the endless printing of paper money. True enough, there is a difference in the types of promise. The national debts—ours, for instance, totaling $36,500,-

* Source, National Bureau of Economic Research. Estimates of Simon Kuznets. Real estate, total gross rentals.

ooo,ooo—represent a type of promise, a good part of which, by its very terms, is to remain unfulfilled for a stated period; whereas the promises represented by rent must currently and continuously be completed. Nevertheless, both are large aggregated groups of promises. They are therefore comparable as mere promises. And it is deliberately that I make this particular comparison, in order to illustrate the degree of reliability manifested—in the one case, at least. The $129,000,000,000 were promises made almost wholly by plain unassuming individuals, like yourself. Except for the most trivial portion, *they were all fulfilled!* The proportion of promises unfulfilled in this field of rent, as compared with the total completed, is so inconsequential that it probably would not reach a hundredth of one per cent.

In other words, the practically infallible reliability of individuals, which we saw to exist in labor relations, in the production of most of the wealth in the world, and in the distribution of the greater part of it to consumers, is matched once more here!

But we intimated above that there was some differentiation here, that made these deferred exchanges especially charming for the economist to contemplate—aside from their antiquity. This is because of one curious aspect of them: they are almost infallibly performed, yet it appears that in no other type of deferred exchange—at least where individuals are the promisors and not governments—is the sense of obligation so attenuated and weak. Nobody loves a landlord, and in all history nobody ever has. The deep antipathy in the relationship, on the part of the promisor, is evident as far back as human records show there was private ownership in land. The feeling ran as deep and was as widespread in ancient Palestine, as revealed in the Mosaic Laws; in Attica and other Greek States before the Solonic Laws; in Rome all through its history; in every land and every time where there has been tenantry, as it is clearly general today.

This deep antipathy of tenants should be contrasted with the psychological attitude of the promisor in the other types of deferred exchanges we have examined. In the labor relationship it is a rare thing

80

for the promisor, the employer, not to be deeply sensible of this particular obligation. He may, in other respects, be pretty insensitive to labor. But if he did not pay his men, after they had performed work for him, he himself in his conscience would count the delinquency a fraud.

Again, when an economic enterprise—or a consumer—obtains goods by the giving of promises, if he is the least bit sensitive, he has the incompletion of the promise very much upon his conscience, and would certainly regard *a deliberate incompletion* not far removed from theft and robbery.

No such natural and personal responsibility is felt by the tenant to his landlord, except in rare cases. The relation between the parties is, ordinarily, one of a hardly concealed antagonism.

Yet the amazing fact stands that, in spite of this genuine antipathy on one side and manifest distrust on the other, the economic promises represented by rent are as infallibly fulfilled as others like them. What is the explanation of this?

We can at least account immediately for the landlord's distrust. It is justified. It arises, without any question, from the absence of any true sense of obligation to him. He would be merely obtuse not to be aware of this; and his experience of it leads him to every possible protective action against it. For he is no different from everybody else who is the party that first relinquishes his property in a deferred exchange. His principal concern is that *the second half, where he and not the other fellow is to be benefited, shall be completed.*

So far as the tenant's absence of any sense of obligation is concerned, it arises (in my own belief) from certain psychological factors of which he is wholly unconscious. *The things we use we come to feel we own.* The aura of our personality colors them completely. For the time being, certainly, no matter where *legal* ownership may lie, we do possess them, with all that possession means. Now the legal distinction between possession and ownership is far too metaphysical for a workaday mind ordinarily to make. In other words, it is not quite so plain, as it might be, precisely what we are paying the landlord *for*. Oh, yes, the theorists tell us it is *for the use* of this home we have fashioned and have become so deeply attached to; or for this land which by the sweat of our brow we have come to identify as our own. Or some other old beetle-browed Socrates tells us we are paying the landlord, simply because he is *depriving himself* of the use of the home or the land for our benefit. But now what chance have these pallid intellectual considerations to survive in the face of the strong sense of personal possession, *which comes from years of use*, in the case of a home; and from that even stronger sense of possession which comes from *growing the crops by our own labor*, which have to be turned over to the landlord, in the case of farming? This sense of partial, often principal possession, of the home or land he rents, certainly dulls the edge of obligation in the tenant; and it would seem, with a good color of plausibility, to account for his strong antipathy against the landlord. For every time we hand over money to a landlord, consciously or not, we feel we are paying for something that in some way *is as much our own* as his! Particularly is this true if we are handing over a share of crops grown. This is my own explanation (for what it is worth) of the first half of this enigma.

But why, in the face of such deep antipathy, are the promises represented by rent so invariably fulfilled that the exceptions do not count? Logically, default should be frequent. The explanation must be that the *compulsion to full performance* here must be particularly strong. We must find the answer to this enigma, then, by trying to discover what that compulsion is.

I believe that here, in rent, more than in any other economic area, *the fear of compulsion by the State* is principally operative in effectuating completion of the promise.

A few comparisons here are most revealing. Looking at the larger picture, so far as it has been unveiled in this analysis, it appears that in the case of the employer of labor, anticipated compulsion by the State has practically no effect at all in inducing him to complete the promise. So little so that his promise is usually oral, not written.

In the case of economic enterprises which obtain tangible forms of wealth by promises, anticipated compulsion by the State plays a very

82

minor role in completion. The principal compulsion in this case is the economic penalty.

In the case of the individual who buys consumers' goods on credit, neither the economic penalty nor the fear of compulsion by the State is a noticeably strong force in completion. The latter becomes so, if the individual fears it will become known to his neighbors that the State had to step in to compel him to do what any honest man should. If it is strong at all, then, it is only so when it can be tied in with this *social penalty* for non-performance.

In contrast with all these, I say, in the case of rent, fear of compulsion by the State seems to flow deep and strong. That is why the landlord—in his obviously disadvantageous position, arising from the antipathy to him—so carefully prepares for recourse to the State.

For not unreasonably—when we come to think of it—the State gives the landlord two shots at us. First, if we fail to complete the promise to him, he can sue us for payment, and if he wins, the State will seize what wealth we have, sell it, and complete the exchange we have left uncompleted. This, however, is not a particularly fearful procedure. If it were all the protection the landlord had, he would almost certainly be in bad case far more often than he is, for in most cases there is all too little for the State to seize. But in addition, the landlord is given another recourse. If we fail to complete our promises to him, it seems not unfair that he should have his property back for his own use. Accordingly, he calls in the State, as the phrase is, to *dis*possess us. The sheriff throws us and our furniture into the street; and with this event on the record, no other landlord—at least immediately—is likely to let us have his abode or land for a promise. Now this, indeed, is serious business to any human. The fear of being without shelter, of possibly being rained upon and being cold, even for a short time, seems to be one of the most terrifying of prospects to modern men. Here is a penalty for non-performance with spikes in it—one of the worst, in our estimation, that can be visited upon us.

Closely allied with it is another hardly less terrifying. We live in the most intimate relations with our neighbors. Everything we do is under their eyes. It is no light matter, in these circumstances, to have

83

the sheriff throw us in the street. The fact of non-performance of promise is then heralded to the world. The shame in our situation is profound. It is these *social penalties*, so closely tied in with the legal one, which give the landlord the whiphand he has, and which chiefly account for the enigmatic fact that the promises represented by rent are infallibly performed, although the sense of obligation in this field is so notoriously weak.

This explanation accounts for the extraordinary lengths to which poor people will go to pay their rent. Rent comes first. Food and everything else, if necessary, will be sacrificed. It accounts, too, for the phenomena of rent strikes. When, in rare circumstances, a large number of families in a tenement, or in a small neighborhood, for some reason participate in not fulfilling these particular economic promises, the social penalty which we have mentioned—that dread question of what the neighbors will say—lifts like a great weight from their souls. Who under these circumstances would have any compunction in not paying a landlord rent? The separated drops of quicksilver resentment against him coagulate into one mass at once. Let him hale us all to court, if he will. Even if the State backs him and throws us into the street, that other dread, of being without shelter, seems less terrifying when all our neighbors share the experience.

It is hardly strange that the land we work, or the little home we dwell in, should thus become the core of a special cluster of psychological phenomena; nor that they should find a final representation in important economic differences. Nor are the phenomena we have considered the whole picture of these differences. For rent itself is not the sole type of deferred exchange that has to do with land and buildings. There is another—of inestimable importance in the affairs of men. It is loans on lands and buildings, secured by what is called a "bond and mortgage." These, too, have their peculiarities.

7

*The Vital Differences Between Short and Long
Promises—And Why the Long Promises That
Center Around Land Have Produced the
Same Type of Events as Far Back
as There Are Records*

IN examining loans on land and buildings—commonly referred to as mortgages—we come for the first time, in this inquiry, to a consideration of the differences between half-exchanges that remain uncompleted for a short time, and those in which the second half is not consummated for a long time.

There is little about the affairs of humankind more important than this simple fact: namely, that the lapse of time before the second half of the deferred exchange takes place may be either short or long.

For this mere *lapse of time* before the performance of economic promises will be found to determine the very nature of many basic human customs and institutions, the existence of which we now take for granted as part of the environment we are born into. Moreover, the most vicious political quarrels arise from failure on the part of men to take into account the necessary differences which lapse of time makes in the performance of economic promises.

On that basic Roman road we spoke of metaphorically in our Introduction, here is a coign of vantage where we can survey a great deal that happens in human affairs lying in a rational relationship. All the considerations of so-called finance center here—in the length of the period economic promises cover. The operations of modern institutions, like banks and insurance companies; the fiscal activities of governments; yes, even modern money—all find a great deal of their explanation in this matter of the length of time economic promises run before completion. Innumerable economic events, too, have most of their mystery dissipated when they are examined under the white light of this simple distinction. For *the interdependence of short promises and long ones* has as much to do with determining the sequence of economic events as any other factor in modern life. We shall get more than a fleeting notion of the importance of this interdependence of promises when we come to study the activities of banks and governments, and even more when we examine, in a later chapter, that congeries of events we call the Business Cycle. In fact, the economics student can station himself at this eyrie at any time—nor is it a bad spot to repair to first when he is mystified by any particular problem—and he will seldom fail to observe, in this mere matter of the length of time an economic promise runs, some new and illuminating aspect of human events.

What is the principal difference between an exchange deferred in completion for a long time and one for a short time?

The first and most important one is that the exchange deferred for a short time is much more likely to be completed.

In short, the stark question of completion of the promise is very much bound up in *how long the promise runs*.

Thus both parties in every half-exchange must be sensitively aware of what may happen before the second half of the exchange is to be completed.

Well, what sort of thing may happen? Anything; give your imagination free play. The promisor can die. Or he can *forget*, purposely or not, that he has this particular exchange to complete. Or the resources, which both he and the other fellow thought were ample to insure completion, may fail to eventuate. His wealth may be filched from him by someone smarter than himself. Or it may turn out not to be a form of *exchangeable wealth* at all. (We shall see how

86

easily, in Chapter Seventeen, this surprising *dénouement* can occur in modern times.) Or his very philosophy may change, if sufficient time elapses, and he may become a cheat, whereas before he had been an honest man. Who can foresee what will occur? The only certain thing about life and circumstance, as they unfold, is uncertainty and change. Accordingly, the person who relinquishes his property in the first half of a deferred exchange is manifestly taking a risk of ending up with no benefit.

Clearly, what this amounts to is that when men enter into deferred exchanges, they are trying to see into the future. Now, let us look at experience. The past we can be not too uncertain about; but how far and how successfully can we see into the future? We function as rough-and-ready prophets all the time, but what we really do—if one reflects upon it—is to assume that the future, if not the same as the past, *will be so little different from it* that we can base our present acts on that assumption. How often is this tacit optimism justified by the event? The answer may be found in the circumstances of all your life, in what you know about the experiences of your friends and neighbors, in the newspapers you read daily—particularly, the business and financial sections, which you so faithfully ignore. About the only thing to be said on this point is that we can be *righter*, in this effort at prevision, over a short period than over a long one.

When the period is long, we are extremely likely to be wrong in assuming that the future will not be noticeably changed from the present. Indeed, it is remarkable if no serious error is made in this regard.

Now, at what point are the mistakes made in these long deferred exchanges? We have seen abundantly the two prime considerations of all deferred exchanges. The honesty of the promisor—his basic philosophy, which we describe by the inclusive word *character*—is not so likely to change, although we have suggested, and it is not meant as mere cynicism but as a curiosity to be observed, that even this may occur. Where error is most likely, however, is in the estimation of *sufficiency of resources* on the part of the promisor to complete the exchange. Here is where miscalculation most occurs.

87

Moreover, let us be well aware, *this error is made on both sides*. Both the person promising to complete the exchange, and the person first relinquishing his property, may be entirely wrong on this point. It is seldom that one or the other of them is not, and it may be as serious for the one as for the other.

Now, this *likelihood of miscalculation* is the outstanding feature of long-term deferred exchanges. It is a minor aspect, very much less certain to be present, in the short-term deferred exchange.

This, of course, makes a vital difference in the details of the two types of deferred exchanges. Men are not stupid—at least where their immediate interests are concerned. They finally shape their actions to their experience. They become fully aware of this greater likelihood of miscalculation when long periods elapse before economic promises must be fulfilled. Accordingly, in long-term deferred exchanges they try to protect themselves from their possible mistakes.

They do so in two ways. First, the promisor is ordinarily obliged to put up a forfeit, in case he fails to complete the exchange. Today we call it "security." This security is very seldom a feature of a short-term deferred exchange—only when incompletion seems likely, as in the instalment contract, protected with a "repossession clause."

Second, because of this likely miscalculation, men are forced to rely to a much greater extent upon the State to insure ultimate completion of the long exchanges. Accordingly, all long-deferred exchanges are highly formal and precise in their nature. Every eventuality is thought of and prepared for. It is put down minutely on paper what the nature of the promises are, and what is to be done under all the circumstances that can be imagined. This, incidentally, is the chief business of the legal profession. Thinking up eventualities may be said to be the stock in trade of our lawyers. This observation, I hasten to say, is not made invidiously. Anyone who has sat through long hours, watching two opposing lawyers think of everything that can happen in the near and distant future, can only be lost in bewildered admiration over the precision of their imaginative processes.

Another very important difference between long and short promises is that, in short promises, *the honesty of the person being trusted plays the major role* in the transaction. In the long promise it can be —and indeed often is—ignored. Lenders can accept certain types of long promises—for example, mortgage loans—even though the borrower has shown himself time and again to be as shifty as Beelzebub. The reason is that in long promises *complete reliance is had upon compulsion by the State*. It is true, of course, that the powers of the State can always be invoked to see that a short economic promise is fulfilled. But calling in the State—"bringing suit"—is both a disagreeable and a long-drawn-out process. Moreover, it is not always a one-hundred-percent assurance of completion of an exchange. By sad experience men have come to know that justice often is somewhat myopic. For that reason, in short-term deferred exchanges, the State's compulsion is always regarded as a final and remote contingency in the mind of the two parties. For when the State steps in, one certainty is that delay also steps in; and with short promises quick completion is of the essence of the matter. The borrower's honesty, therefore, and not the State's powers, must be the *principal* reliance in every short economic promise.

On the other hand, where the need of the party who relinquishes the property is at a minimum; where time makes little or no difference to him; and where by careful prevision of the lawyers the State will assure—with no element of uncertainty—the eventual carrying out of the agreement, the honesty of the trusted party can be ignored. It can be ignored, *because it plays no part in the completion of the exchange*, which will inevitably be completed whether the trusted party be honest or not.

But perhaps the most important difference between long and short promises is the psychological one. This certainly should be accorded a far more serious role in political and economic theory than is given it. Yet ordinarily the fact is hardly even observed that *the promisor is likely to forget the first half of the exchange when its last half is deferred for a long period.*

It seems to pass out of his mind that the other person has actually relinquished property to him, receiving nothing. This is particularly true if the property he has thus obtained has been consumed or lost before he has completed his half of the bargain. The other party, then, ceases to be either a benefactor or a friend. "For loan oft loses both itself and friend." Indeed it does, and here is the principal reason for it—this forgetting of the first half of an incompleted exchange by the party who first benefits! Few things could be more obtuse than to account this a mere interesting curiosity of human nature. It lies at the root, often, of abysmal political differences among men, where animosity could hardly run stronger; and it soon shows up, in any analysis, as one of the basic determining factors in the sequence of economic events.

Now, it is a highly significant social fact that this unquestioned animosity between the two parties in the relationship is seldom a feature of the short-term deferred exchange. Ordinarily the relationship there is thoroughly amicable. It is a fair and revealing question to ask, therefore, why the animosity should exist merely because the completion of the exchange has been deferred for a long time.

The explanation of this, I think, can be found in two sources. First, because of the miscalculations we have mentioned as being so frequent a feature of the long promise. Soon enough it appears that one or the other had made a mistake and that the future is not to be quite what had been envisaged. The other seems then to be benefiting *more* than had been intended. The party who made the mistake, on either side, feels outraged in his sense of justice; and, of course, this is vented, not in any sad deprecation of his own lack of foresight, but in animosity against the other fellow.

The second underlying cause is that while the first half of the exchange may conveniently be forgot, the second half unfortunately cannot be forgot. The promisor, in particular, must remain vividly and continuously conscious of it. Soon enough it becomes, in its disagreeableness, the only thing he is conscious of. He comes then to regard it *as a control of his actions*, and this is something against which one of the deepest human instincts rebels—an animal instinct, indeed. In the experiments our behaviorist psychologists have made with newborn infants, they discovered that almost the first clear reactions

90

in their tiny subjects—the first thing they scream about and struggle against with all their puny strength, is any attempt to keep a part of their bodies immobile—that is, to control their actions by force. This instinctive animal revulsion against control—try, if you would like to see it demonstrated, to hold a cat motionless with your hands—carries through, without any question, from the physiological to the more recondite psychological areas of human action. We will not be *unwillingly* controlled. Even when, outwardly, we seem to accept the control that our accidental environment imposes upon every one of us, if it is not a willing and an understanding acquiescence neuroses ensue—as the psychoanalysts show. This deep-going instinct, which is aware of nothing but the control—operating in us unconsciously, more often than otherwise—seems to me certainly to be a factor in the psychology of long-term debtors. Incidentally, I believe, it very largely accounts also for the unconscious animosity, wherever it exists, of laborers to their employers. And vice versa!

Were the first half of the exchange not forgot, it seems unlikely that such an unreasoning instinct would come into play; and, in fact, we can observe that it is not present in short-term deferred exchanges. There, the first half of the exchange, having occurred but a short time before, is sharply remembered and the obligation felt. This undoubtedly is the reason why it is never short-term debtors, but always long-term ones, who are involved in agitation over the abrogation of their promises. The long-term debtors wholly forget the benefit they received. Usually, *they forget the first half of the exchange altogether*, and become thoroughly unwilling to complete it. So long a time elapses from the first half of the exchange, that their role in it becomes no part of an exchange at all, but tribute, exploitation, a form of slavery. This animosity of long-term promisors is certainly a "blind economic force" of the first importance, though not of the type the commentators usually refer to. But reasonless or not, it is real enough. It determines the nature of the action of large bodies of men.

We can pass here from the general to the particular. This animosity of promisors is particularly present in the long-term exchanges that center around land and buildings—the loans of money secured by what we call mortgages. There is no type of long economic promise that is older; and as far back in antiquity as we can go, the economic events arising from the relationship appear to be the same as they are in our supposedly advanced stage of civilization. Before examining this particular relationship in some detail, it may be illuminating to glance at a first-cousin to it, a type of deferred exchange that is just as old, but is now extinct—the curious institution of debt-slavery. This was a human custom once as widespread and as deep-rooted as the mortgage loan.

It seems incredible to the modern mind that the penalty for non-performance of an economic promise should ever have been slavery. It was so; and—even more incredible to modern thought—the penalty was not one imposed by a tyrannical superpower, the State; it was a voluntary penalty. He who suffered it did so of his own will. This custom, and the habit of thought explaining it, was as common and as deep-rooted in the dim past of the race, as that involuntary slavery which arose from warfare. It can be found wherever we have records of early civilization—and, of course, it should be realized that records themselves came very late, comparatively, in the career of man on the planet. In India, Babylon, Syria, Palestine, Egypt, Greece, Rome, Italy—all over the Mediterranean littoral, and all through Northern Europe, among the early Slavs, Teutons and Celts —it was a common feature of economic life that a man—and as often as not, the other members of his family with him—became the slave of another, if he could not pay his debt; that is, if he could not fulfill an economic promise involved in a half-exchange.

The custom becomes less irrational and barbarous when we attempt to acquire the manner of thought of these distant ancestors, which was of course largely determined by their conditions of life. In the first place, we must realize that slavery itself—the ownership of human beings—was counted as no more immoral than the ownership of any other animal. Where constant warfare was the normal state, slavery was a condition in which any man, at any time, might find himself. There, but for the grace of God, went everybody. High birth made no difference. The only thing that ever saved the wealthy from it was the corollary custom, equally well-established, of ransom. Slavery was thus a relationship to which everyone was accustomed.

Only by transporting ourselves into this utterly alien point of view, are we able—with our passionate acceptance of individual freedom as the sole way of life—to conceive of men willingly putting themselves into slavery, merely because they could not pay a debt. What happened, simply, was that individuals put up their own persons, and the members of their families, *as security* in case a deferred exchange was incompleted. This would occur only where their own persons constituted the only property they could offer as forfeit. Economic promises in those distant days were fewer. The certainty of completion was less, the vicissitudes of fortune greater. When, then, one man came to another, seeking to enter into a deferred exchange, the most reasonable question would be, "How can you assure me the exchange will be completed, and that I will not be relinquishing my own property to you in vain?" *The question is precisely the same, not one whit different, from that which is asked today in any long promise.* The first thing the borrower would offer as forfeit would be land, cattle, or slaves. These were the principal forms of wealth in primitive days. If he had nothing else to put up as pledge, he proceeded to put up himself or the members of his family. Debt-slavery in its beginnings was highly conditional. It was either for specified periods, or—as in Greece and Rome—it ended when the fair value of the debt, with interest, had been covered by the period of the servitude. Later, however, it developed—in most places—into full slavery, indistinguishable from the involuntary type.

Common institution though this was, can it be imagined that men would have put themselves and their children in such jeopardy, unless they fully expected, in every such instance, to complete the half-exchange they entered into; and then, time and time again, would prove to be completely wrong in their estimate of the future? Thus we see exemplified—in this earliest form of long economic promise

93

—that miscalculation of the future which we identified as being characteristic of all long economic promises.

Moreover, since freedom itself was at stake, we can rest assured that the other concomitant of this type of exchange was also very much present—the deep animosity on the part of the borrower, who would have good reason to forget the first part of the exchange in his vivid awareness of the second half.

It was this animosity, indeed, we can now see, which finally put a quietus on this system. It was Solon in Athens, around 600 B. C. who prohibited all such deferred exchanges, where the borrower put up his own person or his family as security in an economic promise. His name has become synonymous with wisdom, but it is obvious he was representing public opinion rather than leading it. An ever-increasing number of Athenian citizens, chiefly farmers and shepherds, found themselves in this situation. Only with this predominant opinion of defaulting promisors behind him could Solon (who with Moses must rank as one of the great revolutionists of the ages) either have conceived or carried through this deep-going social reform, quite comparable to the revolution in 1917 in Russia. For, without compunction or compromise, it completely overturned a basic human custom many thousands of years old at the time. The revolution was followed soon after by other Greek states, and a century or so afterward in Rome, although the custom persisted in desultory forms for many centuries later.*

Solon inflicted the death-wound upon the system of debt-slavery, and in time it died away, to become extinct. But at the same time he dealt just as radically—so he thought—with the *pledging of land* as

* Caroline Singer and Cyrus Leroy Baldridge tell me of a curious relic of this primitive custom still to be observed in Ethiopia. They were surprised to see defaulting debtors following their creditors around the streets, *and chained to them!* This, of course, may be considered as much a relic of the institution of ransom as of debt-slavery. The debtor gets freed from his chains, and the public disgrace of the situation, only when the debt is satisfied—the half-exchange completed; the disgrace and the economic loss, presumably, being depended upon to make relatives or friends come across. Imprisonment for debt, so marked a feature of eighteenth-century and early nineteenth-century life in England, would probably—on tracing—be found also to have had its roots in the primitive customs of debt-slavery and ransom.

94

security for the completion of deferred exchanges. Yet the very system he dealt with is as alive today as it was in his time, and as it had been a couple of thousands of years before him, as shown both by the Old Testament and by the Code of Hammurabi. It is not only the same system now as then—it has the same recurring problems! You know what a bond and mortgage is. If you are a farmer today, have little cash, own your own farm, and want to put up a structure or to buy some farm implement, you borrow the money. That is, you enter into a deferred exchange. Let us say you receive $2,000, not from a bank, but from another more prosperous farmer. You promise, on your part, to give back the $2,000 to the lender in seven years—let us say—and in the meantime to pay small sums of interest, $60 every six months. This looks easy to you. Seven years is a long time off. Sixty dollars every six months is nothing. However, the lender (being himself a farmer and knowing something about the uncertainties of this ancient pursuit) says: "How am I to be sure the $60 will be forthcoming regularly through this long period, to say nothing about the $2,000 at the end of seven years?" You say, "Old fellow, my farm can be sold today for $5,000. You know the value of farmland hereabout, and that this is true. If I don't pay any one of these paltry interest items, or if I don't pay you the $2,000 at the end of seven years, I will allow the State to step in, sell the farm, pay the $2,000 to you with any unpaid interest items there are; and all that is left over from the sale is to come to me."

This is the bond and mortgage; it is a simple deferred exchange, with land or a dwelling put up as forfeit in case the exchange is incompleted. No procedure could seem more sensible nor fairer all around. And it has always been pretty much the same. The Attic farmers, in Solon's day, went through the same reasoning and the same process as you did. The pledge in your case is registered with the proper local government official. In Solon's day a pillar was placed at the corner of the land to declare to all and sundry that it had been put up in pledge of an economic promise. These pillars are still being dug up every now and then throughout Greece.

You know from the newspapers—even if you are not a farmer who has had the unpleasant experience—what frequently happens. To make the interest payments, the only way the farmer can get money is to sell crops. But the amount of money he anticipated from the sale of his crops may not materialize. He may be unable to pay one or two of the interest payments. Under the agreement the deferred exchange can then be terminated by the sale of his property.

Or, while he may be able to meet the interest payments, the payment of the principal at the end of seven years proves difficult. Here he may have been relying upon another eventuality: that his land may have gone up in value, or at any rate be no less. Therefore, to pay the $2,000 at the end of the period all he has to do will be to borrow it from someone else, if not from the same farmer who originally lent it to him. But here, also, it is all too easy to miscalculate. This estimate of the future value of his farm depends wholly upon the value of the crops he and others can obtain from it. But, as we have said, the price of crops may be 'way down. Instead of being worth $5,000, the farm at the end of seven years may be worth only $2,500, and he may find it extremely difficult to discover somebody to lend him $2,000 to complete the old exchange. Accordingly, the farm would have to be sold, under the agreement.

This precise pattern of reasoning, and this precise pattern of events, have happened time and again in human history, in connection with deferred exchanges secured by mortgages. We see the long promise itself. We see the reasonable protection set up for the benefit of him who first deprives himself of property. We see the miscalculation of the future on both sides. We see the deep animosity of the person who has to complete the exchange. We see the ultimate forced transfer of ownership by the State to complete the exchange. And we have the same social disturbances every time!

Solon met it in the forthright intellectually honest old Greek way. Not only had the Athenian small farmers gotten themselves, a predominant number of them, into jeopardy, by pledging their personal freedom for the completion of deferred exchanges; a large proportion of them also had pledged their lands, and had the slenderest chance of completing the exchange. Solon decreed that all existing agreements of the kind be abrogated forthwith and the pillars at the corners of the land-holdings be torn up. What did this mean? Merely that the last half of all these exchanges should be incompleted; it was the same thing as today tearing up all mortgages would be. It is one of the first examples—in the existing records, anyway—of the attitude, toward economic promises, of power-groups which control governments. We shall have occasion later to look at some others.

In Solon's direct fashion, and by other means, all through history down to the turbulent present—which, by the way, is perhaps less turbulent in this respect than other periods—agriculturists who predominate in a State have sought to free themselves from the completion of the deferred exchanges represented by these mortgage transactions, when they became difficult to complete. It occurred many times throughout Roman history. It is one of the oldest economic problems, forever recurring. Solon, of course, did not solve it. After he had freed the Athenian farmers from their promises, in a few years all was again forgot and they entered into new ones, putting up their land (of necessity) as forfeit for completion of the last half of the exchange. Otherwise, obviously, *they could get no one to give them money in the first half of the exchange.* The mortgage pillars reappeared throughout Attica.

It may be instructive at this point to open your Bible. "At the end of every seven years thou shalt make a release," declared Moses. "And this is the manner of the release: Every creditor that lendeth aught unto his neighbor shall release it; he shall not exact it of his neighbor or of his brother; because it is called the Lord's release."

Who could have been the ancient debtors Moses was legislating for? Only peasant farmers and shepherds. None others in primitive days would have had occasion to enter into long economic promises.

Accordingly, this sabbatical cancellation of debts, from the very fact of its recurrence, was clear recognition on the part of this ancient Hebraic realist, of the apparent inevitability of peasants and herdsmen involving themselves in half-exchanges they could not complete.

When I read this passage recently, I thought: "Ah, Moses was a

97

great humanitarian, he considered the little man always. Here in this provision he demonstrates it. But as an economist he was not so shrewd as he might have been. For it is clear, if he decreed that deferred exchanges should be canceled every seventh year, the only effect would be to kill them in the making at that time. All lending would stop every fifth or sixth year, in anticipation of the seventh. For who would give away his wherewithal, money or goods, in the first half of an exchange, when there is this absolute certainty that he will never get it back?"

But then I read further, and came upon this. "If there be among you a poor man . . . thou shalt not harden thine heart, nor shut thine hand from thy poor brother: But thou shalt open thine hand wide unto him, and shalt surely lend him sufficient for his need, in that which he wanteth. *Beware that there be not a thought in thy wicked heart, saying the seventh year, the year of release, is at hand; and thine eye be evil against thy poor brother, and thou givest him naught; and he cry unto the Lord against thee, and it be sin unto thee.*"

How shrewd and wise! What this audacious social inventor—more imaginative and more ambitious than Solon—was clearly attempting to do was to prevent the *recurrent* difficulties in which men become involved through not being able to fulfill long economic promises. He was attempting a *permanent* solution of a problem which, even at that time, must have seemed eternal—to protect men against the consequences of miscalculation of the future. He was doing it, as rulers always have, at the expense of the creditors—by canceling the last half of these long-deferred exchanges, at seven-year intervals. But then, in order not to render his society stagnant, to avoid choking off all deferred exchanges, he sought to throw a religious aura around the necessity of lending to those who need it—in the seventh year, as in all others. It did not work, as the fulminations of later prophets well indicate. Religion is as weak a reed as can be found as a reliance for orderly economic activity. But, nonetheless, must we admire the audacity of this combination of economic realist and dreamer.

98

Thus, we see that a thousand years before Solon, Moses was giving his deepest thought to straightening out the troubles caused by long promises based on land; and then, 2,500 years after Solon—about six years ago, in this land of progress *par excellence*—the same acute problem was agitating our legislators. These solons, being neither so bright nor so bold as their namesake, muddled around with the problem, magnifying the distress and trouble no end, as compromisers always do.

It is instructive, however, to see wherein the precise parallel lies between ancient times and what happened to farmers in this country within the past twenty years.

We must observe, first, the increase that occurred in the volume of this type of deferred exchange, based on agricultural land. In 1910, the amount of money borrowed on mortgages—where farmland and farm buildings had been put up as forfeit—totaled $3,300,000,000. About twenty years later (in 1928) this had almost trebled. It was then $9,500,000,000.* In 1930, there were 6,288,000 farms in the United States and about 40 per cent were mortgaged. What was the underlying reason for this increase in borrowing? Had farmers got themselves into more difficulties during this period? Was it this necessity that sent them to the modern moneylenders? Later some agriculturist apologists talked as if this might have been the explanation. But lending does not increase to those in difficulty. The reverse happens: lending to them stops; it tends to diminish, not to increase. The explanation of the increase was that mere miscalculation of the future—on both sides!—which we have seen to be an almost inevitable concomitant of all long-term deferred exchanges.

What happened was that, owing to the World War, prices of all agricultural products grown in the United States rose enormously. With them, the value of agricultural land and buildings mounted. It went up from a total, in 1910, of about $35 billion† to a total of about $66 billion in 1920.‡ This was the simple reason for the tre-

* *Long-Term Debts in the U. S.;* a publication of the U. S. Department of Commerce, Page 107.
† *U. S. Statistical Abstract, 1936,* Page 570.
‡ *Long-Term Debts in the U. S.,* Page 109.

bling of mortgage loans in such a short period. Farmers simply found that they *could* borrow more money on their land and buildings, since they had risen so greatly in value. The obvious reason they did so was because they were again (as most participants in long exchanges do) assuming the future would be like the present. They thought that the prices of crops, and therefore the exchange-value of agricultural land, would remain high; and accordingly, that they could always easily complete these deferred exchanges, and that they would never lose the land they put up as forfeit.

Of course, *the lenders* made the same calculation—or miscalculation. They were not diabolically interested, as farm-apologists often represent the mortgagee as being, in taking away the farmer's precious home and farm. Their point of view was the normal and reasonable one of getting the last half of the exchange completed, since they had divested themselves of their own property in the first half. It is a fairly safe statement to make that very, very rarely nowadays would lenders on agricultural land (since they consist now almost wholly of banks, insurance companies, and the government) enter into such an exchange at all, if there were even a fair chance of having to take over the farms. Lenders on farmland do not expect this to happen, any more than the farmer does.

The miscalculation was particularly egregious in this period we are looking at. Gross farm income, which had been nearly $17 billions in 1919, fell to less than one-third this amount—about $5 1/3 billions by 1932. The value of farm land and buildings in the United States dropped from a high point of about *$66 billion in 1920 to about $33 billion in 1935.** In other words, it was cut in half, going back to less than it had been in 1910. But, in the meantime, of course, the outstanding mortgage loans did not decrease. These have nothing to do with the current value of land. They are simply the total sums *lenders have divested themselves of,* and expect to be reimbursed for. They remained in 1932 at over $9 billion while the value of farmland had dropped to what it had been a generation before,

* U. S. Statistical Abstract, 1936, Pages 576 and 601.

and the average price of farm products had become less than a third of what it was in 1920!

But now see how deeply undermined and how precarious was the important eventuality of completion of these promises, when the resources, which were being depended upon for completion, were so enormously lessened. We can trace the result in the history of the times. We see banks by the thousands, in agricultural districts, closing their doors because these particular long-term deferred exchanges could not be completed. We see the farm-holdings of insurance companies rising, a large proportion of their funds thus becoming "frozen"—by which we simply mean that they cannot be exchanged for the sums originally given. We see this affecting the bond market, through the forced sale of bonds held by banks and insurance companies, to obtain cash. We see farmers organizing to stop the normal and ancient processes by which this type of deferred exchange gets completed, by compulsion of the State. That is, we see the deep underlying animosity of the promisor in this type of exchange flaring up again—as it has done through all history—in complete forgetfulness of the first half of the exchange. We see the government getting involved in the deferred exchanges. We see the agitated political counsels that arise from all this. Our muddled modern solons begin speculating about "money," the root of all evils, and soon they are in such a complete mental haze that miracle it is that any sensible thing gets done. We see them, impelled by these distressed promisors, adopting such astonishing economic practices as to destroy wealth already grown, curtail the production of new wealth, and to propose (and even go some way toward doing it *) to free everybody from completing half-exchanges, so that these few, who might lose their land, would not have to complete theirs. One need only recall, or reread, the newspapers from 1930 to 1935 to be aware of the preponderant role played in the mad economic *mélange* of those years by farmers who had entered into deferred exchanges which, because of their own miscalculations, they could

* I am referring here to the monetary acts passed by Congress at the time. The major intention of these was to relieve the farmer; the Congressional debates, the President's messages, and speeches of Cabinet members, all make this clear.

not complete, and who were ready to believe any madman, so long as they did not have to complete the exchange by losing their land. There is no question that this marked minority of the population (it was one, as we shall see) were allowed to be influential, out of all proportion to their importance in our economy, in the political policy and action of the time. But not the least valuable thing to observe about all this is that the whole set of phenomena was typical. These particular long-term exchangers, all through history, have made trouble when they could not perform their promises, and when the time came for performance to be accomplished.

Agriculture is an important, but not by any means the predominant, industry of our people. While farmers all were distressed by the Depression, so was everybody, and far more industrial labor than farmers. Actually 60 per cent of the farms in the United States in 1930 *had no mortgages on them at all!* That is, about 3,700,000 farms were quite free of this dread form of debt. But were the 2,500,000 other owners, who had put up their land as collateral at the time, all in fear of losing it? Not at all. It was harder for all of them to pay their interest charges—just as it was harder for everybody to complete exchanges during this period. But no other type of debtor was so vocal nor quite so well organized as the farmers, so that their particular difficulties came to appear less bearable than those of others.

But the real debt situation of farmers—both during this period and normally—is put into its proper perspective by comparing it with the mortgage loans that had been made on urban land and dwellings. A little digging into the statistical records immediately reveals—what reflection would show—how much more important in our modern economy are these latter deferred exchanges. The structures used for commerce and industry have not been reliably counted, but so far as dwellings are concerned there are little short of nineteen million of them in the United States. Of these, about 8,700,000 are mortgaged.* The money lent upon them totaled in 1930 about $22,000,-000,000.† To it must be added, to get the whole urban picture, about

* Source, Federal Home Loan Bank Board.
† *Long-Term Debts in the U. S.,* Page 136.

$15,000,000,000 lent upon the security of commercial structures, land used for industrial purposes, and vacant land.*

In other words, on city land and buildings there was a total of uncompleted promises of about $37,000,000,000 in 1930. *This was almost four times the volume of promises based on agricultural land and buildings.*

It will be seen from the figures that the owner of urban land and buildings is of somewhat more importance in our modern economy —so far as these deferred exchanges are concerned, at any rate—than the much more vocal farmer. He makes less noise about his troubles. But is this because he gets into less trouble? He gets into the same trouble—and for the same reason. He enters into these long-deferred exchanges, and just as frequently as the farmer, he *miscalculates* what the future course of events will be, fails to complete the exchange, and as a result loses the property he has put up as forfeit.

The farmer goes wrong, when he does, as to his future income from the crops he will raise. Either the crops do not materialize in the volume he expects, or their price goes down. His urban counterpart goes wrong, if he is a landlord, in estimating the future rent obtainable from the dwellings he owns.

Usually, the principal income of the landlord is from rent; we saw, in the last chapter, that over half the homes in the land are rented by those who occupy them. Now, rents of course, can change, just as the price of crops can. They do change. For example, in the three years between January, 1929 and December, 1931, it is estimated that rents on the average fell 14 per cent.† This fall was greatly accentuated later. In 1932–33, one estimate is that rents had fallen from 40 to 50 per cent.‡ A little worse for the building owner than having his income in rent thus reduced in amount is having it cease altogether. If no homeowner wants to use his dwelling, or if no business firm wants to use his commercial structure, the income he had counted upon is not zero, but less than zero. For he has both to pay out money to keep it in repair, and still more money for taxes. It is

* *Ibid.*, Page 136.
† Source, National Industrial Conference Board.
‡ *Internal Debts of the United States,* by Evans Clark, Page 83.

clear enough how hampered he must become in meeting that dread deferred exchange, with its inexorable pressure upon him, represented by the mortgage loan. Finally, like the farmer, he often completely miscalculates (when entering upon the half-exchange) the future value of the building or land. It is upon this, of course, that he is depending *to pay the principal* when it comes due. What he invariably expects is that its value will be as great, and that therefore the lender will enter into a new long-term exchange for the same amount. If the original lender will not, he expects that somebody else will. This is an invariable psychological ingredient in the mental state of those who enter into these long-term deferred exchanges based on real estate. On both sides—we must repeat.

We Americans particularly are addicted to this optimistic point of view of the value of real estate. It is impossible for us to conceive that buildings or land will do anything other than increase in value, or at least remain the same. Oh, yes, of course, one will occasionally come across an old Sourface, who would sell his country short, simply because he has had some peculiarly bad experience. But as a principle upon which universally we base our actions, real estate values are never expected to decrease. It always comes as an economic surprise when they do. The explanation of this psychological state—though no justification for the obtuseness in it—is that over the long pull throughout our history, it has been true. Land values *have* always continued to go up in this country—when total values are taken, when all values are averaged, and when intervals of time are eliminated. The trouble is *our anticipation always outspeeds the event.* The particular bit of land with which our fortunes are involved seldom reaches the value we anticipate until after, often long after, we had based our calculations upon the increase. The history of real estate values in every tiny community, of the tens of thousands in the country, is one of a continuous hill-and-valley movement, *with the grade itself ever upward.* Whenever there is a downturn, there is calamity among starry-eyed land speculators, who expect the movement to be a straight grade, forever up. This clear notion among Americans that the grade of real-estate values

104

is always up, and never down, has made us pre-eminently the most confirmed land-speculators in history.

With the richest land in the world opening up for the taking, and with the most astonishing industrial era in all history having our broad acres for its chief theater, how could it have been otherwise? The first settlers began to indulge in this speculation as soon as they were well placed and found themselves being followed by others. No one can read our early colonial history properly without being aware of this continuous speculation, which was forever in the background of economic and political events. Few among our revered Founding Fathers were not up to their necks in land-trading. Washington himself was not only one of the great land-owners of the day, but before the Revolution the chief preoccupation of his life was real-estate operations. They covered vast tracts of land in what is now West Virginia, Kentucky and part of Ohio. The mere area covered by his operations, by comparison, would make any modern real-estate man a piker. Patrick Henry, the great patriot, though not so grandiose an operator, had all his fortunes even more deeply involved in real estate, and some of his activities might be said today to border on the shady.* Robert Morris, the financier of the Revolution, engaged in land operations in his later years that were comparable to the operations carried on by the wildest Stock Exchange gamblers we have ever had; he ended penniless in a debtors' prison on account of them. Franklin, of course, with his eye ever on the main chance, did not neglect this one. There are many other examples. Men traded in land then as they do in shares of stocks today. One of the most salutary things one can do is to read the records of the Constitutional Convention, delve into the personal history of the makers of it—whom we have endowed with aureoles—and learn how much this document, now holy to us, had both its provisions, and its actual adoption, determined by men who were great land-speculators at the time.

As the united nation became more sure of its destiny in the early

* He was prominent and active in a land company which sought to profit in the "Georgia Land Frauds," notorious at the time. See Chapter VI, *The Great American Land Bubble*, Sakolski.

decades of the nineteenth century, and as new land opened up westward, the speculation time and again went to fever height. We find the history of this preserved in the term "land-office business," representing the most active selling and buying that could possibly go on. The phrase arose from the mad scramble that occurred whenever the Government Land Office opened up new territory, to be obtained for a dollar or so an acre. It was land that was rarely seen by those who bought it, and which they never expected to see. It was grabbed up, to be sold at a much higher price later, to that mythical person—usually a foreigner—who was supposed to want it so much more than the buyer.

This indigenous tendency to land-speculation is as much a feature of our life today, though now somewhat hidden, as it ever was. It does not so often break out into mad excesses, although in the nineteen-twenties in Florida, there was such an outbreak, quite typical of the ones which occurred frequently in our earlier history. What has happened is that real-estate speculation, with its attendant *miscalculation of the future*, is now overshadowed, when it occurs, by much more exciting speculation in other fields.

For example, let us look at the last twenty years or so. It is within our own lifetime. Few would say that real-estate speculation was a particularly outstanding economic feature of that period. But in 1912 the real-estate of the country, farm and urban, was the basis of loans totaling around $10,800,000,000. Eighteen years later, in 1930, these loans had become $46,300,000,000. *They had more than quadrupled!* And, of course, this represented only an increase of the loans. What far astronomical regions, beyond this, total real-estate values in the country had soared to, nobody knows reliably. Such an increase, over a twenty-year period, would probably match any like period in our history, whatever their excesses. This speculation went on unnoticed by all but a handful of persons. They were academicians —closet-economists. The fact that it was unnoticed, it seems to me, is perhaps even more socially significant than the speculation.

Of course, we have long ago become inoculated against amazement over such sums. The only way to get any significance from

106

figures like this $46,500,000,000 is to try to become aware, in general terms, of what they represent in the dynamics of human society. In this case, they reveal the *great extensity* of this special kind of economic promise. For they are all promises! They are not dollars—remember that. They are *a mere measure of men's promises* in this field, the yardstick being dollars. They also demonstrate, of course, that ancient inborn tendency of men to miscalculate the future, which is a mark of all long deferred exchanges, and particularly—on our beloved shores—of exchanges where land and buildings are put up as forfeit.

Indeed, these loans of $46,500,000,000 can serve as an outstanding illustration of the sort of miscalculation of the future that goes on in our economy. The loans had dropped in 1934 to about the neighborhood of $38 billions.* About $8½ billions of it, in other words, *went out of existence in four years!* Very little of this was finally completed by payment of the money. *Most of it became completed through foreclosure.* The promisor lost his land or building, and the debt was thereby canceled—the exchange ended.

We stated, as a general proposition, in the beginning of this chapter, that it was a characteristic of long promises to be much less certain of completion than short ones. Here, in the first of this type of long promises that we consider—the real-estate mortgage—this becomes demonstrated by the figures.

We saw the infallibility in the performance of promises, on the part of individuals, in every other economic area. Performance, under the worst circumstances, always hovered close to 100 per cent. Now, here is a field where that remarkable record of the individual is very badly broken. The reason is apparent. It is not the integrity of men that fails here, but that other necessary reliance of the deferred exchange, *sufficiency of resources;* and this occurs because of miscalculation as to what those resources will be, under the unforeseeable circumstances of the future.

In measuring the degree of reliability manifested in this field, the experience of city and country may well be separated.

* *Long-Term Debts in the U. S.,* Pages 106 and 136.

As to farms, taking the six-year period from 1927 to 1933, about 13½ per cent of all American farms changed hands, either through foreclosure of mortgages or through bankruptcy.* How many of these changes in ownership resulted from foreclosure and how many from bankruptcy does not appear in the statistics. But, since, through this period, about 40 per cent of all farms were mortgaged, this means that *about one-third* of the farmers who had entered into this type of long-term deferred exchange, putting up their land as forfeit, failed to complete the exchange and lost their land during this period.

On their face, the figures for urban real estate do not appear quite so bad. But this, almost certainly, is mere appearance. One informed estimate shows that in the ten-year period, from 1926 to 1935, about 9 per cent of all urban land and buildings changed ownership through foreclosure.† Roughly, about 50 per cent of all urban structures were mortgaged in this period. This would mean, therefore, that about 18 per cent of those who entered into these obligations failed to complete the promises, and lost their property.

But all this is putting too fair a face on what really happened in the years when the last business cycle was at its nadir. In fear of the farmers, the politicians in a great many States put legal obstacles in the way of farm foreclosures. Moreover, very widely, those who held the mortgages *did not foreclose on them*. This latter course was particularly true of urban property. Banks, insurance companies, building and loan associations—and later, the national government—who among them constituted the principal holders of mortgages, were not merely lenient; they were loath to exercise their full rights. What good were farms to them, if they could not be rented to other farmers? And what good were homes and commercial buildings, if they could not be rented? To take them over would merely put the banks, insurance companies and building and loan societies deeper into the real-estate business, in which they were not anxious to get any more involved than they already were. Accordingly, it was quite common

* *Farm Real Estate Situation, 1932–3;* U. S. Dept. of Agriculture. Period is from March 15, 1927 to March 15, 1933.
† Source, Federal Home Loan Bank Board.

practice, all through this period, for mortgage-holders not to insist upon the letter of these contracts; to allow the promisors to pay what they could, and keep the property. There were many interesting instances, indeed, where the debtors had to force the creditors to take over the property, because these latter wanted to avoid the legal expense of foreclosure—as well as taxes and other expenses—all of which amounted to more than any income that could be anticipated in any near period of rental.

Because of this development, probably a better measure of performance, in this particular type of long promises, consists of estimates as to the degree of delinquency in payment. As to farmers, one informed estimate is that in 1933, 45 per cent of the number of mortgaged farms, and 52 per cent of the total debt, was in arrears as to either principal or interest.* As to urban property, again the information is more fragmentary, but the delinquencies (wherever studied) were strikingly large. One estimate was that in 1933 "almost two-thirds of urban mortgagors are now unable to make the payments specified in their bonds." † In another study of sample cities (none, unfortunately, among the largest, where the delinquency was almost certainly greatest on business property) the delinquency varied from 20 per cent in some cities to 50 per cent in others.‡ Notorious among the defaulters were companies which had sold real-estate bonds, all secured, of course, by real-estate mortgages. There was enormous loss here to innocent investors, who had been lured into parting with their money—in deferred exchanges, of course—by such slogans as "no loss to any investor for so-and-so many years." No nation-wide tabulation has been made of these particular delinquencies, but in one State where 3,234 such issues of bonds were studied, 2,641 of them—over 80 per cent!—were in default.** Aside

* Sample data for 12,000 farms compiled by the Bureau of Agricultural Economics, quoted by *Long-Term Debts in the U. S.*, Page 12.

† *Internal Debts of the U. S.*, Evans Clark, Page 20.

‡ The general distress of these borrowers is also indicated by the fact that the government, through the Home Owners Loan Corporation, took over $3,000,-000,000 of these mortgages from the holders; about 18 per cent of all outstanding mortgages; and this measure of relief was only extended to the small borrowers.

** *Long-Term Debts in the U. S.*, Page 144.

from common recollection, all the figures demonstrate that the degree of performance of this kind of promise was shockingly poor.

We can come back to general principles to see the reasons. It was principally due, as with all long exchanges, to miscalculation of the future. "Debts were incurred," says Evans Clark, of this period, "in the confident expectation that values and income would continue to increase with the years. Precisely the opposite result occurred."

Now, even during this period, of probably the greatest economic disturbance in history, performance of short promises hovered not very far from 100 per cent. Instead of being practically infallible, performance in some fields would drop, at the worst, to three or four per cent below perfection.

No more striking demonstration is ever likely to be afforded than that which occurred in these few years, of the difference in certainty of completion between economic promises made for a short and those for a long period.

Of course, it must be observed by the economics student here that these high percentages of default on urban and farm mortgages are very far from being measures of loss. They are merely measures of the *non-performance* of this type of long promise. It must be remembered that after foreclosure, or bankruptcy, or composition of the debt in some way, the lender either became owner of the property, or was liberally recompensed in some other way. For example, when the government took over defaulted mortgages through the Home Owners Loan Corporation, the mortgage-holders received bonds guaranteed by the government, which were salable in the open market for practically face value. Or when the mortgagees foreclosed and received the land or building, it was almost always worth a fair proportion of the amount originally loaned. In other words, *the total loss* ultimately sustained on mortgage loans is quite another matter from *the measure of performance* of these long promises. *The forfeit still serves its primitive purpose* of protecting against loss him who first gives up his property in a half-exchange.

Merely to see what their outstanding characteristics are, we have been looking at these deferred exchanges centering around land and buildings—those we call rent, and those we call mortgage loans—as if they were more or less isolated in our economy. Of course they are not. They are a part of that inconceivable complex of all human activities, which we are trying, in this piecemeal fashion, to present to the understanding. What we have been doing is, like Dr. Carrel, to separate an organ out of a body, keeping it artificially alive, and watching it operate by itself. But the organ belongs in the whole body. In life it is inextricably related with others, in a thousand ways, which can only be seen when it is in its proper environment. So with these congeries of half-exchanges centering around real estate. When we study them, not separately, but as part of our living society, we can see how they are dependent upon all other exchanges, and all other human activities.

For example, so far as farm mortgages are concerned, we see how both the making of the promise and its completion are dependent on the prices of the farmers' products, and these on other human relations in an endless chain.

So, too, in the case of rent and mortgages on urban homes, they are determined, both in their origin and in their completion, largely by the income from labor—of the tenants. This is then governed by something vague called "conditions in the labor market"; and this in turn by that mysterious entity called "business conditions"; and this, in turn, is determined—by what? Perhaps later on, in studying Business Cycles, we can get some glimpse. The whole is a mass of interrelations, but it is no jumble. What jumble there is it may be wiser to lay first to our own imaginative deficiencies, before impatiently ascribing it to any fundamental anarchy in the system. The "anarchy," in short, may be in our mental processes.

We cannot here trace with exactitude all the interrelations this particular area of deferred exchanges has with others; but two important ones, at least, it is advisable to become aware of, because of the insight into our society it may add, at this point of our study.

The first is the close relation mortgage loans have with our banks, insurance companies, and other fiduciary institutions. These long promises are made largely *to* banks, insurance companies, building and loan associations, and the like. If incompleted, these institutions suffer. Now, the promises *they make* in turn rest to a great extent upon *these* promises. In the next chapter, we shall look a little more closely at what happens on account of this particular interdependence.

The second important relation of this type of exchange is with industry. One of the key occupations of men—in the classifications of economists—is inextricably tied up with it. It is the construction industry. The reason for this inextricable relation is that very little *new building* nowadays goes on unless a mortgage loan is arranged in advance. Modern building, ordinarily, *is done on borrowed money*. This amounts to saying that somebody, first, has to make one of these long promises, and some cold financier has to estimate that the promise can easily be fulfilled, before large numbers of men begin with pick and shovel, and then with trowel and trip-hammer, erecting the building; and before other men in distant regions begin manufacturing the cement and molding the steel, and doing the thousand and one other things necessary to the erection of the smallest home. You see how swiftly, as soon as you turn up this or any other economic soil, promises immediately appear, and support all the activity.

How much so, in the case of the construction industry, it may be illuminating to uncover, as an example. From 1930 onward, in this country, it began clearly to appear that most of the then-existing vital deferred exchanges, based on land and buildings—totaling $46,-500,000,000—were going to be difficult of completion. Who had been relinquishing their property in the first half of all these exchanges? Who had been *most immediately* relying upon this mass of promises, which began now to take on so dubious a color? Our banks and insurance companies, principally. That is the principal source of modern mortgage money in the United States. Now, with the old deferred exchanges of this type becoming so questionable, what chance did new deferred exchanges, based on land and buildings, have with the bankers and insurance companies? Precious little. Lending money on mortgages had already begun noticeably to decline in 1928. In 1929 and 1930 the decrease was accelerated. During the depths of the depression, in the three succeeding years, lending in this field went almost to zero. In Greater New York, for example, mortgages recorded dropped from $1,797,000,000 in 1926 (the high point) to about one-fifteenth of that sum, $136,000,000 in 1933.* With the long promises of this type then showing the record of fulfillment which we have uncovered, it would have been mad of lenders to trust *new promises of the same kind* just then. But—observe now!—it was these very borrowed funds which had largely supported the construction industry in the past. With that support gone, what happened to building in the United States?

No better illustration can be afforded of the dependence of activity upon great bodies of promises. But only, be it noted, *upon promises that men consider certain to be fulfilled.* In 1929, leaving out construction initiated by national and local governments, the amount of money spent privately in labor and materials for building was $8,700,000,000. This was not, be it understood, the high point. The construction industry had actually begun to decline the year before, in 1928. In 1930, this amount slid down to $6,700,000,000. In 1931, it tobogganed by roughly another 2 billion to $4,600,000,000. In 1932, it was cut in half, going to $2,200,000,000. And in 1933 it reached its low point: it was then $1,900,000,000.† After that it began, very gingerly, to rise.

Building in normal times is among the first four of our largest industries. At its low point, there was not one-quarter as much private construction going on (as distinguished from government-initiated work) as in 1929. No other branch of economic activity showed a like decline, nor anything like it. The only other field of activity even approaching such a reduction was metalliferous mining. When we consider, not building itself, but the materials that go into building, the decline between 1929 and 1932 was 66 per cent.‡ Again, no other *type of goods* experienced such a decline in production.

* Figures compiled from *The Real Estate Record and Guide.*
† Source, Bulletin 58, National Bureau of Economic Research, *Production in Depression and Recovery*, Charles A. Bliss, Page 6.
‡ *Ibid.,* Page 7.

Or look at it from the point of view of income received from construction, by everybody, including laborers employed. In 1928 this income was $3,147,000,000. In 1933 this had dropped to $623,-000,000, about one-fifth of the 1928 figure.* Here again, this was by far the worst record among all branches of industrial activity in this country.

There are some economic theorists who find, in the varying fortunes of the construction industry, the prime cause of Business Cycles. We can pass no comment now on the validity of that thesis. One thing only seems clear from this analysis. The varying fortunes of that industry certainly have the closest relation, if not their cause, in the sums of money lent on mortgage. This in turn depends, not merely on the amount of unused capital seeking an income in the market, but, just as much, upon the reliability of the promisors. The reliability of promisors in turn rests on calculations, sound or not, of their future resources. But the circumstances of the distant future —which so affect future resources—upon what does this depend? Upon the whole complex activity of the society. This is the sort of The-House-That-Jack-Built reasoning which one immediately gets into, in trying to find "causes" of Business Cycles; or of any other widespread economic phenomena.

Nevertheless, some headway to comprehension of the whole can obviously be made. If one wants to follow the story of The-House-That-Jack-Built, one can do so. The strain on the imagination becomes geometrically greater, but it is possible to go some distance. In human affairs, it is at least helpful to understanding merely to observe with precision what goes on—as we have tried to do in this particular economic area. One general observation certainly seems justified by the revelations: that again *promises which are believed underlie and explain all the activities,* both in the case of rent and mortgage loans. Whether or not the promises are fulfilled is the principal factor that determines the nature and the sequence of the economic events.

* Source, Bulletin 59, National Bureau of Economic Research, *Income Originating in Nine Basic Industries, 1919–34,* Simon Kuznets.

8

How Banks Constitute the Focal Point of the
Interdependent Promises of Men

THE deferred exchanges centering around land have a particularly intimate relation, in our country, with those which center around banks. Our loose end of truth, which has slowly been unraveling, leads now into one of the most complicated knots in our economy.

I am reminded of a fanciful notion of Christopher Morley, in that fateful March of 1933, when complacent citizens were suddenly aghast to find that those penny-in-the-slot machines, which our corner banks constitute for us, all had signs on their windows: "Temporarily out of order."

Mr. Morley came into his office completely upset. "It's high time," he remarked, "somebody prepared a Guide to the Earth for the Perplexed Martian."

Certainly one of the first things such an unspoiled intelligence would notice about men is their quixotic behavior with their money. They slave without thought of themselves to obtain a little, but when success crowns this effort, immediately they give it away—to bankers.

This may appear a mere quirky—a Morleyish—way of looking at the matter. But when we "put money in the bank," or "have money in the bank"—as we express it—the starkest fact about the action is that we entirely relinquish possession of it. Yet the expression itself indicates a continuing belief in ownership. This, of course, is a mere additional exemplification of that tendency to blind ourselves to actualities by the words we use. The phrase reveals that, unconsciously, many of us regard the particular bank with which we deal as a sort of huge distortion of the little receptacles, in which, as children, we dropped our pennies and nickels. In some special little cache of this enormous adult bank, we conceive of our money being retained safely, ready to be handed over to us whenever we ask for it. Informed persons know better than this, of course. But very few, even among these—when it comes to the point—speak or reason as if they knew better.

Examine for yourself the actuality. It is only too familiar to you. You have in your wallet a sum of money. If you will trace back, you will always find you have obtained this money by means of an exchange. You have given in exchange for it either some of your work, physical or mental, or some possession which you formerly owned. You take this money to the window of a bank, with a little notebook which you call your bankbook. You hand the money and the book to the man behind the cage. He makes some hieroglyphics, often indecipherable, in the book, and hands it back to you. You then walk away, with an unaccountably satisfactory feeling of being somehow a little wealthier than you were before. You have, as you say, "more money in the bank." Wealthier! Look in your pocketbook: what have you?

The undoubted fact is that *you have nothing at all tangible to show* for this money which you owned a moment before, and which now the bank owns. All you have, plainly, is a mere promise of the bank to give you an equivalent sum at a later time. Even this promise—it should be noticed for clarity's sake—is of the most informal character. Did you take the precaution to get, when you handed this particular sum of money to the cashier, a written promise that the bank would return an equivalent sum? You did not. But perhaps when you first opened up relations with the bank, you then obtained a written agreement, signed by the president or treasurer of the bank, promising to repay you, John or Susan Citizen, for any sums you left with him in the future? Search through your papers; you will find none of that character.

What originally happened—you will recollect—was that you en-

116

tered the bank and simply told the banker you wanted "to open an account." He was graciousness itself in accepting your money. He at once gave you in return for it—the little bankbook! Possibly he even expressed a hope that you would come around frequently, and give your money to him in this fashion! He said not a word about promising to return it to you, and much less did he give you a written promise to that effect. The truth is that he assumed, and you assumed, that as a matter of course he would repay these sums whenever you requested: such is the customary relationship between depositor and banker. Thus there was a promise, but it was neither written nor oral. It was an unspoken promise, *it lay in the custom!*

It is clear enough that what we have examined here is another deferred exchange, of precisely the same character as those which have been analyzed in the preceding chapters. It is an exchange, now, not of labor for money; nor of goods for money; nor of the use of a building for money. *It is an exchange of money for money.* On one side of the exchange, you relinquished possession of your money to the bank—totally. On the other side, there was a promise of the bank *to complete the exchange,* by giving you an equivalent sum of money, or perhaps a little more as interest, at a later unspecified date. These are the simple basic facts about every such transaction.

We have said that the promise involved in this relationship was neither written nor oral; it lay in the custom. That generalization is true. But what throbbing implications lie buried alive under this stony abstraction! What do we mean by "custom"? Here we mean, without any question, that the fulfillment of the promise to complete such an incompleted exchange is, in the experience of men, so certain, so infallible in its performance, that you and the banker, and all other men, feel that it is even unnecessary to mention the promise in speech or in writing.*

* This custom is enforced by common law, not by statute law. Most people—and I have even found some lawyers—assume that affirmative statutes exist, with a clear compulsory provision requiring a bank to return money given to it by a depositor. If any such provision can be found in the banking statutes of any of our states, it is safe to say it is a curiosity. The relationship is not even that of a trustee; it is a pure debtor-creditor relationship, so hallowed now by custom that the fulfillment of the second half of the exchange has become a

How lost in amazement would a Martian be over this additional revelation of the degree of reliance which human beings have come to place in one another! Here, without question, is the explanation of that apparently puerile notion of so many of us that we "have money in the bank." That is seen to be, as soon as it is thought about, a fallacious statement. It not only does not describe the facts, it is a mischievous misrepresentation of them. But, from this view, it becomes impossible to dismiss it as a mere demonstration of men's stupidity. The fallacy is explainable, as others we have seen, by the surface appearances of what goes on in our society. We give money to the banker and we receive a like sum in return whenever we ask for it. The final upshot of the transaction, then, is just *as if* we had money in the bank. The reliance we have in one another is here so complete and unquestioning that we utterly ignore the promise, the performance of it, and all the momentous significance of this faith in one another which, in this field, has become so profound that it is now all but unconscious.

But is performance here so inevitable that such unconsciousness on the part of all of us is justified? Most certainly not! A good case could be made out for the thesis that the economic history of the past three hundred years—which has seen the complete development of this institution, the modern bank—has been more affected by the completion or incompletion of this kind of promise than by almost any other factor; and notoriously has this been true in our own beloved land within the past ten years. Customary or not, this kind of promise is one that it is fatal to be unconscious of, particularly if an unconfused comprehension of the mechanics of society is our quest. For nobody nowadays can remain unaffected, on one side by the performance of the promise, and on the other by non-performance, when this occurs.

Precisely because of this universal unconsciousness, perhaps first it is advisable to point out that again the same psychological elements

long unquestioned part of what is called "common law." If one reflects, there is no more rationality specifically in the statutes to require a banker to return money given to him than to require any business man or consumer to hand over money, in the last half of a deferred exchange, for goods he has received.

are present in this relationship as in all the other deferred exchanges of ownership which we have so far examined. Naturally you would not relinquish your hard-earned money like this to every Tom, Dick and Harry. Indeed, it is very unlikely that you would trust even your dearest friends in this fashion.

I suggest that you stop reading at this moment and carry out a simple experiment with yourself.

Sit back in your chair and run over in your mind all the individuals whom you know.

Write the names down, and think carefully about each one of them.

Is there a single one amongst them, to whom you would thus relinquish all your money, retaining no power over it whatsoever?

Would you divest yourself completely of ownership in it and vest total ownership in him, to do with what he will?

And, in turn, would you accept from him a mere verbal promise to give you an equivalent sum whenever you requested it?

This question is asked seriously, not rhetorically. For only by such *ad hominem* comparisons is it possible to appreciate with true clarity, and in their full force, the underlying psychological factors that are involved in our social relationships. For you will be a very rare and fortunate person if, after trying this simple experiment, you can put a cross beside a single one of your dearest relatives and friends with whom you would go through this suggested process, without the most nervous qualms. Yet every day, astonishingly, you follow this apparently mad procedure with a banker whom you know hardly more than by name, and of whom (as a separate individual) you certainly entertain no higher opinion than you do of some dear relative or friend. You do it with all the money you can gather together, and you are perfectly composed in taking the action!

Why do you do it? The explanation we have seen elsewhere. You do it because you are utterly certain the deferred exchange, which is what this action is, in actuality, will be completed infallibly whenever you desire. You assume two things: first, that the bank has ample resources to complete the exchanges; and second, that it will always prove to be honest enough to complete them upon demand. But of course it is not precise to say that you merely "assume" these things. How, actually, do you come by this unquestioning faith? *It rests upon past performance only!* Invariably, your own experience has been that the bank always has completed the deferred exchanges it has entered into with you—that is, it has always honored your withdrawal checks. Infallibly also—so far as you know—it has done so with many other people. Both its solvency and its integrity, in this respect, have thus been demonstrated to you by its innumerable past actions. Once more we see how all the past makes the present what it is.

The bank must be, in this respect, even more than a Caesar's wife, above suspicion. There must not be a grain of tarnish upon its record of completing those vital half-exchanges in which it is trusted. If it fails to meet a single demand for completion of such an exchange, and the fault is clearly that of the bank and not of the depositor, all the infinitely scrupulous performance of the past is forgotten. All the thousands upon thousands of occasions it has completed such deferred exchanges go for naught in the eyes of its depositors. A panic "run" ensues. Like wildfire the news spreads from one to another of those who have trusted it. In droves they descend upon it, all demanding that it do the same thing—complete the second half of the deferred exchanges it has entered into with them.

In no other country in the world has this happened so frequently as in the United States. From our earliest days as a united nation, bank failures have been an ineradicable disease of our economy. In the past forty-five years nearly 18,000 banks failed in this country. We became so used to them that even in good times they were not noticed. "All through the prosperous decade of the '20's," notes a writer in the London *Economist*, "there was a continuous epidemic of bank failures . . . the average rate throughout the nine years to 1929 was 627 bank failures." We of this generation have seen the worst outbreak of this economic disease in our history, and possibly, in world history. In the fifteen years between 1921 and 1935, inclusive, there were 13,648 bank suspensions in the United States, involving deposits which totaled $7,800,000,000.* Between 1921 and 1929, 18½ per cent of all our banks were closed up; and then between 1930 and 1932 an additional 21 per cent of those remaining! Nor will anybody of this generation ever be likely to forget those fateful—but to the cold economist—fascinating few days before March 4, 1933, when practically every bank in the United States was on the verge of experiencing a "run." Presently, by order of the President, every bank was ordered closed and remained closed for varying periods, until this panicky excitement could be allayed. The normal prevailing order, of belief in the banks' ability to complete their deferred exchanges, built up by a long record of infallible performance, had to be restored in the population. There have been few demonstrations of mass psychology, operating in the economic field, more clear-cut and fascinating than this.

Why could the particular banks that failed us at one critical moment not complete their exchanges? Simply because they were in the same situation as ourselves. They too were on the other, *and last end*, of half-exchanges, which they had entered into with the money which collectively they had received from us. Too large a number of those upon whom they had been relying to complete these deferred exchanges were not able to do so. These individuals or corporations failed in their promises to the bank, and then the bank failed in its promises to us.

Now, it is this *interdependence of promises* which is the key to most economic events. Every unit of economic enterprise in the modern world, no matter how tiny, is an isolated spider web of incoming and outgoing promises. The completion of its own promises depends wholly, under ordinary circumstances, upon the promises made to it by other firms and other individuals. The most illuminating view to take of a bank is to regard it as a far larger spider web where this crucial *interdependence of promises* is revealed. Each bank is a focal point where the promises of thousands of men converge, are exchanged, and depend upon one another for fulfillment.

* Source, *U. S. Statistical Abstract*, 1936, Page 252.

Every bank, in a sense, is a local market for money, in which nothing but deferred exchanges—of money for more money—takes place endlessly. Like a good many other human enterprises, banking has been invested with an air of mystery for the layman. This arises from nothing but that unfamiliarity with other occupations that we commented upon in our Introduction. In their essence, a bank's operations are of the simplest nature, and even in the largest banks, they call not for any uncommon intelligence, but for two qualities in an exceptional degree: probity and caution. In the first of these, probity, the banker is little different, if at all, from the rest of us—as this whole study indicates. It is in the latter respect, caution, that bankers fail most often, for that indeed does call, in the modern world, for some slightly difficult operations of the intellect. Our own American bankers have the worst record in the world because they are the least cautious in the world.

This bad record may be instructive to analyze in a little detail, not only because its lessons come so near home—nor even because of the satisfaction there may be in licking our wounds—but because of the special light it can throw on this whole subject we are delving into: the role of promises and their performance in human affairs.

The bad record seems, first, to be inextricably associated with the number of banks we have. While over 13,500 banks in this country, between 1921 and 1933, slammed their doors in the face of their depositors, during the same troublesome period in all of war-rent and inflation-ridden Europe, there were perhaps not half a thousand cases where this happened. In the most stable lands, like Great Britain, France, Holland and Switzerland, in whose category of financial strength we certainly belong, whatever failures did occur were of the most trifling character. In Canada, whose entire economy is most comparable to ours and therefore furnishes the most striking contrast, there was only one bank failure in the period, to compare with our 13,500.

What a remarkable fact for a Martian to try to fathom! Do Americans as individuals enjoy losing their money?

122

But this fact of endemic loss here, and little loss elsewhere, is linked with another fact no less startling. We have at the present moment about 15,750 banks in this country. In Great Britain, there are only 35 having the same type of relation with the general public; in France and Germany together there are not more than 500, including the smallest private banks; in Canada there are only ten.

There can be little question that the explanation of this economic peculiarity of American society lies in the large number of our banks, as compared with other countries.

If you suspected that our little individual bankers were not so bright as they might be about banking, you would not be far wrong. But that is too easy and general an explanation—we love to blame individuals—for so deeply significant an economic phenomenon. Where precisely do our bankers go wrong? What mistakes do they make that the larger bankers in other countries do not? What mistakes does our very system of banking, authorized by us through our intelligent legislators, make possible and actually encourage? These are no academic questions. Losing money through a bank failure is no pleasant experience, as millions of us can testify. Instead of blaming individuals—the particular little bankers who seem immediately responsible—or instead of regarding such events as strange economic visitations, which must be borne like floods and dust-storms, if most of us took the trouble to understand their simple causes, we would no longer suffer them; and bank failures, which have never ceased among us, would become as much an economic dodo of an event as it is in lands more civilized than ours in this respect.

The basic causes clearly have to do with *the interrelation of promises made to and made by banks*. What that interrelation is appears, quite simply, when we examine the different interesting kinds of deferred exchanges, of which every bank is a perpetual center.

The banker makes first what he calls "commercial loans." These are loans made for comparatively short periods—that is, involving *short promises*—to enterprisers who are engaged either in producing or distributing goods. We saw, in Chapter Three, how every production enterprise hands out its property freely, in a curious sort of selective largesse, to its favored customers. Frequently these enterprises run short of the money needed to meet the promises in which they themselves are being trusted.

They go to the banker and ask him for what they need. He proceeds to hand over the money, just as you handed over yours to the bank, and as the business man handed over his property to his customers. What does he get in exchange for the money from the enterpriser? A piece of paper, the business man's so-called promissory note. One more promise!

Now, of course, no more than you do, does the bank relinquish ownership of its property in this fashion, unless it is certain that the particular promises made to it will be performed. Indeed, it is in a peculiar position. It must be far more cautious even than you are in entering into such a half-exchange. It must be far more cautious even than the credit man, who hands over his firm's property in a production enterprise or in a department store. For it does not wish to lose its own property—no more than you or the credit man. In addition, the half-exchanges, in which it happens to be the trusted party, are "on demand" exchanges. They have no date. They must be completed immediately, without a moment's delay, when completion is asked for. Nor can it ever know when completion will be asked for. In other words, so-called bank deposits are very much *short-term promises!*

All the bank's resources, therefore, must be watched with perpetual scrupulousness. Accordingly, when a commercial loan is being sought, the bank examines with the most minute care into those two factors which we have already seen are the basis of every deferred exchange: first, the business man's integrity, and second, his solvency. By the latter term is simply meant whether all his tangible property, and all the deferred exchanges in which he is trusting others, if and when realized in money, would together add up to more than enough to enable him to fulfill all the economic promises he himself has made. This can easily be determined by the banker through an itemized ex-

124

amination of what the business man owns and what he owes. The question of his honesty is different: that is a matter of the record. His past actions alone will reveal that story.

If the bank itself has had no previous experience with him, it seeks in every possible direction to find out whether in the past he has infallibly carried out his promises to complete deferred exchanges. If there is even one suspicious incident in his record, the red flag of caution flies at once. And if there is a clearly flagrant case of non-completion of a deferred exchange—if, for instance, the seeker of the loan has had to be sued by some bank or business house on just such a promissory note as he now offers, and a judge or jury had rendered the verdict against him—the chances of his obtaining the loan are practically nil. Only the most extraordinary explanation of such an incident would enable him to obtain it.

The truth is that it is extremely seldom bankers are obliged to refuse a loan on account of the questionable honesty of the party who asks for it. The reason for this is that any person with a clear instance of fraud in his record knows it is idle for him to ask a bank to relinquish its money to him in a half-exchange. He may do so and may succeed once, by pulling the wool over a particular banker's eyes —by keeping hidden, in short, the fact of his previous dishonesty. Once, however, that record becomes known, his credit with banks ends even more promptly, if that were possible, than it does in other quarters.

Since the bank finds that most business men can be relied upon to fulfill their promises if they are able to, its chief concern ordinarily centers about the determination of that ability. Here lies the real secret of modern banking. The banker's judgment and experience, as it is exercised upon the highly diverse forms of enterprise which seek his money, are focused chiefly upon this question. The banker's relation to business, indeed, is that of the critic to literature. If he is perspicacious, he is able to assay the nature and merits of an economic enterprise more truly, certainly more dispassionately, than its creator. What happens, in actuality, is that the long-headed experienced banker has found certain measures by which an enterprise of any character can be judged, and these measures, by and large, give an extremely reliable picture as to whether or not the loan-seeker is likely to be able faithfully to complete his deferred exchanges. The good banker always applies these yardsticks, and is unhappy if he must vary from them.* When he applies them, and as a result is left with even a little doubt as to the ability of the loan-seeker to complete the exchange, what he does is to suggest a type of deferred exchange which is different, in an important particular, from the ordinary "commercial loan."

In effect, he says to the loan-seeker: "We are not in the least concerned about your integrity. We do not, however, see eye-to-eye with you about the financial condition of your business. If too large a proportion of your promisors fails you, you will then not be able to meet all your own promises to complete deferred exchanges—and ours will be among these. We do not see why we should take this risk. Accordingly, we make you this proposition: we will let you have the money you need at present; but in the meantime give us a conditional ownership, so to speak, in such and such property which you say you own, and which you do not need at present. If and when you complete the exchange, we will release the property from this conditional ownership. If, however, you fail to complete the exchange, you must give us the right to sell this property. We will then apply the receipts to completing your exchange with us, and will hand over any balance that remains to you."

This is the so-called secured loan. It is precisely, of course, what takes place in those deferred exchanges called mortgages. It is precisely what took place when men put up their own persons as forfeit to complete an exchange, in ancient times. The reasoning is as deep-

* The most important one among them is what the banker calls the "ratio of current assets to current liabilities." These terms simply mean how much does the business man owe that is soon payable, and how does this compare in amount with his quickly available resources. The ratio, safely, it is generally considered, should be two to one in a stable industry. This ratio would change in more speculative industries. Of course, the crucial thing to be determined here is how good are the current assets being added up. The greater portion of them always consist of *promises of other firms and individuals,* and their certainty of fulfillment must be judged carefully.

rooted as the practice of exchange itself. For it has its roots in the same consideration—an attempt to make as certain as possible that a half-exchange will be completed.

The bank's secured loan, of course, is still in every respect a deferred exchange. The property which is held pending the completion of it, the so-called security, is not owned by the bank. The bank cannot do anything it pleases with it, which is the ultimate criterion of ownership. It merely has been given the right by the owner to exchange it for money *in a stated event*—namely, if the particular exchange is not completed within a specified time. On the other hand, neither can the real owner do with it what he pleases, as he can with other property he owns. It is, in a sense, sequestered property, held by the bank for its protection.

Since a forfeit is asked for, it is evident that distrust as to the eventual completion of the deferred exchange is present whenever a bank makes such a "secured loan." Our Martian might imagine, since it would seem that the banker would lose nothing by always requiring such protection, that all loans would be secured. Not so. On June 30, 1937, for example, unsecured loans for all banks in this country stood at around $7,000,000,000.*

There is an explanation, of course, of this apparent anomaly. To ask for "security" in some cases might be actively resented by the borrower as a reflection upon his integrity. He would almost surely go and borrow elsewhere, where his mere word would be honored, as he expects it to be. This fact may be taken as merely another demonstration, somewhat in reverse, of the degree of reliance men have come to place in one another's economic promises.

When bankers cannot divest themselves of their money by handing it over to business men on so-called secured and unsecured loans, they give it away in another quarter: to corporations or units of gov-

* This statement is based on figures of the Comptroller of the Currency for all "insured banks." I am using the word "secured" loans above in a broader sense than is usual. Technically the "secured loans" reported by the Comptroller are those where stocks and bonds only are put up as security. Total loans, on the date given, came to over $17,000,000,000. Included in these were $7,165,000,000 "commercial and industrial loans, otherwise secured and unsecured." The greater part of these were unsecured promissory notes of business enterprises and individuals.

ernment. Of course, every banker would bridle to hear it said that he gives away the bank's money. In the terms they use, they "invest" the money. But this is merely another good obscuring word which keeps men from understanding the simple actualities of what they do. For when banks "buy" corporation or government bonds, what they really do is to enter into a long deferred exchange with corporations or governments. Again, it is an exchange in which *they first give up their money unconditionally*, totally relinquish ownership of it, and then receive a mere promise that the second half of the exchange will take place—years hence! It is perfectly all right, of course, to call this procedure an "investment," if one is in the habit of doing so. But it is again fatal not to be aware that in reality it is not a thing, in essence, but a deferred exchange in which a long promise intervenes. These long promises of governments and corporations are of such a special nature that they cannot be examined hastily; they deserve a chapter each to themselves, for things happen with regard to them which are both peculiar and important.

We are now in a position to observe, in a broad fashion, the necessary interdependence that exists among men's promises, of which every bank in the world is a focal point. On one side are the promises *made by* the bank. They consist almost wholly of that kind which is made to you and me. We call them "deposits," a word with a pleasant aura of self-deception, for it makes us feel as if we really retained possession of something, when we give our money to the bank. The most important characteristic to be observed about these promises made by the bank is that *they are all short promises*. They must be completed at once, upon request.

On the other side are the promises *made to* the bank: first, by business men on secured and unsecured loans, and second, by corporations and governments. Some of these are short promises, namely, those made by business enterprises; ordinarily, these are completed in sixty or ninety days. Others are long promises: those of governments and corporations. A third kind, in a sense, are in-between: they are both short and long promises, where the bank tries to protect itself

128

against incompletion by a forfeit that has been put up, the "security."

Now, the essential business of banking can be described in a phrase: it is determined by the obvious relation between these promises *made by* and *made to* the banks. So that his own promises can be fulfilled, the banker must see that all the promises made *to* him shall be fulfilled. All, or practically all. If *any substantial part* of the promises made to him are definitely unfulfilled, then he has no recourse but to default on the promises made to us. He fails.

At this point, the analysis we made in the preceding chapter—of the difference *in likelihood of completion* between long and short promises—lights up beautifully what happens in American banking. It explains, almost entirely, that peculiarity of our economy, the bad record of our bankers, the incredible number of our bank failures, as compared with the rest of the world.

For example, one of the principal kinds of deferred exchanges our banks enter into consists of loans on land and buildings. They are extremely long promises. They seldom run for less than three years, and often as high as fourteen years. We saw, in the last chapter, how very dubious they often are as to completion in full. Even aside from this dubiousness, they are a peculiar form of promise for a banker to accept. For it would seem that he would very much hamstring himself in fulfilling his own short promises, if he allows his money to go out in long deferred exchanges, which he has no right nor opportunity to end when it suits his convenience. Hamstring is about the word to use for this practice, and surely it would be taken as one of our most light-hearted curiosities by a Martian. For this hare-brained procedure we Americans not merely allow our bankers to follow; it is a recognized part of our banking system and has been for one hundred and fifty years. At regularly recurring intervals it has taken its almost inevitable course and resulted in bank failures by the thousand. And now, after the most disturbing of all these economic upheavals—in which it would almost require an economic moron not to observe the important role it played in what happened to the banks —this happy tradition has remained quite unchanged by our politicians, although they tinkered enough over our banking laws in other ways. It is still part of our latest amended banking act that the Federal Reserve member banks may lend money on real-estate mortgages. Needless to say, every one of the forty-eight States allow their chartered banks to do the same. Over the border, in Canada, where there was only one bank failure *at a time when 13,500 of our banks closed* —and where there was as much industrial trouble as we had during the last Depression—*commercial banks are not allowed to lend on real estate*. Abroad, the sensible bankers are not restrained by law, but they simply do not *allow themselves* to follow this practice.

It is important—in order to understand our own American society better, but even more for theoretic reasons—to identify the particular operation of this cause among the several that were clearly responsible for our bank failures of the past two decades. It can be identified most easily by seeing *just where* the bank failures happened. They happened principally in small communities, rural and otherwise, where there was little if any industry, and where—to make any profit —the banker was compelled to give out an undue portion of his money for long-term promises, resting ultimately on the value of land or buildings. The banks that began in great numbers to fail, as an anonymous observer in the London *Economist* remarked, "were the smallest variety of rural bank, and the cause was *in the main* [italics mine] the collapse of land values in and after 1921 and the slow deflation of agricultural pipedreams which occupied the whole of the '20's." * He does not happen to mention in this connection, although it was of course the fact, that simultaneously—as we indicated in the last chapter—the value of urban real estate had been even more swollen during the same period, and that thousands of banks in small towns and large cities had tied up enormous sums of money in these long promises on real estate, which so soon were to be proved dubious of fulfillment. "The real run on American banks," this same acute commentator observes, "can be dated from the failure of the Bank of United States in December, 1930. This was the first time a large bank in a large city had closed its doors. From that time the tide of suspicion mounted. Failures continued at an increasing rate, and the

* Supplement, *The Economist*, October 3, 1936.

size of the bank affected was growing." Now, the Bank of United States—as developments quickly proved—was involved to an almost incredible extent in loans based on real-estate values in New York City. Later on this same observer makes another interesting comment on what happened: "The Detroit banks closed on February 14, 1933, and within three weeks the bank 'holiday' had spread to every State in the Union." In the investigations that ensued, it transpired that these Detroit banks again had, incredibly, tied up large portions of their resources in promises which depended for fulfillment upon real-estate values.*

No thorough investigation has been made of the causes for the failure of the 13,500 banks which closed in this country between 1921 and 1933; but it would be a surprising thing, were it possible at this late date to undertake such an analysis, if it did not develop that in practically every case—to some extent, and often to a very large extent—the closing of the bank was related to the fact that it had undermined its ability to meet its *short* promises to depositors by accepting *too many long promises*, the fulfillment of which depended in the final analysis upon real-estate values. Some indication of this is given by a statement of the Comptroller of the Currency, under whose charge suspended national banks come. In July of 1935, the receivers of these failed banks owned, or held mortgages upon, *over forty-five thousand pieces of real-estate property*, which of course the failed banks had dropped in their laps! †

But this undue reliance of bankers on the particular long promises represented by mortgage loans is far from being the only diffi-

---

* I find an interesting and certainly the correct explanation of this in an article in the *Atlantic Monthly*, January, 1937, by Arthur Pound, entitled *As Goes Michigan*. He says: "Major industries in Michigan, with large reserves built from profits, seldom borrow considerable sums from local banks; if and when they borrow, they go to New York for money, for they want big money and cheap money for long-range programmes. As a result, commercial banks in the principal automobile cities have little or no outlet for funds on local paper of best character, with repayment certain at near dates. To get rid of the savings poured in upon them by temporarily flush workers and merchants, the banks fell naturally into financing real-estate mortgages in an amount and of a quality not consistent with sound commercial banking. In the clutch of circumstances, these loans were frozen far too solidly for the solvency and morale of alternately high-spirited and downcast communities."

† Seventy-third report of the Comptroller of the Currency, 1934-1935.

culty incautious bankers allow themselves to get into. We must look at those other long promises, so beloved of bankers, represented by the bonds of corporations and governments.

The banker has great numbers of these; whole "portfolios" of them, as he himself puts it. The money is paid out, and won't come back for a long time, just as it is with the mortgage loan. In the latter case, it may be repayable in three years, whereas in the case of a bond it may not be repayable for as long as ninety-nine years! A pretty long promise to depend upon, in case a large part of the promises made by the bank have to be fulfilled in a hurry.

But, of course, in meeting his own promises, the banker is not relying *on the completion* of these long promises. Naturally, there is no way in which he could get them completed ninety-nine years in advance, if necessary. *He is relying upon being able to re-exchange them with somebody else, if he has to in a hurry, for at least the same price he has paid.*

It seems safe; but how safe is it? It is clear that the amount of money the banker can get in the market for these long promises depends principally upon two things: first, the general estimate, among informed persons, as to *whether or not* the long promise will be faithfully fulfilled when the date of completion arrives. And second, the quantity of these long promises that are being offered, as compared with the ability and willingness of buyers to exchange money for them.

Now, in order to be able to meet any abnormal volume of his own promises immediately the banker must be able *quickly* to exchange long promises of this kind for money, and he must be able to do so *at no great loss.* Preferably, of course, in case of such need, he wants to be able to make the exchange at a profit. His next preference is to break even. But two untoward things may happen. First, informed persons may come to the conclusion that these long promises *may only be partially fulfilled*, if at all; in this case, naturally, they will not give as much money for them as the banker did. They may count the promises as wholly worthless, indeed, and offer nothing for them. Or, second, the promises may continue to be just as certain of fulfill-

132

ment as before, but at the moment the bank must exchange money for them, *nobody can be found who wants them,* and the bank (under the compulsion to get money at once for them) may have to offer them at a lower and ever lower price to find buyers. This particularly may turn out to be the case, if a great many banks find themselves in this position *at the same time.* There may be a glut of this kind of long-term promise on the market, and "sacrifice" prices have to be offered, in order to get them exchanged for money.

This was precisely the situation which arose in this country in the three years of 1930, 1931 and 1932. With their portfolios full of long-term promises, which they had either bought outright, or taken over on secured loans which had failed of fulfillment, banks were faced with a slowly accelerating demand for fulfillment of their own promises. People were withdrawing their deposits. The only recourse of the banks was to exchange the long-term promises called "bonds" for money. The insurance companies, too, found themselves in the same position—for an interesting reason which we shall analyze in a later chapter. But it became clear that a good many of the long promises would only be fulfilled in part, if at all. This general realization, together with the fact that more and more banks and insurance companies were obliged to exchange their bonds for money, completely undermined the bond market. The final event was that, contrary to their expectations, many banks could not obtain in money as much, *or even nearly as much,* as they had given away for the promises in the first instance. Accordingly, they could not meet their own promises; they failed.

The essential point for the student of human affairs to observe about all this is *the close interdependence of the promises.* Naturally, when short ones are dependent for fulfillment upon long ones, they become affected by that greater undependability of long ones, which we demonstrated in the last chapter as well as here, and will demonstrate with other examples later. It all comes down to our tendency, as we showed in the last chapter, to expect the future to be like the present. In the case of banks, as we see, almost their entire trouble (when they get into it) can be localized with the long promises that are made to them; first, those involved in real-estate values, and second, those long promises of governments and corporations, which have to be exchanged when money is needed, and do not—for the reasons outlined above—bring in as much money as was anticipated.

"The inconsistency of borrowing short and lending long," says one of the ablest students and practitioners in this field, "has constituted a basic weakness in the banking system and has subjected long-term assets to violent deflation when banks have had to sell these assets rapidly to meet the demands of time depositors." * Another comment seems pertinent here, made by one of the surprisingly few students who have thought it necessary to inquire exhaustively into this vital field of the causes of bank failures: "To maintain that it was the breakdown of the business structure which caused the banking system to collapse is putting the cart before the horse. It should be recognized that the accumulation of our banking troubles during the twenties was to no small extent due to the effective way in which the breakdown of the business structure, locally or regionally, was used as a smokescreen for the errors, abuses and malpractices which developed with the entrance of commercial bankers into the securities markets." † That is, the trouble was caused by the notions of many brash bankers, upon whose promises innumerable persons were relying, that they were able to judge the reliability of the promises of corporations and governments, of whose operations they were in reality utterly ignorant.

We finally come to a fairly clear explanation of the enigma with which we began: why it is that 13,500 banks could fail in this country in a given period, while none failed in other comparable lands, with the same type of industrial organization and undergoing like economic difficulties. Our little bankers simply did not know their business! They simply have not the experience, in these modern days, to keep a careful and wise relation between the promises *made by* them and the promises *made to* them. That is the simple key to

* W. Randolph Burgess, in *The Reserve Banks and the Money Market.*
† *American Bank Failures,* by C. D. Bremer.

banking, which anyone can observe; and it is apparent that most of our bankers have not yet grasped it.

It may be a matter for interesting reflection here, among those philosophically inclined, to ponder over a simple but highly significant fact. We officially recognize the deficiencies of these thousands of bankers of ours. We hedge their operations about with the most careful laws. What they may and may not do is set forth, oh! so precisely, in the statutes. We have examining officials visiting them without notice to see that they keep to these laws. Nor can anyone say they are not sensible laws, for the most part. On the other hand, abroad, in what we consider more socialistic lands, there are few such laws. The foreign banker is subjected to no such detailed governmental control, either of his actions or of his judgment. *He imposes them upon himself.* They are matters of long banking custom, not of law. Yet this country has 13,500 bank failures in fifteen years, and Europe a bare fraction of this! What this strange fact discloses every man will decide according to his philosophy; or as the Greeks used to say in their treaties, "according to the custom of the country."

Nothing is more economically dramatic than the failure of a bank, but the very drama in it may give a distorted notion of what occurs in the day-by-day progress of our society. We must analyze here, as we have elsewhere, the *degree of reliability* manifested by men in this special area of economic activity. Because of the distressing record of bank failures in this country, it might well be imagined that men do not begin to show here the same remarkable measure of dependability that they manifest elsewhere.

On the contrary, an analysis of the figures reveals an almost incredible degree of reliability.

It must be clearly seen that what we are striving to obtain here is merely the ratio between the performance and non-performance of promises. How often are the promises of banks fulfilled, and how often not? We must therefore get a figure, on one side, of the total sums which were promised by banks, *and paid,* and compare these with the sums which were promised, *and not paid*. It would be faulty reasoning, and would not truly reveal the degree of reliability shown by banks, to take the money lost by individuals through the closing of banks *over a protracted period*, and compare these losses with the total deposits that happen to be in the banks *on any single day*. This latter ratio would only be useful in helping to give us some idea of the percentage of wealth lost by individuals through bank closings, as compared with the *average* wealth held in banks.

For example, suppose we take a single bank which closed on December 31, 1932. Let us assume that on that day it was on the trusted end of deferred exchanges with depositors, totaling $1,000,000. Assume, further, that after it was closed no depositor received a penny of this sum. But during the ten years preceding, let us say, the bank had never failed to meet its deferred exchanges with depositors. Deposits would be made with it and drawn out; they would be made again, and again drawn out. Each time this happened, of course, the bank fulfilled the promise it had made in the deferred exchange. It is the total *of all these promises fulfilled in the past*, as compared with the promises of $1,000,000 *fatally unfulfilled* on December 31, 1932, which would give us a true measure of the degree of reliability *manifested over a period* by this particular bank.

Now it happens that some figures are available to supply us with such a comparison. In the six-year period of 1929 to 1934, inclusive, which saw the two extremes of the last great business cycle, the total amount of deferred exchanges which banks completed with their depositors—that is, *the total of their fulfilled promises*—was at the very least $3,000,000,000,000.* During the same period, the money tied up (not lost) by all depositors through bank-closings—

* This figure is arrived at in the following fashion: The Federal Reserve Board publishes figures for 141 cities, of what are called "debits to individual accounts." These consist of withdrawals made by depositors, or charges against depositors. Of course, whenever a withdrawal by a depositor is made it means that the bank *has fulfilled* an economic promise represented by that amount. To get the total of such promises fulfilled for the period by these banks, these total yearly debits are added, from them is subtracted the sum of all deposits in these banks at the beginning of the period, and to them is added the deposits on hand at the end of the period. Of course, if figures for all banks were available (instead of those in 141 cities) the aggregate would be considerably increased, and the record of performance even better. See *U. S. Statistical Abstract, 1936*, Page 269.

136

that is, the total of unfulfilled promises—was $6,400,000,000. This latter figure constitutes a little more than one-fiftieth of 1 per cent of the first. In other words, it is fair to say that the record of fulfillment of banks, on their promises to depositors, is 99⁹⁸⁄₁₀₀ per cent perfect.

But even this one-fiftieth of 1 per cent is an unfair picture, in measuring the reliability banks have demonstrated. The $6,400,000,000 tied up in the closed banks during the period was not all lost, by any means. This was simply the total amount owed to depositors *at the moment* these banks closed. All of the banks which closed still had some assets, which were gradually liquidated and distributed among the depositors, and this process even yet is going on.

Moreover, an additional pertinent fact should be observed. *This record includes the worst economic period in our history.* During this six-year period 8,559 banks suspended operations, with these $6,400,000,000 tied up in them. If we chose any normal six-year period, the record of fulfilled promises, as compared with their unfulfilled promises, would be infinitely better.

An equally striking picture of the reliability manifested in this particular area of human relationships would be provided, if we were able to obtain exact figures about the losses sustained by banks on all loans. Unfortunately—and very curiously—no authoritative study seems to have been made as to this question. Chester Arthur Phillips in his book, *Bank Credit*, refers to the fact that in 1892 a Comptroller of the Currency estimated that such losses of banks, at that time, only amounted to one-two-hundredth of 1 per cent. And he himself remarks that the loss of one-hundredth of 1 per cent would be accounted serious by a banker. But there can be no question that non-performance of the promises, represented by commercial loans, is trifling.

The whole record—both of banks and their borrowers—shows that the scrupulousness of men in dealing with one another, in this particular field of human activity, approaches the finest extreme. The promises run into inconceivable billions, thousand of billions over a period as short as twenty years, and—as we saw—with practical invariability these promises may be counted upon to be fulfilled.

9

How Bank Promises Are Used as Money Far More
Than Money Itself, and How the Creation
of Bank Money Is Controlled

THE history of banking, usually presented in tomes that are among the dullest in our libraries, should constitute one of the most fascinating strands of human history. For it is clear that the development of the custom, of entrusting banks with money, would trace out the gradual extension among men of the practice of carrying on their economic life by means of half-exchanges. To follow the detail of this evolution, and to observe its necessary consequences in the common life of men and women, would be as absorbing a spectacle as all history can unroll. Only the most backward individual, economically speaking, now keeps his money himself. This wholesale trusting of one another with our most cherished possession, our money, has slowly evolved as a system, until our whole complex civilization clearly rests upon it. Indeed, it is responsible, as much as anything else, for what we regard as the complexity of modern life. Yet time was when the very reverse was true, when many of the conditions of ordinary life were determined by the central fact that every man kept his money on his own premises; when, in short, this particular type of half-exchange which we describe by the words "deposit banking" did not even exist.

We can barely touch upon this evolution here. A better place to do so will be when we inquire into that enigmatic subject, Money. But at least one thing may be noticed at this point. As in the case of

138

the specialization of markets, the present universality of this custom *has been a comparatively recent social phenomenon*. Careless writers frequently refer to banks and bankers in antiquity. They were not the kind of banks we know. There was occasional custodianship of wealth, and of course this reveals in very ancient times the same reliance on human honesty as exists today. The great Hammurabi, in the laws he codified for Babylon about 4000 years ago, gives the clearest evidence of the well-established existence of this relationship, for some of his laws have to do with control of the custodianship of gold, silver and other forms of wealth. But custodianship of wealth must have been very occasional, and—where it occurred—was certainly an indispensable relationship. He who entrusted his wealth with others did so only because he could not himself, in a world of thieves, properly guard it. There were also large lenders from the very earliest times. The temples of Babylon, for example, made loans, not of money, but of goods. The Mosaic laws are explicit on the matter of lending, showing how common the relationship was. Both Greece and Rome in their heyday, particularly the latter, had their specializing lenders. Knightly orders, like the Templars, were often lenders to Kings and courts and cities. The Catholic Church, through its business agents, was perhaps the greatest of all lenders in the Middle Ages. Also, a great many monasteries lent money.

But these lenders of antiquity *lent their own wealth* to the borrowers—not other peoples' wealth. This is the vital distinction between an ordinary lender and a banker. Whenever they acted as the custodians of money, as the Knights Templars did, for example, or as the Kings of England in the Tower, they were considered and counted themselves *to be custodians only*. Rarely were they supposed to touch the money left with them, and the last thing expected of them was to lend it to anyone else. For the most part, they were mere ancient safe-deposit boxes.

Banks, as we now know them, originated in Europe, largely in Italy, in the Middle Ages. They had their real roots in the economic scoundrelism of rulers. The amoebic banker was in some cases the money-changer—and, apparently to a less degree, the worker in precious metals, the goldsmith. We shall see later, in our chapters on Money, why in the Middle Ages it was made necessary—by the fraudulence of rulers with regard to coinage—for men to bring their money to the money-changers, to pass upon its value; or to goldsmiths, to melt it down, assay its value, and make it up into ornaments. These persons necessarily had stores of precious metals on hand; that which they themselves owned, and, if they were goldsmiths, that which they were working upon for others. They were obliged to keep it as well protected as today a bank does its cash. It was a natural development, in a turbulent political world, for wealthy persons increasingly to leave their gold and silver coin with the money-changer or goldsmith, for safer custody than they themselves could provide. This was particularly true with important money-changers, who frequently were under the close protection of the ruler, and often were given the concession of minting the ruler's money. The money left with the money-changer was, of course, subject to call at any time; and it is well to note our loose end of truth reappearing here at the beginnings of modern banking: this most precious of all human possessions would, of course, never have been so left had not the owners found, by previous experience, that the custodians were wholly reliable and would always relinquish the money, upon a mere request to do so. Modern banking began when the custodians—the money-changers and goldsmiths—by agreement with those who trusted them,* proceeded to lend out their own money, and that which was left with them by others, interchangeably.

Now, this trusting of money-changers and goldsmiths with the custodianship of money, which in time they were allowed to lend, became more and more to be the practice, among persons of some wealth, in the fifteenth and sixteenth centuries in large cities like Venice, Genoa, Milan, Rome, London, Paris, Amsterdam, and other European trading centers.

* See Chapter Sixteen. In the case of Italian money-changers the lending originally was not by agreement; it was a violation of trust, and was stopped by law; this constituted one of the first instances of governmental control of this economic relationship.

An often misunderstood, and certainly an unhonored portion of these first individual bankers were Jews, who had been forced into money-dealing because no other occupation was allowed them. They were among the few trustworthy elements in the mediæval population.

Incidentally, there are few strands of European history more important to follow, and less generally familiar to informed people, than the vital role of the Jews in that history. They had, in Palestine, been predominantly handicraftsmen and farmers. Upon dispersal over all the Near East and throughout Europe, they were—by pure circumstance—placed in a favorable position for much the most important economic activity of the first thousand years of the Christian Era: international trading. It was a natural development for Jews in widely separated localities to know one another, have more confidence in one another than in the surrounding population, and thus to trade with one another. Accordingly, they early became important, out of all relation to their numbers, in inter-city exchanging of goods. But equally operative in fashioning their activity was that trend of cultural circumstance which practically forced them into money-lending. One of the most strongly held tenets of the early Christian Church—reinforced by all the mediæval authority of Aristotle—was that the acceptance of interest on money loaned was a sin. No economic notion could possibly be more damaging to the body politic, for its clear effect (we can see today) was to *compel the hoarding of capital by religious tenet*. This completely killed, in the making, perhaps the most necessary form of deferred exchanges: those of money for more money at a later date. This, perhaps, is the most necessary form of half-exchange because, through promising, it permits of every man's accumulated wealth *being utilized for the benefit of the whole society*.

So vital an economic function could not, of course, allow itself thus to be atrophied. Accordingly, business activity, for almost fifteen hundred years, found ways of circumventing this religious interference with economic progress. Even the Church itself, and monasteries galore, managed somehow, by subterfuge, to enter into

141

lending. But the Jews were, nonetheless, by this Church interdict against interest, propelled, in a sense—by an economic vacuum—into money-lending. The Church clearly had no control over them. It was almost inevitable, therefore, for many Jews (at any rate, those who acquired a little money) to go into money-lending as a pursuit, and into the associated activity, money-changing. They would both do it on their own initiative, and without doubt frequently with Christian friends as silent partners, men who could not publicly and personally engage in lending; who—not to endanger their souls— had to accept what they called "profit" and not "interest." The historical evidence is fairly clear, also, that the general trustworthiness of Jews in this relationship, as compared with current business morality at the time, had a great deal to do with their early preeminence in this field, a preëminence they soon enough lost when the Church interdict progressively became a dead letter.*

For all the many thousands of years prior to this crucial social development of the beginning of this deposit-and-lending system, it should be realized that almost every human being who lived his span upon the planet always kept what little wealth he could garner together in the form of gold and silver coins hidden away on his premises or person.† It is because they were hidden so well that we have such abundant and excellent specimens of ancient coins in our museums. Now, when this custom of relinquishing money-property to banks became gradually more extended, not many generations had to pass for the recognition to arise that the banker was performing a public function; in other words, that a few individuals were entering into the most vital relationship with a very respectable proportion of the population. In our own day, it is practically the entire population they deal with. That dominating part of the population, in its organized form as the State, began then to intervene *to control the banker* in these particular half-exchanges.

* A good recent book, throwing some detailed light on this subject, is *The Jews of Germany*, by Marvin Lowenthal.
† There seem to be instances referred to of a deposit-and-lending relationship in Athens and to a greater extent in Rome, but it was far from being common practice.

How that intervention began, the precise forms the control has taken, the increasing degree in which it has been exercised, would make up a large part of the history of banking. The control took in the main the direction that might be expected. It specified courses of action the banker was required to follow in order to make as certain as possible that *he would always be able to complete* the half-exchanges in which he was being trusted.

Originally, it is interesting to note, the protection was almost entirely directed against outright dishonesty. For bankers did not always manifest the scrupulous integrity they show today. Far from it. After its first honest beginnings (it had to be honest, observe, to have a beginning) the practice of banking in many countries became what today we call a "racket." Sharpers came to recognize that it was a beautifully easy way to gull the innocent. For example, even as late as the Civil War in this country, a certain little publication used to appear, and had to be kept continuously up to date, which was more important to everybody, particularly shopkeepers, than even the newspaper. It went by the colorful name of *The Ready Detector*. Its *raison d'être* was to guard careless people against accepting notes issued by banks, which had no good money to redeem them with, but which had not the slightest scruple in issuing the notes. But, gradually, egregious dishonesty, such as this, wholly disappeared from the practice of banking; the banker's name became synonymous with probity, and we have wholly forgotten that at one time it was in the same questionable category as the words, Wall Street, a few years ago. As this change occurred, the State's safeguards in the field of banking were built up more against the incaution of bankers, proceeding either from greed or from poor judgment.

When they are analyzed, the ponderous technicalities of our banking laws and customs sift down into mere applied common sense. Almost in their entirety, in one way or another, they are designed to accomplish two things: to prevent the banker from entering into *too large a volume* of deferred exchanges, as compared to the resources he has; or into deferred exchanges of *too risky a nature*.

143

Perhaps the most basic and most important of these banking laws and customs relate to so-called bank reserves. What are they? They are requirements (either set up by law, as in our own country, or decreed by custom, as is the case largely abroad) that banks shall keep on hand, in the form of actual money, *a prescribed proportion* of the total amount in which they are being trusted by depositors. The bank may not lend these so-called reserves of cash. The reserves must be on the premises, or close by immediately available. Reserves naturally are always set high enough to give the bank plenty of leeway. There can be, there must be, no single slip in this record of inviolable performance of promises. In the United States, at the present moment of writing, the money reserves required of Federal Reserve members vary, with the location of banks, from 14 per cent to 26 per cent of their "demand deposits," and 6 per cent of their "time deposits." These reserves (in our country) are not kept on the bank premises, but must be deposited by each member bank with the Federal Reserve Bank of its district.*

Unfortunately—for those who shy away from technicalities—it is important here to be a little more detailed, and not so general, in our study of the necessary relation between the reserves a bank must keep and the loans it may make. The arithmetic, however, is simple, and it is inestimably important—as we hope to demonstrate—for everyone to understand the operations of the banker at this point. What occurs right here has the most far-ranging social and economic consequences.

If a bank only has to keep as reserves, for example, 25 per cent of the money it receives as deposits, obviously it can use the remaining 75 per cent to enter into the various types of deferred exchanges we have previously looked at—secured and unsecured loans, and so-called investments (which are really loans) in corporate and govern-

* "Time deposits" are those which do not have to be met upon demand. That is, the bank, by previous agreement with depositors, is given a specified period, if it wishes to avail itself of it, before it is required to complete the half-exchange. The above figures of reserves seem to indicate a marked difference in character between time and demand deposits. This is an absurd assumption, made by both bankers and depositors, which is analyzed, and its pernicious consequences clarified, in Chapter Eleven.

ment bonds. But a simple analysis soon reveals that this means a larger volume of possible loans than would first appear. One might think that if a bank received $1,000,000 from a depositor and had to keep 25 per cent of it as a reserve, the amount that it would be enabled to lend would be the remaining three-quarters—that is $750,-000. Not at all; it can lend far more, for a simple reason which soon becomes apparent.

When a bank lends money it seldom gives the borrower the cash at once. The borrower must keep his borrowed money somewhere. It would be—to say the least—ungracious of him not to keep it in the bank which has lent it to him. It is very seldom that any cash at all leaves the bank at the precise moment of a loan. *The bank's so-called deposits are simply increased by the amount of the loan.* Only slowly does the borrower withdraw from the bank the money he has borrowed, *and seldom does he withdraw it all.*

But now let us see, mathematically, what happens. If the bank's "deposits" are increased by the amount of a loan at the time the loan is made (and we have seen they are), the bank, assuming the reserve it is required to keep is 25 per cent, may lend out 75 per cent *of this additional deposit.* We started out with the supposition that the bank had received a new cash deposit of $1,000,000. So long as that deposit is retained by the bank, so long as it is not decreased by withdrawals, if the bank's required reserve is, say 25 per cent, it is theoretically enabled to lend not $750,000, three-quarters of it, but three million dollars! In other words, *by its own action through loans*, it can theoretically *increase its own deposits* so much.

Now, a very tricky thing happens at this point. It is so tricky that up to a few decades ago bankers themselves did not recognize it. As a plain layman you need not be ashamed, accordingly, to find it a little difficult to understand the details. Yet that it is incalculably important to understand will soon appear. We said that, *theoretically*, if a bank had to keep reserves of 25 per cent, it could add three times the amount of any new deposits, through the making of loans. In actuality, however, *no single bank* can do this. In practice, it turns out that a single bank can only safely lend *a little more again* than the amount of any new deposit. In other words, when a new deposit of $10,000 is received by a bank, it can only safely make loans of a little more than $10,000. The reason for this is that, while the borrower at the moment of a loan leaves the money in the bank and thereby increases the bank's deposits, very soon he must begin drawing upon these deposits to pay his bills. This withdrawal obviously *reduces the total* of the bank's deposits, and therefore the total sums it is allowed to lend.

But here is where the tricky phenomenon, referred to, occurs. While *no single bank* can quadruple its own deposits by loans (assuming the average reserve requirement to be 25 per cent) the loans of each single bank, lending up to the limit its reserves allow, *can and does pyramid the deposits of the entire banking system up to that limit*. Let us attempt to see what these words mean in actual events.

Assume the borrower "withdraws" *actual dollar bills* from the bank which has lent it to him—instead of doing so by writing out a check. What does he do with the money? He pays a bill with it. The recipient of the money then deposits it in his own bank—Bank B. All is simple enough to this point. Bank B's deposits are thus increased and Bank A's are precisely the same as before it made the loan. It is clear, therefore, *that Bank A's loan has increased Bank B's deposits!* But now Bank B, with increased deposits, can also safely make added loans, up to a little more than the amount of the new deposit. It proceeds to do so to another borrower. That borrower withdraws the money, and pays a bill to a man *who deposits it with Bank A*. Ah! Bank A now indeed has a new deposit, *and can lend a little more than the amount of it*. Again, it proceeds to do so. Back and forth, in this fashion, the loans of one bank increase the deposits of another; and the limit of the deposits that can be created, *by the banking system as a whole,* is determined by the proportion of reserves that all banks, on the average, are obliged, by law or custom, to keep.

Whether or not, as an inquiring citizen you comprehend clearly the details of this process,* it is certainly not difficult to grasp the

* A good book, explaining in detail this somewhat hidden and involved process is *Bank Credit,* by Chester Arthur Phillips.

146

social significance of it. For it is clear that, by this process, our banks bring into existence by their own actions, through the making of loans, a very large portion of what individuals in our modern society *use as money*.

We are face to face here with a fact which is so pregnant with significance to human affairs that no one who wishes to comprehend our modern society may allow himself to be unaware of it. These particular half-exchanges which banks enter into, with their depositors and lenders, have a peculiar quality shared with no other type of deferred exchanges, except certain ones which are entered into by governments, and which we shall examine later. The peculiarity is— as indicated above—*that bank promises are universally used by men as money.*

A fog of mystification often surrounds this area of economic activity—but it is not a natural, it is a man-made, fog. The basic processes are simple enough to understand. All anyone has to do is merely to observe what commonly takes place, and not let himself be fooled by the words he uses. What takes place is certainly not hidden.

That most bank deposits *are used as money* in modern society is an obvious truth to anyone who cares to notice it, and it has long been one of the commonplaces of economics. Bank deposits, in what are called commercial banks, perform precisely the function that bills and coins perform; that is, *so far as use goes*, they are indistinguishable from bills and coins. In other words, men commonly *relinquish* very valuable things, and perform arduous and long-sustained labor, and they will *accept in exchange*—just as they will accept the bills and coins which we call money—an order upon a *bank to transfer bank deposits* to them. This order is what a "check" is; read any check you make out, or receive, and you will realize that it constitutes a mere transfer of bank deposits.

The word "deposits" undoubtedly fools many people here. It calls up to them visions of piles of coins and stacks of paper money. But actually this is not what the word modernly means at all. "Deposits" simply mean the total sums of money *promised* by the bank to those who are trusting it. If it were never thought of as money, *but as*

147

mere bank promises, which the word now actually means, a great deal of mystery would disappear from economic events. Ultimately it is mere bankers' promises, consisting of words—and not something substantial—*that we accept* for the precious things we own and relinquish, or *offer to others* in exchange for the coveted things we wish to own.

Let us take a simple case here for illustration, and you may be sure it is like all others. You have a "bank account." What is it? It is a promise of the bank to give you so much money at any time on request. You want to buy a suit of clothes. You go into a store, where —let us assume—you have long been a customer, and very soon you walk out with a suit of clothes. It is your suit, no longer the store's suit. Now, what have you given for it? You are not one of those who carry rolls of bills in their pockets. What you did was to sit down and write out a check. What was the check? It was *an order to your bank* to give fifty dollars, let us say, to Mr. Clothier.

Now what did this gentleman do with the piece of paper? Did he present it at the bank's window and get the fifty dollar bills? He did nothing of the kind. Let us assume, not to go into unnecessary details, that he is a depositor in the same bank as you. At the end of the day, then, all he did was to take the piece of paper to the bank window. When the busy cashier saw it he merely wrote a probably indecipherable notation in Mr. Clothier's bankbook. Later, some other bank clerk made two entries in the bank's records. One of these entries indicated that the bank *no longer promised* to give you fifty dollars. The other indicated that it *now promised* to give Mr. Clothier fifty dollars. You also, incidentally, in your own records, noted that the bank no longer promised to give you fifty dollars, but had been instructed by you to give them to Mr. Clothier.

Now, what actually has happened in the entire transaction? It was obviously an exchange. You have your suit on the one side. What has Mr. Clothier received on the other? A promise. Not your promise, *but the bank's promise.* No coins or bills passed. Nobody, during the entire procedure, has even seen coins and bills. What really has happened is that the bank had previously entered into an incom-

148

pleted exchange with you, and you now instruct the bank, when it completes the exchange, to do so with Mr. Clothier. *But it remains an incompleted exchange!* The promise of completion is merely now made, not to you, but to Mr. Clothier.

Thus, what occurs *is a mere transfer of bank promises;* checks are simply the written instruments by which this transfer takes place.

Now, *the greater part of the exchanges of wealth which go on in modern society are in this category.* It is estimated that between 90 per cent and 95 per cent of the exchanges among the reliable people of our nation involves the acceptance of a bank's promise on one side of the transaction, instead of real money. In a country like the United States, bills and coins are used ordinarily only in small retail transactions, and for the payment of wages and salaries.

It follows, from this analysis, that the total of these bank promises—"bank deposits," subject to check—which are in existence at any one time—plus the total amount of actual coins and bills that are in bank vaults, in the safes of business enterprises, in men's wallets, women's bags, and hidden in bureau drawers and under mattresses, all together comprise the total of *what men use as money* in modern society. For these two categories of things are what men are now ready to accept for the wealth which they relinquish, and the labor they perform, in those countless exchanges which make up civilization on its economic side.

In every civilized country today bank deposits subject to check are much the larger item of these two components. For example, in our own nation, on June 30, 1936, the total bills and coins in circulation (outside of those held in the United States Treasury and the Federal Reserve Banks) was about $6,250,000,000. On the same date the total bank deposits throughout the nation were about 8½ times as much, $51,000,000,000.* This mere difference in the existing quantity is enough to indicate, aside from common experience, how much more, in a finely organized society like the United States, we use bank promises as money than we do those tangible pieces of paper and metal, which most of us think of as alone constituting our

* *Federal Reserve Bulletin,* February, 1937.

money. It is indicated by some other interesting figures. Over 2½ million checks, on the average, are handled *every day* by the twelve Federal Reserve Banks in the United States.*

Now, we must be sharply aware that these bank deposits, these mere promises of bankers, *come into existence in two different ways.* When you go into a bank and leave your hard-earned dollar bills and coins with the cashier, the bank promises to pay you back. That is one way these bank promises come into existence. But when a bank makes a loan to a business man, it promises to let him have money up to a certain amount. That is a second way these bank promises come into existence. In other words, we are back to the point we made before: a very great portion of these bank promises, which are used as money, come into existence through the bank's *own action.*

But it is perfectly obvious that the portion so created is absolutely indistinguishable from, and just as utilizable in obtaining tangible forms of wealth, as the bank deposits which do not arise from loans, but from the fact that you and I leave money at the bank cashiers' windows.

Bankers themselves keep very much in mind this distinction as to the *source* of the "deposits" they are said to hold; and, for economic understanding, there are few matters more necessary to observe clearly.

For example, if you were to bring $1,000 in bills and coins to your bank, that—you would say—constituted "real money." What happens to it? Let us assume these very bills and coins do not leave the premises, but remain in the bank's till. Now, at the moment you hand in these precious trivialities, over in the carpeted corner where the bank president sits, a business man is asking him for a loan of $1,000. The banker with solemn circumlocution says, in effect, "Sure." Does he now fetch the thousand dollars in bills and coins which you just brought in, and give them to the business man? He could, but he does not. What he does is simply to write the figures, $1,000, in the business man's bankbook.

This—you will recall—is precisely what the bank cashier did with

* *The Reserve Banks and the Money Market,* W. Randolph Burgess.

150

you, when you handed in the tangible bills and coins. It means that the business man can come, in the future, and get that sum in bills and coins, whenever it suits him to do so. In short, we *say* the bank's deposits are now increased by $2,000 as a result of these two trans-actions. For the bank now owes you $1,000, and it owes the business man his "deposit" of $1,000—a total of $2,000. But, of course, the bank has received no bills and coins from the business man. It has only received a piece of paper, a note, saying that at the end of ninety days he will deliver that sum to the bank. The only bills and coins represented in the two transactions are still your $1,000.

What then is the *other* $1,000 represented by the business man's "bank deposit"?

Both the business man and the banker *speak* of it as money. Cer-tainly, the procedure will enable the business man to use this amount of bank promises as money. He will be able to use it in precisely the same way as you use your bank promises. He will pay his bills with it. But is there a total of $2,000, in actual bills and coins, representing these particular two transactions? Most certainly there is not. There is only $1,000 in bills and coins. The $1,000 represented by the busi-ness man's deposit is nothing tangible at all, like your deposit of bills and coins. We refer to it as dollars, simply because we measure it by the real dollars, and because actual bills and coins *can presumably be obtained* as a result of it, if anybody wants to do so. *But actually, it is clear, it is something with no material existence!* It consists wholly, as we have analyzed, of promises—of promises which no doubt will be fulfilled all around, but which still remain insubstantial!

This insubstantiality, which consists of words, but which is quite as potent in creating utilizable bank deposits as coins and bills, is termed by the economists "bank credit."

Perhaps the essential fact to grasp in this set of circumstances is that modern banks *no longer lend money.*

Again, in short, at this point we are ordinarily led into confusion of thought and observation by carelessness in speech. *What the banker lends the business man is really the bank's credit.* By this is meant that it allows the business man to apportion to other people

151

(in exchange for goods and labor) a certain specified amount of the bank's promises. This distinction to be made, between the actual money and the bank's promises to pay money, is crucial, because it has the most widespread economic and social consequences. Not to grasp it is to remain blind to one of the most vital features of modern life. We can perhaps see it more clearly if we consider, for example, the difference between an old money-lender of the sixteenth century and a modern banker. When the old money-lender lent money, *he lent money*. The borrower walked away, with heavy bags of clinking metal, and when he paid the loan, he brought back bags of metal. When the modern banker lends "money"—as we say—he lends nothing of the kind. The borrower walks away with nothing substantial. He walks away merely with the banker's promise to give him money. Then he proceeds *to transfer that promise* to someone else, and himself obtains goods or services for it. He makes use solely of the bank's promise, not of its money. In short, the modern banker *lends bank credit*—bank promises—to the borrower, not money.

The actualities in the occurrence may also be seen by taking another approach—and perhaps it is the basic one.

Throughout this inquiry we have been analyzing various kinds of half-exchanges.

First—in the labor relationship—there was the exchange of labor on one side, and a promise to give money on the other.

Second, there was the exchange—in Production and Distribution—of goods on one side and a promise of money on the other.

Third—in the case of rent and mortgages—there was an exchange of the use of land and building on one side and a promise of money on the other.

Fourth—in the case of one kind of bank deposit—there was the exchange of actual money on one side (on the part of the actual depositor) and a promise to give money on the other.

Here, fifthly, are bank loans. What really are they, when we look at them from this point of view? *They are mere exchanges of promises for promises!* On one side the bank promises to give the business

152

man money whenever he asks for it; on the other, the business man promises to give the bank a little more money at the end, usually, of sixty or ninety days.

This view, I think, reveals best what bank credit really is: an exchange—not of money for money—but of promises to pay money for promises to pay more money! But there is all the difference in the world between the two kinds of promises. *The bank's promises can be used as money!* The business man's promises cannot. That is the real reason, observe, why the transaction occurs at all.

In other words, what the bank does is to let the business man *substitute the bank's credit for his*, with which to obtain goods or labor. For 6 per cent interest, it lets him *use its promises for money*, up to a specified amount.

To sum up, then, banks themselves create—by lending to business men—a large part of those bank deposits which are commonly utilized as money. How much of our commonly used money, using the word, money, in this sense, is so created? How much of the bank deposits of the nation consists of this type of deposits *which banks themselves have created by mere loans to business men?* Hold your seat! On June 30, 1936, the total amount of bank loans outstanding— which were being transferred from ownership to ownership, as if they were real money—was over $20,500,000,000.*

The magnitude of this figure is no problem, nor is the fact cited here to terrify the innocent. The truth is that if all human promises were kept as infallibly as this particular type of promise that is used as money, the mechanism of society would purr along much more beautifully than it does. The fact and the figure are brought out here in accordance with the simple purpose originally set forth for this inquiry: merely to disclose *the nature of the role* that promises play in modern existence, and to show as precisely as possible how they play it.

It is undoubtedly the better part of valor, however—in such a panoramic purpose—not to go into too great detail here. Bank credit

* *Federal Reserve Bulletin*, February, 1937, Page 129.

—that is, bank promises used as money—is very closely allied to government credit, some forms of which are likewise used as money. The two together lie at the root of a number of the problems which laymen find so bewildering in what currently happens to the human race. These problems, every layman may be pleased to hear, are not without their bewilderment for economists. This, indeed, is one of the outlying frontiers of economics, which we mentioned in our Introduction, where disputation among the doctors of the science goes on merrily—and not unhealthfully. For honest dispute here, as everywhere, is likely in the end to lead to agreement upon truth which can be corroborated to the satisfaction of everybody. But it is, at the least, helpful, in illuminating the nature of our society, merely to become aware of the basic facts here, and particularly to observe that in their ultimate nature neither bank credit nor government credit are at all mysterious: they consist merely of *promises to complete half-exchanges*. Having taken this one plunge here, so to speak, and with this firm sand of indisputability still beneath us, it seems advisable to step back temporarily, and to defer venturing further into these breakers until our later analysis of Money itself.

There is, however, one very important associated group of facts which should be noticed at this point, because they are so easy to overlook. We have seen how banks create bank deposits by their own loans, and thereby increase the quantity of *what is used as money* in the nation; and that this bank credit, used as money, then passes from person to person and is just as utilizable in obtaining any form of modern wealth as the bills and coins we handle. Now, this portion of bank deposits that is created by bank loans *goes out of existence quite as easily and simply as it is created*.

If bank deposits are increased by the making of a loan by a bank, it is also true that bank deposits are *decreased* by the ending of this deferred exchange, by the payment of the loan on the part of the borrower. Just so much less bank credit is then extended by the bank, so much smaller become bank deposits, and by so much the existing purchasing-power of the nation is depleted. Unless the bank makes a new loan to supplant one which has been completed, it is

154

fair to say that just so much of the existing purchasing-power of the nation is wiped out—*every time a business man completes a loan.**

It follows from this that the decision of economic enterprisers to borrow from banks, and the decision of banks on the other hand to lend, have a great deal to do with *the total amount of effectual purchasing-power* which exists on any day in the nation.

Now, this is a state of affairs which has the most profound significance to every one of us. The amount of effectual purchasing-power in existence, at the command of each individual and each enterprise, has everything to do with the total amount of exchanges that are entered into in the society—exchanges of goods for money, labor for money, money for money.

For example, what you will buy at any moment, or even think of buying, depends upon the cash you have in your pocket, plus the bank deposits that are owed to you by the bank. That is the present *effectual purchasing-power* which you as an individual can command. Multiply your single case by many millions, and you have the total existing effectual purchasing-power of the nation. When this total effectual purchasing-power is depleted, the total exchanges of the nation lessen—just as yours lessen, when your purchasing-power becomes smaller.

Accordingly, the importance, to the nation as a whole, of the amount of lending that is being done by banks, is obvious. For when a bank decreases its loans for any reason—or when business men decrease their borrowings—through the effect upon the bank deposits that are then in existence, the total volume of economic activity going on within the nation is very decidedly affected.

How vitally it may be affected is disclosed by some interesting

* It is just as well for the inquiring citizen to understand that the same thing happens whenever a bank sells one of its "investments"—a bond—to a purchaser other than a second bank. To appreciate this, follow the process. You have a deposit with your corner bank. You want to buy a $1,000 U. S. Government bond. The bank has one in its vaults. What does it do? It cancels its promise to pay you $1,000, and gives you the bond. You put the bond in a safety deposit box, and there it lies. What is it? Merely a piece of paper saying the government in so many years will give you $1,000. Another promise. But, in the meantime, the bank's own outstanding promises, its deposits, *have been decreased* by $1,000; and those promises ordinarily, as we have seen, would be utilized by you as money, and by other persons to whom you transferred them.

figures. On December 31, 1929, the total loans of banks in the United States (not including the long-term loans to governments and corporations which they term "investments") were $41,918,-000,000. On December 31, 1933, the total loans of these banks had decreased to $21,977,000,000.* A drop of almost exactly twenty billion dollars! It is true that while this was happening, new purchasing-power (through bank deposits) was being created in other ways —principally through the borrowing done from banks by the United States Government. In spite of this, through the four-year period, total bank deposits decreased about $16,750,000,000. This astronomical decrease was due almost wholly to the drop in bank loans.

In other words, throughout this period of four years which we have come to call "the Depression," some $16,750,000,000 of purchasing-power *was extinguished* in this country by this process!

This is a lot of billions, even to those who have become immunized to the word. If we take the purchasing-power of the nation as consisting of its bills and coins in circulation plus bank deposits, the above figures mean that during the four years *about thirty per cent* of it was wiped out. Forget the billions for a moment. If you had $2,000 in the bank at your command, and suddenly lost $600 of it, you would decidedly enter into fewer exchanges. You would economize. You would buy fewer things. You would engage fewer persons to do things for you. This would surely be the effect upon your actions, if about one-third of your personal purchasing-power were extinguished. Precisely the same effect, on a grand scale, might reasonably be expected if 30 per cent of the total purchasing-power in the nation were extinguished.

In other words, the relation between these two sets of circumstances is apparent: the enormous drop in bank loans between 1929 and 1933 and the resulting extinguishment of bank deposits on the one side, and on the other the appalling decrease in the amount of business being done throughout the country, of goods being produced and of labor being employed. All of us in the past five years *have* been aware of the second set of circumstances, through the

* *United States Statistical Abstract, 1936,* Page 241.

actual suffering we had to endure as a result of them. On the other hand, very few of us have been aware of the first set of circumstances, with which the second is so clearly linked.

We should be careful not to confuse ourselves here. In particular, we should understand that we are considering relations, not "causes." To disclose the connection between the amount of bank loans and bank deposits that are in existence, and the state of well-being or ill-being of the nation, is not to say by any means that the Depression in this country was *caused by* the lessened volume of bank loans. This great drop in bank loans, which took place during the Depression, and the consequent extinguishment of purchasing-power, might just as easily be thought of as being *the effect* of lessened business activity as its cause. Or both phenomena may best be comprehended as resulting from other "causes." The whole notion of cause and effect in economics is a ticklish one to raise, because of the maddening intricacy of the relations that must be studied—all of it, incidentally, in the imagination. Later, in an examination of what the Business Cycle is, it may be possible to obtain a little more detailed comprehension of these relations between bank loans, bank deposits, so-called "purchasing-power," and the well-being of the nation. Here the matter is brought up, not to add to mystification—as it unfortunately may, by this somewhat fragmentary treatment of it—but to italicize a point that most decidedly needs emphasis.

It may have seemed a highly academic matter—oh, so unimportant!—to explain a few paragraphs back that the payment of a bank loan, that the mere ending of this type of deferred exchange, decreases the total of bank deposits and therefore of the nation's purchasing-power. Academic! You see what tragic facts it was so intimately associated with in the past few years.

At one time during that period there was a certain bank, in a city perhaps a thousand miles from yours, which for any one of a dozen reasons—either because of its own internal troubles, or because of the questionable resources of a certain business man—refused to continue to lend money to him. It refused to renew a loan to him of $50,000. It was quite within its rights, and probably wise—from the point of view of its own depositors—in taking this action. But by doing so, it wiped out of existence $50,000 worth of purchasing-power that was being used. Because of this, the business firm had to curtail its usual orders to your firm. You knew nothing about this occurrence then, and never have. Probably you may never have heard of the bank or the business man. But when this distant banker said, "No," it was at that moment you fatally lost your job—with perhaps half a hundred other unfortunates. Do you remember how you felt at the time? Or if it was not you who was struck by that particular bolt of economic lightning, perhaps it was Mr. Smith next door. Perhaps it was that "No," which he never heard, spoken to someone of whose existence he is still unaware, which doomed him, by a rapid-fire series of consequences which he could easily have traced if he were an economist, to lose the home which had been his pride for half a lifetime. It was this unheard "No" which broke his spirit, made his happy wife a harried woman, took his son and daughter out of college, and set them pounding the streets for jobs they could not find.

Certainly there is nothing academic, there is something profoundly personal, about understanding in detail the processes by which events of this character are brought about.

The Center of the Vast Spider Web of Promises in Each

Nation—Its Central Bank; and How It Ties up the

Promises of Individuals with Those

of Governments

BANK LOANS are nobody's business, we should all be inclined to say, except that of the particular bank and business man involved in each case. But we saw, in the last chapter, that since they are bank promises which pass from person to person like money until the loan is paid, they are very much everybody's business. Whether or not a particular promise of this sort is made, and whether or not it is completed, affects many more people than the two directly involved in the relationship.

We must go back to a simple statement about these loans, made some pages back. In the hurried way we all read you probably paid little attention to it. Offhand, indeed, the statement would seem to be of not the slightest importance to you or to anybody else. We said that the bank's so-called *reserves* determined the total amount of loans it could make, and then we said that these reserves are kept on the premises, "or close by immediately available;" and that in the United States, member banks of the Federal Reserve System *are required* to keep these reserves with the Federal Reserve Bank of its district. There are twelve such Federal Reserve Banks.

Well, of what consequence is this apparent technicality?

Of course, the first thing to be remarked about it is that your corner bank—if it is a member of the Federal Reserve System—instead of having from 14 per cent to 26 per cent of real money on hand to meet the millions of dollars of promises it has made to you and other depositors, probably does not have on hand 1 per cent in so-called cash. How can it have? It is required by law, as you see, to keep these reserves of cash with the Federal Reserve Bank of its region, which is quite likely to be in another city. All it keeps in its till are the comparatively trivial sums of money needed for the payment of wages and salaries by its depositors. These packages of currency are drawn out toward the end of each week, and begin coming back to the bank immediately, a little dirtier, principally from the retail merchants among its depositors.

This situation—that your corner bank has entrusted all its reserves to another larger bank and keeps very little cash on hand itself—would certainly seem to weaken it—so far as the performance of all its own promises are concerned. Actually, it does not. It strengthens your bank, in any emergency that may arise—but for reasons too detailed to elucidate here. For, if we followed them, they would involve us too much in the daily business of central banks and commercial banks. For the simple purpose of following the in-and-out weaving of promises, by which modern men live, the principal point to remark upon here is that your bank, if it is a Federal Reserve member, *has substituted for money* a mere credit with another and larger bank. But we were talking about its reserves. What are its reserves, in these circumstances? Are they great piles of money? The word "reserve" might lead one to think so. Actually, again, they consist of nothing material. *They are mere promises of the Federal Reserve Bank of its region.* Just as you have your bank's promises to pay money, and it is all you have, so the Federal Reserve member bank has the promise of its regional Federal Reserve Bank to pay it the "reserves" it has deposited—and that is all *it* has!

In short, a new vista is opened up here of an enormous field of deferred exchanges. In one way or another, it involves literally thousands of billions of dollars yearly. The curiosity a Martian would note down here—to report home about us—is that the ordinary citizen is totally unaware even of the existence of this vast area of human promises. Much less has he an inkling of the indirect processes by which they condition—it may almost be said, by which they determine—every aspect of his entire existence. This ignorance of so vast a field of men's promises, and the almost universal indifference to them, is itself a social phenomenon of the first importance. Its explanation seems clear enough. The ordinary man knows nothing about this area of promises *because he is never personally involved in them.* They are entirely outside his daily experience. This, in short, is one of those key occupations of men, which we mentioned in our Introduction, and which we are all content to leave to specialists. But the explanation must go deeper than this. Is it not clear that, here again, we could not remain indifferent to promises so crucial to our whole lives *were it not that they were infallibly fulfilled?*

A simple fact will indicate how completely we depend upon this particular area of promising in our everyday living, without knowing about it. About two-thirds of the bank deposits of the United States are in the banks that are members of the Federal Reserve System. These member-bank deposits totaled over $34,000,000,000 on June 30, 1936.* There were exactly 6,400 such member banks on that day. Now, these banks—since they owed us $34,000,000,000—had received exactly that much, in coins and bills or promises, from you and me and our millions of fellow-citizens. What had they done with the sums they had received? The greater part *they had given away* in exchange for the promises we identified in the last chapter; in secured and unsecured loans to business enterprises, long promises called "mortgages," and other long promises they called "investments." But surely they had not given all of it away for promises. If they had, where would we get off in any emergency? We saw, in the last chapter, that it is in our behalf they are required by law to keep reserves. They must do so, for the very purpose of meeting all their promises to us infallibly, and in those countries where this is not the law, custom and prudence dictate that they shall do so. Accordingly, on June 30, 1936, you will find that these 6,400 member

* *Federal Reserve Bulletin*, February, 1937, Page 129. All deposits of one bank with another are excluded from these figures.

banks had indeed entrusted something over $5,500,000,000 to the twelve Federal Reserve Banks placed in strategic spots throughout the country. *These* were their reserves—in addition to the trivial amounts each one kept in its till to meet demands of its depositors for actual currency.

Now, ask yourself a simple question. All the other funds of these 6,400 banks had been given away for short and long promises. If the Federal Reserve Banks turned out to be unable, for some reason, to keep these promises to the thousands of member banks in the banking system, what chance would there be of those banks keeping their promises to you and to me?

The question reveals again the interdependence of promises one upon another. We all completely ignore these activities represented by the daily relations between member banks and the twelve Federal Reserve Banks. From what we read in the papers, what a dismal and arid field it seems! A field of rocky figures and dollars only! It is upon this sort of activity old Carlyle would have spit his scorn— and who would object? But *if a single one* of these promises were unfulfilled on demand, oh, how swiftly we would all know the consequences! In short, there is no area where human promising goes on that is of more crucial importance than this, which only a handful of human beings at present pay any attention to, and which yet conditions the life and welfare of almost the entire two billion members of the race.

For, of course, this intimate relation of the greater part of American banks (as measured by resources) to our Federal Reserve Banks is not an uncommon one. Our Federal Reserve System—with its twelve regional Federal Reserve Banks, united through the Federal Reserve Board—is simply the American form of so-called central bank. Every civilized nation has a like central bank, with which its government and its banks enter into the most crucial deferred exchanges. The United States was one of the latest to become civilized in this economic respect. In our early decades we did indeed have a good central bank, but about a hundred years ago we allowed our politicians to dismantle it; and then characteristically, when we again set one up, we compromised in doing so. After three-quarters of a century, which witnessed the most unparalleled industrial growth of any nation in history, our recurrent troubles with money and banking became just too much to bear. It was borne in upon our solons that we really had to be civilized and have a central bank. But then, typically, we allowed one of our usual "pressure groups" to bull-doze the politicians into not making our central bank what it should have been.* The pressure group consisted of those small bankers, whose record we analyzed two chapters ago. What animated them? Why, they wanted to be free to make economic mistakes of the kind previously identified, and which we alone, among the important peoples of the world, suffer from. We paid handsomely for this freedom of the little bankers and will continue to pay for it, so long as they can continue successfully to hold the high sign over our politicians, as they have, to this day and hour. Over 9,000 of these bankers still remain quite free of the sensible control and support the Federal Reserve System can give them.† If we rule out sheer economic stupidity on their part, we can be sure that no public interest, only the barest concern for a little more personal profit, can keep them from this action, which all their more responsible fellow-bankers in this country have taken.

The explanation would boil down in the end—not to be invidious against these stubborn little bankers—to that general ignorance

* I refer here, in particular, to the fact that the formulation of the system, in President Wilson's administration, was a notorious compromise, by means of which most of the small state banks successfully kept themselves out of our unified banking system. There had always been chartered national and chartered state banks; and the latter have always been far more numerous, less experienced, less rigorously controlled, and—on the whole—have had far smaller resources than the national banks. The one thing most of these state banks wished to avoid was to come under a system where their responsibility would be properly tightened up. W. Randolph Burgess says, in *The Reserve Banks and the Money Market:* "No change in our currency and banking system would have been accepted which involved any general disturbance *to the existing practices and the vested rights* of this great number of banks" [italics mine]. In the quarter-century this patchwork system has been in operation there have never been as many as 10,000 banks associated in our Federal Reserve System. In the year their number was nearest 10,000 (in 1922) there were over 20,000 banks outside the system. Among no other advanced industrial people is there so loose and indirect a relationship between subordinate banks and the central bank.

† *Federal Reserve Bulletin,* Page 129, February, 1937.

which prevails among men, about the true nature of their relationships which we remarked upon in our Introduction, and of which, of course, this is only one more manifestation. Here it is merely part and parcel of the ignorance which prevails universally about the nature and activities of central banks; an ignorance which a great many commercial bankers, if it is any consolation to know, share with all the rest of us. Only a bare few thousands of persons among the two billion members of the race know anything about central banks, and not many more than this care to know. "The profession (of central banking) suffers," wrote one of our own most studious practitioners in the field, "from the limited general understanding of its principles and practices." * This is putting it conservatively—even, in one sense, curiously. The profession suffers! Of course we can imagine some sensitive central bankers gloomy and unhappy at not being properly understood by those complacent mortals in whose behalf they are forever losing sleep. But sadder than this, the *nation itself* suffers grievously; each one of us suffers without knowing it, because of the "limited general understanding" in this particular direction.

For there is no more critical point in modern human relations. Here in the central bank, in every country, the interdependent promises of men converge more than they do anywhere else; so that, at its central bank, the most comprehensive view and the deepest insight can be obtained into the economic activities of every people. If every little Conservative and every little Communist born into this world of men had to spend a year or two of his happy school days merely watching, under the instruction and guidance of informed men, what took place in the central bank of his country, oh, how different the world would be within one short generation! Don't say the children would not understand it, when they can grasp the principles of the elementary sciences. They would be watching the actions of men, and observing the considerations that inspire them, and when these are seen and known, there is nothing recondite in them that cannot be grasped by any human being.

* W. Randolph Burgess, in *The Reserve Banks and the Money Market.*

What difficulty we may have, in understanding the activities of central banks, principally arises—as we suggested—from the fact that personally we never deal with central banks. This difficulty can be surmounted if we make an imaginative use of the daily experiences we do undergo with our corner banks. Almost exclusively central banks deal with other smaller banks and with governments. Only in a few countries do they deal direct with individuals and industrial enterprises. Now, the common daily experiences you have with your corner bank are very little different from the common daily experiences your corner bank has with its central bank. You can well apply the one to understand the other.

You deposit your money in the corner bank, receiving a promise in exchange; in the same way, your corner bank gives its so-called reserves to its central bank, receiving promises in return.

You transfer your bank promises (through checks) to settle your deferred exchanges with other individuals. Your bank settles its incompleted exchanges in the same way, by means of checks drawn on the central bank. The central bank merely makes a notation on its books that a promise for a specific sum is transferred from your bank to another one. This mere *transfer of a bank promise* is what happens, you will remember from Chapter Nine, when an individual pays any bill by check.

The invariably faithful performance of your bank's promises to you depends upon the unimpaired reserves your bank keeps; in the same way the faithful completion of the central bank's promises to its depositors depends upon the unimpaired reserves the central bank keeps on hand. In the case of our own Federal Reserve Banks, they must keep on hand 40 per cent of the promises they make to their depositors.

Finally, just as you go to a bank, if you are a business man, to borrow money when you need it to fulfill your promise, so your bank goes to its Federal Reserve Bank to borrow.

The parallel, we see, is complete. Everything you do with your corner bank, the corner bank does with the central bank. The central bank is thus a "bankers' bank." But it is more than this.

It is always the bank, in each country, *through which the government carries on its financial activities*. First, on one side the government deposits money with the central bank. Now, we saw in the last chapter what the word "deposits" really means. Deposits are mere *promises* of a bank. They are just as much so here, when they are made by the central bank to the government, as when little fellows like you and me are dealt with. They are merely promises for a few more billions of dollars—that is the only difference.

But the central bank not only makes promises to the government, by accepting its so-called deposits; *the government also makes promises to the central bank*. Whenever any government wants to borrow, it either does so from its central bank (that is, it gives short or long promises to the central bank) or it uses the central bank as its agent to place the promises with other smaller banks, or with individuals or corporate groups.

Thus, what takes place in every central bank in the world is simply the swapping of promises on a grand scale. The mist which for most of us hangs over this economic region can best be dissipated by considering the promises in two broad classifications: those *made to* the central bank, and those *made by* the central bank.

Take first the promises *made to* the central bank. Who makes them? First, other subordinate banks; and second, the national government. These promises consist of loans.

First, let us consider the subordinate banks. Why is it necessary for them to do any borrowing from—any promising to—the central bank? The answer at once appears, from reflection upon what we have seen of the activities of your corner bank. It has done a great deal of promising to its depositors on one side, and on the other has relinquished a great deal of its property to enterprisers in short promises, and to real-estate owners, corporations and governments in long promises. An occasion may arise when there is an unexpected influx of demands for the completion of its own promises—those to depositors. It must always be prepared for such an unexpected situation. When it occurs, your bank draws upon its own deposits with the central bank. That is, it asks the central bank to complete a por-

166

tion of the half-exchanges the two have entered into. But, remember, its deposits with the central bank may not go below a certain figure —a fixed proportion of its own promises to its depositors. This proportion constitutes its "reserves." What then does it do, if it must exceed this figure? It borrows from its central bank. That is the necessity for the promising in this case.

Now, what is the nature of the promising? What your bank does is merely to take some of the promises it holds—business men's promissory notes—and turn them over to the central bank, with its name under the name of the business man. This is called "rediscounting" a promissory note. What is this but putting up security, a forfeit as in the old institution of debt-slavery, that the bank's promise to the central bank will be fulfilled? That is, when this promise of the business man is fulfilled, the money received must be used to complete the bank's promise to the central bank.*

The effect of the situation is that *the promises your corner bank holds* can be utilized to obtain money from the central bank, when your corner bank needs money in any unexpected amount. What would happen if this were not possible? Your bank, when faced with an unexpected volume of demands to complete its own promises, would in such a case be obliged to sell in a hurry its so-called investments, which are really long promises. It might have to do so in such a hurry that it could not get nearly as much money as it had given for them, which would also impair its ability to meet its promises in full. Because it is always able to borrow immediately from its central bank, if the promises which it holds are good promises, *banks can do more lending than otherwise they would.*

Now, when a bank borrows from its central bank, does it receive money? It could, but it does not. What happens is that it receives promises from the central bank. *Its "deposits" with the central bank are merely increased.* But you will remember that this is what happened, when we watched a business man borrow from a bank. He too did not receive money; he received the promises of the bank,

---

* Banks can now also borrow from their central bank on other security—but there is no need to go into too much detail here.

and then he proceeded *to transfer those promises* to someone else. Bank-borrowing from a central bank is no different. When a member bank is under the necessity of borrowing, it receives not money, but mere promises of the Federal Reserve Bank. It then uses these promises, these increased "deposits," in lieu of money, to meet the demands made upon it by other banks.

Precisely the same thing happens when the government, and not banks, borrows from the central bank.

It is instructive to follow in detail what happens when any government borrows from its central bank. What it receives is just what your corner bank receives when it borrows—the mere promise of the central bank to pay it money. The government then proceeds to transfer this central bank promise to its soldiers and sailors and government employees, and its suppliers of material. It does so by writing out a check, as you do.

The government's check is an order to the central bank to transfer its promise—the central bank's promise—to some individual. Let us say you are one of these lucky individuals. You take the government check to your corner bank. What does your corner bank then do? It makes a notation in your passbook that *it now promises you* this much more than it did before. It gives you this promise, in the form of a bank deposit, in exchange for the government's check. But what does it do with the government check, which constitutes the transfer of a Federal Reserve Bank promise? It takes it to its own Federal Reserve Bank which—to simplify the procedure a little —may have been the very one which issued the promise to the government in the first place to pay this amount of money. Does your bank now, at last, get money from the Federal Reserve Bank? Nothing of the kind. Again it can, but it does not. It receives, in exchange, another promise from the Federal Reserve Bank, a so-called deposit, and the Federal Reserve Bank at the same moment *cancels a promise to this amount which had been made to the government.**

* For illustrative purposes here, I am using our own Federal Reserve System to indicate what happens when any government borrows directly from its

The upshot of the matter is that your bank's "deposits" with its Federal Reserve Bank *are increased* and the government's "deposits" *are decreased* by the same amount.

Now, the government promise still remains unfulfilled, you will notice. A Federal Reserve Bank promise was given for it and that promise, as it ended up in all the transferring, is now made to your bank. *It is counted as part of your bank's reserves.* Since money can be got for it by your bank from the Federal Reserve Bank, it is counted 100 per cent as cash reserves. And, as we saw (in Chapter Nine) your bank is then allowed, on the basis of it, to create (under present reserve provisions) between four and six times as much bank credit, in the form of loans to business men. Then, as we also saw, this bank credit (which consists of nothing but bank promises to pay money) can also be used by individuals to carry on exchanges of goods and labor.

What then has happened, to summarize the entire matter, is that the bank deposits of the nation, which are universally used as money, *have actually been increased by the amount of the government borrowing;* and then this actual increase, in turn, can—if necessary—be multiplied about fivefold at present (through lending by banks) and the nation's total purchasing-power, in the form of bank deposits, thus increased. It is this process which explains why government bor‑ rowing from banks, from an economic viewpoint, is so inestimably

central bank. Actually, at this moment, the direct borrowing, as I describe it above, is prohibited in this country. It was allowed in our emergency monetary laws of 1933, and therefore the illustration is justifiable, but in 1935 an amend‑ ment disallowed direct lending by the twelve Federal Reserve Banks to the Treasury. Nevertheless, these Banks can and do *extend credit* to the Treasury. This Federal Reserve credit to the Treasury stood at over $2,500,000,000 on December 31, 1937. The system is that the Treasury promises are sold first to member banks (and to a slight extent, citizens); and the Federal Reserve Banks then buy the government promises from the member banks, prin‑ cipally. The final upshot, obviously, is the same as if the Treasury borrowed directly from our central bank, which is done so frequently abroad. Why the prohibition, the ordinary citizen might logically ask. It is because, typi‑ cally, in this country, our solons think that because direct central bank lending to our Treasury is now prohibited, they have blocked this route to modern monetary inflation, which I explain in the following pages. In any presumed emergency, it seems certain, this slender obstruction would be blown down, with one slight woof, as it was in 1933.

important. For it ends up by vastly increasing the quantity, not of money, but of what is principally used as money in modern society —bank promises.

This automatic increase of purchasing-power that follows government borrowing from banks—either from central banks or from subordinate ones—*does not occur when a government borrows from its individual citizens.* Why is this? Follow out the processes—as they occur in nature, so to speak—and it becomes clear. You have a bank deposit of $10,000. It consists of nothing but a promise of a particular bank to pay you so much money. You now receive a circular from the government offering you a government bond of $10,000. The "bond" is the government's promise to pay you so much fourteen years hence, let us say, with small amounts of interest in the meantime. This is a simple proposed deferred exchange: you are pretty familiar with them by now. You decide to enter into the deferred exchange. And what does it consist of, actually? You accept the bond: that is the government's promise. In return, you give the government your check. But what is the check? It is a *transfer* of your bank's promise to the benefit of the government. The government then transfers that promise to whatever purpose it pleases. *No new bank promises have come into existence.* Therefore the total effectual purchasing-power of the nation has not been increased.

Thus, there is all the difference in the world between a government financing its needs by borrowing directly from its citizens, and financing them by borrowing from banks. The main difference is that, in the latter case, the effectual purchasing-power of the nation is automatically increased, and sometimes enormously so.

There is an extremely important difference between the loans made by a central bank to its subordinate banks, and those it makes to governments. In both cases, since the central bank's promises are increased and those promises are passed from person to person in lieu of money, the effectual purchasing-power of the nation is increased. But when the individual bank borrows from the central

170

bank, *it does so for a short period!* We saw that ordinarily it put up security, and within a short time the loan is always canceled. When payment occurs, just so much of the Federal Reserve Bank's promises immediately go out of existence.

In other words, the increase in the national purchasing-power which takes place as the result of member-bank borrowing is a *temporary increase*. It is called into existence by the needs of industry and goes out of existence when that need is over.

In contrast with this, when the government borrows from the central bank, *it is an exceptional event for the loan soon to go out of existence*. The promise remains all but permanently incompleted. True, the term of it may expire, but ordinarily it is then immediately replaced by another loan. Government borrowing from central banks, therefore, almost always *permanently increases* the total effectual purchasing-power of the nation.

What's bad about this, if anything? Central bank promises, coming into existence, through being swapped for government promises, become used by men as money, and remain in existence, *so long as the government's promise is unfulfilled*. But while they may be used in lieu of money, this does not change their character as economic promises. They are half-exchanges, which the central bank has to complete. If the government borrows so much—that is, if it increases the central bank's promises so much—that the central bank finds it impossible to fulfill its promises, all interdependent promises likewise will be undermined.

We come here upon a fact of the most salient character. It is one that is completely hidden to the average citizen: *it is by this route of borrowing from central banks that modern governments initiate the processes we now call inflation*. What we have done, of course, is simply to uncover the method. Later on, we shall examine more precisely what economic promises have to do with inflation; indeed, how it is *unfulfillable promises*, of governments and central banks, that cause all the disturbances and readjustments that are associated with the word "inflation."

This new highway to inflation—a highway with all modern improvements, quite different from the rude ones utilized by rulers in less civilized times—is now a very easy one to travel. We can understand how easy it is, by identifying another vital difference between the central bank loans made to smaller banks, and central bank loans made to governments. In the case of the subsidiary banks, the central bank *can refuse to make the loan*, if it feels the promise is unlikely to be fulfilled. Or it can refuse to make the loan, *if it feels its own resources are already too much overburdened with promises.* Not so with government loans. The central bank is completely at the mercy of the government. For all the world, it is in precisely the same situation as persecuted Jewish bankers in mediaeval cities: they were compelled to lend to their rulers. Seizure of their wealth, torture and even death, were frequently the only alternatives. Now, modern governments always use the central banks as their agents in the placing of loans. The central bank tries to find individuals who will lend to the government, giving up their wealth in exchange for the government's promise. This is the least disturbing thing that can happen when a government borrows, for (as we saw) total bank-promises are not increased when *individuals* lend to governments. But if the loans cannot be so placed, and the government—in a dire emergency—needs the money, there is no recourse but for the central bank to accept the government's promise, and give its own in exchange. We have had central bankers, in recent years, who have stood up to their governments, refusing to be gouged *ad libitum*, in this fashion. Their influence is moral, and nothing more. They cannot control the government's needs, and whenever—in the government's view—the needs become crying enough, in every case the central bankers succumb to this *force majeure*. They lend all the government requires. If they do not, they are quickly replaced by other individuals who will. This new highway to the wealth of mankind—by the route of promising to central banks—is one that no modern government in the world will allow its central bankers to block. In our chapters on Money, we shall see, interestingly enough, how the route was originally opened up. I am inclined to call it a robber's route.

172

But what is wrong—what is dangerous—about permanently increasing the promises of the central bank in this fashion? The danger is revealed (and the role of the central bank in our economy is additionally illuminated) when we examine the other broad classification of promises that are made in this area—the promises *made by* the central bank.

Nothing could be clearer than the connection between these two sets of promises. The promises made by a central bank cannot be fulfilled unless those *made to it* are fulfilled! You have asked, and it is a profound question, in your innocence, what is wrong with enormously increasing the promises of the central bank, and thus increasing the effectual purchasing-power of the nation? The answer is that the promises are promises, and must sooner or later be fulfilled. What are the promises? They are central bank promises *to pay money*. Upon what does their fulfillment depend? Clearly, it depends upon *the amount of money* the central bank has on hand, plus what it can get. If the amount of money the central bank has remains the same, and its promises to pay money increase—particularly, if by forced lending to the government, the central bank's outstanding promises *increase permanently and enormously*—its ability to complete all these promises is manifestly undermined. Promises to be believed must be performed—let us never forget that. It is as true here as elsewhere in our society.

The first kind of promises *made by* a central bank we have already looked at. They are its so-called deposits, and—as we saw—they are made to other banks and to governments. In the case of subsidiary banks, we saw how vital they are. The final reserves of the banks, to repeat, consist of nothing but the promises made by the central bank, and of course if they were ever incompleted the whole system of promising, of which banking and modern business consist, would collapse in chaos.

The second principal kind of *promise made by* the central bank will, in all probability, surprise most persons: in that it should be

173

considered a promise at all. Several times here we have said that when a bank needs money from the Federal Reserve Bank, it can get it. Ordinarily, it is content to receive the central bank's promise, represented by an increase in its "deposits" with the central bank. But it does deal in currency nonetheless, and frequently it needs currency. Does it get money? Never, nowadays.

We are perilously close here to the inner mysteries of money itself, which we shall have to elucidate in a later chapter. The government—its power, its policies and its actions—is certainly involved in these modern mysteries. All we may do here, because it is at present pertinent, is to point out a simple fact: namely, most of the so-called money which an American bank receives from the Federal Reserve Bank are mere pieces of paper called Federal Reserve Notes. This constitutes the bulk of the "paper money" we are so familiar with. Everybody calls these pieces of paper "money." But they are just as much money, and no more so, than the bank deposits of the central bank which are transferred from ownership to ownership. For like these bank deposits, *they are bank promises,* and nothing else. They are the mere evidence of our central bank's promise to pay money —an incompleted promise, observe!—and not the money itself.

Take out one of these bills, and read it. It says: "This note . . . is redeemable in lawful money at the United States Treasury or at any Federal Reserve Bank." What! Redeemable in lawful money? Is this itself not lawful money? It is not. "Lawful money" is gold and silver coin, and nothing else. The note, as it most plainly says, is merely a promise to pay lawful money, a promise made by our central bank, and guaranteed by the government. There is the promise and the guarantee on the face of the note itself. Now, of course, we all regard such notes as money, just as we do gold and silver coin and other pieces of paper issued by the United States Treasury. But an habitual acceptance of the Federal Reserve Notes as money does not alter the fact that in actuality they are central bank promises, which are simply being used, commonly and thoughtlessly, as money. In the basic respect, that they are mere bank promises, they are indistinguishable

174

from the bank deposits (another form of bank promise) which are also transferred from ownership to ownership, through the medium of checks.

Here then is the second kind of promise *made by* the central bank. How great in volume are these promises? On December 31, 1936, the Federal Reserve Notes outstanding, in banks and passing around from person to person, were about $4,250,000,000.

It is perhaps interesting to note here, parenthetically, that most of us thoughtlessly assume that paper money consists wholly of government promises. Not at all. Paper money far more often consists of central bank promises. The government is closely involved. For one thing, it is only by government permission that the central bank can issue such promises. But this was not always so, as we shall later see. Paper money *originated* as bank promises, and it is an interesting historical and social fact that it still consists, principally, of central bank promises. It is the central bank, in short, which issues the promise, and which must complete it. Therefore it is the central bank's resources that must be examined, if one would learn how good the promise is, and what chance there is of ever receiving real money for it.

Perhaps we are in a position now to put together the pieces that have been collected, in this particular picture puzzle which central banking constitutes for the average person. The promises *made by* the central bank must be fulfilled—infallibly. They may never be broken. There can be no fear they may ever be broken. Every activity of the whole society finally depends upon their complete fulfillment. But upon what does their fulfillment depend? Plainly enough, upon two things: upon the resources, *the actual money*, which the central bank has upon its premises, plus the resources, the real money, which it can obtain from the promises which have been *made to* it. One is as important as the other.

Let us pass here from the general to the particular. For illustrative purposes, consider the situation of our twelve Federal Reserve Banks on December 30, 1936. On that date, the promises *made by* them consisted roughly of about $7,000,000,000 made to depositors, plus, roughly, $4,250,000,000 made to the holders of Federal Reserve notes: a total of about $11,250,000,000. What resources did they have, with which to meet these outstanding promises, if it became necessary?

First, on that date they had cash on hand of something over $9,100,-000,000. Something parenthetic must be noted here about this "cash." Almost the entire amount—to be exact, $8,851,878,000—consisted of so-called gold certificates. Gold certificates are paper promises of the United States Government that it is holding in the Treasury the precise amount of gold specified and that it will deliver this gold on demand to the holder of the certificate, whoever he may be. Since 1933, *the latter part of this promise* has been abrogated, so far as individuals are concerned—but not so far as the Federal Reserve Banks are concerned! But because of the so-called emergency, which occurred in that year, Federal Reserve Banks, no more than individuals, have been allowed to *hold* gold. All the gold must be held by the government. The Federal Reserve Banks may obtain gold from the government, if they have to ship gold abroad or deliver it to a dentist or jeweler for industrial purposes; but they may not have gold on their premises. Their actual money resources, therefore, do not now consist of gold, but of the United States Government's promise to pay them about $9,000,000,000 of gold. Before 1933—it should be understood—*they would have had the gold itself*, and perhaps in more placid times than the present they will again have it.

In addition to these promises of the government to pay them about $9,000,000,000 in gold, the Federal Reserve Banks held about $2,500,000,000 of promises made to it by the United States Government and by other smaller banks; and, again, almost all of this—to be exact, $2,430,227,000—were promises *made to* it by the Government.

We thus see that the promises made by our central banks—roughly $11,250,000,000—total the same as the promises *made to* them; for, of course, we must count the $9,000,000,000 of gold certificates as government promises.

From this simple analysis, it appears that our Federal Reserve

176

Banks were in an extremely strong position on December 30, 1936. By that is meant that there would be very little likelihood of their not being able to fulfill their promises. If all their promises came in upon them at once—and it is an interesting thing to remark that all but the tiniest proportion of the total of $11,250,000,000 does consist of deferred exchanges where performance can be demanded at any time—they would have little difficulty in completing them. To do so, first, they have about $9,000,000,000 in gold, assuming the government would give dollar for dollar in gold, as it promises to. Second, they have about $2,500,000,000 of other promises. Of these, as we saw, all but a fraction—$2,430,000,000—also consisted of our government's promises. The balance—a trifling $53 millions—consisted principally of banks' promises. These latter were certain to be fulfilled. They had to be, or the banks involved would close up. Even if the whole of them were not fulfilled, hardly any trouble would be caused the central bank.

But if the $2,430,000,000, promised by the government, were not likely to be paid in full, then indeed the Federal Reserve Banks would have difficulty in meeting their promises. And if that other larger section of government promises, represented by the approximately $9,000,000,000 of gold certificates, were not fulfilled by the government, where would our central banks be left, so far as fulfilling their own promises is concerned?

What is disclosed by this simple analysis, in other words, is that the final ability of the Federal Reserve Banks fully to meet the promises made by them *depends entirely upon the fulfillment of the promises made to them by the government.*

Now, an essential fact for every citizen in the world to recognize is that *every central bank in the world* is, in the way we have indicated, dependent for the fulfillment of its promises upon the promises made to it by its government. We saw that every central bank, in turn, was the center upon which converged all the promises of other banks and business enterprises. *Thus all promises in the society rest finally upon government promises*—principally those made to central banks.

177

We can get a pretty clear notion, then, of why an ugly danger rears its head when a government begins borrowing heavily from its central bank. The illustration we had, of our own central bank, it would be unwise to regard as typical. No central bank in the history of the world has ever had so much gold as our Federal Reserve Bank system, presuming the government will ultimately give the Federal Reserve Banks gold for the certificates they now hold. And the additional amount our government owed our central banks was comparatively paltry beside the resources it could raise, if it had to, by taxation: a mere $2,450,000,000. Now this is an extraordinarily safe condition for a central bank to find itself in.

Let us consider a reverse condition—and we may be sure we can find plenty of governments, in the past twenty years, that could sit for the portrait. Assume a case where a central bank has only $500,000,000 of gold on hand. Its government is in need. It borrows and borrows again; and then once again. It must do so through its central bank. What does the borrowing mean? We saw that it simply meant a swap of the central bank's promise for the government's promise. The government uses the central bank's promise to get goods and pay its employees. The central bank promise remains in existence. The whole effect of the process is *simply to increase the total of central bank promises*. Thus, the relation between the promises made by and made to the central bank is rendered abnormal and dangerous. Let us assume the central bank is able to hold on to its $500,000,000 of gold. Because of what has happened, *more promises are outstanding against it*. It is true the so-called resources of the central bank are also increased, but what do the new additions consist of? More government promises! Are these reliable resources? Will these promises eventuate in real money? Can real money be obtained for them anywhere? If not, the central bank's promises must be defaulted upon—for they are promises to pay money, lawful money, gold or silver coins. Well, the mere fact that the government is *continuing to borrow* from the central bank throws a very informing light upon whether or not real money (or forms of wealth

178

which can be exchanged for real money) will eventuate from the government's promises.

In this way, the central bank's condition—by which is meant its ability to meet its promises to pay real money, gold coin—is so weakened that its promises become suspect by the initiate. But what are its promises? We saw what they were: aside from bank-deposits, *they are the central bank notes which are being passed from hand to hand as money*. They are usually the principal form of currency in the country. They begin to depreciate in value. We need go no further at this point. The resulting social and financial disturbances are well enough known to this generation. To go further in our analysis here would plunge us too deeply, when we are still not as properly prepared as we should be, into the peculiar problems of modern money.

The principal thing to observe here is clear. It is the failure of government promises—or expectation of failure in the judgment of careful men—which causes modern currencies to collapse; and by the tracing out of the promises, we have seen that this takes place, ordinarily in modern times, through the failure of the central bank's promises. The government, by *force majeure*, increases the promises of the central bank to such a point that they cannot be completely fulfilled. A complete readjustment, then, of all the promises in the society must follow; and since everybody is involved, on one or the other side, in promising—in both long and short promises—nobody can be unaffected. But we must defer, to later chapters, a closer examination of this sort of development.

The ordinary citizen need not be ashamed if he does not see everything that happens in central banking in sharp and clear detail. The strain upon the imagination here is immense, particularly when one has no personal experience in the field. Even among the practitioners in it, and among economists, there is by no means complete agreement upon the interpretation of events that seem to have their beginning somewhere in this area. The exposition as to what goes on, which has been given here, is obviously of the most general character. As we indicated—aside from government—this is perhaps the keystone occupation of men. What the few central bankers of the world do, the judgments they make, and incidentally how clear their understanding is of the processes by which human society operates, sooner or later has its effect upon the lives of every individual in their nation.

For example, it is clear enough from our analysis, even though we did not go into it exhaustively, that it is they really who determine the amount of purchasing-power in existence in each nation. It is bank promises, we saw, which are principally used as modern money, and the central bank in each nation *can completely control the amount of bank promises* outstanding at any one time.*

Our panoramic purpose is sufficiently served if a simple truth has been grasped, by the ordinary citizen who is not a specialist, from these few pages. The prime business of this whole study is to disclose how great a part men's promises play in human affairs, and to see as precisely as possible how they play that part. Our loose end

* There are three devices that are used by central bankers to control the total amount of bank credit that is being passed around from ownership to ownership in place of real money: First, by lowering and raising discount rates—that is, the amount banks must pay the central bank, when they want to borrow money from it. The more interest they charge, the less, ordinarily, do the subordinate banks want to borrow; accordingly, the less central bank credit, usable as money, would be created. Second, by buying and selling the long promises of governments and enterprises, so-called investments. Since it pays for these merely by giving credit on its own books, the central bank thus lessens or increases the amount of its own promises outstanding, and these—as we saw—can be counted as "reserves" by smaller banks and in turn control the total amount they can lend enterprisers. Third, the central bank occasionally is given the power by the national government—our own central bank has had this power within the past few years—to change the proportion of reserves smaller banks are required to keep against their deposits. The detail by which these several devices operate to control the amount of bank credit in existence—and therefore the current amount of purchasing-power in existence—can be learned from any book on central banks. A thorough and simple one, on our own central banking system, is *The Reserve Banks and the Money Market,* by W. Randolph Burgess. This detail every citizen should be familiar with, for the amount of effectual purchasing-power in existence in the nation at any time affects the daily activities of men and women as much as anything one can think of. The central banker is the man who can turn this spigot on and off. It seems to be a rather important matter, therefore, for everyone to understand both how he does it, and precisely what considerations, what problems, he must bear in mind in making such portentous decisions.

of truth led us inevitably into this complex region, which most of us instinctively avoid. It was impossible to stay away, and it is enough for our broad purposes, if we can acquire a fairly clear comprehension of the vital promissory relations that lie here, at the heart of modern economic life: the complete interdependence of promises between the government, the central bank, all the subsidiary banks, and at the end the simple economic promises, in which you and I are involved on one side or the other. There they are—all fatefully intertwined.

II

How the Promises Made to and Made by Insurance
Companies Differ from Those of Banks

THE invention of insurance rests upon the discovery of the means by which men can protect themselves, not from the immediate harshnesses of raw Nature, but from those which they anticipate Nature will visit upon them in the future. That discovery is the realization that a loss of wealth that would be disastrous to a single person becomes inconsequential *when it is shared by everyone in a large group*. Each one in the group therefore contributes a small sum, so that should the anticipated natural calamity occur to any one of them, he is reimbursed, *and each one then loses little*. Insurance, in short, is a deliberate sharing of economic loss, and one of the most intelligent forms of group action that men engage in—one of the few really intelligent ones, it might even be said.

The Greeks, in their maritime loan system, seem to have been the first to use a crude form of marine insurance. But the institution, as we now know it, really grew out of the adventurous enterprises of merchants from the fourteenth century onward. "Doth not the wise merchant," said Nicholas Bacon, in Elizabeth's time, "in every adventure of danger give part to have the rest assured?" Many decades later insurance against losses from fire began to develop. Insurance against death was not organized until well into the eighteenth century, and for years was confined to comparatively small groups within the population. But the institution of insurance, as modern men know it, has had its principal development in comparatively recent times. Indeed, only within the past seventy-five years has this

182

social invention become so far-flung in its operations that practically everybody in the population is affected by it, in many ways, consciously and unconsciously. In advanced nations it plays almost as important a role in human society as the bank, although a more retiring one, like that of a rich "silent partner" in an economic enterprise.

How, precisely, does the half-exchange play its part in this wide field?

In the first place, every insurance policy, when it is examined, merely sets forth the details of a deferred exchange of money for more money. At fixed intervals, you agree to give the insurance company specified small sums. You do so, and you get back what? A paper receipt, nothing more. The money is gone, so far as you are concerned. It now belongs to the insurance company. You keep this up over long periods. Indeed, on life policies, you keep it up, in certain cases, as long as you live. Literally and actually, you have nothing to show for the money but written promises. These promises are incorporated in detail in the insurance policy. It says, in effect, that in exchange for these sums of money the insurance company promises to pay you other sums—*in the future.*

Precisely when? At no precise date at all. Simply when a specified contingency occurs: when you have a fire, if it is a fire insurance policy; when and if something is stolen from you, if it is a burglary or theft policy; when you have an accident, if it is an accident policy; when you die, if it is a life insurance policy. In the last event, the exchange is completed, unfortunately, a little too late to benefit you personally. Manifestly, the most implicit reliance is placed in all these transactions upon the integrity and resources of the insurance company. The insurance company—and let us not forget, as we are inclined to, that they are run by men—is trusted just as blindly and utterly as the bank is trusted.

Few persons are aware of the astronomical volume of these promises that insurance companies undertake, and which they are being trusted by almost all economic enterprises and by tens of millions of individuals to complete. On December 1, 1935, the amount of life insurance alone in force in the United States was almost $101,000,-

183

ooo,ooo! * This is one measure—and by no means complete—of the volume of promising that goes on in this single area of human affairs. For, observe two things: first, this figure only includes life insurance in force *in the United States*. And second, it does not include any other forms of insurance—fire, burglary, marine, tornado, and what-not.

On the nearest comparable date, the total deferred exchanges which all the banks in the United States had agreed to complete—so-called time and demand deposits—were not half this amount; they were about $49,000,000,000! †

Now, of course, so far as the insurance companies were concerned, the completion of this unimaginable mass of promises was spread out over a long period of the future. Only a serious nation-wide catastrophe, when a large part would become fulfillable all at the same time, would present serious difficulties in their ultimate completion. On the other hand, the banks were in a position where the promises were currently fulfillable—not in the event of a stated happening, but at the pleasure of all the trusting individuals.

This vital difference in the date of completion makes an enormous difference in the nature of the deferred exchanges the insurance company itself proceeds to enter into, in which it is the *trusting* party —that is, in its so-called loans and investments. Since its own promises are, for the most part, long promises, the insurance company *can accept* long promises from others.

Nevertheless, an important qualification must be made here. Very few persons, even among our legislators, realize that the modern life insurance company's obligations do not depend entirely, by any means, upon our dying in an orderly fashion, according to ratios which have been laboriously calculated by a cold-blooded life insurance actuary. In late years, life insurance companies have, in one portentous respect, become very much like banks.

As we have pointed out, one of the great drawbacks of that type of deferred exchange, which we call a life insurance contract, is that

* *Best's Life Insurance Reports,* 1936.
† On December 31, 1935; *Federal Reserve Bulletin,* February, 1937.

184

its completion comes slightly too late to be of any direct benefit to the person who has been doing the sacrificing on the other half of the exchange. It is all outgo, no income—a strain upon human nature at its best. But back in 1907, as a result of the historic Armstrong Investigation in New York State, in which Chief Justice Hughes first came into considerable public notice, practically all life insurance companies—in the United States—were compelled to put into their contracts what are called "cash-surrender and loan privileges." This made most of the money paid to an insurance company very much like the savings put into a bank. The ubiquitous insurance agent was not slow in pointing it out.

The insurance policy which includes the "cash-surrender and loan privilege" is simply a deferred exchange, in which *a double set of contingencies* determines the date of completion of the exchange. Different amounts are specified, depending upon which contingency first occurs.

The insurance company now says to you in one of these policies: "Pay us so and so much each year. If you die (Contingency Number One) we will pay this large sum to those whom you specify (Amount Number One). However, you may find it necessary to transfer that protection from your own grieving heirs to yourself. If you do (this is Contingency Number Two) at any time after the first year, we will pay you back a stated portion of the sums you have paid." The amounts specified to cover Contingency Number Two are, needless to say, not the face value of the policy, but always slightly less than the total amount previously paid in.* This "cash-surrender or loan value" of the policy *for any date* is stated explicitly in the policy.

As a result of this interesting double-liability, the sums which the life insurance company receives are made, at the will alone of the policyholder, like his so-called savings in a bank.

Now, such deferred exchanges, fulfillable on demand, are loaded with dynamite. If completion is called for at an inopportune moment, if the calls are bunched insanely by millions of people—like a

* With the exception of endowment policies in their later years.

run on a bank—the insurance company will be caused some difficulty, to say the least.

This fact is so important—though few persons are aware of it—that an illustration is in order. The total "cash-surrender value" of all the life insurance policies in the legal reserve companies in the United States was a little under $18,000,000,000 in the beginning of 1933. This was one kind of deferred exchange they were being trusted in. At the same time the deferred exchanges they were required to complete in the event of deaths totaled about $109,-000,000,000 at that time.* The first figure, of the money they had to pay on demand, may give some notion of the worry that can be caused insurance companies, if any undue number of their policyholders suddenly ask to have those exchanges completed that are embodied in the "cash-surrender" provision of life insurance contracts.

Precisely that situation did arise during the fateful months of 1932 and 1933 in this country, and it is highly instructive for this study to examine what happened, again because of the light it throws *on the interdependence of economic promises.*

Insurance companies, of course, do precisely what banks do with the money they collectively receive. They promptly hand it over to others—in deferred exchanges. They do not keep it in vast vaulted stores of cash. But only a small portion of the deferred exchanges in which they themselves are being trusted—that is, their obligations in case of deaths—*are likely to come to completion at any one time.* Indeed, they can calculate—from the mortality rates—with an amazing precision how much these obligations will total in any year, almost in any month. In the meantime, under normal circumstances, the demands made upon them for the completion of the other type of exchanges in which they are trusted—those embodied in the "cash-surrender and loan" provisions of the contract—are comparatively not large.

Accordingly, it is perfectly safe for life insurance companies, under normal circumstances, to allow the larger part of their money to be tied up for long periods.

* *Best's Life Insurance Reports, 1936.*

186

They therefore buy mortgages on real estate far more than banks do. At the end of 1932, about 36 per cent of the resources of all legal-reserve life insurance companies was thus tied up in mortgages. They also give out money in exchange for long-deferred promises of counties, municipalities, States and central governments; roughly, 8½ per cent of the funds they had received had thus been used at the end of 1932. Finally, they invest in long-time promises of corporate enterprises of every character. About 37 per cent of their funds was so tied up at the end of 1932. In addition, about 18 per cent of their funds had been lent to policyholders. On that date, actually only 1½ per cent of all their resources was in the form of so-called cash.* But this latter is a decided misnomer. Without doubt, practically all of this 1½ per cent was also out in the form of half-exchanges—*with banks*. This small portion simply differed from the others in that the companies could call upon the banks for *the immediate completion* of these particular half-exchanges. Because of this advantage they are carelessly called "cash."

Now, what happened in this country during this interesting period of the Depression from late 1929 to 1933? The demand upon the insurance companies for the completion of those exchanges *fulfillable because of deaths* remained at pretty much the normal ratio, although it increased slightly because of suicides. But, owing to bank failures and other losses, an increasing number of policyholders began to avail themselves of Contingency Number Two in their contracts. They began, that is, ultimately to follow the original advice of the companies, something the companies never expected them to do in any volume—that is, to consider their former premium-payments as "savings." Some borrowed their own money from the insurance companies. Others completely terminated their policies, asking for all their money back under the "cash-surrender" clauses. Policyholders' borrowings on policies from those companies which operated by license and charter in New York State (representing at least three-quarters of the total life insurance of the country) totaled over $9,000,000,000 in 1931, 1932 and 1933. In addition,

* *Proceedings of Association of Life Insurance Presidents*, 1936, Page 93.

187

$3,250,000,000 were paid on policies which the policyholders closed out, demanding their cash. This was a total drain on the companies of over $12,250,000,000. In the previous three years similar demands had totaled about $5,000,000,000 less than this.

Thus, demands upon the insurance companies for immediate cash (having nothing to do with deaths) were increased far above the normal. Where were they to get this additional needed money?

As we have seen, at the end of 1932, only a trifling 1½ per cent of their resources was immediately available. The *one-third* of their funds which they had given to borrowers on mortgages could not be recovered for long years. This was true, likewise, of the *one-tenth* of their funds which they had given away for government promises. It was similarly true of the *one-third* of their funds which they had given to corporations for promises. Now, of course, these last two categories—government and corporation bonds—were long-term exchanges which were *ordinarily easily exchangeable for money*. They could be sold. But here the insurance companies ran into the same difficulty banks had to meet, which we examined in Chapter VIII. A good many of these bonds were long promises of corporations and of governmental units that seemed *very unlikely* to be fulfilled *in toto*. Also, even to sell the good ones at a fair price might prove difficult, if there proved to be no buyers.

One source of income the companies could rely upon: the current payment of premiums by those policyholders, who were continuing to trust them in these half-exchanges. Nevertheless, the insurance companies were in a quandary. They sold what bonds they could, to raise cash. But you will remember that banks were doing the same thing in the same period—and for the same reason! There were so many institutional sellers of bonds and comparatively so few buyers, that the bottom dropped out of the bond market. The fact is that these very institutions, banks and insurance companies, which were then selling bonds, had formerly been the principal buyers. If they could not buy in real volume, who could? In the meantime, the demands upon the insurance companies for the completion of their short economic promises continued to accelerate. There can be little question that the actual exchangeable value of much of the long promises they owned had dropped so low that, *from any strict accounting standpoint,* some of the important life insurance companies would have been considered insolvent at this period.*

The crisis came, as the bank crisis did, in early 1933. Just as the demand from policyholders took on the portentous blackness of a hurricane run, the States stepped in. Led by New York State, they allowed the insurance companies to refuse, if they so pleased, to honor any demand upon them for the completion of the enormous mass of promises represented by the "cash and loan value" provisions in the policies—$18,000,000,000 of promises at the time! †
This was an action unprecedented in American history, and undertaken—be it observed—not by the national government, but by the States. For, curiously, the national government exercises no control over these financial enterprises which, as we have seen, are in some ways little different from banks, and are involved in just as great a volume of deferred exchanges of money for money as banks are. The action was clearly unconstitutional, a high-handed abrogation of contract, and an unwarranted infringement upon the rights of any individual policyholder. But there was no doubt of its wisdom from an economic point of view. It saved the insurance companies. Saved them to do what? To meet one type of deferred exchange they had entered into under their *double-entendre* contracts—that is, to pay death claims. Their current incoming cash—from those policyholders who were continuing to trust them—was ample to enable them to do that. It was not for six months—not until demands upon insurance companies for immediate completion of deferred ex-

---

* What happened was that the insurance commissioners of the various States, upon whom devolves the duty of determining the solvency of these institutions, met in convention in 1932, and decided that, so far as the insurance companies were concerned, the prices offered on the stock exchanges for many of the bonds and stocks they held were "not fair market value." The insurance companies were allowed to put a value upon them, which *was an average of the quoted market value over five preceding quarterly periods.* This was rational in view of all the circumstances; particularly since the commissioners were valuing securities which the companies were holding, not selling; but it is not—as stated above—as strict accounting as is normal.
† Payments up to $100 were allowed, where need was proved.

changes had so lessened that they could easily be met from current income—that the old order was restored.

This story has been sketched briefly here, to illustrate—as it does strikingly, by experience—the intricate interdependence of the various types of half-exchanges one upon another, and to show again—as we did with banks—how dangerous it is, when those who make short promises accept and rely too greatly upon long ones.

Long since now all has been forgotten. One will sometimes even hear it claimed by a zealous insurance agent, with charming effrontery, that the record showed that insurance companies were "safer" for individual savings than banks. One interesting result, however, has followed from this experience—quite unnoticed by the general public. The dynamite that underlies life insurance contracts, with their present double form of liability, *is still there!* The companies, however, have attempted to protect themselves somewhat against it. With but very few exceptions, since this dramatic episode of 1933, new insurance contracts allow the insured person to draw out most of his money at any time, but they give the company sixty or ninety days' leeway, if they wish to avail themselves of it. The company's reserves, in short, are no longer comparable to the "demand-deposits" of banks, but to the so-called time-deposits of banks. It may be said, in short, that while the dynamite remains under most life insurance contracts, with their double form of liability, a long fuse has been laid to it. The hope is that if another emergency like that of 1933 arises, the spark can be stamped out before the dynamite gets set off; before the "cash surrender or loan values" have to be paid out in any undue quantity.

How ostrich-like! How characteristic of our American tendency to compromise about any change that seems a little disagreeable, after the immediate need for it is over! Once more it illustrates our wishful thinking and our curious readiness to believe that the future will never be very much different from the present.

For, if there was one single thing that the Depression demonstrated in this country, it was that the so-called time-deposits of banks are not of the slightest protection to a bank in an emergency.

190

Nor does this need experience; the slightest reflection, upon the underlying relations a bank has with its depositors, would indicate that time-deposits afford the bank no protection. The moment the promisor avails himself of the right to postponement which the time-deposit allows, flatly saying that he will not complete a half-exchange for thirty, sixty or ninety days, he trumpets aloud, for all the world to hear, his own belief that these vital half-exchanges are becoming *uncertain of completion.* At once, quite naturally, everybody who had trusted him in the first half of such exchanges descends upon him with demands that they be completed. If they cannot be completed immediately, then they must be completed as quickly as possible. In the meantime, no one is moronic enough to trust the banker in new half-exchanges at such a moment.

For that reason, during the entire period of the Depression, it was suicidal for any bank, with time-deposits, to avail itself of its legal rights. The storm-cellar which they had rigged up—and, incidentally, it has always been a characteristic feature of our banking scene—proved to be right out in the open air, when the hurricane came. There it has been all the time, and there it remains for everyone—except our intelligent statesmen—to see. For our Banking Acts have always assumed, and still do, that time-deposits are different from demand-deposits, that they provide some safety to banks, and that therefore smaller reserves of cash can be kept against them; and, consequently, that other long promises (in the form of long loans) may safely be relied upon to support these hypothetical longer promises of the banks. The trouble, plainly, is that *in normal periods* time-deposits are not regarded as long promises. They are considered just like demand-deposits. The bank will complete them at any moment upon request. Accordingly, in abnormal situations, they cannot suddenly be changed into long promises—not even thirty, sixty or ninety days long. *They must be as short as they normally are.*

"Time deposits under present practices," says one undoubted authority, "are in effect payable on demand, and yet they have to be employed in long-term assets, which are subject to fluctuations in value, and often cannot be liquidated properly without adverse effects." * This says in a nutshell what we have been demonstrating. It sets forth one of the basic weaknesses of the American banking system, long recognized by everybody who has dispassionately reflected upon it.

Now, of course, it is as true of the insurance company as it is of the bank. The cash-surrender and loan privileges of life insurance contracts, which involve obligations not far short of $20,000,000,000 at this moment, remain like the demand-deposits of commercial banks. To change them, by changing life insurance contracts, to something like a bank's time-deposits, is merely camouflaging the danger. For before invoking this privilege in the next great emergency, insurance companies will undoubtedly be compelled to do what banks did from 1930 onward. Rather than announce to all the world that they are in danger, thus bringing down upon themselves a flood of demands that will geometrically multiply their difficulties, they will let these time-deposits continue to be regarded as demand-promises. The first protection they will naturally seek will be to dump their long-term promises on the market—their investments in government and industrial securities—to get what money can be got for them.

One thing, in fairness, should be observed in this connection. The insurance companies in 1932 and 1933 would hardly have found themselves in this quandary, arising from the dependence of their short promises upon long ones, had it not been that most banks at the same time were in the same difficulty. It was the accelerating flood of bank failures from 1930 onward that compelled a great number of people to look to the "savings" that had accumulated in the cash-surrender and loan provisions of their insurance policies. Accordingly, if by some incredible good fortune—before the next great Depression descends upon us—our banking system were shored up in this respect, it is highly unlikely that the insurance companies would find themselves again in this danger. The banks, in other words, would provide an almost impenetrable first line of defense

* *The Reserve Banks and the Money Market*, W. Randolph Burgess.

192

for the insurance companies. What chance there is of this eventuality of sensible banking reform, looking upon both our past and current history, you can judge as well as the next man. My own personal view is, unless politicians change their nature, that we can fairly count upon, some time in the future, precisely the same sort of experience we had with banks and insurance companies from 1930 onward. Few economic events, in their general features, can be predicted with more certainty. For the very conditions ultimately involve the events. Short promises cannot depend for fulfillment upon long ones, without all kinds of trouble ensuing in time.

What does the record show, as to the measure of human reliability, in this field of insurance? We must proceed to take that measure here, as we have elsewhere.

There was, of course, the one lapse in the extraordinary emergency that we have just outlined. There, as we saw, the States absolved the insurance companies temporarily from fulfilling their short promises, in order to enable them infallibly to fulfill the long ones. No policyholder ultimately lost money as a result of this measure. All long promises—death claims that had to be fulfilled—were kept; and soon all short ones were again fulfilled upon demand.

Aside from this one passing cloud, the record of the life insurance companies in the United States is practically spotless.

A reliable authority on life insurance statistics, after an exhaustive inquiry, reports only two failures of life insurance companies, which involved an ultimate loss to the policyholders: * one company went into receivership in 1879, the other in 1934. It is true that a number of small companies went into receivership during the past Depression. But in every case, except one, their resources were sufficient, if they did not have to be sacrificed by immediately selling their investments in the market, to cover death claims—that is, the long promises. These resources, accordingly, were always taken over by larger companies, who (to their own advantage, of course) kept the policies in force, and thus no policyholder lost. The loss that oc-

* Best's Life Insurance Reports.

curred in the two genuine failures, when compared with the billions of dollars of insurance that are in force, and with the promises that have continuously been met by death claims and cash withdrawals, is so infinitesimal that it is not worth trying to dig into the records, in order to calculate the tiny fraction of a per cent that it would be.

We can add this record, then, to the others which we have been gathering. Once more, in this field, we see that the fulfillment of economic promises runs barely short of complete perfection.

12

How Our Loose End of Truth Explains the Rise of
Corporations and One of the Most Deep-Going
Changes in the Long Career of Human
Beings on the Planet

O UR portrait of the *genus homo* has been rather flattering so far. It is about time, the misanthropes will say, we reached for the black pigments, if only by way of contrast. Otherwise, we shall be accused of seeing human society through rose-glasses. But any roseate hue is really due only to the fact that we must faithfully paint what is there. If we consider individuals—in this particular matter of promise-performance—there have been no uglinesses so far to represent, except miscalculation of the future. But, of course, they exist; and now we begin to come upon them.

Insensibly we have been approaching what writers in the nineties used to refer to as the Temple of High Finance. It is a place of such forbidding mystery that even today modest laymen assume that only the high priests can enter and comprehend the mysteries that go on. But peek within, with what bravado you can muster: and lo! its votaries seem to be following the same simple principles of action as we have seen operating everywhere else in society. Strip away the mumbo jumbo, and the basic considerations are the same that inspired you and your baker, when you walked off with a cake in the beginning of this book, and promised soon to give him one dollar. Our loose end of truth, which fully explained that simple event, will elucidate quite as much here.

A brief but exact definition of High Finance would be that it consists of incompleted exchanges of very large sums of money—instead of small ones—for more money at a later time.

Surely, at some time or other you must have strolled contemplatively through the towered streets surrounding Wall and Broad Streets in New York, or through the equally small area around Threadneedle Street in London, and wondered what all these intent and hurrying men were engaged in doing. Where is each one going— to do what? Inquisitively—if you were a Martian—you would wander through these massive structures. Here you would see unsmiling men conferring in high-ceilinged and carpeted spaces. There would be others in solitary, almost bare, cubbyholes, as studiously engaged in poring over some document as a monk with his breviary in the Middle Ages; and there still others in mad, gesticulating crowds. What are they all doing? It would be found, upon separate analysis, that almost every individual, among these alert and keen-eyed thousands, is attending to some detail involved in a half-exchange still to be completed, or in worrying about one to be entered upon. The promises of men, and the completion or incompletion of them, would explain these puzzling human activities almost in their entirety. What they are all so intent upon is the future, and how it will affect the completion of their own, or other men's, promises.

Let us see, more precisely, the nature of some of these promises. They are not hidden; they are merely obscured to us—like so many others we have examined—by our thoughtless acceptance of them.

It is, of course, the corporation carrying on an economic enterprise with which, principally, we have to deal here. Ever since Lord Coke, in the reign of King James, delivered his famous comment upon it, the corporation has been assumed to be, in some sort, a mysterious entity. "The opinion of Maxwood, Chief Baron, was this, touching Corporations," said Lord Coke, "that they were invisible, immortall, and that they had no soule; and therefore no subpoena lieth against them, because they have no conscience nor soule; a corporation is a body aggregate; none can create soules but God, but the King creates them and therefore they have no soule; they cannot speak nor

196

appear in person, but by attorney, and this was the opinion of Maxwood, Chief Baron, touching corporations."

What a useful opinion—for the corporations! This quaint concoc-
tion of economics, law and theology has ever since colored a certain
type of reasoning about corporations. If one discards it wholly,
which is justifiable in a modern realist, and considers merely the human pattern of the corporation, any normally bright child can understand both its nature and its activities. Sometimes referred to as a
legally fictitious individual, the corporation is simply a group of individuals who together own and carry on, through officers whom
they designate, some enterprise engaged in the production or distribution of goods, or in the rendering of services. This group has been
granted by the State certain prerogatives which individuals do not
enjoy. The principal prerogative of the group, and the one which explains both the rise and the continuing existence of these behemoth
enterprises, has to do—as we shall presently see—with the question of
the completion of half-exchanges.

But, before looking into this, it might be advisable to acquire a
mental image, if it be possible, of the role the corporation, as a social
institution, has come to play in human affairs. Its only present rival is
that entity which we call the State. It is not unilluminating, indeed,
to liken corporations to small States. Says one commentator: "Black-
stone very aptly called them little republics, though he could have
been more faithful to history if he had called republics 'big corporations.' " *

If we regard the *field of economic activity* of the corporation as
comparable to the territory of the State, the figure of speech may
help to reveal quite a little about corporations; particularly, if we
conceive of an unsettled ancient land, like Greece, with hundreds of
fiercely independent little city-states, each one ready to carry on dep-
redations over the border in any direction, whenever need arose or
good opportunity offered for the acquisition of more land or cattle
or slaves. A difference is that the modern corporation is far more dis-

* John P. Davis, in *History of Corporations.*

ciplined in its internal organization. Some are tiny, like a minute Greek state perched on a hillside or on a rocky islet; they range over only a small segment of economic territory. Others compare with an Athenian or Roman Empire in the scope of their economic operations, covering large portions of the earth.

Corporations have their armies like States—civil and not military. These armies not only compare in numbers with those of States; but, in their discipline and their beautiful coordination of special skills in men, they are ordinarily superior to the armies which States have immemorially maintained.

Figures may make this comparison more revealing. Take the American Telephone and Telegraph Company. It is a group of 715,-000 owners, who, theoretically, choose their officers by a prescribed voting system. Athens in its palmiest days had not so many citizens as this. In addition, this corporation may be conceived of as having an army of 294,362, working together with an incredible discipline and efficiency. No single Greek state ever had so large an army, and there are few nations on the earth today which have peace-time armies greater in number than this. Or take the Pennsylvania Railroad, an army of 100,000 people—quite aside from its owners.

It is doubtful whether any military organization, large or small, even approaches the smooth, everlasting efficiency which such economic peaceful armies as these manifest daily in their continent-wide operations—without notice, much less astonishment, from anyone. Nor are these examples untypical of the modern business corporation.

There are now literally tens of thousands of these established little economic republics, with their civil armies large and small, recognized in each nation, favored in each nation. Every one of them is preoccupied, more or less, with a single economic objective. Each one of them battles principally with those that are engaged in the same objective, although sometimes it is in economic war with those that are different, but which yet may indirectly threaten its existence. Sometimes, like the Greek city-states, these economic units establish

198

ententes cordiales with one another, portioning off the territory—the economic territory, in this case—where each may range without interference by those strong enough to threaten it.

It is men organized in groups of economic armies like this, who now carry on the most vital activities that make and keep human civilization what it is. Such is the broad picture that would finally appear of the place of the business corporation in the modern human scene.

Now, it is helpful to reflect that time was—and the time lasted for almost all of the hundreds of thousands of years men and women have been other than tree animals—when their purely economic activities, providing themselves with the wherewithal to remain alive and enjoy living, were carried on *as individuals and families*. Economic enterprise from time immemorial has been individual. Occasionally, it is true, during the past two thousand years, a comparatively few individuals would associate themselves in that form of economic enterprise which at present we call a partnership. But partnerships in the olden days were far more often family enterprises than otherwise.*

Now, of course, individual enterprise is far from extinct. We can observe it still prevailing, deep-rooted in its long past, in agricultural production; in small retail shops; in minor production enterprises; among handicraftsmen, like plumbers and watchmakers and carpenters; and in service-occupations. It is the first and natural form for economic enterprise to assume, as each individual becomes aware of the necessity of pitting his senses and skills against an essentially hostile world, as all his deepest instincts as a living creature tells him that

* Partnership in economic enterprise is as natural as individual enterprise. But it has always had a peculiarly fascinating psychological background. It arises, with hardly any question, from the need of individuals to give one another support, if it is only moral. To attempt to do something new by oneself is infinitely more difficult a task than where another is by one's side; very few persons have the moral courage and complete self-reliance to be solitary in a new venture and to dispense with the assistance of anybody who can be found with like interests. This can be observed in the history of existing economic enterprises. It is a rarity that they are begun by individuals acting alone. Where they are not corporations, they begin as partnerships. But the need for this latter form of enterprise is far more psychological than economic.

it is. But natural as individual economic enterprise is, and widespread as it still is, it has become very much the second fiddle, as an institutional form of economic activity in the modern world; and it seems clearly on the evolutionary road of slow, although perhaps never entire, extinction.

Men now carry on their most vital activities, in the production and distribution of goods, *as groups;* and the groups are the economic republics, with their peaceful armies, large and small, which we call corporations.

For example, there are about 470,000 active economic armies, large and small, operating in the United States alone.* In the year 1930, when the American government took a census of business enterprises in this country, *it was revealed that over ninety per cent of all the goods manufactured in 1929, finished and semi-finished, were manufactured by corporations.* Ninety-five per cent of all the metals mined was done under the aegis of corporations. Seventy-five per cent of wholesale trade was carried on by corporations; and close to fifty per cent of all retail trade. And, of course, so far as concerns railroading, the provision of power, and all other public utilities, practically 100 per cent of it is carried on by corporations. When all income produced, including agriculture and service, is considered, *half of it* was attributable to corporations.

This predominance of the corporation in our economic life would be true of every other industrial nation. One might be tempted to cite Soviet Russia as an exception; but, except so far as ownership of the enterprise is concerned, the trusts which operate as units under the Soviet government, each one attending to the production and distribution of special commodities or services, are in nowise different— so far as their human organization is concerned—from the far-flung corporations which function in other countries. Quite as much as business corporations—and in the same way—they must be sharply distinguished from individual enterprise. Indeed, in Russia, this development of *group economic activity* has extended more than any-

* The total number of corporations reporting to the Bureau of Internal Revenue in 1935—covering 1934 operations—was 528,882; of these 59,122 were inactive. *Statistics of Income,* 1934.

where else in the world into the last real stronghold of individual enterprise, agriculture.

It is doubtful whether in all the history of Man a more radical change in his essential way of life has taken place than this—from the production and distribution of goods by individuals to their production and distribution by groups, large and small, specially created, recognized and favored by the State as corporations. *This momentous change has taken place almost entirely within the past one hundred years!* The change was the clear result of a social invention, and it is an invention particularly interesting to this inquiry, because *the question of the completion of deferred exchanges lies at the bottom of it.*

This is no more the place for a survey of the history of corporations than it is of banking. But enough must be sketched of it here to see the nature of this momentous development. From the earliest days, no doubt, groups of men in any large community naturally would associate themselves for one purpose or another. But it would be a mistake to imagine that these associations of antiquity were anything like what we mean by the modern business corporation.* They were sometimes associations for religious purposes; or they were among men of like activity in a single community. These groups were recognized by the State; they often acquired specific rights and undertook specific duties; but each one in the association remained an individual producer or distributor or artisan. This was true likewise in the Middle Ages of the guilds of merchants and artisans. All these organizations were more comparable to modern unions than to the modern business corporation. This latter had its real origin during the fifteenth and sixteenth centuries in Europe. Its development came about as the result of a growing international trade. In England, where the record of the development is most clear, the corporation began to put forth buds, as an institution, in the reign of Elizabeth; and to ob-

* Both Greece and Rome, in their heyday, developed organizations which seem to approach our corporations *in structure*, but not in activity. They were organizations in which "shares" were sold. In Rome these seem to have consisted principally of companies which bought the privilege of taxing conquered people. Some of Cicero's letters give a clear picture of the situation. See *Social Life At Rome*, W. Warde Fowler.

serve the part that deferred exchanges—and, therefore, economic promises—played in its rise and subsequent evolution, we should at least glance at what was happening in the world at that time.

We have seen already that there had always been, from the earliest days, traders among men—half adventurers, half business men—who would travel at the risk of their lives, by caravan and frail vessel, to distant parts of the world, in order to bring back to their own people strange forms of wealth. This was particularly true around the littoral of the Mediterranean. As far back as there are records, there are indications of active trade among peoples far removed from one another—and a great part of it had to be by vessel. In the Egypt of 3000 B.C., there have been found objects and materials that must have come from abroad, before the rise of the Mycenean civilization in Crete. Later the trade relations between Crete and Egypt were constant. Still later the Phoenicians, Greeks, Carthaginians and other peoples laboriously rowed their little vessels all over Homer's wine-dark sea, and far beyond it. The Athenian Empire of course, and later the Roman colossus, was built up on trading, policing and control of the seas, just as much as the present British Empire was. Thus, trade with foreigners, for many thousands of years, represented much the most important form of economic enterprise among men. Production remained individual and small. Most men still produced chiefly for their own needs. It was the merchants, the foreign traders, who supplied the liveliest economic activity in ancient centers like Cnossus and Ur and Nippur and Babylon and Thebes and Tyre and Sidon and Troy and Athens and Carthage and Rome and Alexandria and Byzantium, and a dozen other ancient centers of population.

Now, all through that long history of foreign trading, the traders *were almost in their entirety individual enterprisers.* They dealt, for the most part, among themselves. They were precisely what we now call exporters and importers. They came, separated as they were over the world, more or less to know one another; and, without doubt, it was first among merchants, dealing with one another in different countries, that the half-exchange, with its crucial promise, became a well-established economic procedure. When we come to the Mid-

202

dle Ages, more and more did the foreign trader flourish, the merchant exchanging his goods with other merchants in other lands. Venice, Genoa, Milan, Marseilles, Barcelona, Hamburg, Amsterdam, London—and a hundred other ports—were forever black with caravel and galleon, moving slowly and majestically "with their woven wings." Trading with foreigners, in the Middle Ages, was the only form of economic enterprise by means of which any large accumulation of wealth could be amassed. By the fifteenth century international trading had become so thoroughly and widely organized over Europe that a highly significant development began to occur.

Antonio's difficulties with Shylock provide a good fictional illustration of the situation that must normally have prevailed. Why did Antonio have to borrow from Shylock, whom he so abhorred? Here are the picturesque references thrown out by Shakespeare, who gave no thought to economics, but whose perspicacious eye missed nothing human:

Salarino: Your mind is tossing on the ocean;
   There, where your argosies, with portly sail—
   Like signiors and rich burghers of the flood,
   Or, as it were, the pageants of the sea,
   Do overpeer the petty traffickers
   That curt'sy to them, do them reverence,
   As they fly by them with their woven wings.

Salanio: Believe me, sir, had I such venture forth
   The better part of my affections would
   Be with my hopes abroad. I should be still
   Plucking the grass, to know where sits the wind,
   Peering in maps for ports, and piers, and roads;
   And every object that might make me fear
   Misfortune to my ventures, out of truth
   Would make me sad.

Antonio: Believe me, no: I thank my fortune for it,
   My ventures are not in one bottom trusted,
   Nor to one place: nor is my whole estate

Upon the fortune of the present year:
Therefore my merchandise makes me not sad.

Not then, but soon. We may assume, taking the prosy economic view, that his property had all been given away in long-term deferred exchanges. He expects some of the exchanges to be completed soon—within sixty days, he later says. When Bassanio comes to him to borrow money in order to make a show before Portia, Antonio supplies this financial statement in poetry:

Thou knowest that all my fortunes are at sea,
Neither have I money nor commodity
To raise a present sum; therefore go forth;
Try what my credit can in Venice do; . . .
Go presently inquire, and so will I,
Where money is. . . .

Bassanio goes to Shylock and that economic realist sees the situation in its true light.

Shylock: Antonio is a good man.
Bassanio: Have you heard any imputation to the contrary?
Shylock: Ho, no, no; no, no;—my meaning in saying he is a good man, is to have you understand me he is sufficient; *yet his means are in supposition:* he hath an argosy bound to Tripolis, another to the Indies; I understand, moreover, upon the Rialto, he hath a third at Mexico, a fourth for England,—and other ventures he hath, squandered abroad. But ships are but boards, sailors but men; there be land-rats and water-rats, water-thieves and land-thieves; I mean pirates; and then there is the peril of waters, winds, and rocks. The man is, notwithstanding, sufficient;—three thousand ducats;—I think I may take his bond.

Antonio, completely divested by his own acts of his property, enters into a ninety-day deferred exchange with this economic realist, believing that his own long-term deferred exchanges will be com-

pleted before the short one. The old, old story of the way most op-
timists court bankruptcy.

Speculative voyages like Antonio's, in Elizabethan days as in all
previous times, sometimes took several years. As frequently as not,
with water-thieves and winds and rocks abroad, they were never
completed. The risk indeed was so great that, as we have seen, the
momentous institution of modern insurance had its origin in these
very circumstances. With this in mind, the significance of what began to occur in Europe, and particularly in the active and adventurous England of Elizabeth, can be better appreciated.

Enterprises in foreign trade became possible which, *because of
their volume*, involved such large sums that few individuals had sufficient aggregated capital to undertake them. Aside from this, individuals with enterprising ability—mariners and adventurers—began
increasingly to appear, who had little or no capital. The adventuring
of such persons had to be "backed." The natural thing to happen,
under such circumstances, it would seem, was for groups of persons
to pool their resources—to finance, as we say—a particularly promising trading enterprise to some distant nation. This is indeed what
happened in the maritime cities of Europe from the fourteenth century to an ever-increasing degree up to the time of Elizabeth and
James I, when the development became particularly active in England.

But the necessity for large resources was not the only causal background of these associations of men in overseas enterprise. "There be
land-rats and water-rats, water-thieves and land-thieves." Pirates
throve more when cargoes became richer, and out in the lonely sea,
who would ever know if a respectable English or Spanish or Venetian
merchantman temporarily turned pirate and a weaker vessel met on
the way would be *spurlos versenkt*—for its mere cargo. The borders
of morality, from the most ancient times, had stopped at the shore.
It became more and more necessary for honest merchantmen to
travel in fleets, for protection, not against water, wind and rocks, but
against black piracy. Of course, this problem was as old as sea-trading
itself. Necessary policing of the sea against little pirates had been the

205

foundation of the Athenian Empire,* and was later a function assumed by every sea-going power.

These associations of merchants, in single ventures, were at first a loose form of partnership. Each merchant had his own stock of goods on board the vessel, traded them, and brought back what he could. These in England were so-called Regulated Companies. An easy evolution from this procedure was for each merchant to contribute to a common stock of goods, and receive profits—or endure loss—in the proportion of his original contribution. These were the so-called Joint Stock Companies; the stock of goods then was property common to the group. Another development soon occurred. Groups of traders began to receive from the sovereign *monopolistic rights* to trade with certain foreign peoples. Any merchant, not belonging to the group, sent his vessels to such regions at his peril. Elizabeth and James I granted a large number of such foreign trading monopolies. Thus, the famous East India Company, receiving its momentous charter the last day of the year of 1600 from Elizabeth, was a group of merchants, who were specified originally by name and who had the sole right to trade with India. Trade with Russia was carried on monopolistically by another group, trade with Turkey by still another. There were quite a few of these groups of merchants and court favorites.

At the beginning, it was single voyages of fleets of vessels that were financed by these groups, and settlement was made among the associates *at the end of each voyage.* But ownership of some forms of wealth—for example, often ships—remained in common. Moreover, incompleted exchanges were a necessary part of sea-trading. They often had to be entered into by the group as a whole. Time and time again, then, the burning question would arise, Who is responsible for the completion of these promises made by the group as a whole? How far was each member of the group responsible? Was it a partnership, where each member could be held for all the promises—could be compelled indeed by the State to perform them? Now, this from the days of Rome had been the law, with respect to individuals

* *The Greek Commonwealth,* by Alfred Zimmern.
206

associated together in strictly economic enterprise. This was often true, even where the economic aspect of the association was not primary, but incidental. "In a rough way, the members of mediaeval gilds and municipalities were held primarily responsible for the debts of members, whether incurred in personal transactions or in transactions relating to matters of common concern." * Fancy the individual members of a modern Chamber of Commerce, or of a labor union, each holding himself responsible for the personal debts of his fellow members. Or of John and James Citizen being haled into a modern court to pay municipal debts!

If this was to be the case with such large and extensive sea-trading adventures, enterprise was smothered before it began to stir. For no individual, and particularly no individual of integrity, would place himself under the risk of having to complete deferred exchanges—by the compulsion of the State or otherwise—that were far greater in sum than his own resources. A social invention was necessary to free large enterprise in such a situation. It was found in the so-called limitation of liability.

England was a little late in applying this principle to the enterprises that were beginning to transform her into a world power. It was in mediaeval Italy, largely, that the principle seems to have had its first application to business, and it seems really to have arisen, most interestingly, from the necessity of evading the strong canonical injunction of the Middle Ages against the acceptance of interest.

On the Continent there were two principal forms of mediaeval associated business enterprise. One was called the *societas*. It was like our partnership. The old, old principle obtained that each partner, like a blood brother, was responsible for economic promises made by the other. The second was called a *commenda*. It appeared to be a form of partnership, but in reality was merely a device by which one party lent money to another. What the lender received was *called* profit, not interest—and therefore no purgatory lay in wait for him. His profit, ordinarily, was fixed, like interest; it was three-fourths of what resulted from the venture if he put up all the money. Later

* *History of Corporations*, by John P. Davis, Volume II.

on, in these business contracts, more than one *commendator* appears. They invest money in specified amounts in the enterprise. The same old question arises—to what extent is each member responsible for the economic promises made by the group? The *commendatores* had no voice in the management of the enterprise. They cared to have none; at bottom they were lenders, not enterprisers. In time, then, the principle became solidly adopted that only the managers of the enterprise were personally liable for all the promises of the enterprise, and the *commendatores* were only to be responsible up to the amount of money each one put in. Early in the 1400's in Florence it seems that the *commendatores* were given this privilege, and all through Italy the business practice spread in the fifteenth and sixteenth centuries. It became common throughout Europe, though not in England. "It was through the *commenda* that the idea of a society in which the capitalist could invest, and limit his liability, came into the commercial law of Europe." *

Here, indeed, was the crucial social invention that, perhaps as much as any single factor, transformed our society into its modern forms. The *commenda* was of course known to English merchants, although not practiced as a form of enterprise. But its significant *limitation of liability*, not only in England but elsewhere, was recognized as the rational way out of the chief difficulty that stood in the way of the extensive enterprises that were being carried on, where large aggregations of capital were needed—more capital than any single merchant had, or cared to risk.

In Holland and in the England of James I, particularly, the joint stock companies—so-called, because originally the stock of goods on the vessels was jointly owned—began to thrive, when this social invention was applied to them. They became specifically endowed by charter with this invaluable privilege. In England, Lord Coke, with the typical English tendency to rationalization, was a particularly strong legal supporter of the idea. Today we take his references to the corporation as being without "soule or conscience" as condemnatory. But there was economics, not ethics, in his rationalization. He

* W. S. Holdsworth, *Juridical Review*, Volume 28, No. 4.

knew well enough, most surely, what his doctrine meant to English merchants and to English enterprise. The doctrine completely freed large and ambitious enterprise, which otherwise was hog-tied by old custom and law. With the thongs cut, one is tempted to remark, the hogs could range and wax fat. Soon the principle was applied whole-sale by James I and succeeding sovereigns. Court favorites in particular were granted charters—usually monopolies—to do a hundred things, and when they were in groups they were freed from personal liability for the promises made in the name of the group.

Now, this remains today the prime prerogative which the State confers upon the business corporation. The group of persons who compose it may own property as a unit, and may carry on productive or distributive or service activities as a unit. But only as a unit may they be expected by others, or be compelled by the State, *to complete the half-exchanges they enter into.*

Without such protection, obviously, no person would associate himself in such organizations as our modern business corporations, dealing as they do in millions of dollars. In England, these groups of persons are called, more descriptively than ours, "limited liability companies." The liability of each individual is limited to the amount he puts into the enterprise. One interesting requirement is usually made: the group must give notice always, to those who trust it in deferred exchanges, that the responsibility of each one of its members is thus delimited. This necessary warning is the explanation, which you may sometimes have wondered about, for the Ltd. and Inc. tacked on to the names of most of our corporate megatheriums.

Thus, we see that the simple matter *of the completion of deferred exchanges* is historically the seed, and is now the great trunk, of that vastly extended system of corporate enterprise which carries on the most vital functions of our modern life.

There is one special type of deferred exchange which corporations enter into, and which is of great importance in the modern world. It is that involved in the corporation bond. Why does a corporation borrow money from you on its bond? What does it do with it?

These simple questions uncover an extremely interesting set of social details.

These specially empowered groups of persons, carrying on an enterprise together, often find—or their officers find for them—that it would be beneficial for all concerned if their operations could be extended. To do so, they must acquire more property of one kind or another—new machines, buildings, land, a mine, ships, a railroad, or what-not. In short, they need more "capital." Well, why don't they get together among themselves and contribute it? They normally do, when not much is required. Only too often, however, the sums necessary for the new ambitions of the group are far too large for its original members conveniently to find. The next obvious thing for them to do is *to add more persons to the group,* and thus increase their resources. They proceed to do this, too—when they can. That is, they increase their capital stock, by permission of the State, and proceed to exchange it for the money they need.

Here, however, they run into an interesting but common attitude toward economic enterprise. The persons with available money whom they approach, say: "Sorry; we want no share in your enterprise. If you want our money, the only way we will let you have it is in a deferred exchange! In short, we will trust you, and the fortunes of your enterprise, only up to a point, and only if we are put in a favored position. Promise to give us back an equivalent sum later on—five, ten, twenty, even fifty years from now, and in the meantime as a reward for helping you out, pay us small sums as interest every six months or every year. The only requirement we will make of you, aside from finally completing this exchange, is that every year you will pay these sums of interest before each one of you as a group receive any earnings from the enterprise."

This is the explanation of the corporation bond, and reasonable enough the position is. The corporation, with the money thus given it, in these long-term deferred exchanges, proceeds to obtain the property it needs to carry on the additional operations it has in mind. That is, money borrowed on bonds is supposed, in good industrial practice, to be spent on "capital facilities"—on property which will not be consumed, *but which will be useful in producing more goods.* The property, however, belongs to the corporation, not to the bondholders, responsible as these latter may be for its being. But what in the meantime is their situation?

They have given away the property they owned, their own money. They have received what, in exchange? A so-called corporation bond. What is it? Precisely the same, in nature, as a business man's note, although it is engraved and printed with handsome curlycues all over it. The amusing purpose of this artistic effort is to throw some aura of inherent value over the piece of paper. Of course it has none. In itself it is not worth a hundredth of a penny. It merely sets forth, usually in unreadable type and in great detail, the terms of the promise. Read it through with a good lawyer and a dictionary at your side (you will need both) and the final translation will be as follows: "To the person who has given us this money, we promise to give the same amount at such-and-such a place and such-and-such a time, and in the meantime small added sums, called interest, at such-and-such a place and such-and-such a time."

It is again, in short, a promise of later action—a deferred exchange of money for a little more money at a later date.

Like the loans made by a bank, sometimes these bonds are secured, sometimes they are unsecured. When they are unsecured, the person who has given away his money is simply relying upon the corporation's integrity and ability to carry out all the terms of the promise. When they are secured, the corporation specifies in the bond the particular property owned by it, which it stands ready to forfeit for the benefit of the bondholders, if it fails to carry out the promises.

Now, it is illuminating to examine what the considerations are that induce you and others to give up your money for these pieces of paper. Do they differ in any way from those which explain and animate the other types of deferred exchange we have examined? Essentially, no; but to some degree, yes—because of the difference in circumstances. This slight difference it is worth looking into, for it leads to some interesting revelations.

For the purpose of our own inquiry, the most interesting aspect of this type of half-exchange must be, What role does reliance upon the honesty of individuals play in such a transaction? Lord Coke told you the corporation has "no conscience nor soule." Actually, we have seen the corporation is a group of individuals. Have they no souls? But there may be tens of thousands of them, they are unknown and unknowable, and they have been careful to put us on notice that individually they disclaim responsibility for the official promises of the group. Their honesty as individuals, therefore, *has nothing to do* with the performance of any promise the corporation may make.

We are, however, in a position to scrutinize carefully *their actions as a group*. Corporations, like individual enterprisers, enter into endless deferred exchanges. The record of what happens in them is kept. If that record divulges any serious lapse of performance, quickly it becomes known and the trusting of the corporation ceases as effectually as it would with an individual. Now, if a corporation is not trusted in deferred exchanges, it requires more resources to carry on all the exchanges it must necessarily engage in. Therefore, it is quite as suicidal for a corporation as it is for an individual, to fail to complete its deferred exchanges scrupulously. But icy necessity alone dictates the performance of its promises. There is no vestige of what we may call personal integrity here. No sacrifice may be expected of any of the members of the group, in case the promise is unfulfilled. They put everybody on notice, indeed, that they will not make the slightest sacrifice.

But if personal integrity plays no role at all, it is clear that reliance must be had upon the two other factors that govern the completion of every deferred exchange. We have seen what they are: first, the resources available to the trusted party to fulfill the promise, and second, the fact that the State may be called in to compel completion.

What then must be the mental processes of the man who unconditionally relinquishes his property, his money, and accepts the particular kind of written promise we call a "corporation bond"?

It must first be seen that corporation bonds are in that large group we have called long promises. They are very long promises. Sometimes they run for ninety-nine years. The most important thing the lender must be concerned about is *the ability* of the corporation to complete these long exchanges. To determine this properly involves a genuine study of the enterprise; what it expects to accomplish with the money it is borrowing on bonds; what it already owes, compared with what it owns; how well its operations have been carried on in the past; who are the personnel in control; in what way have they demonstrated their management ability, and justified the faith imposed in them by their unknown owners; what have been the past earnings of the enterprise, and what reasons are there for believing—or doubting—that they will continue to be as good or better; who are the competitors of the enterprise—the other large or small armies it must contend with; and are they likely to be able, in any way, seriously to affect the fortunes of the enterprise?

Reliable answers to all these questions require experience of a wide order, cool and dispassionate judgment about men and affairs. It also requires, obviously, an intimate knowledge of accounting—that is, of reading without being misled—by persons who are sometimes not above trying to mislead—the records of its operations which a corporation must keep.

No less important is the other consideration the long-time lender of money must keep in mind before he relinquishes it to a corporation for a piece of paper. When personal honesty is the principal reliance in the completion of an exchange, the appearance of the State in the transaction is regarded as a remote contingency. The fact seems to be, as this study has already traced out, that the greater the reliance upon personal honesty the less thought there is of the State, and the more informal the transaction. The less honesty can be relied upon, the more careful and formal the agreement becomes. Finally, in the case of a corporation bond, where the question of personal integrity is completely eliminated, the possibility that the State may have to step in some time during the long period before the final completion of the exchange becomes something that must be very seriously considered.

That is why all the terms and conditions of the promise—what may and must be done under all sorts of circumstances—are set forth with the most minute particularity in the bond and its accompanying legal documents. Accordingly, the lender must also be in a position to judge, under these legal hieroglyphics, *whether this protection is really adequate*—that is, how thoroughly it insures completion of the exchange.

Now, the truth of the matter is that there are very few individuals who can acquire all the necessary information, and have wisdom and experience enough to analyze it, in order to pass safe judgments upon these long-time promises of corporations. Banks and insurance companies, which relinquish a large part of their money to corporations on bonds, keep voluminous records and employ specialists who make such judgments for them. But so far as individuals are concerned, even the wealthiest, with the rarest exceptions, rely either directly, or at one or two removes, upon the so-called investment counsel and the investment banker.

The "investment banker" represents expertcy in this field built up into an institution. He is a person or a company which has specialized in determining the ability of corporations and governments to complete the half-exchanges represented by their bonds. The so-called investment bank has "customers" with which it is continuously in touch. They consist of wealthy persons, of banks, insurance companies, and other institutions, which have troublesome recurrent accumulations of money, and do not know what to do with it.

If the investment banker is satisfied, upon analysis, that a corporation will be amply able to complete the deferred exchanges represented by a proposed bond issue, he can and does guarantee to find the money for the corporation. This is called "underwriting" a bond issue. The investment banker assures the managers of the corporation, in other words, that if he cannot sell the corporation's bonds, he will himself lend it the money. For this, needless to say, he receives a rake-off, frequently a handsome one. Now, in actuality what he does, it will be seen, is to guarantee *to find persons or institutions* which will lend the corporation money in exchange for its promises to pay. Investment bankers are thus salesmen, go-betweens,

214

in finance. If you want to add to your stock of antipathies against the great bankers, whom perhaps, in common with Henry Ford, you regard as the devils of our otherwise holy age, call them "middlemen," and you will be accurate. They play precisely the same function in the field of money which the retailer performs for the producer of goods.

Because of his close connections with persons and institutions with troublesome accumulations of money, the investment banker has come to play a highly vital role in modern society. It is ordinarily he, and not the commercial banker, who is meant when we refer to our "invisible government." When investment bankers are able, far-seeing and wise, the function they play is of enormous value to society. This is because their peculiar position enables them to *direct the flow of capital* into enterprises that are socially beneficial. It is this which gives them their power, and in this resides their responsibility. When they are incompetent—and frequently enough they are; when they are concerned less about protection to those who are relinquishing money on their advice than with their own gain or acquisition of power—these few mortals can bring misery to millions, by paralyzing the orderly processes of our society. There is no doubt that an appreciable portion of the unusual virulence, in the United States, of the worst depression on record, can fairly be traced to the poor judgment—and sometimes treachery to those who trusted them—of certain American investment bankers during the ten-year period following the close of the World War.

Through this period, incidentally, an interesting development occurred that should be noticed here. The ordinary commercial banker always felt, and sometimes he still does, that he was quite capable of appraising properly those long-term loans which he calls "investments." Actually, except in the rarest cases, he is no more of a reliable specialist in this respect than any experienced business man. During the period from 1920 to 1929, quite a few commercial bankers in our large cities acquired Napoleonic complexes in this regard. With hundreds of millions of deposits, they were in intimate contact with enormous springs of idle wealth. They could see no rea-

215

son why they should not perform the brokering function of the investment banker. They became more and more active, accordingly, in underwriting promises of foreign governments, and of large domestic enterprises which were highly speculative in nature. Some of them actually covered the country with salesmen, inducing smaller banks and wealthy individuals to lend money to these governments and industrial enterprises. Aside from the risk of involving themselves in these long promises, at a time when they themselves were bound by short promises to their depositors, the advice these bankers would give to their own depositors and others could hardly be impartial, when they themselves were so involved in the ventures.

What might have been expected happened. In the short period from 1919 to 1929 alone, over $75,000,000,000 of long promises, made by domestic corporations, foreign governments and municipalities, were peddled and finally sold by bankers in the United States.* Not a bad selling record for eleven years! What did most of these banking intermediaries know about this perfectly stupendous mass of promises? Precious little, as both the event and later investigation proved. Literally billions of dollars were thus irrevocably lost by trusting citizens, as a result of this increasing assumption, by careless commercial bankers, of the expert and highly responsible duties involved in wise and honest investment banking. At least one salutary result of the Depression followed from this experience. In the Banking Act of 1933, it was provided that no bank in this country could both receive money from depositors, in short-term exchanges, and at the same time act as the agent in the procurement of money on long promises from corporations or governments. In other words, the demarcation between banks of deposit and investment banks was made clear and complete by law in this country. This is simply an added method of control of incaution, as it may appear in some megalomaniac commercial bankers.

An almost exact measure in dollars of the degree to which men now rely on one another's promises, in this field of the corporation bond, is obtainable. It is disclosed, simply enough, by the total

* *U. S. Statistical Abstract*, 1936, Page 292.

amount of bonds of corporations which are outstanding. In the United States, on December 31, 1934, it was not quite $37,000,000,-000.* All of this—let us not forget—represented real wealth which had been turned over by the owners to these groups of persons. For what? For pieces of paper which constitute *nothing but promises.*

Large as these sums are, it is still only a minor manifestation of the full extent to which men rely upon one another's integrity in this comparatively new human field of collective enterprise.

We have seen that business corporations are groups of persons owning and operating a specific enterprise together. We have seen also that our most vital economic activities are now carried on by these groups. As a corollary, a very appreciable portion of the tangible forms of wealth of the human race is now owned by corporations. In the United States, for instance, the Bureau of the Census estimated, in 1922, that the country's wealth, including its finished and partly finished goods, its raw materials, its homes and the personal possessions in them, its money, its buildings of all kinds, its machinery, its means of communication, and so on, could be valued as then exchangeable for $321,000,000,000. No analysis was published as to how much of this was owned by corporations, but there is little question that at that time the lion's share of it was, and that a larger share is now, fifteen years later.

We must be precise here in our distinctions. The groups of persons constituting each corporation "owned" all this property. They owned it, however, *only as groups.* No single one of them owned any single item of it. Acting as a unit, through their officers, they could do whatever they pleased with the property. This is the final criterion of ownership. Acting singly, none of them could do as he pleased with any part of the property, or enjoy the use of it exclusively in any way. The corporation alone owned the property. Now, considering this from the point of view of the individual, what in reality does each one own? We say he "owns shares" in the corporation. But it is apparent that the corporation's property can-

* *Long Term Debts in the U. S.,* Page 6.

217

not, as a practical matter, be shared unless it goes out of existence. In that case all that it owns can then be swapped for as much money as it will bring, and that money can then be shared among the corporation's owners. What each individual does own, it is clear, is nothing tangible at all. *It is merely the right to obtain a stated share* of any money the corporation earns, and the right to obtain a stated share of the money-proceeds that would result if the corporation went out of existence. These rights are testified to, by a piece of paper called a "stock certificate." It has our name upon it as the owner, if we are the fortunate possessors. It states the total number of shares which exist, and the number of them which we own. It is a mere *evidence of ownership;* and so it is generally called.

Men will give, and do give, as one of the commonest acts of business, large sums of money for these pieces of paper. At one moment they own the money. The next moment, after an exchange, they own the piece of paper. That, it can be said, is the only tangible thing they own; for that, indeed, they can do with as they please. It merely avers, to all and sundry, that the owner of it is a member of the corporation.

Now, while corporations—for reasons we have seen—must ordinarily be owned by large groups, necessarily they must be run by small ones. Every business enterprise, whether corporate or not, represents a little autocracy, in which ordinarily one person (sometimes in large corporations a few) is the Pooh-Bah who directs what is to be done. As a practical matter, it is obvious that the vast mass of corporate owners cannot manage the enterprise they own. The affairs of every corporation must be "controlled" by someone. These persons acquire control through a voting system. He who owns most shares, if he wishes to exercise his right, has most to say. But it is extremely seldom that the persons *who actively conduct the fortunes* of a corporate enterprise own all, or even a majority, of its shares. That portion of the shareholders who own most, almost as an invariable rule, through sheer lack of interest, *abdicate control of the corporation* to an interested clique which owns less, and frequently very little. In the case of our large corporations, it

218

is a rarity that share-owners even know who are conducting the enterprise they own. Much less do they know anything about its operation, or take an active part in the management of the property they own jointly with others.

But what does "control" of a corporate enterprise involve? It *means doing with the corporation's property practically anything the controller decides,* short of a defalcation which can be proved. If they can present a remote justification in business necessity, the controllers of the enterprise cannot be held liable by the entire body of owners for any action they may take, no matter how unwise it may be, nor how much it dissipates the joint property of the owners. The owners trust the controllers utterly, with no supervision over what they do, no knowledge of what they do, nor ordinarily even any knowledge as to *who they are!*

It seems as if confidence of men in one another's integrity could hardly go much further. That it is abused, time and again, goes without saying. In fact, in this field of corporate enterprise, we have at last come upon the one area of human activity where fraud, dishonesty and general unreliability—while it is by no means the rule —is at least more prevalent today than in any of the other areas of human action we have so far surveyed.

The unreliability is not manifested so much in the incompletion of *specific promises of action.* In the ordinary conduct of its affairs— when a corporation enters into deferred exchanges with laborers, suppliers, or banks—it completes them carefully. Otherwise it will no longer be trusted, and would have to go out of existence. For not the hugest corporation in the world has enough money to carry on its operations, if it had to "pay in advance," if it always had to be *the trusting party* in a deferred exchange. Such is the necessity it would be faced with, if it welched on the promises embodied in these half-exchanges.

Nor is the unreliability of the corporate enterprise manifest—to any unusual degree—in those long-term deferred exchanges represented by corporation bonds. A measure of its comparative reliability here is obtainable in the record of defaults on corporation

219

bonds. At the end of 1935, about 16 per cent of all railroad bonds were in default as to interest; about 6 per cent of public utility bonds were in default in 1933, which was the worst year for this type of bond; and about 13½ per cent of all bonds of industrial corporations. Comparing the total of corporation bonds, about $37,000,-000,000 in 1935, with the amount that was in default, shows a percentage of about 9 per cent.* In short, about 91 per cent of these long promises remained unimpaired, in spite of the worst industrial depression in history. Moreover, it must be observed—as we did with mortgages—that non-performance here does not necessarily mean ultimate loss. When a bond is defaulted upon, the property being held as security is sold, and the bondholders are supposed to get *something*. Here, incidentally, a great deal of shady work also goes on—among bankers, trustees, corporation managers and even in our courts—as revelations in recent years have abundantly shown.† Nevertheless, this 9 per cent record of default, on these particular long promises, is not a highly disturbing record of unreliability, and when we compare it with the long promises represented by mortgages, it is not so bad. To be fair, perhaps it should principally be laid to the same cause as the defaults on mortgages—not to dishonesty, but primarily to miscalculation of the future.

Dishonesty and unreliability, where they appear in the corporate field, manifest themselves almost entirely in the relations *between the controllers of the corporation and its owners*.

Its owners, as we have seen, are many. In the large corporations they are numbered in thousands, often in tens of thousands. They

* *Long Term Debts in the U. S.*, Pages 10–12.
† The Securities Exchange Act of 1934 directed the Securities and Exchange Commission to study and report to the Congress on this matter of "reorganization" committees. It has not yet covered all the fields, but five full reports have been made to the Congress. No more revealing documents, as to the untrustworthiness common in this economic area, have been printed. In addition to the Commission's necessarily formal presentation of what ordinarily goes on behind the scenes, when these long promises of corporations are defaulted upon, there have been a number of books, magazine and newspaper articles covering specific occurrences. Two particularly interesting books, revealing at least a little of the covert responsibility of some judges, and the much more direct responsibility of lawyers, in this sort of situation, are *Upton Sinclair Presents William Fox*, by Upton Sinclair, and *The Investor Pays*, by Max Lowenthal.

are unknown personally to one another and to the clique in control. The whole set-up is completely de-personalized. Under the circumstances, it may be understandable from a psychological point of view—though none the less reprehensible—that often the autocrats in some of these groups come to regard the enterprise as their own. To say that they "loot" the enterprise may not be an entirely fair description of their state of mind. More nearly it is one where they rationalize themselves into the belief that the values created, and the gains obtained, are largely the result of their effort, and that therefore it is not unfair if, by some roundabout method, a large part of the gain should accrue to them. Whatever their state of mind, they often proceed to actions which amount to plain stealing of a good part of the property that belongs to their stockholders.

For seventy-five years this well-recognized state of affairs has been far from uncommon—indeed, at certain periods, it has been rife —in the management of large corporations in this country. The devices used in this plundering of innocent and trusting owners are always barely within the sunny side of the law. They are many and devious, but in the main they follow three general directions.

First, the controlling clique may vote itself unduly high salaries or bonuses. Second, knowing in advance of certain conditions of the enterprise which will increase the exchangeable value of its shares in the market, they purchase at a present low market price the shares of other stockholders, who have no means of knowing of the favorable conditions. Or, knowing of conditions affecting the company's earnings adversely, they divest themselves of stock they own at a present high market price, and then later re-acquire more of it from stockholders who did not know of the adverse conditions and who bought it at the higher price. Third, they make the corporation enter into unfavorable contracts with other companies which they themselves control. That is, they mulct their stockholders by decreasing the company's earnings, *through unnecessarily increasing its expenses,* and they themselves benefit—through other companies —by this increase of expenses.

The economics student must beware of succumbing to indignation, or to any other emotion, lest it cloud his capacity for the straight view. But he can at least observe that here is one noticeable Augean stable that still exists in our economic life. If the men of Wall Street want to know why its very name is synonymous in this country with a high and devious brand of fraud—an imputation many of them seem to bewail—they can find it here. The opinion is justified by the record. This sort of unreliability, *unknown elsewhere in our economic life,* for seventy-five years has been publicly identified with Wall Street. For there most of it centers.

Why, it may be asked, are men less reliable—why are they inclined more to dishonesty—in this field of human action than in others? It cannot be because they are more subjected to temptation. Who, for example, could be more subject to temptation than a banker? Nor does it seem wholly satisfactory to account for it by the de-personalization of the corporation, by the fact that the autocrats of these enterprises do not know the real owners and come to regard the enterprises as theirs. They know better. They are men of the world, not ninnies; and if some of them rationalize their actions, for their own conscience, there is no reason why an unimpassioned student should let himself be fooled by the philosophy a thief uses to fool himself.

The principal explanation, it seems clear, why instances of utter unreliability are more rife here than elsewhere, is because the perpetrators of these acts are in a position *to keep hidden* the demonstrations of dishonesty. They suffer neither loss of esteem socially, nor any economic loss, as a result of their actions.

We have seen in other fields how instantly any manifestation of dishonesty is followed by what amounts to an economic boycott of the perpetrator. No one will thereafter enter into half-exchanges with this clearly dishonest person. Dishonesty, therefore, as was pointed out—in the field of production and of distribution—constituted the suicide of enterprise; and this is true because it cannot be hidden from general knowledge. But this is not the case—the reverse, indeed, is the case—in corporate management.

A faithless clique in control of a corporation can rely upon many things to keep both the nature and the results of their actions from becoming known to the stockholders who trust them. First and foremost, they rely upon the complete *lack of interest* which almost the entire body of stockholders manifests in the detailed operations of the enterprise. They can also frequently hide behind the smokescreen of incomprehensible legal verbiage, in which a certain type of lawyer, although sworn to justice, abets and instructs them. Again, they can take action through dummies, or through members of their families, so that the cheating of stockholders is not in the records of the corporation itself. Finally, whatever records there are, they themselves make and keep, and under circumstances where disclosure has become imminent, there have been many who did not scruple to see that the records were destroyed; always accidentally, of course.

In spite of the fact that flagrant dishonesty manifests itself more in corporate management than elsewhere in men's economic relations, we must not blind ourselves to the vastly larger picture, in which this is the first real flaw that we have come upon. The social reformer concerns himself quite properly with abuses, and seeks to set up safeguards against them. The provisions of our Securities Exchange Act of 1934 constitute precisely such an effort and unquestionably, in time, together with like efforts, will be effectual in cleaning up this smelling Augean stable.

But the speculative economics student will also be interested in the almost incredible degree to which this system has come to extend in the modern world—a system by which, as a common action, men put a large part of their possessions at the complete disposition and mercy of others, whom they do not know and never inquire about. For such a prevailing and astonishing confidence, it must be clear from the whole trend of this study, can only be explained by the fact *that on the whole the confidence has not been abused*. The evidences of dishonesty, many as they have been, fortunately are still only occasional, *when the whole record is taken*. In a land like Great Britain, where justice is not dispensed with a cocked eye, it is rare.

This is the large, and—too often in comment and reasoning—an ignored fact, which we must fasten our attention upon, here and elsewhere in studying deferred exchanges, if we wish to comprehend and evaluate the actual relations that exist among men; and no less, it must be added, if we wish in wisdom to try to change them.

13

Government Promises and How They Compare in
Reliability with Those of Individuals

W E saw, in the chapter on central banks, that governments, like individuals and corporations, enter into extensive deferred exchanges of money for more money at a later date. The exchanges involve even larger sums than in corporate finance. The piece of paper, which is the evidence of the unfulfilled last half of the deferred exchange, is predominantly the government bond. Sometimes, when the deferrence of the exchange is for a short period, it passes by another name than bond. Sometimes these government promises are called Treasury Notes or Treasury Bills. But all these deferred exchanges of governments, both sovereign and subsidiary, have some special aspects, which make them, perhaps, more necessary to be scrutinized than any other promises which pass among men.

Let us first have some notion of their extent.

A striking indication of this is furnished by the operations of governments during the World War. Through that four-year period, it has been estimated that the money outlay of all the governments involved totaled about $270,000,000,000. Of this about $186,000,000,000 was borrowed.* *Only a small proportion of this enormous mass of promises, originating with the War, is still outstanding!* Most of it has been canceled, in ways we shall soon examine.

The above figures might, by an apologist, be taken as a distorted picture of a world that was then in emergency. But the extent of deferred exchanges in this field would appear no less staggering in

* Harvey E. Fisk, *Inter-Ally Debts*.

more orderly days. Take this present peaceful year of our Lord, with only a mere civil war in Spain going on and a new type of "undeclared war" proceeding—boldly, cynically and, as always, stupidly—in the Far East. The latest available figures show that on December 31, 1936, the total recorded borrowings of all sovereign states—those to which they admitted in their financial statements— were in the neighborhood of $149,000,000,000.* Remember that this only includes a small proportion of the internal debts incurred by the World War. It does not include quite a few billions which are hidden—Germany has been doing a great deal of hiding, for example. It does not include the promises represented by the paper money of each country. Nor does it include a few other billions of war debt, owed by one government to another, which are now frankly ignored in the records.

Nor does this enormous recognized total include the borrowings of the subsidiary units of these sovereign States. Yet these, of course, must also be placed in the category of deferred exchanges of governmental units. This last group piles up an unimaginable total of itself. For example, in the United States on June 30, 1937, the debt of the national government was about $36,500,000,000, represented by bonds and other pieces of paper, not including currency. On the same day the debt of States, municipalities, townships, counties, agricultural assessment districts and other small units, was in the neigh-

* *Statistical Year-Book, 1936–37, of the League of Nations.* Figures on public debt, pages 274–285, are taken for each nation, and transformed into dollars according to the table for rough conversion of currencies, using the exchange rates in 1936, the rate for December, 1936, being used. Page 12. This total of $149,000,000,000 is a poor figure, since the stated debt of many nations is far from up-to-date, as given. The present total is almost certainly far greater. The above figure includes, for example, an item of only $5,750,000,000 against Germany. Reliable estimates, which include its "secret debt," increase this to at least somewhere between $15 and $18 billions. Incidentally, the year before, in calculating total national debt for 1936 by the same procedure (using the previous year's *League of Nations Yearbook*) it came out to about $172,000,000,000. What! Did the governments succeed in paying off $23,000,000,000 debt in that one year, modestly, with no one knowing about it? The difference, on a quick analysis, turned out to be principally due to two factors: certain governments simply admitted to less debt, and also, that particular year had seen drastic devaluations. Russia, France and Italy alone, by "revaluing" their currencies, accounted for about $18,000,000,000 of this decrease. Profitable government business for one year!

borhood of $18,000,000,000. It is estimated on good authority that in this country there are more than 180,000 communities and districts * large and small, which with a mere bagatelle of exceptions, enter into deferred exchanges of money for money at a later date. Most of these are long promises—so-called bonds. How much the total subsidiary governmental promises of *all* the nations of the world sum up to, nobody knows.

Since the War, the common citizen has come to bandy billions like this with light-hearted familiarity. Unimaginable in actuality, they constitute mere words to him. There is no reality in them. But, of course, every one of these countless billions of half-exchanges, which governments and their subsidiaries have entered into, is counted upon to be completed by somebody, who now holds but the promise of the action. If they are not completed, trouble will ensue among those who have been betrayed in their faith, and this economic trouble will spread from those who are afflicted, as swiftly as a plague spreads. If we could have a long era of world peace, perhaps *a fair portion* of these promises might be completed. The probability of this good fortune may be assayed by anyone who reads the current newspapers. But assuming we have a long peace, the upshot will then be pretty serious *for those who have to carry out the promises.*

In this connection, it may be of interest to you, as an average American citizen, to know that you and your family are already contributing $447 every year to support your central and local governments—"with further large increases in prospect." Quite a sum for anybody to pay out, without knowing about it! †

The truth of the matter is that, in ways few of us understand, we, the plain people of the world, have had our names signed as the parties responsible for the carrying out of this unimaginable mass of promises to complete half-exchanges, represented by governmental borrowings. We have handed blank checks to the dignified politicos,

* *Long-Term Debts in the U. S.*, Page 179.
† Source, National Economy League, New York; Petition to the President, dated April 5, 1937.

in their top hats and cutaways, who have talked us into delegating power to them; and they have gone the limit in filling in the sums, while we have gone our happy-go-lucky economic way.

This is the first, almost incredible, aspect of this type of deferred exchange—*that those who are obliged to fulfill the promises are completely unconscious of the fact!* This, of course, is true of no other type of deferred exchange that goes on among men.

This fatal ignorance, of course, arises from the total absence of understanding among men (except for a few) as to the modern processes by which they are governed. That is Jones' business—not ours. We lightheartedly leave it to those who have chosen this field for the specialization of their activity. But see what a fine mess of our affairs these particular specialists, the politicians, make! If all public officers, executive and legislative, were required to pass a primary examination in economics and finance, it is a safe prediction that not one in a thousand of them in this crucial fiduciary position, where we have placed them, would qualify. One finds it difficult, both from their speech and actions, to discern that more than a bare handful of them are even aware that they are occupying a fiduciary position; that when they make promises, these are made in behalf of other people; that the promises have to be fulfilled; and that we and our children will have to fulfill them. For how otherwise are governments' promises to be completed? Governments create no exchangeable wealth. The promises can only be completed *by the seizure of wealth in the future from those who do create it.* But those from whom it must then be seized for this purpose—the old, old story about long promises—*totally forget the first half of the exchange,* when somebody gave up his wealth in a deferred exchange in the firm belief that it would be returned. The ultimate performers of the promise, forgetting this or knowing nothing about it, make a great fuss about being milched and "exploited" for bloated bondholders, and often they so scare the politicians that, by ways open or devious, these latter welch on the promises; and, of course, make a virtue of doing so.

But then *who* holds the promises? If, indeed, it were a few mere

228

wealthy bondholders, whose way of life would thus be slightly changed by the default, perhaps no widespread damage would be done among men. The trouble is that government promises are held mostly by banks, insurance companies and like institutions, each one of which is—as we have seen—*the focal point of a whole immense tissue of other promises.* These other promises, short and long, depend for fulfillment upon the faithful carrying out of the government's promises. Neither the common politician, nor the average man who suffers him in the pathetic belief that he is a specialist, has the faintest notion about this intricate interdependence of promises, in which the government promise plays so vital a role. Accordingly, the politician goes irresponsibly ahead and piles up the promises by the billion.

A second very curious—and highly important aspect—of this type of deferred exchange is that it differs from others in that the promise, *for the most part, represents no form of tangible wealth.*

Comparison with other types of half-exchanges makes this clear. Consider long promises alone. For example, the promise covered by a mortgage bond is represented by the building or by land. Frequently, in the case of the building, the money given in the first half of the exchange was actually used to erect the building. In any case, the promise (of which the mortgage consists) has its clear representation in a home which can be lived in; or in land upon which food may be grown. If the promise is unfulfilled, *this visible form of wealth is then transferred to the holder of the promise.*

Likewise, all promises which go under the name of "corporation bonds" represent tangible forms of wealth. A public utility company, borrowing money to put up a plant to produce electricity, uses the money to erect the plant; and there it stands, purring away. The bond merely represents it. If the promise is unfulfilled, *the holders of the promise get the plant.* In the United States all except a trifling proportion of the approximately forty billion dollars' worth of corporation long promises, called bonds, is represented by machinery, railroads, land, buildings, stocks of goods—all forms of wealth that can be seen with the eye and touched with the hand. For the most

229

part they are the kind of goods we identified in Chapter Two, production-goods, which are utilized to bring forth the other type of goods and services which men consume and enjoy. They are forms of wealth which have a more or less long life. Accordingly, they can well be represented by more or less long promises. The bonds, no less than stock certificates, may thus fairly be considered, *indirectly*, mere evidences of ownership of tangible forms of wealth. Those who own the bonds share in what is produced by the production-goods, which the bonds represent.

But now what form of tangible wealth do government promises represent in this fashion? True, a small portion of them are offset by some form of productive wealth: those where the money was utilized in roads, reservoirs, useful buildings, parks, and like forms of public wealth. Indirectly—and very often with great directness—these do assist in the production of other forms of wealth, *or of service*, which can be enjoyed. A substantial part of the promises of our subsidiary units of governments does consist of these forms of publicly owned real wealth. If citizens must give up money in exchange for them, and if the promises—which the bonds represent—are finally fulfilled before time itself destroys the form of wealth, no more rational objection can be made to this type of economic promise than to those represented by corporation bonds.* But unfortunately, these genuine forms of public wealth often are destroyed long before the promise offsetting them is fulfilled. The promise then represents, it might be said, forms of wealth no longer in existence. More unfortunately than this: a very great portion of government promises *even in the beginning represents no tangible form of wealth.* The real wealth which the first party in the exchange gives

* A good example of this is the Holland Tunnel which connects New York and New Jersey. Its construction was paid for by the issuance of bonds. Every user pays fifty cents for the right to go through, a great time-saver for travelers and commuters. Trucks pay more, the service to business men being even more obvious. The receipts are being used to pay the interest on the bonds, *and also to retire the bonds.* Thus the promises, represented by the bonds, will be fulfilled long before this form of genuine public wealth will go out of existence or have to be replaced. This self-extinguishing feature of the original promise is true of a great many forms of public wealth owned by local governments; it is outstandingly true of public water-works.

230

up to the government is utilized in some completely unproductive fashion. For example, in the World War, a good part of the $186,-000,000,000 borrowed was spent in keeping tens of millions of men alive while they tried to kill one another, and most of the balance was transformed into a species of wealth which was immediately blown to Kingdom Come. In peacetime, too—by sheer waste and misdirected energies—real wealth which is given to the government in these half-exchanges is so utilized that *nothing tangible remains in existence* to represent the promise and to produce new wealth by means of which the promise may be fulfilled.*

What is bad about this? Look at all other deferred exchanges and you soon see. Since in other deferred exchanges, the promise is represented by a form of tangible wealth, it can be completed—and is, in fact, completed in its second half—by a transference of either that particular form of wealth which it represents, or by some other form of tangible wealth, equally acceptable to the first party. In other words, these promises for the most part are fulfilled—practically all the short ones, and almost all the long ones. When this happens, *new ones can take their place in an endless round,* just because this reliability of men has been demonstrated. But where the promise—as in the case of the government promise—is *unrepresented by any real form of wealth,* what can be transferred to the trusting party in the necessary last half of the exchange? True enough, the government seizes some wealth, and transfers it *in partial payments* of these promises (interest payments). But it never dares seize enough to fulfill the whole promise. *What is transferred, usually, is merely another government promise.*

In other words, most of these crucial government promises *never get extinguished—except by cancellation!* Practically all other eco-

* The greater part of the federal debt added in the years from 1931 to 1937 is in this category. The total federal promises increased by about $19 billions in this period. Very little real wealth is left to show for it. A good part of this money was disbursed for relief to unemployed, to farmers for curtailing production, and in taking over old promises—of banks and individuals on mortgages—which can never be fulfilled, and a good part of which is already canceled. The greater part of this wealth is as much gone as the ammunition shot off during the World War. Only the promises remain.

nomic promises, those of individuals, get extinguished by fulfillment.

When the bond issue of a government becomes due as to principal, what does it do? It enters into new deferred exchanges with the same or with other borrowers. It then cancels the old promises, and goes on with the new. The total of its long promises remains the same. The process is so easy that the government's promises *keep on aggregating*. "Like an improvident spendthrift," wrote Adam Smith, "whose pressing occasions will not allow him to wait for the regular payment of his revenue, the State is in the constant practice of borrowing from its own factors and agents, and of paying interest for the use of its own money." Its borrowings finally run into the astronomical totals we have seen, and—soon or late—the question of *ultimate fulfillment* of the promise cannot be averted with a new promise. Then comes disaster. It arises, as we shall see, because of the interdependence of all economic promises upon one another, and in particular of other economic promises upon these of the government.

Performance of the second half of the government deferred exchange is put off and off and off, until only scholars, and persons whom we regard as cranks, are aware that performance is a vital part of the transaction; or that any promise is involved; or that transference of good solid wealth took place in the first instance. The truth is—observe!—that everything disagreeable about the promise is conveniently forgot, both by those who entered into it and by those who must complete it. Perhaps we must not get into psychoanalysis to explain economics; but there is the interesting fact for our psycho-analysts to ponder over.

Now, why should a State—or a subsidiary of a State—borrow at all? We touched upon the actual borrowing in Chapter Ten; now we can examine carefully precisely why it occurs. The State assumes the right, and it certainly has the power, to seize the property of the individuals who comprise it, and every organized government in history, under one device or another, has invoked this assumed right and used this power. Why, then, is it necessary for the State to borrow?

232

To answer this question, one must see unconfusedly into the true nature of the relationship that exists between individuals and the State.

That relationship is sometimes shrouded in metaphysical and mystical concepts. Ideas that are tied in with the words Duty and Destiny and Race and Patriotism are spun about it. Possibly some little enlightenment—at any rate, about the amusing human tendency to rationalize—may be gained by exploring in these conceptual labyrinths. But for the plain person a straight pragmatic scrutiny of some obvious facts may provide a little better illumination about the relationship.

"L'Etat, c'est moi!" said Louis XIV. Plainly he was identifying the well-organized control he had acquired over a clearly defined group of people, the French people, with the natural power resident in that group itself. Time proved his error. Indeed, even while his will reigned absolute, in those fields where it was exerted, there existed an amorphous and a more extensive power, upon whose territory, arrogant as he seemed, he actually never too far infringed. "L'Etat, c'est moi!" says the modern citizen in a democracy, "I and the millions of others, who by contiguous residence and other more or less definite criteria, comprise our distinct group." His statement is more nearly in accord with all the phenomena than that of the King.

The State, as a working notion, may be conceived of as a clearly separated community of individuals, acting together and animated by whatever peculiar ideational stimuli they may by tradition acquire. The ideational background may include, as it did often enough in ancient days, the notion that *those who wielded the power* which an organized community possesses, are identified in some way with the Deity. This involves the corollary notion that the will of all the individuals who comprise the group should be wholly supine; or at least subservient. In this way the actual wielders of power come to confuse themselves with the State, in their thinking. But no matter how absolute the ruler, nor how supine the ruled, it seems necessary to distinguish between those who wield power in the State, by suf-

233

ferance or choice of its citizens, and the community which creates, and in which resides the power, by the very fact of its organization. That is, it seems that a clear distinction must always be made between rulership, which represents the human means through which the inherent powers of the State are exercised, and the State itself.

This distinction, both in practice and in political philosophy, is unfortunately not always made. In ancient days, rulership was most frequently individualized in monarchs. Now it is hydra-headed. We call it "the government." Yet it is far from infrequent among these less absolute rulers—as it was with ancient ones—to confuse the concept of the State with that of the government. The identification of the ruler with Deity still occasionally colors our notions about those who immediately rule us, and we are supposed, by this ancient and half-conscious tradition, to pay the supreme duty of submission to the dictates and judgments of those who currently represent the State. Socrates was a democrat, if ever there was one. He could easily have averted death, the Dialogues indicate. His calm acceptance of it, and the reasons he gives, in spite of the maddening illogic in his condemnation, provides an interesting illustration of this particular philosophical view of the relationship between the individual and the State. Contrasted to it is that of Thoreau, who clearly distinguished between the government, the State, and the individual, and who regarded it as his duty, far from submitting, openly and publicly to disobey "the will of the people," whether properly or improperly exercised by their representatives, provided it infringed upon prerogatives he as an individual preferred not to relinquish. "The will of the people" was invested with no element of divinity for him; no more than that of a king would have been. Far less would he submit to those frequently muddle-headed individuals, who presumed, by the interpretation of old law or the creation of new, to decide what that "will" was. Thoreau's point of view certainly more commends itself to an American and a modern.

The least confusion in this field seems to arise from recognizing that actually "the will of the people" is coterminous with the powers of the State. This public will may be temporarily supine, as it is under a terrorizing autocracy, Old or New Style. It may be deceived into acquiescence, as it is when it follows demagogues. Or it may be misled by shibboleths. It may be blundering, uninformed, unclear, fashioned by a thousand conflicting considerations, conscious and unconscious—as an individual's will is. Yet it remains always, and always has been, the supreme force in any community. Our rulers merely are those who fashion, guide and take advantage of it. A definition of rulership might be that it consists in the control of a large group of individuals *through concordance with the common will*, unclear as this latter may be.

This seems to constitute the final hard core of phenomena about the State and rulership in it. But an additional steely fact must not avoid our observation; namely, that the supremacy of the State over the individual rests upon the superior force of numbers. The great symbol of the State is the police and army. No organized community has ever existed without one. No single individual can set himself up, successfully, against the grouped strength of all his fellows. The ultimate function the State performs is to provide the protection individuals need against one another. There is no inherent "right" in the individual to own property, or even to remain alive. In Nature force makes right. The "inalienable right to life, liberty and the pursuit of happiness," and to the ownership of property, are "rights" only in a human society, in a group. The word "right" here in actuality merely describes a set of social conventions, by which individuals in a group agree not to allow single ones among them to run amok and prey upon the others. When the group itself, for any reason at all, wishes to do so, it recognizes no inalienable "right" in the individual, but will take away his life, liberty and property with no ethical compunction whatsoever.

Over countless centuries men have found that only by living in organized communities can they enjoy some measure of security in their possessions and way of life. This, then, is both the explanation and the primary function of the State—to provide *a favorable environment* in which the economic action of individuals and groups, the activities which keep them alive and happy, may proceed and flourish.

Such an environment is above value, of course. In enlightened self-interest, the individual will help to maintain that common environment against anything which may threaten its continued existence. But what is his *strictly economic relationship* to this community, which is the State?

We conceive of it, philosophically, in two ways. One is that the community, the State, is all-supreme. The group itself owns everything. When individually we own anything, we do so by its privilege. Accordingly, the reasoning goes, the community has the right *to take away* what in the final analysis it possesses. The other conception is that as individuals we enter into a sort of bargain with the particular organized community, of which we are a part. In return for this invaluable protecting environment which it affords, we offer it a portion of our means, as it needs economic support. These two conceptions usually form the justification for what we call the State's "power of taxation."

Take your choice. They are both, in my own private opinion, mere engaging rationalizations. For while it may now be clear that it is to the self-interest of everyone to support the modern community in its functioning by economic contributions, this surrounding of the right of taxation with an aura of duty, or of bargaining, or of supreme "right," which the community does or should possess, has rather scanty historical evidence to support it; and such evidence as there is consists much more of what men have said than of how they have acted. The "right of taxation" seems to have evolved as much out of stark and unadulterated forcible seizure *on the part of ruling groups,* as out of social agreement of any kind. It seems at least a somewhat sounder theory, in that it explains more history. It explains plausibly, in particular, why States—through their rulers—came to borrow.

The absolute ruler of ancient times made no bones about forcible seizure of property. He never borrowed. He took what he wanted from his subjects. In short, *he applied to his own subjects the practice which prevailed as to all foreign groups.* War for pure pillage was part of the accepted *mores* of the human race until our more re-

236

cent centuries, and under the thin disguise of economic rationalizations, it still is. Foreigners were recognized to have no rights, either to life or property, which need be respected. The law of the jungle was the prevailing and governing law of all inter-community relations in our past. So far as whole nations are concerned, are they very far out of this stage? The fact that, up to a point, men acquiesce in this survival of jungle law, *as it persists in the form of taxation*, should not blind us to the probable origin of this supposed "right" of the State to all the property of its citizens.

As applied to his own subjects, time came when the absolute ruler of ancient days began to find forcible seizure a dangerous procedure. For if he seized too much, from too many individuals, the prevailing "will of the people"—whose power he was in reality wielding—might turn against him and he might lose the perquisites of that power. Yet means were necessary, large means, to support the myrmidons upon whom he immediately relied for power. Apply this key to historical events, and it will make clear a very great deal. The game of rulership over the ages, from this point of view, developed into a nice calculation of how much could be seized, and from what individuals, without inviting sufficient rebellion to endanger the ruler's power. If the necessary means could not be seized from other communities, by warfare, it had to be seized from his own subjects. Who among them, and how many among them, could be plucked with the least squawking? That has been the immemorial problem of ruling individuals and ruling groups in every community, large and small, in history.

The economic needs of rulers and ruling groups have, in all the past, been enormous, but when this extensity began to coincide with the fact that they could not safely tamper with the "will of the people" *by taking too much from too many people by forcible seizure*, it was then that States (through their rulers) began to borrow. Wherever borrowing began, there may be said to be a recognition, by that very fact, that the rulers—individuals or groups—were somewhat unsure of their position, and that real absolutism no longer existed. The very difference, indeed, between absolutism and more

237

democratic forms of government—where, through various devices, the final power of the State at least theoretically rests upon the decisions of all its citizens—can be measured by the degree to which the power-wielding group in the community relies upon taxation—that is, seizure—or upon borrowing, to obtain the wealth needed for its economic purposes.

By this means it can be seen that, while our modern forms of dictatorship have gone far, they have not proceeded the whole way back to ancient absolutism. True, they tax their citizens, both directly and indirectly, far more than they borrow from them. "Forced loans," like those the Italian Fascists and the German Nazis engineer, are indistinguishable (except for the falsifying screen the words constitute) from direct seizure. Nevertheless, our present false-face Napoleons still bear very much in mind the ancient rule of the game of government: that it is perilous to take too much property from too many people, who are the units in constituting "the will of the people." Much safer is it to obtain the necessary means by giving them *more promises* for their property or labor. It is instructive to note that the present admitted debt of Germany is about $5,750,000,000, of Italy about $5,500,000,000, of Russia about $2,800,000,000.* The actual, not admitted, debt is far greater.

The Russian debt, particularly, ought to give thought to those who regard the government's power as so supreme. The Soviet government is accounted the example, *par excellence*, of the supremacy of the State over the individual. A none-too-clearly defined group, the proletariat, are presumed to be the real rulers. But who owns these billions of Soviet State promises? Principally individuals and the Savings Bank, to which individuals have given their money

* Some additional light on these "admitted" figures is decidedly necessary. In the first place, Germany's real national debt, if the secret figures were included, would almost certainly be not less than $15 billions, instead of $5¾ billions. Italy's $5½ billions is more accurate; the year before it was $8½ billions. That is, Italy "devalued" in 1936. Russia did even better. Her $2.8 billions was over $12 billions the year before. In 1936 she reduced the gold content of the ruble by over 75 per cent, with very few people in the world knowing anything about the fact, and fewer understanding what difference it would ultimately make to Soviet citizens, who were blindly trusting their leaders. Incidentally, this is a 1933 figure of national debt which Russia "admitted." What has been added in the past four years perhaps no foreigner will ever accurately know.

—in return for promises, as in other benighted lands. Two things happen. The Savings Bank—there are about 60,000 branches of it—gives the money to the Soviet Government, in return for the government's bonds. *An exchange of promises!* But the individual must also accept these government promises. It would be highly dangerous, personally, for anybody holding a Savings Bank deposit not to subscribe to the State loan. Nevertheless, inducements are required—as in every other land—to make the individuals happy in doing so. Eight per cent interest is paid on these loans, one of the highest interest rates paid by any government to its citizens! But even this is not sufficient. One large portion of the loan is a premium loan: it has a lottery feature; and this portion is far more popular than the other.*

Now, it is illuminating to ask, Why does this most absolute of modern rulers, the so-called dictatorship of the proletariat, go to the trouble of borrowing from its citizens? Why does it hide this roundabout acquirement of the individuals' possessions, as it does when it borrows from the Savings Bank; for, of course, the average Russian citizen has no notion what this lending ultimately means, even if he is aware that it takes place. If the State needs the wealth for its purposes—as it does, or it would not borrow—why does it not seize it out of hand? The reason unquestionably is that this would be playing the game of government most inexpertly; the ruling group dares not do so openly, for fear of endangering the power it wields.†

The answer, then, as to why States borrow when they have the

* "One of the Savings Bank's most important functions is to mobilize the resources of the people for investment in state loans, investment in which, though nominally voluntary, is in fact almost compulsory. Owing to the urban housing shortage and consequent lack of privacy, workers deposit their salaries or wages in the Savings Bank in preference to carrying the money about on their persons. The *whole* [italics mine] of the Savings Bank's liquid assets is invested in a special branch of the State loan."—Page 86, *Soviet Money and Finance*, L. E. Hubbard.

† The interesting details of Russian finance of the past twenty years, and the remarkable degree to which it has come to conform in every respect to the orthodox financial practices of all other States, including all the malpractices—is revealed in the analysis made in Mr. Hubbard's *Soviet Money and Finance*. This selection of the Soviet State as an example among modern dictatorships is not an invidious one; it is made here because of the common notion that this particular State is so all-powerful. Other modern dictators have an equally

so-called right to seize what they need from their own citizens, seems clear. It is that a real distinction exists between *the ultimate power* which rests in a community, and the extent to which this power is exerted, by the individuals or cliques which necessarily must manage the affairs of the community. Theoretically, the two should be coextensive. In practice, the power of the political managers is decidedly limited.

What then happens is that, controlling the community, they embark upon ventures which require more property and man-power than they can commandeer from individuals, without undermining their position of supremacy, which is always to some extent insecure. How temptingly easy it is, in such a state of affairs, to make use of that fine habit of faith which has now come to exist among men, through the extension of the practice of half-exchanges! How much safer it is to gull their own citizens, by the giving of promises, than to seize the needed means out of hand!

This, perhaps crudely presented, is to my mind the principal explanation of that enormous mass of deferred exchanges which the plain people of the world unknowingly have signed themselves to complete.

But there are still other unique features in these deferred exchanges of governments, which are necessary to distinguish, if we are to see the whole human scene in something other than fog.

No one, as we have seen, will ever enter into a deferred exchange which he does not fully expect to be completed. In every field of economic activity, we have identified three matters which men invariably take into consideration in judging, so far as they are able, the eventuality of completion. First, the honesty of the trusted party; second, his present available resources and future probable ones; and third—if these two fail—they may then call in the State to compel completion.

false front of secure power. It is perfectly apparent, to any but the most unintelligent in matters of government, that their power rests finally upon force, far more than upon acquiescence.

240

Now, curiously, the first of these considerations, honesty, which almost everywhere else is the principal one, plays so slight a role in the half-exchanges of governments that it can be ignored, except for philosophical speculation. The cold fact is that men acting together in a community, large or small, are just as dishonest, just as unscrupulous in breaking their promises, as they dare to be at any one time. Governments always, small or large, will get away with what they can, up to the point where the supremacy of the ruling power is endangered. No such thing as personal integrity, the satisfaction of being reliable, and the shame of betraying faith, appear other than microscopically in governmental economics. This may be a hard pill for the patriot who is a sentimentalist to swallow, but no clear-eyed person, looking at all past and all current history, may doubt it. True enough, the stigma of a broken promise is occasionally felt somewhat by some persons in the group. All one may say about this is that it is perhaps an indication of incipient "group honesty." Up to this present year, it has played a quite imperceptible role in governmental action. The interesting thing, for the speculative observer is, to mark the fine inventive fancy which peoples, large and small in number, display in *finding reasons* for not carrying out promises made in their name, which have become disagreeable to carry out. Beautifully, in some higher considerations, the group always finds itself to be right, and those who expect the promise to be fulfilled, to be wrong or unreasonable.

But if honesty plays so insignificant a role in the completion of the economic promises of governments, may not full reliance be placed upon the other two factors which ordinarily ensure completion?

Certainly not in one of them. In the case of all other deferred exchanges, in the event of incompletion, the powers of the supreme government may be invoked, as a last resort, to compel completion. But if the State itself fails to complete one of its deferred exchanges, who or what may be called in to compel completion? Manifestly, a little difficulty arises here. Large strong States used to try to compel small weak ones to complete such deferred exchanges. The history of Central and South America, in particular, is full of instances in which the United States and European Powers used actual force, or the threat of force, to compel some struggling government "to honor its bonds." But large strong States are a little hesitant to employ such tactics against one another. It has at last even become a dangerous and unpopular procedure with weak States. And, of course, where it is its own citizens whose faith a State has violated, there is no hope of completion by means of any outside compulsion. How then about inside compulsion? But a State cannot be sued without its consent. In other words, the question of *completion by compulsion* may not even be raised against a State, if it ever wishes to avoid the issue. In minor matters, as a sort of concession to current morals, the State may indeed allow its citizens to present "claims," and will put up some front of dispensing justice; but redress is practically hopeless if any real inconvenience to the State would be caused by the completion of its half-exchanges. The State knows no moral law. It knows and follows only jungle law.

Theoretically, it is true, this does not hold of the subsidiary units of governments. They indeed may be sued. They may be haled into the courts of the supreme government, in an effort to compel them to complete deferred exchanges. But, as a practical matter, men have found they cannot get very far in this direction. For these subsidiary units are always allied with the supreme government. Frequently, when they get into unusual difficulties, the supreme government, by some neat new legalism, will make it either impossible or extremely costly for those seeking completion of the half-exchange, to obtain it.

In this respect, the experience of bondholders of so-called "municipals" in this country during the years from 1929 to 1935 is illuminating.* All but a few of our 180,000 subsidiary taxing units in the country were very unhappy some time during this period. Their

* The term "municipals," in financial parlance, refers to the bonds of all subsidiary units of governments, including those of our forty-eight States.

deferred exchanges, represented by bonds and similar instruments, were at a total of over $17,000,000,000 in 1930. This was the total of merely their written promises. It was quite aside from the continuing deferred exchanges of money for labor and supplies, which represented an additional total drain of incalculable billions each year. Everybody in the country felt poorer than for decades. Thus, *the seizable wealth* of citizens was smaller in total. Moreover, the temper of citizens was such that it was more than ordinarily dangerous (for the governing groups in each separate small community) to seize by taxation what was needed to complete the exchanges. Accordingly, the *current available resources* of the subsidiary units of government shrank to an extraordinary extent. Some of the largest of them failed to meet even the interest on their bonds. An interesting situation, particularly, arose in the second largest city in the country, Chicago, where even the city's deferred exchanges of money for labor could not be met out of current funds and city employees were paid in scrip—that is, in promises, which were exchanged for money (often at a discount) in the expectation that later they would be honored. The general apprehension as to the ability of these subsidiary governmental units to complete their exchanges was mirrored in bond prices, which, even in the case of the wealthiest cities, dropped alarmingly. It was shown also in the difficulties they had in finding individuals or groups to trust them in new deferred exchanges. Whereas, in the seven years up to and including 1931, these subsidiary governmental units had been able to borrow an average of about $1,400,000,000 a year, in the three years 1932, 1933 and 1934, they were only able to borrow an average of about half that amount yearly.* A tabulation made in 1935 showed that over 3,200 taxing units, all issuers of bonds, had defaulted on the payment of principal or interest.†

All of these defaulters could have been haled into court to compel completion. The citizens in each community, through their officials,

* *U. S. Statistical Abstract*, 1936, Page 292.
† *Long-Term Debts in the U. S.*, Pages 181 and 182.

were certainly responsible for payment. Their property as individuals, since it was subject to tax, was thus legally available (in theory) to cover completion of the exchanges. Yet, actually, it was rare for any of these 3,200 groups to be brought into court. Would that have happened with 3,200 defaulting individuals or corporations?

The reason was that the creditors found legal barricades had quickly been raised. Either the State legislature would step in with its supreme power and protect the group in the defiance of its ultimate obligation, or the community itself would make difficulties by changing its tax ordinances. Ultimate compulsion by legal means, difficult at best, soon appeared so uncertain that it was not worthwhile in time, expense, nor effort, to attempt it.* Congress ultimately passed an amendment to the bankruptcy laws enabling these subsidiary governmental units to arrange with their creditors *partial completion* of such exchanges, a law later, by some typical reasoning of our present Supreme Court, declared unconstitutional by a five-to-four decision. Prior to that happening, however, creditors had already—in almost all cases—begun to make adjustments with the governing groups, taking what they could get. They played upon what little group honesty existed, or upon considerations of future self-interest, which were to some degree present. In the meantime, however, the supreme government had, to all practical purposes, abro-

* For the difficulties placed in the way of holders of municipal bonds which defaulted during the thirties, see report of the Securities and Exchange Commission, on the study of Protective Committees for municipal and quasi-municipal obligations. The ordinary difficulties in the way of collection on municipal defaults are also indicated in a chapter on Creditors' Remedies, in *Municipal Bonds*, by A. M. Hillhouse. Says the author (Page 276): "After judgment an execution issues and is normally returned unsatisfied *(nulla bona)* because no municipal property or moneys is found upon which a levy can be made. In six states—Maryland, Michigan, Illinois, Pennsylvania, Louisiana and Wisconsin—no property of a municipal corporation, either public or private, can be reached by its creditors. . . . The only property that can be reached in other states (except the New England group) is the 'private' property of the municipal corporation. The distinction between 'public' and 'private' property of municipalities is not clearcut, varying somewhat from state to state. But attachment of the private property of a municipality is a hollow remedy. The proceeds that might be realized therefrom are usually insignificant compared with the amount of bonds in default. The instances in which anything is collected by levy upon a municipality's property, or upon some alleged proprietary fund, are few."

gated its power to compel completion of deferred exchanges in the case of its subsidiary units.

Thus we see, curiously enough, that neither honesty nor any ultimate form of compulsion can be relied upon in the eventual completion of deferred exchanges with governmental units, supreme or subsidiary.

Only one of the three criteria normally present in other deferred exchanges is present here: namely, the resources with which to complete the exchange. These resources, theoretically, should always be ample. They rest upon the taxing power of the community. All the property owned by individuals in any community is, in a sense, on pledge to complete its deferred exchanges. The vital question then arises, *what is the pledge worth?* These available resources are, in actuality, limited by that highly practical consideration of government which we have already pointed out: namely, the extent to which individuals will allow the ruling group, then in power, to seize their wealth without rebellion. If the ruling group seizes too much of the citizens' property—if, in the usual terms, taxes become too high—the citizens may turn out the current political managers at the first opportunity, substitute others, and refuse to stand for the seizure of too much of their property.

Thus, the ability of governments to complete any deferred exchanges represented by their bonds rests not at all upon the total wealth of a particular community. *It depends upon how much of it as a practical matter of rulership is seizable.* Is the community borrowing so much that it will never be able to seize enough from its citizens to complete the exchange? This is what the governmental bond expert must look into and determine.

In the case of subsidiary governmental units, it is interesting to note how much, in expert opinion, this consideration limits the available resources. The law in Massachusetts, governing investments which savings banks are allowed to make, provides one illustration of this. No savings bank in that State may enter into a deferred exchange (that is, buy a bond) with any subsidiary governmental unit

245

in the United States if the total outstanding obligations of that unit are *more than from three to seven per cent of the total assessed value of property in the community*. It would appear from this that the experts who framed this law estimate that from three to five per cent, of real estate values alone, is the limit of their property which citizens in general will allow to be taken from them, without becoming restive, turning out their ruling group and substituting another, which will seize less property from them, and which will thus throw into question the eventual completion of the exchange.

All in all, it seems there is reasonable ground for suspicion of these economic promises, which governmental units, both supreme and subsidiary, make to their citizens. For if simple honesty will play no part in the completion of the promises; if there is no agent of eventual compulsion that can infallibly be relied upon; and if even the resources to complete the transaction, while theoretically ample in total, may be governed by the fitful wind of political circumstance, the degree of uncertainty about the completion of these deferred exchanges should be a high one. Yet, curiously, in the money markets, they have, in the past, often been considered among the least speculative of all deferred exchanges. Why is this?

The real reason can be found in what we have already pointed out: that these economic promises, unlike others, tend to be perpetual. *Full completion is never asked for.* For example, when a government borrows $1,000,000 at 4 per cent, it seldom has to repay the million dollars—and it seldom does! If it can succeed in paying a mere $40,000 a year, it can keep the principal part of the deferred exchange juggled in the air forever after. Nor is this juggling a mere potentiality—an unused reliance of the governments, invoked only in an emergency. It is the explanation of the financial legerdemain that is carried on by every central government, and by all but the tiniest proportion of subsidiary governments, in the world today.

What a beautiful system! What long, long ropes of waste it gives our politicians, before they get tangled up and tripped! Because of course they all do get lured on, until an unforeseen set of circumstances arises where the principal part of the promise must be com-

246

pleted, not with another promise, but *with a form of real wealth!* Then comes the deluge.

In short, when principal—and not interest—is considered, government promises are the most speculative and uncertain of all economic promises, if we mean by speculation (as we should) whether or not the second half of the exchange will eventuate in as much real wealth as the amount given in the first half. Of course, this is true only over a long lapse of time; but then these are long promises.

In the past pages, we have been carefully acquiring—wherever it was possible—a picture of the degree of reliability men manifest in various fields of economic activity. It has been a rough approximation, necessarily, because of the scantiness of data. Nonetheless, there can be no question that it is pretty closely in accord with the facts.

We saw that simple men and women, in a low-income stratum of the population, dealing in instalment contracts during the worst economic maelstrom in our history, completed no less than 97½ per cent of the promises involved in their deferred exchanges.

We saw those citizens who are somewhat better off, allowed credit from retail stores, completing 99⁴⁄₁₀ per cent of their promises.

We saw exchanges of money for labor so inevitably fulfilled that the participants did not even record them in writing.

We saw men, in production and distribution, handing over hundreds of billions of dollars' worth of goods for promises, and about 99 per cent of these promises fulfilled, even through the most disturbing depression in history.

We saw that far more billions were paid in the promises constituting rent, over a short period, than governments obligate themselves for; and that the record of performance again was practically 100 per cent.

We saw banks with a record of fulfillment of promises to depositors close to 100 per cent, although these also totaled hundreds of billions, and in spite of the difficulties many bankers got themselves into through their incaution.

247

We saw the business men to whom banks lent money on promissory notes, with a record of fulfillment falling short of complete perfection by perhaps one-one hundredth of 1 per cent.

We saw insurance companies, dealing also in tens of billions, again with a record of fulfillment close to 100 per cent.

Even with soulless corporations, on their short-term deferred exchanges, a record of 99 per cent performance is found.

In every area of economic activity except two—the long promises represented by mortgages, and corporation bonds—the fulfillment of promises by individuals hovers so close to 100 per cent that it is fair to say that individual dependability, in the performance of economic promises, approaches the infallible.

What now, by comparison, does the record show of the reliability of governments, in respect to their economic promises—to say nothing of any other kind?

Take first the record of subsidiary governmental units.

It is not a bad record.

We must use our own country as an example, because it is the only place any figures are available. Unfortunately, in the most authoritative study made of them, the data as to defaults on these promises are frankly stated as being meager. One record is quoted as showing that 3,238, out of our 180,000 taxing units, were in default as to either principal or interest at the end of 1935. There have been varying estimates as to the proportion of the total money in default. For example, one investigator figured 5 per cent at the end of 1934, and another 7 per cent in the summer of 1933. A third estimate is that somewhere between 5 and 10 per cent was in default in 1935, and still another that a full 10 per cent was in default at the end of 1934. Of course, we must calculate the same here as we did with corporations. These bonds that are in default as to interest cannot be counted as incompleted promises. For an adjustment is later made, in almost every case. The holder of the promise receives a new one for a lesser amount, or at a lower rate of interest. Thus the amount finally lost in these deferred exchanges, when compared with the total, is

248

very little. If only 10 per cent of all this type of bonds were in default at the end of 1934, only a part of this would be ultimately lost. So that we must come to the conclusion that, in the case of subsidiary units of government, the record of performance is almost comparable to that of individuals. It is not disturbingly below 100 per cent.*

Unfortunately, sovereign States show no such glowing record. Here are a few pertinent items. On December 31, 1936, American citizens had lent money to *forty nations* on their deferred exchanges. Of these, *twenty-three* had defaulted on part or all of the promises. The total sum in default was 36 per cent of the total relinquished in the first place, and promised in exchange!

These, it should be observed, were merely the deferred exchanges these nations had entered into with American citizens; the ones that were payable in dollars. Needless to say, the same nations had entered into quite as huge—if not in some cases—a huger volume of long-term deferred exchanges with their own citizens. What the record of non-performance is upon these internal promises is not fully available.

The League of Nations in one of its publications gives the total long promises of all the sovereign States. They added up, as previously stated, to about $149,000,000,000 in 1936. Sixty-two governments were listed in this record. Of these, *twenty-seven were in default at the time*, either as to principal or interest. This is over 45 per cent.

This is, of course, only the record of the promises *still existing*. But following the War, there was a well-nigh universal welching on the part of governments in the deferred exchanges they had entered into with their own citizens and foreigners—both by direct repudiation and by monetary subterfuge.

Prior to the World War, the national debt of the active belligerents was about $32,000,000,000.† During the conflict, probably about $186,000,000,000 more were borrowed. Except for that which was borrowed by Great Britain and the United States from their citizens, almost the entire balance of this enormous sum of close to $218,000,-

* The figures above are summarized chiefly from *Long-Term Debts in the U. S.*
† *The Inter-Ally Debts*, Harvey E. Fisk, Page 324.

000,000 has not been paid, and will never be paid, to those who trusted the promisors. Russia wiped out all her debt out of hand. Germany canceled the astronomical billions she had borrowed from her citizens by paying it in a valueless mark—a grim joke. Austria did the same. France and Italy wiped out from 80 per cent to 90 per cent of what they owed their citizens, and lately have wiped out a good portion of the balance. All the smaller nations of Europe involved in the War on both sides—Belgium, Jugoslavia, Greece, Rumania, Turkey—followed the same course of action.

Another example of the attitude of sovereign States to their promises is that involved where States borrowed from one another, instead of from individuals. A great deal of this took place during the War, of course; but few people realize that very large sums were advanced by one government to another, *after the War was over*, for relief and reconstruction. This was particularly true of our nation. In any case, Great Britain and the United States were the principal lenders to other governments. On March 31, 1936, the amount owing to Great Britain (not including unpaid interest accrued) was £2,565,638,000—about $12,250,000,000, at the present rate of exchange. Nineteen governments were the promisors. In our case, the amount of promises stood at a little less than $12,500,000,-000 at the end of 1935. Twenty governments were the promisors. It is, of course, notorious that only one, little Finland, is regularly meeting its promise to us. In the case of Great Britain—which is defaulting with us, and, typically, being righteous about it—the same practically total defalcation on the part of all the promisors is the case.

Let us not be confused here, either by sympathies or by antipathies. No doubt reasons can be found—some are obvious—why nations, in their extremity, refused to honor these long promises. But explanations of why this non-performance eventuated, whether they appeal to us as being well founded or as mere rationalizations, are one thing. *The non-performance itself is another.* It is the latter fact which we must keep our eyes upon as an economic phenomenon of the extremest significance. The truth seems to be that, for whatever reasons their apologists may find, modern States may be expected never to complete their half-exchanges, *if and when they find it to be to their better interest not to do so.*

This is made even plainer and more indisputable by occurrences throughout the world in the past eight illuminating years. The simplest form of economic promise which governments make is that evidenced in their bonds. These are clear promissory notes, for short and long terms, in every respect like those which a business man gives a bank. But there is another, an even more important type of deferred exchange, which States enter into with their citizens—*that which is involved in their national currencies.* It is a type of economic promise which few persons understand. But let us make no mistake about our ruling groups. They understand it well enough. They are perfectly aware that both their paper money and so-called token money represent promises in a deferred exchange. By the manipulation of these particular deferred exchanges, States can defraud those who trust them, citizens and foreigners, as effectually, and much more safely, than by open and honest repudiation of a promise recorded in a bond. They can invent words for it like "devaluation" and "reflation," which because of the obscurity generally surrounding this matter, may even earn them the sympathy, if not the applause, of a large part of those who are being cheated.

Now, the stark fact is that every important sovereign government on the planet, since 1929, wiped out a good part of its promises by this device, and several of them have used the device more than once. Our own nation, let it stand forever to our shame, was among these respectable pocket-pickers—*for the first time in our history as an organized nation;* and with us, the airiest and most inventive rationalizer of all, Great Britain. Needless to say, this device of governments works successfully only because almost all of those who are gulled do not understand what is happening. An increasing number of citizens, it is true, have come to be able to appraise in some measure its final outcome. But few comprehend its *modus operandi*, and that it takes place through the incompletion of promises in deferred exchanges. We shall examine these deferred exchanges, represented by national

251

currencies—obviously the most critical of all economic promises—in the five succeeding chapters.

In the meantime, one thing appears even from this swift survey: that the unreliability of States is a clear, a startling, and a predominating set of facts in our present economic scene. The truth is that whole volumes could be written, and ought to be for the sake of the record, about the ingrained dishonesty of rulers through all history. It stands in the sharpest contrast to the integrity and sense of responsibility of the individual, which has been built up through long social evolution. Its deep evil, in disturbing the orderly progress of human living, is obvious.

One large fact, which has clearly appeared from our survey, is the complete interdependence of economic promises one upon another. When one is unfulfilled, not only one but many others may have to be unfulfilled. We have seen the enormous extent of governmental deferred exchanges. They run into unimaginable billions. There are few individuals in the world who are not directly, or at one or two removes, dependent upon these governmental promises. The economic promises we make to one another as individuals almost infallibly we keep. But the economic promises which governments make may almost as infallibly be expected—if we allow sufficient time to elapse—to be broken. That is the hard fact.

Those who have been in late years in such dreadful doubt about our economic "system" will do well to examine carefully this part of the social machinery. What social system—capitalist, communist, or whatever one wants to call it—can possibly work with government ethics in this status?

It is just as if, through the ages, men have been slowly building an economic arch. It is well and solidly based. It rests upon the fulfillment of promises, and therefore upon an accepted responsibility, which, as we have seen, has come to approach the finest extreme among individuals. But the capstone of the arch, *the governmental promise*, proves never to be anything but clay. It crumbles, time and again, upon pressure; and then men, patient as bees, proceed to raise the structure again. That it is the capstone, and how infirm it is, will ap-

252

pear even more clearly when we examine, as we now must, the half-exchanges which modern governments enter into under the mystification of the word, Money.

14

A Simple Explanation of Money, with a Little History,
Revealing How Its Modern Mysteries Principally
Arise from Failure to Distinguish between a
Promise and a Thing

WHAT is money? At least one statement can safely be made about it: that it is the controlling economic factor in the life of every one of us. "The great affair," says Adam Smith, "is to get money." The entire course of our lives is ordered by money. No single thing is more interwoven with human experience. Yet nothing seems so poorly understood by men as money. The most fantastic fallacies are, and long have been, current about it. For the great mass of people, the subject is shrouded in the densest and most pernicious ignorance; pernicious, because we allow persons in power, as ignorant as ourselves, often to take astonishingly stupid action about our money—without interference. Nor is this a modern phenomenon. For the approximately twenty-five hundred years that governments have had a close relation to money, the same confusion about it—both on the part of the masses of men who use it, and rulers who presume to do things about it—is clear and consistent in the records.

This long-continuing, and still universal, ignorance about money is a genuine enigma. One might deduce, from the fact, that money by its nature is a particularly difficult thing for the human intellect to fathom, that an uncommon order of intelligence is required to comprehend both its nature and its problems. But as soon as anyone, of ordinary common sense, applies himself to the subject, the greater part of its mysteries (though perhaps not all) dissipate like mist. The trouble really is that few persons really apply themselves to an analysis of the subject. We all assume, since we deal constantly with what we *call* money, that our personal experience tells pretty much all there is to know about it. This might be so, *if we really analyzed our experience*, which is precisely what we do not do. It is the old story of the prime source of confusion in thought: our actions become utterly habitual, and the original considerations which inspire them are completely forgotten.

We said, parenthetically, in a previous chapter, that most of the puzzlement about money can be found in our own psychology. This is true, and since the chief mystery about money is in our own state of mind, its solution will be found there. The mystery has its central source in two fallacies which have bedeviled men in this matter from time immemorial. Both of them involve the relationship of governments to money, a relationship that is seldom seen with clarity.

The first of these fallacies arises from the fact that we are utterly oblivious to the role deferred exchanges play in this field. We have seen elsewhere in human affairs how, by habit, the fact that a half-exchange is taking place is obliterated to our consciousness by habit. This is more perniciously true here than anywhere else. Few of us observe that what today we use chiefly as money *are mere promises to pay money on the part of governments or central banks*. Accordingly, without thought, we identify the promise with the money. Soon we shall see how that identification, pregnant with endless social trouble, has come about.

The second of the fallacies is like a Siamese twin to the first. It has its origin in a notion which we analyzed in the last chapter: that the powers of government are coextensive with the full powers resident in the community that is governed. We saw that, while in theory they may be, in practice they are very much limited. With regard to money, this notion results in the anciently accepted belief, an almost ineradicable one, that governments have the power *to create money*, whereas this is not true at all. The whole society, ex-

255

pressing its true will in its actions, alone can create the money of the society. This truth is seldom now observed, simply because under normal economic circumstances the rulers' notion as to what the money of the community shall be *coincides* with that of the ruled. But instances are legion in history where rulers and subjects have disagreed as to what the money of the community should be. Invariably, it is the subjects who settle the decision their way. Later we shall have occasion to look more closely at this clash of will, between rulers and ruled, over what the money of a community shall be.

Let us examine the first of these fallacies, the common confusion between *promises to pay money* and *money* itself. To be able to make the distinction, obviously we must be able to identify what money itself is.

It is at this turning that most of us wander off into the mazes that surround the subject. And no wonder! For the stark fact is that, although we say we do, few men today have any experience with real money itself; and, although we think we do, none of us have any real money in our possession. Most of the individuals in industrial nations, like the United States, Great Britain, France, Germany, Russia and Japan have never even seen the real money of their nation. Even the wealthiest men nowadays own no money and seldom see any. What we handle, what we deal in, what we say we own, *consists almost entirely of promises to pay money*—promises made by our governments or by our central banks.

But, surely, this is mere quibbling. What hundreds of millions of people use *as* money must, in common sense, be considered money. If modern men commonly use government and central bank promises as money, as at one time the ancients used cattle, and Indians used beads, and Virginian colonists used tobacco, then why may not government and central bank promises be called money? They do all the work, they perform all the functions, they answer all the purposes, that gold or any other commodity can supply as money.

There is no more pernicious point of view than this, because it has all the deceit of verbal logic in it. The viewpoint is blind as a bat to

256

a simple fact. These promises perform all the functions of real money *only because they are promises to give real money, and because the promises not only are believed, but under ordinary circumstances are invariably fulfilled.* Otherwise, they would not be believed. Nevertheless, they remain promises—that is, a few words inscribed in the laws or on a piece of paper. *And the promises may not be fulfilled!*

Now the distinction between promises, consisting of mere words, and a clinking weight of gold or silver, is palpable. If the promise to give money be not fulfilled, the person relying upon it then finds that he has—what a word is—nothing! If what a community of men uses principally *as* money is an insubstantiality, a mere promise of the State or a central bank to give real money later in a deferred exchange, it is a little perilous to consider the difference between the promise and the money mere quibbling over words. So tens of millions of persons have found, by sad experience, during the last two decades! Even after the experience they did not know what had happened. They simply ended up with nothing that could be exchanged for other forms of wealth or labor: this last great fact was all they knew. They did not realize that what had occurred was that a promise men had believed was definitely unfulfilled. Manifestly they did not realize this, *because they were unaware of the promise.* They were unconscious that they were on the last end of a deferred exchange—with their governments; a dangerous condition of mind to be in at the moment the last half of the exchange was going to be canceled, by trickery or *force majeure!*

But if we are always to distinguish in our reasoning between money and promises to pay it, we are under the necessity of being able always to identify the thing itself.

The best background for this necessary realization is to know something about the history of money. In its essential character, money has never changed. Real money has always been—and still is— a tangible and useful form of wealth. It is always a commodity that is so widely desired in any given community that all the members of the community will unworriedly exchange other forms of wealth for

257

it, and also contribute labor for it, because of the certainty in their own minds that it will be accepted by others, in a later exchange, for some other desired form of wealth, or some other kind of service.

Thus, the most useful knowledge the average citizen can have about money is its history. I said, some pages back, that the most romantic book in the world remained to be written about the History of Peddlers. I change my mind: it would be the full story of money. What men desire most is most revealing of them. They have always desired their money most. What, then, the money of men has been, in different times and different places, is a beautiful revelation of the manner of life and thought of the common man throughout all history. The changes that have taken place in money would mirror, better than anything else, the changes that have occurred throughout the history of human society.

This particular inquiry—as with trading, and banking, and the corporate enterprise—can go into this subject only with the utmost brevity. But at least it is necessary, for an unconfused observation of our modern life, to do so much.

It is, of course, of recordless groups in the dimmest past that the economist must generalize in outlining the beginning and evolution of money. But his generalization is no mere spinning of logic. It is well-buttressed by the discoveries of anthropologists and archaeologists, scanty as these are; by the history of men that is preserved in their words; by paintings of great antiquity and literary references; and finally by authoritative records of travel among semi-primitive and primitive communities, whose way of life could be little different from that of our most distant ancestors.

Money is obviously associated with exchanges of property, and that in turn is based upon specialization of occupation. In primitive days, when this specialization was in an incipient stage—as we saw sketchily in Chapter Four—exchanges of property probably took place more between clans than between individuals. It probably evolved out of the practice of making gifts. When strangers visited a settled tribe, or roving groups met peacefully together, hospitality was the rule. This deeply-rooted custom of gifts is mentioned time and again in the Bible, and it is still a tradition of the desert.

Obviously, under such circumstances, the things that would be offered as gifts were most likely to be those of which the givers had an excess, and the recipients had none. It is easy to imagine how this practice, an engaging manifestation of friendliness—in fact, a demonstration of the deep instinct which makes man, like the ant and bee, a social animal—came to evolve into a frank unashamed swapping of needed article for needed article, of excess for excess. Here is the matrix out of which specialization of occupation could emerge, could become more and more general, more and more refined.

This exchange of needed commodity for needed commodity, of excess for excess, is the condition underlying the beginnings of money. It constituted, of course, barter. Jevons gives an interesting instance of it in the opening of his book, *Money and the Mechanism of Exchange:* "Some years since (he writes), Mademoiselle Zelie, a singer of the Théâtre Lyrique in Paris, made a professional tour around the world, and gave a concert in the Society Islands. In exchange for an air from *Norma* and a few other songs, she was to receive a third part of the receipts. When counted, her share was found to consist of three pigs, twenty-three turkeys, forty-four chickens, five thousand coconuts, besides considerable quantities of bananas, lemons and oranges. At the Halle in Paris, as the prima donna remarks in her lively letter, this amount of live stock and vegetables might have brought four thousand francs, which would have been good remuneration for five songs. In the Society Islands, however, pieces of money were very scarce; and as Mademoiselle could not consume any considerable portion of the receipts herself, it became necessary in the meantime to feed the pigs and poultry with the fruit."

The prima donna's experience—it should be observed—was a case of bartering products for her labor. Most original barter was not of this sort; it was a swap of product for product. We can today see an ancient picture of it going on, in Egyptian paintings dating back to

2500 B.C. It was, of course, far older than this. It was earthwide, for necessarily it was the first form of exchange.

We do not need today to go to Central Africa or deep Australia, among unlettered savages, for present instances. Much of the foreign trade of Germany, under the clever Dr. Schacht, constituted true barter—a swapping of commodities for manufactured articles, without the medium of modern forms of money. But we can look even closer than that, in our own particular front yard. Barter still survives, one of the deans among our economists points out.* In 1920 more than a quarter of the 6,450,000 farms in the United States were cultivated by tenants who paid as rent a share of the crops. What do they really do in such transactions? Having no money, like Mademoiselle Zelie's happy audience, they pay for the use of the land in cotton, corn or other crops.

It must not be imagined that it was by any reasoning among men that this universal state of barter changed, in any given community, to one in which a money was deliberately or even consciously decided upon. One can understand both Money and History better by realizing that every money, in a sense, *has grown to be money*. The role of time is all-important where any money is concerned. A long period of barter would elapse, preceding the final emergence of any form of wealth as money. During this period, it would gradually come to stand forth as a commodity which practically everybody in the community wanted *in and for itself*. The process is completely psychological. Because of this universal desirability, men in the community would come to realize that it was a *third thing* for which any two other things *could with virtual certainty be exchanged*. Even if the owner of it did not need it, even if he already had an excess of it, he could safely accept it in a swap; because if later on he wanted something else, he was sure that this thing being used as money *in turn would be accepted* for what he wished to obtain.

This is what the economists mean by saying that, through its practically universal acceptability in a given community, money is that commodity which constitutes *the medium of exchange*. Perhaps a

* Wesley C. Mitchell, *Business Cycles: The Problem and Its Setting.*

slightly more precise definition would be that it is always a widely desired commodity which will be accepted or offered *in an intermediate exchange*, so that the exchange of any two other commodities may ultimately be effectuated. By using it in an intermediate exchange, *men can divest themselves of what they own and obtain some other thing they want—from some other person, at some later time.*

To perform this office of being an intermediary in the exchanges of all kinds of wealth and labor, the primary quality the thing being used as money had to possess, for any given community of men, was thus *general acceptability*—common esteem as a thing of value.

A second and hardly less important quality of a useful money is *durability*. A commodity quickly perishable, like fish or fruit or eggs or meat or milk, has never evolved into a money in any community. On the other hand, numerous *more durable* agricultural and animal products have, as we shall see.

A third necessary quality in an ideal money is that it should be easily *divisible*. Assume that cattle constituted the money of a community, as they did for long ages all over Asia and Europe; and that the owner of a cow wanted to acquire a single piece of pottery. His judgment might be that a dollar-cow—shall we call it?—should exchange equitably for three such vessels. However, we have assumed that he does not want three, he only wants one. How is he going to get the one? On the other hand, let us assume that he would be willing to accept three pieces of pottery for a cow, but the person with whom he is dealing has but one to exchange. How can the exchange take place? So long as live cows remain the money, such exchanges could not take place. It is clear from this that *the indivisibility of cattle* made them none too ideal a medium of exchange. The more practicable the divisibility of the commodity being used as money *the more numerous are the exchanges* that can take place in the community. Accordingly, the more extensive may specialization of labor in the community become.

Still another desirable quality in an ideal money is *portability*. It should be easily transferable from place to place, although there have been plenty of moneys which were not. But one reason, without question, why cattle continued to be money for so long, was that they could be easily moved.

A still further quality—and decidedly important in its effect upon the number of exchanges which money makes possible—*is homogeneity of substance*. When cattle were money, for instance, individual oxen and cows differed in desirability. This condition must have tended greatly to diminish the volume of exchanges. With the units of money themselves varying in value, many exchanges of property must have been impossible, and every exchange must have involved haggling not far removed from barter. This is true in some districts of Central Africa today, where in certain regions cattle are still the medium of exchange, as they used to be all over the known world. It is apparent likewise in the colonial period of our own history, when various commodities other than metal coins were our forefathers' money. "If a cow will pay taxes," says Sumner, "the leanest cow will be given. If corn will pay a debt, the corn which is of poorest quality, or damaged to a certain extent, will be given. If a large number of commodities are made legal tender, the poorest quality of that commodity which may be cheapest at the time of payment, will be given."

There can be little question that one of the reasons, though by no means the principal one, why gold and silver ultimately became the world's money was because of their homogeneity of substance. Divided into however small parts, each part in quality is the same.

At different times, at different places, the most diverse varieties of commodities and utensils have been used by men as money. It is this variety which contributes the glamour to the history of money. For, as we said, what a community selects—no, selects is a poor word—*what it grows into accepting* as money reveals, as nothing else can, the common conditions of living, the habit of thought, and the status of civilization of the community.

It may be instructive here to survey briefly the multitudinous moneys that have been used, dividing them into broad categories.

First—as we have mentioned—it is clear, from the records, that in

262

ancient times both animals and animal products constituted prehistoric money. This was true over all the wide areas of Asia, Africa and Europe, wherever men passed from a hunting into a pastoral stage. Cattle then constituted the chiefest form of wealth. Abraham and Lot offer good examples. They were both rich in flocks and herds, so rich that when pasture was scarce, they had to separate to preserve the peace among their herdsmen. They did so, and of course each took his money with him—cattle. The value of everything *was measured* by cattle. Across the Aegean Sea, Homer writes of a different world and time, about a thousand years later, when the value of everything was still measured by oxen. And then perhaps another thousand years later, Caesar breaks into the far land of Britain, and remarks how rich the chieftains are—in cattle! It was their money, as well as their chiefest form of wealth.

But other living animals have also constituted money, as cattle so widely did. Where slaves were a principal form of wealth they were often used as a fixed measure, by which other forms of wealth could be valued, and for which they could be exchanged in accepted ratios. Why not? Apply the criteria we have identified as being desirable in money. Slaves were as generally acceptable as cattle; they were somewhat more durable than cattle; they were quite as portable or transportable; and they were no less divisible nor homogeneous in substance. In short, they had almost the same advantages and disadvantages, *as a money*, as cattle had. The only drawback about them in comparison with cattle, was that there was no residue of value, if they died or were killed. For, of course, cattle had another value: they could be eaten, and their hides were useful. Cowhides, oxhides, sheepskin and goatskin, all at one time or another have served as money. Furs and skins were probably money in paleolithic times, A. R. Burns suggests.* These things represent, of course, a different category of money—*animal products*. Beaverskins, for example, constituted money at one place or another all through the wilds, in the early settlement era of North America. Horns of cattle, elephant tusks, whale teeth, feathers—all have served, in some place and time where

* *Money and Monetary Policy in Early Times.*

they were commonly owned and widely valued just like gold coins, as commodities *in comparison with which* other forms of wealth were measured in value, for purposes of exchange.

Whenever agriculture came to predominate as a way of life, as may be expected, *grown products* with some quality of durability and divisibility, have been money—wheat, oats, barley, wine, olive oil, salt, cubes of Benzoin gum, tea—to mention but a few. Particularly interesting examples of this to us, in our own history, were the early years in Virginia, when tobacco was a recognized money;* and further south, rice played a similar role. Even paper money—promises to pay rice and tobacco on demand—were issued upon these commodities and circulated as promised money.

No less fascinating a category has been the innumerable common utensils which have circulated at one time or another as money. Notoriously, there was the roasting spit that was common in the early Greek world. Six of them, all one could hold in the right hand, made a drachma (handful), which is still the name of the unit of Greek currency. Bronze and iron spits were also used as money among the Etruscans. Battle-axes too served as money in antiquity, and in that wonderland of the ancient world, Minoan Crete, tripods and cauldrons in different sizes were used to measure values. But instances of manufactured articles need not be confined to the ancient world. Few people in our own country know that, during the fifties and sixties in the Far West, blankets constituted a true medium of exchange among the Indians and traders who ranged the land. Pieces of cotton cloth have been used as money as far apart over the planet as Africa, Siberia and Peru. For hundreds of years, knives were money in China. They began to be used about the time coinage was being invented thousands of miles away, in the Greek Archipelago. A curious form of money this seems today, but what a story it tells—of the usefulness and deep appeal of this common tool—to those who first saw it as something new in the world. Spades and other small implements

* John W. Vandercook, explorer and traveler, tells me he has found tobacco still being used as currency in places as far apart as New Guinea and Liberia. In the former place it is still our Virginia tobacco, in rolled sticks of a uniform length and weight.

were also used in China as money; and iron shovels and hoes were once money among the Malays! Is all this to be taken as a mere revelation of the primitive mind? But the canny Scotch, some of them, used *handmade nails* as money up to the time of Adam Smith 150 years ago!

This use of *manufactured utensils* as money may indeed go back to the Stone Age of Man. "It would be interesting to discuss," says Jevons, "the not improbable suggestion of Boucher de Perthes, that, perhaps, after all, the finely worked stone implements now so frequently discovered were among the earliest mediums of exchange. Some of them are certainly made of jade, nephrite or other hard stones, only found in distant countries, so that an active traffic in such implements must have existed."

Another obvious category to be noticed—important enough, for out of it emerged modern money—is metals. As men began to discover how to mine and make use of them, they naturally became a principal form of human wealth. The most prized metal, almost from the beginning, was gold. It was in use among the Egyptians by 3400 B.C. Pictures from the days of the Old Kingdom often show scales in which precious metals are being weighed. In Egypt a thoroughly established form of money, for long centuries, was gold rings, each one of a fixed weight. They are found in abundance in the tombs of the Pharaohs. But not only there. Egyptian relations with Minoan Crete were of the closest character and gold rings were also money among the Minoans. When Schliemann almost miraculously discovered the treasure of Troy, over 12,000 gold rings were part of it. And when the Mycenean tombs were located by this same amazing excavator, merely using Homer as his guide, again rings and spirals in great quantity were found. They were all in fixed weights —they constituted money! But gold also passed as money in *bars* of fixed weights, and in the form of oxheads, also in standard units of weight. In short, since gold in this part of the world, was replacing oxen as money, it was cast to represent oxen. This was not only done with gold, but with bronze, copper, iron, and other metals. These latter passed in the form of ingots of fixed weight. but the shape was that of an oxhide!

265

All this, although occurring a thousand years and more before Jesus, was the development *in a comparatively civilized world*, where exchanges of wealth were becoming a well-established procedure. Metals were used as money, perhaps even more widely, not as ingots, but without fixed form. "Hoards of such broken metal, merely amorphous, or cast in the form of bricks, bars, plates, and the like, are forthcoming from all kinds of places, from Assyria to Ireland, and at all periods from the ninth century before to the fifth century after Christ. . . . A later development is shown when the metal is cast in the form of more or less regular ingots or bars, sometimes ornamented. Such bar money, which could be broken into smaller pieces and weighed, is found at all times down to the Middle Ages; it was the most convenient method of keeping bullion, whether intended for conversion into coin or not." * When so cut, it was done carefully—even in the most ancient times—into units of fixed weight. The name for the English coin, shilling, comes from this. A *skilling* was a cutting from a metal bar.

Finally, there were the commodities that could be utilized for ornament. "A passion for personal adornment is one of the most primitive and powerful instincts of the human race," says Jevons, "and as articles used for such purposes would be durable, universally esteemed and easily transferable, it is natural they should be circulated as money." The most conspicuous form of this ornamental money— aside, of course, from gold, which has a utilitarian as well as an ornamental value—was the little cowry shell, which comes from a small mollusc found on shallow shores of the Indian Ocean. It is counted by some numismatists as probably the first form of money, and spread in use all through the East Indies, through the populations of Asia, and down the West Coast of Africa. It is still being used as money among some of the natives.† It was common in ancient China, it has been found in the ruins of Nineveh, and dates back, most prob-

* *Cambridge Ancient History*, Volume IV.
† The remarkable degree to which these shells circulate and their universal appeal among primitive people, no matter when they lived nor where they are, is attested to by the fact that John W. Vandercook found them being prized thousands of miles from their source, among the Carib Indians, in Guiana.

ably, to long millennia before that empire among continent-wide populations.

Comparable to it were the wampum beads of our own Indians These beads were of two kinds, one white from a periwinkle shell, the other black from a clam shell. The black ones were more valuable and exchanged for two whites. They were arranged in strings or belts. They become a coordinate money—with beaverskins and English and Spanish minted coins—among our Pilgrim Fathers, who not only used them in trading with the Indians, but in trading among themselves. They were made legal tender; that is, they had to be accepted in the last half of deferred exchanges. But our ancestors, of course, were much more civilized than the stupid honest redmen: they very soon began to counterfeit the wampum!

At this point in our sketchy history we must halt. When we begin to talk about counterfeiting, and about metal bars and ingots of fixed weight, we are almost to the point in history where rulers began to have a close relation to money. It was when they did, that confusion among men, over money, began. The source of that confusion—the second great fallacy that has always bedeviled men in this matter—we shall consider in the next chapter.

Up to this point, it will be noticed by the reader, all these curious and fascinating commodities and objects that have been mentioned, are—so to speak—natural moneys. They just grow, like Topsy. They arise from the needs of men, and from the natural processes, through which a growing social organization would go, in which the occupations of men are becoming more diversified.

Now, it is an essential fact, which the economics student must never allow himself to forget, that in this long and absorbing prehistoric and early historical record, these original moneys—whatever form they took—invariably were not alone things of value, but in each case *a very widely desired thing of utility or adornment* in its community. Without a sharp recognition of that truth an unconfused understanding of our own problems of money is impossible. *For it remains as true today as it has ever been,* although the truth, for a

267

variety of reasons, is hidden under appearances, which we must uncover. What we must do, to understand money in the present day, is to strip away the appearances which now enshroud this simple nugget of fact.

To recapitulate, then, it is clear that money originally is always a commodity, an article, wanted in and for itself by everybody. It is a commodity with a utilitarian or ornamental value. That is its *primary* quality. That is what makes it the money of a given community. It does not become money by will of the group, by any deliberate concert of opinion, but as the result, it may be said, of social circumstances. The universal esteem in which it is held results in its being *much more exchangeable* for other forms of property than anything else. It then becomes that intermediate article in exchange (between all other exchanges) which we really mean by the use of the word, "money." But we must distinguish: this social value of the commodity—for that is what it is—is originally only a secondary *and derivative* value, clearly arising out of its primary quality: namely, that it is valued in and for itself, ordinarily more than anything else, by the members of the community.

Now what happens? Slowly a crucial psychological change toward this commodity which is their "money" occurs in every community. As the diversification of labor becomes further and further refined, due to the very services (it must be noted) of the article being used as money; as the goods which owners are willing to exchange become more varied in character and greater in abundance, this secondary social value, of the article being used as money, comes more and more *to overshadow in importance*—in the eyes of a large portion of those using it—its original inherent value. Originally people accepted it in exchanges solely because they wanted it for itself. In time they come to accept it principally because they find it can be exchanged readily and easily for anything else they may want. The commodity thus becomes valued *chiefly for its social utility*, simply because it can be used as a money—not because of its inherent utility, for individual use or adornment. Nonetheless, it must be observed clearly, no money—genuine money we are speaking of, not promises

268

to pay money—ever loses this quality of inherent value. This is true, even though the inherent value may be ignored *by a large number* of the collectors of the money, who concentrate only upon the social use to which it may be put: as the best means of carrying on intermediate exchanges.

For clarity of comprehension we must be careful not to lose sight here of the role which the diversification of occupation plays in bringing about this vital change in the mental attitude of the members of the community toward the commodity which has become their money. Upon analysis it appears, indeed, to be the principal factor in the change. In the early stages of growth of any society, a commodity becomes money *because it can be enjoyed or used by practically everybody*. Cowry shells would prettify everybody, man and woman. Wampum belts were displayed on the person. Cows and sheep could be utilized as a form of wealth by everybody in a pastoral civilization; they were largely the means by which people kept alive. The many animal skins that have been money in the past could be fabricated into clothes by every family, and they were. Spits could be used for roasting by everybody, battle-axes for killing, tripods for religious purposes, pottery for storing liquids, knives in a hundred useful ways. Ingots of lead and copper and iron and bars of gold and silver all could be beaten, by early men, into weapons, tools, vessels and ornaments; and each man, each clan, did this for itself. Thus, the members of any community, in which any particular commodity became money, could *see* and *feel* its inherent value. For all of them—with rare exceptions—made individual use or acquired individual enjoyment from it. No fact about the early history of money is more important to grasp than this.

It is easy to see, however, as occupation became sharply specialized in the later stages of a community, how this would become less and less to be the case with the given commodity which had become the money. What use, for example, would a shepherd have for an ingot of iron? His days and his skill were spent on the hillside, watching sheep. What use would an ironmonger have of half a dozen cows, or of a pile of oxhides? His days were spent in fashioning weapons

269

and tools. It was thus inevitable, as specialization of occupation slowly proceeded, that the commodity being used as money should be wanted, not primarily for itself, *but for what it would bring in exchange*.

In short, it is clear that this pregnant change in the mental attitude of members of a community toward their money, *which made its derivative utility its chief utility*, both arose from and proceeded apace with the increase in diversification of labor in the community. We see to what extreme lengths this profound change in mental attitude has gone today with gold—which is practically all the world's money. True enough, it is still universally prized for ornamental purposes; but its derivative social utility, as money, has overwhelmingly become its chief utility.

Is there any need to go further? We seem to have acquired sufficient of an answer to the question which inspired this highly generalized excursion into history—namely, *what is this money*, which we must always carefully distinguish from promises to pay money?

It is now—and it always has been—a thing, a commodity, durable and ordinarily easily divisible, which was so deeply desired for its own inherent value by everybody in the community that by a process of natural social evolution it came to be utilized in intermediate exchanges of wealth.

For about three thousand years (although they were known and valued long before that) the use of silver and gold has been spreading over the earth until, for long centuries now, they have become the predominant money of all the more civilized communities. For a good part of this period silver was more in use than gold, which was comparatively so scarce that it was more applicable to large exchanges of property. But in the last century gold has become the supreme money of the two billion inhabitants of the earth. It is now, indeed, the official money of every important group of people in the world, except the Chinese.

It would serve no purpose here to proceed to an examination of the historical and psychological factors which have resulted in this predominance of gold as the money of mankind. It is a predominance comparable to that of man over the animal world. Nor can we consider the special problems which have arisen by reason of this event. Whole libraries have been written about these problems. We must present the mere inescapable fact. Those who think a better "hard money" could be found, or a more rational money could be devised to carry on human affairs, may take up their quarrel with all the thousands of years of history, with the habits and the ways of thought our countless billions of ancestors have deposited within us. After their quarrel, they must still lump the fact that this glittering yellow metal constitutes the money of most of the world.

The indisputable fact about our modern world is that everything else we use as money can so be used only because it consists, at one or more removes, of promises to deliver gold in a stated weight and of a stated fineness.

Now, to distinguish between gold, and promises to pay gold, should not be difficult for any normal individual.

But, to the average citizen, old or young, there will always remain an aura of utter unreality about such a distinction. It simply does not accord with his experience to consider everything which he uses as money, not really money, but only promises to pay money. He knows very well what he calls money. If he ever saw it, which he rarely does, he would not call a bag of gold dust, or a bar of gold, money. The word "money" to him *means* the clinking small coins in his pocket, or the crackling new bills he sometimes gets at the bank. They have enough substantiality to him. He is not remotely conscious of any element of promise in them. Why not, says his common sense, think of them as money?

I mentioned this peculiarity to Christopher Morley not long ago. He laughed, and told of an experience he had in the palmier days, when we still occasionally saw gold. A ten-dollar gold piece came into his possession and he walked into a downtown New York shop, bought some goods, and handed the coin to the shopkeeper. This man looked it over suspiciously and handed it back. No persuasion

271

could make him accept it as money. Mr. Morley went back to his newspaper cubbyhole, and wrote one of his *Translations from the Chinese*, as follows:

NOT NEGOTIABLE

Gold is real money;
Bills are not.
Yet, in nine shops out of ten,
If you offer a gold piece
They are vaguely disturbed:
They would prefer the familiar greenback
And anxiously suspect
They are being diddled.
Observe the fable,
You literary men!

And observe the fact, you money pundits!

How the common man comes by this almost ineradicable point of view about money is obvious enough. It is because from the moment, as a child, he is sent to the corner grocery store for a can of beans, *he uses these government or bank promises as money.* All his life through he has no occasion—except in a rare crisis, or as a student, when the matter has a mere dull academic interest—to become aware of the fact that they are mere government or bank promises to pay gold; to inquire, that is, into the nature of what he uses as money.

As soon as he makes such inquiry, speedily he finds *both the promise and the promisor.* For the essential facts about what he uses as money are not hidden. They are a matter of open record. He is merely ignorant about the facts.

Let us see briefly what they are. Take out of your pocketbook what you use as money. Let us hope your pocketbook is well-filled, and that it has every kind of American currency in it. On the table in front of you there would then be pennies, nickels, dimes, quarters, half-dollars and silver dollars: and also a variety of pieces of paper with different names—gold certificates (though you could be jailed

272

for having them), silver certificates, Federal Reserve Notes, Federal Reserve Bank Notes, Treasury Notes of 1890, National Bank Notes, and United States Notes. All these latter are in some slight respect different from one another.

Now, let us get one fact firmly in mind: gold is the money of the United States of America, and a dollar is merely *so much gold by weight*. By the will of the 130,000,000 people of this country, expressed through their representatives, a dollar is now one thirty-fifth of an ounce of gold. *It is nothing else!* It is not one hundred pennies, nor twenty nickels, nor ten dimes, nor four quarters, nor two half-dollar pieces, nor a single silver dollar, nor the piece of paper we call a dollar bill. It is by definition, indisputably, one thirty-fifth of an ounce of gold. This is the official pronouncement of you and your countrymen, even though you may not know it.

One ounce of gold, accordingly, constitutes by definition thirty-five dollars.

Now, let us consider, first, the coins you have put on the table. These perhaps you would most firmly regard as *real money*. What element of promise is there in a common coin? Nonsense!

Let us see! Assume that you are a resident of the District of Columbia, and by some means an ounce of gold comes into your possession. Like Mr. Morley's shopkeeper and most of your fellow-citizens, you do not look upon this gold as money. Money to you has consisted of small coins and pieces of paper. Accordingly you go to the Treasury Building in Washington, and at the proper window tell the clerk you want pennies for it. His eyebrows lift at the request, but you explain (a little self-consciously) that you are just going to experiment chemically with the pennies.

He weighs the gold carefully, finds that it is in fact one ounce, and pushes out at you 3,500 pennies.

You carry the 3,500 pennies to a chemist and ask him to melt them down for you. The result turns out to be about 22.8 pounds of copper, and about 1.2 pounds of alloy. Fine! Your experimental soul satisfied, you now transport all this metal back to the Treasury, go to the same window, and ask for your ounce of gold back. The clerk takes off his glasses, looks you over carefully as a curiosity, and pushes the package of metal back. "Can't be done," he says.

Ah! you remember. The government is not handing out gold to individuals like you. The reason for this you never understood, but you are no crazy Thoreau; you are a thoroughly conforming citizen.

"Then give me thirty-five hundred pennies," you suggest.

"Can't be done," the clerk repeats.

"Why not?"

The clerk gets more interested in you. "Secretary of the Treasury won't let me," he says, grinning. "Otherwise, I'd be glad to."

Oh, of course, you now remember another matter. It must cost the government something to stamp the metal into pennies. But it cannot cost much. Even the government has modern machinery. As a citizen, you decide you might as well stand up to these bureaucrats, who can't conduct the simplest business without getting rolled up in red tape.

"Go in and tell the Secretary," you suggest, "that I'm perfectly willing to have him deduct what it costs to stamp this copper and alloy into pennies. Give me not 3,500 pennies, but 3,250, or 3,000. Take off whatever it costs to make the metal into pennies. That's reasonable, isn't it?"

"Sure is," says the clerk; but he takes the precaution now to see whether he can drop the window in your face, in case you are the violent sort. Then he adds: "I asked the Secretary about this very matter yesterday, when another fellow wanted to do the same as you. He said it couldn't be done."

"Why not?" you sneer. "Government red tape again!"

"Oh, no," says the clerk. "You see, the government can buy this amount of copper and alloy in the market for about 200 pennies. Why should it give *you* 3,500 pennies for it? Isn't that reasonable, too?" And then, as a bewildered look comes into your eyes, he does —for safety's sake—clap the window in your face.

Incredible! To anybody rational the whole thing smacks of Alice-in-Wonderland. You had an ounce of gold and got 3,500 pennies for

274

it. With these pennies, you could have gotten some pretty valuable things in a thousand stores. You received this "money" at its very source, the government you have such confidence in. You melt them down, then carry the complete constituents back to the government, *and merely because it is in another form*—not in little flat round pieces, stamped—the government will give you only $2 for what was $35 worth a half-hour before. Needless to say, a similar result would follow with any other minor coins, if you wanted to make the same experiment.

The whole thing, on its face, seems pretty profitable business for the government. You might well be tempted to call it high-handed robbery of a simple citizen. It does indeed have no sense in it, until you realize what the real difference is between about 24 pounds of copper and alloy *as bullion*, and the same weight of copper and alloy, *when it is stamped as pennies*.

That difference is merely this: that when these various weights of metal *are stamped as coins*, in normal times—not now, for various reasons which will later be elucidated—the government *promises* that it will give an ounce of gold to anyone who presents them.

A promise intervenes when the metal is minted; that is all.

But where is this government promise? You know nothing at all about it. It is not stamped on the coin itself.

It is in our legal archives, and you are simply unfortunate in not knowing about it. The latest government promise, superseding previous ones to the same effect, is contained in the Agricultural Adjustment Act of 1933. This Act, as the economists put it—in terms which would probably be incomprehensible as a promise to you—directs the Secretary of the Treasury "to maintain the parity" of all forms of money with gold.

These words mean that if any person, in normal times, hands the Secretary of the Treasury any one of the following coins or pieces of paper: 100 pennies, 20 nickels, 10 dimes, 4 quarters, 2 half-dollars, a single silver dollar, a silver certificate or gold certificate—he must, without putting up any argument or raising any question, give that person one thirty-fifth of an ounce of gold, *if he is asked for it*. Or vice versa, if they give him an ounce of gold, he must give in return, if requested, any one of these coins or pieces of paper. That is what "maintaining parity with gold" means.

There is no law more important to men in its economic consequences. For let us observe clearly what it is: *it is a promise of the government, and nothing else.* It is the promise of an action. The Secretary of the Treasury, representing the government, is directed to perform this act, unequivocally and infallibly. If he does not, he can be thrown into jail—on all sorts of charges. Treason would be a good one. And, in normal times, *he does perform this act*—although you may know nothing about it. Gold is handed to him by the Federal Reserve Banks and he gives them the specified number of coins or paper dollars for each ounce. Or small coins and paper dollars are handed to him, and without a word he hands out the gold asked for. The transactions of this kind the United States Treasury has, in normal times, run 'way into the billions. Nor is there ever a single slip in the promised action. That is the sole explanation of this Alice-in-Wonderland transaction of yours—why 3,500 pennies will exchange for one ounce of gold ($35), whereas the same mass of metal melted down will exchange only for about $2.00. *The stamp of the government on the metal is its promise*, and when the Secretary of the Treasury sees the stamp, he must carry out the promise, if he is requested to; he must hand you over $35.

In short, he is merely *fulfilling the last half of a deferred exchange.* You may see better that this is a mere deferred exchange, if you follow the process through, in its entirety. Probably a bank first brought the gold to the Treasury, and for it received 3,500 pennies. Because of the promise of the government contained in this Act of 1900—and only because of it!—the bank accepted the coins. It accepted them only because the government promised to give gold—*real dollars*—for them at any time. This was thus a deferred exchange *of gold for gold at a later time*, the intervening promises being represented by the coins.

However, quite clearly, it was a deferred exchange *with no fixed date of completion.* In this respect, it is precisely like the deferred

276

exchanges you enter into when you "deposit" money in the bank. Completion, by the terms of the promise contained in the law, could be called for at any time. The bank hands these coins, representing the last half of a deferred exchange, to you and to me, when we ask it to fulfill its promises to us, those promises represented by our so-called deposits. What do we do with the coins? We hand them to other people for goods or services. The promises circulate. We all use them, by habit, as money. But they are not dollars, or parts of dollars. They are—in the way we have explained—government promises to pay dollars. Remember that, by the will of this people, our real money, dollars, consists of gold alone; that a dollar is a thirty-fifth of an ounce of gold, *and nothing else*. Finally, these coins, representing promises, come back to the Secretary of the Treasury through some other bank; and—until 1933, and it is to be hoped soon again—he would give the promised amount of gold to any bank or individual who asked him to do so, for the proper number of coins. When he does, *the second half of the deferred exchange is completed*. The original promise of the government is fulfilled.

We left you somewhere with the contents of your pocketbook opened up on a table, and all varieties of American money around you. Surely it is unnecessary to point out that what is true of subsidiary coins is likewise true of the various categories of paper money. The only essential difference between them and the subsidiary coins is that the constituent substance of which they are composed—paper—is of even less inherent value than the metal which makes up our various coins. In fact, inherently it is practically worthless. But, also, they are somewhat more clearly the printed evidence of a promise. Even so, the evidence of the promise is not so simply and clearly stated as it might be, and it becomes necessary to refer to other acts of Congress to see what each statement means. When we do, we find that they constitute not a thing in the world but ultimately promises of the government.

In identifying these pieces of paper as promises, at least it is not necessary to do so again with those which are called Federal Reserve notes, and Federal Reserve Bank notes. We took a good look at these in our chapter on central banks. These are, at the same time, both government promises and central bank promises. We saw that on their face they constituted a straight promise to exchange the pieces of paper for "lawful money" at any Federal Reserve Bank or at the United States Treasury; and lawful money, we found, consisted only of gold and silver coin.*

Let us look now at *government paper money* as distinct from central bank promises. It consists of so-called Gold Certificates (of which, at the end of 1936, there were only $95 million outside the Treasury and the Federal Reserve Banks); and so-called Silver Certificates, of which there were $1057 millions outside the Federal Reserve Banks and the Treasury; and $289 millions of United States notes, the famous "greenbacks."

Examine first one of the dollar-bills called a Silver Certificate. Read what it says: "This certifies that there is on deposit in the Treasury of the United States of America one dollar in silver payable to the bearer on demand."

The Mad Hatter might say to Alice, reading this: "That's very interesting. But why does the government certify this? What's the difference to me or to anybody else whether one dollar in silver is on deposit in the Treasury of the United States?" And a good question, too. The dollar in silver is payable on demand; there is the government's clear promise to that effect. But if you went and obtained this bit of metal called "a silver dollar," you would find, in an experiment similar to the one you carried on with pennies, that it contained *far less silver* than you could buy in bullion for the one-dollar in paper. This piece of paper tells about the putting aside of the silver. But the information is senseless without the other bit of

* On December 31, 1936, there were $4,233,000,000 of these central bank promises in circulation. They were carrying on by far the bulk of the small exchanging that falls upon our so-called "currency" to perform. They are primarily central bank promises and should be distinguished from the government promises. In the same category are the national bank notes, of which on the above date, there were $307,000,000 in circulation. On the same date, there were only $517 millions of coins, including silver dollars, in circulation, and about $1,442 millions of straight government paper money, in which our central banks were *not* involved.

278

information we already have: namely, that the Secretary of the Treasury is directed (though he is at present absolved from doing so) to keep both the silver dollar and this piece of paper "on a parity" with gold coin. That is, on the presentation of the bit of paper, he must hand over the amount of gold specified—one thirty-fifth of an ounce. It is only because of this promise of the government—unknown to you though it may be—that the piece of paper can be exchanged by you for the goods you want, or for some service to be performed. It is *not* because of the promise, printed on the face of the paper, that a silver dollar is payable on demand.

This is also, of course, true of the "greenbacks" and the gold certificates. You are not supposed to have one of the latter, but let us say you have tempted fate and kept one as a curiosity. Read what it says: the same as the silver certificate. It merely certifies that gold coin, to a specified amount, has been deposited with the Secretary of the Treasury, and that it is "payable to the bearer on demand."

Now, all this seems quite academic and unimportant, until you look at some associated facts. While you as an individual are not allowed, at this moment, to own these gold certificates, we saw in our chapter on Central Banks *that the twelve Federal Reserve Banks of the nation are*. By act of Congress on March 9, 1933, all their gold was taken from them, and they were obliged to accept in return from the Secretary of the Treasury these pieces of paper called gold certificates. On December 30, 1936, we saw that the twelve Federal Reserve Banks of the country held $8,851,876,000 worth of these gold certificates. They were all pieces of paper, saying precisely the same thing as your illegally-held certificate says. What the Mad Hatter could ask of Alice about the silver certificate, he could ask the Governor of a Reserve Bank about the gold certificate. This great mass of paper lying in the vaults of our Federal Reserve Banks merely avers that about 15,800,000 pounds of gold (on December 30, 1936) were held in the United States Treasury. But the statement of this fact (by the gold certificates) has no meaning without the promise of the government to exchange each piece of paper for the amount of gold printed on its face.

Now, let us ask some simple-minded questions like the Mad Hatter, and not be ashamed in doing so.

Who owns the gold? The United States Government.

How did it come by the ownership? It seized it by force.

What did the Federal Reserve Banks get for the gold? The promises of the government, as evidenced by these gold certificates.

The gold certificates then are not real money, but only promises of the government to pay money? Exactly.

Is the promise being performed? Yes; any Reserve Bank, having to deliver gold abroad or to a jeweler for industrial purposes, or to a dentist to give you a golden smile, finds that the government will in fact give it one ounce of gold for every thirty-five dollars of gold certificates it hands to the government.

Is this the reason the gold certificates can be held, and circulate as "money"? There is no other reason.

They merely represent governments' economic promises.

So do the coins.

So do the silver certificates.

So do the central bank notes—of which, as we saw, the government is the guarantor.

In the last half of a deferred exchange, these promises prove invariably to be completed. Because of this invariability, too, we consider the *evidence of the promise*—the gold certificate or silver certificate or coin—"as good as gold." But when we say our government's paper and minor coins are "as good as gold," we should be profoundly aware of the metaphor in the statement. We are saying nothing but that these government promises, *with regard to gold*, are invariably performed. We may never forget that there is a promise of action; *and that gold must pass in the performance of the action!* We cannot—as so many of us are inclined to, including money pundits who should know better—dispense with the gold (or something else) and just use promises alone as our money.*

---

* I have seen columnists—and not only those who are trying to be funny—expatiating upon the apparent silliness of carrying our great stores of gold in the underground vaults of Fort Knox. A recent play in New York satirized the situation in a whole scene, in which, as the audience laughs itself in stitches,

For here in this field we come once more upon the bedrock fact we have met everywhere in these soundings into our society. As in every other deferred exchange, *the performance of the last half of the exchange is the principal thing that counts.* Some *thing* must pass in the last half of the exchange. It is true that, with governments and banks, another promise may be—and often is—accepted as the last half of the exchange. But only if that promise itself is expected later to eventuate in a tangible form of wealth.

These particular economic promises that are now called "money" can be deferred a long time. They can pass around among many people, each one of whom believes them and therefore does not ask to have them performed. But soon or late, in the ordinary course of a nation's business, they are presented to the government or central bank to be performed. If the half-exchange then is not completed— or if the slightest question arises as to the ultimate completion of all these outstanding promises—the most serious economic consequences ensue. For all other economic promises are dependent for fulfillment upon them.

the President and his Cabinet bewilderingly try to fathom what difference it makes to move the gold from a hole in the ground in South Africa to another hole in the ground in Kentucky. Lying there, as they think, useless and untouched, these great stores of gold seem to constitute a very symbol of unintelligence at the heart of modern existence. If a local earthquake occurred, and the gold irrecoverably sank into the bowels of the earth, and the government then used its censorship powers to keep the knowledge hidden from the whole world, everything would purr along just as before. So they think! But should such a thing happen, pretty soon these wits would certainly be laughing, as citizens involved with all the rest of us, on the other side of their faces. We would have an "inflation" that would make the German experience seem, in comparison, like the fair days of "normalcy." But why? The principal fallacy that confuses these blithe commentators—a remarkable one, for all they need to do is to ask anybody in authority a simple question to discover it—is that *the gold lying in Fort Knox may have to be taken away at any moment.* Under normal circumstances, not a day goes by but demands, often measured by the million, are made upon the Treasury by the Federal Reserve Banks for the delivery of gold. In short, the government is continuously asked to fulfill its promises; *and it must do so, infallibly!* If it does not do so in a single trifling case, we shall see—in coming chapters—what would happen. When one reflects, it is not the fact that gold is lying in Fort Knox that represents a symbol of modern economic unintelligence; but this notion, that it is useless there, becomes indeed a tragic symbol of the profound and pernicious ignorance, about all the modern processes of human life, that prevails even among our otherwise most informed and intelligent citizens.

281

It may not be amiss to re-examine here precisely how this chain of government promises connects up with all other economic promises, and therefore how dependent all other promises are upon them.

We left the Federal Reserve Banks with about $9,000,000,000 worth of government promises to pay them gold whenever it was demanded. Formerly, the government allowed the Federal Reserve Banks to issue Federal Reserve notes *against the gold* they owned. For every dollar of gold the Federal Reserve Bank could issue $2.50 of Federal Reserve notes. Now that the government has seized their gold, it allows them to issue $2.50 of Federal Reserve notes against *every dollar of gold certificates they hold!*

But the gold certificates themselves are mere promises. Surely! So, the Federal Reserve notes are merely our central banks' promises, resting on our government promises.

Now, these Federal Reserve Bank notes are the paper "money" that is most commonly used in daily transactions. This is, principally, what you have always *called* money. These central bank promises can get you pleasant things to enjoy, and induce people to do disagreeable work for you. But only because—in the end—the government promises, on which they rest, are believed in and are fulfilled. For if the Federal Reserve Bank never could get the gold on the government's promise, its own promise to give real dollars to you (a promise in the last few years never asked to be fulfilled) would have to be incompleted.

This, however, is but a small part of the chain of promises linked to these particular government's promises. We saw that every member bank in the Federal Reserve System had deposited its "reserves" with its regional Federal Reserve Bank. We saw (Chapter Ten) that these "reserves" consist of nothing but "deposits" with the Federal Reserve Banks, and that these "deposits" are not money at all. *They are nothing but central bank promises.* Thus your corner bank—if it is a Federal Reserve member—has the promise of its regional Federal Reserve Bank to pay it a certain amount of real dollars. But we saw what real dollars were. According to the law, a dollar is one thirty-fifth of an ounce of gold, and nothing else. Now it transpires,

282

from the foregoing analysis, *that the Federal Reserve Bank has no real dollars.* It only has the promises of the government.

But beyond this, we saw (in Chapter Nine) that bank "deposits" themselves were used as money in our society. But these too, our analysis showed, were not "deposits" of anything valuable, like gold coin. They are simply, stripped to their reality, bankers' promises to pay us all real money. Property and labor are freely exchanged for these bank promises, and on June 30, 1936, they totaled $51,000,-000,000. This was the total of all bank deposits in the United States on that date. These bankers' promises to pay us money rest, as we saw, on their "reserves." What now do we find their "reserves" to be? Real dollars? Not at all. They are nothing but central bank promises resting on the central banks' "reserves." And what are the central banks' "reserves"? *Nothing but government promises to pay real dollars.*

There is the broad but exact picture of our money-structure. When we come to analyze the facts which the words hide, we find that *everything in common use as money in modern society consists of promises that have been made in deferred exchanges.*

The minor coins are government promises to pay gold.

The paper money is either government or central bank promises to pay gold.

The "reserves" of the banks consist of central bank promises to pay gold.

And our "money in the bank," which we transfer to one another by check, consists of not a thing but bank promises to pay gold, which rest upon central bank promises, which rest again upon government promises.

The real dollars are used, oh yes! But seldom by any citizen, no matter how wealthy. And they must be there! For if they are not, and if—every time a bank has to acquire gold for any economic necessity—the government's promise is not fulfilled, down to the last grain of gold demanded—disaster befalls!

You can initiate that disaster by deciding to have a new set of gold teeth. Your little dentist might estimate he needed two-thirds of an

283

ounce of gold for it. *His request for this would travel down this chain of promissory relationships* until it became necessary, as a consequence of it, for a Federal Reserve Bank to present a twenty-dollar gold certificate to the United States Treasury. If that portion of an ounce of gold were not immediately forthcoming from the Treasury upon presentation of the piece of paper, *this whole vast interdependent structure of promises would shake to its foundation.* Few people, among the two billion members of the race, would remain unaffected. In the next chapter, we shall look more closely into what ordinarily causes such events.

One sometimes sees subsidiary coins and paper money referred to as "token money," as "representative money," and sometimes as "fiduciary money," to distinguish them from gold, which is real money. The promise involved is implied by these three terms. Aside from the fact that the terms are far from being in common use, they hardly reveal to the average citizen the true nature of these present universal media of exchange. Far better would it be if in common usage they could be called "promised money." For that is what they really are, and nothing else. If we heard them so-called from our earliest childhood, we would at least be put on notice as to their essential nature. We would be more aware of the actualities of the role our government plays in them. We would not drop into the fallacy, with all its confusing consequences, of identifying *promises to pay money* and *money itself.*

For the ultimate explanation of this fallacy now finally becomes clear. It arises from the simple fact that *we use the same word* both for the promises to pay money and the money. Pennies, nickels, dimes, quarters, silver certificates, gold certificates, greenbacks, Federal Reserve notes—all of these we call "money." So, also, we used to call gold-coin money, when we saw it occasionally, and when we now conceive of it as lying in Treasury vaults. Under normal economic circumstances, they are all interchangeable. But we overlook entirely—few of us indeed ever know—the reason why they are interchangeable. *It is only because of the faithful performance of gov-*

284

ernment promises. Merely because they are interchangeable, we describe them, from our earliest days, *by the same word*. Little wonder is it that the average citizen comes to identify the promise, a few written words in our laws, with the thing. But less excusable is this confusion when it appears in the reasoning of money pundits, where it is common enough, and in government officials and self-appointed leaders of political affairs. There a fiduciary relation with the public, of the most vital character, exists; and by being, for the most part, completely unaware of it, these happy-go-lucky muddlers bring down upon us some of the severest economic ills from which we suffer.

This is particularly true of what is called "fiat money." Many citizens find it difficult to understand why fiat money is more dangerous than any other kind. Fiat money consists of paper promises, issued by governments, *without any backing of gold or silver coin*. In no other respect is it different from other government promised money. It consists of mere promises, as they do. But since there are no present resources in gold behind the money—only *speculative future resources* are being relied upon with which to meet the promises. True enough, the government can in the future seize enough wealth from its citizens to fulfill the promises represented by this fiat money. But such fiat money is dangerous, principally, because the issuer ordinarily does not seem to have any realization that all it is doing *is making promises eventually to pay gold*. But an added pernicious and dangerous feature of fiat money is that those who accept the promise also do not realize they are merely entering into a deferred exchange. The exchanges ultimately must be completed, *all of them*. Somebody who holds the second half of one of these exchanges will ultimately seek to have it completed—by the handing over of gold. If, then, the promisor issues so many of the promises —*as it is inclined to do, because the process is so easy, once it is begun*—that it is utterly impossible to complete all the half-exchanges, the most severe disruption of all the economic processes of the society occurs.

This issuance of "promised money" by governments, with no resources behind it at all, presents a phase of these hidden deferred exchanges of government which we must now examine with more precision. It is only adequately explained by the peculiar notions, which generally prevail, about the nature of the relation which exists between governments and real money. A clear insight into that relationship is commonly clouded by the other fallacy we have already noted: that governments have the power to create money.

15

Why Is Gold the World's Money?

THAT governments cannot create real money is apparent at once from an obvious fact: that gold is the money of practically every civilized nation on the earth and silver the money of the small remainder. Everything else used as money can be so used only because it consists, at one or more removes, of promises to give gold or silver upon presentation of the evidence of the promise.

Clearly, governments cannot create either the gold or silver which thus constitute the real money of their peoples. These metals must be mined. Labor, and other forms of wealth than the metals themselves, are necessarily used up in obtaining them. The government is under the necessity of acquiring possession of them, like everybody else.

It does so in five ways: (1.) By seizure in the form of taxes or fines for punishment. (2.) By selling privileges to its citizens, such as the right to vend peanuts, or to carry on business as a corporation. (3.) By exchanges of property which it owns—such as land. (4.) By itself mining gold. (5.) By borrowing, by issuing its promises to pay gold to those who have mined the gold or silver, or to those who have otherwise come into possession of it.

The first and second of these—seizure by taxes and the sale of privileges—is normally the principal means governments utilize to acquire the real money they need to carry on their operations.

The third, the sale of property, is only an occasional resource. So, also, is the fourth—the mining of gold itself; only Russia now does

287

this on any appreciable scale, since it alone as a government owns valuable gold mines.

But the last means, borrowing from citizens, in modern times is always depended upon, and in abnormal situations *it becomes by far the principal reliance of governments* in acquiring real money.

Although governments cannot create, but like everybody else must acquire, real money from its original owners, this is plainly not true of what we have referred to as "promised money." This latter they do indeed create in abundance. It is apparent, then, that the almost ineradicable notion that governments can create money is linked with the fallacious identification of promises to pay money and money itself. This is why we referred to it, in the previous chapter, as the Siamese twin of that first fallacy.

But is it not true, it may be asked, that governments can create real money—in the sense that they can designate what the money of the community shall be? In determining that gold or silver or some other metal—or something insubstantial—shall be the money of their citizens, they certainly seem to play a dominating role in the creation of the money of the community, in this limited but highly important sense. Our own Congress, under the Constitution, most certainly has the power, by a mere majority vote, with the approval of the President, to dethrone gold tomorrow as our money, and decree that silver or lead or tin or a manufactured compound, or something completely insubstantial like a labor certificate, shall be the money of this sovereign people. The same thing is true of every parliament and every dictator.

We are in the presence here, in my opinion, of almost the trickiest set of phenomena in the realm of economics. They constitute a quicksand in which individuals, from time immemorial, have become bogged and then lost, *spurlos versenkt*, in reasoning about money.

What actually happens in such cases, to generalize, is that the ruling group, designating the money of the community, is merely registering the prevailing will of the people. If, as frequently happens in the historical records, *the action does not so register the prevailing will*, these laws, designating the money of the people, speedily

288

become dead-letter laws, no matter how injurious it may prove to be for the government.

A present example of this clash between the power assumed and exercised by governments, and the greater power resident in the whole community, are the Sunday blue-laws still on the statute books of so many of our States. Another example, fresh in the memory of this particular generation, was our national experience with the Prohibition Amendment, the enforcement of which was utterly hopeless. Not only our present body of law, but all past legal history, is full of innumerable instances where rulers have attempted to exercise control of citizens, and found themselves completely blocked against the superior power of the people as a whole, exercising their will in their own devious but sure ways.

This has been particularly true of all moneys throughout history. It is so infallibly the case that the demonstration of it has been put into the category of an economic law—one of the rare ones, incidentally, that has never been questioned by any school of economists. It goes under the cognomen of Gresham's Law.

Sir Thomas Gresham was asked by the puzzled and worried Queen Elizabeth why it was that, as soon as she minted good gold or silver coins, they at once disappeared from circulation; only debased coins remained in evidence in ordinary commercial transactions. He explained that poor money always drove good money out of circulation. But there seems something paradoxical in this, to us, as it did to good Queen Bess. Why should not citizens prefer and demand a newly minted coin of gold or silver, and refuse to accept a debased coin masquerading under the same nominal value?

The truth is that all those who are alert to what money is—a fixed weight of gold or silver, of a specified quality—*do* actually prefer the good coin. They prefer it so much that, once they get their fingers upon it, they hold it and will only relinquish it when they can be sure to get full value for it in other goods. On the other hand, when they receive coins which—by counterfeit, or by rulers' chicanery, or by mere decree—are supposed to have the same weight, same quality, and therefore the same value as the good coin, but do not actually have it, they quickly pass it on to anybody they can find who will accept it at its face value.* They keep the good, and get rid of the questionable money. Accordingly, the less desired money remains in general circulation, *gradually deteriorating in the power to command other goods and service in exchanges*, as its true character becomes more and more widely recognized throughout the population. To appearances, the poor money is the money of the community, since it is in open use as the medium of exchanges in the community. But *sub rosa* the good coin, the preferred money, is the real money. It is so used in the more important economic transactions, by those who have the sense to know what real money is. That it is the real money is shown by the simple fact that *it is always the measure of value with which the poor money itself is compared.*

Rulers, absolute or democratic, can do nothing about this. By decree, by fines and punishment going even to the extremes of banishment, torture and death,† they attempt to. In vain! In the annals of monetary history, in every country, from the very earliest days, when governments presumed to interfere in this way with the daily

* An everyday example of this, with a foreign but not of course a debased money, is the experience almost all of us have had at one time or another, of carelessly accepting, let us say, a Canadian dime. It would be exceptional for anyone, under such circumstances, to take it to a bank and try to get American coin for it. What most of us at once try to do is to pass it on to somebody else, who, we hope, will be as careless as we have been. If there were more slot machines which took dimes, this would be easier than it is. One of the standing problems of slot machine owners is that they are the silent repositories of slugs, counterfeit and foreign coins. The interesting aspect of this, to the social philosopher, is that slot machines thus make it easy for Gresham's Law to operate in modern times *with regard to token money and counterfeits*. Gresham's Law operates, with modern paper money, through bankers and foreign merchants.

† One example of this in our own history was the attempt of the Continental Congress to make the ill-fated Continental Notes acceptable currency. Anybody who refused to accept them was legally to be regarded as an enemy and precluded from trade throughout the colonies. Another interesting instance, shortly afterward, was the even more determined effort in revolutionary France to make the *assignats* acceptable in French commerce. Those who would not accept them, in payment for goods or debt, were first subject to heavy fine. This penalty was soon changed to twenty years' imprisonment. Apparently ineffective, it was later changed to death and confiscation of all the criminal's property. In spite of these draconian measures, and of the additional fact that a handsome reward was offered for information as to breaking the law (the easiest possible information to obtain) the *assignats* continued to go their swift way to complete worthlessness and unacceptability.

economic swapping of their subjects, there are innumerable clear instances of the invariable operation of Gresham's Law.

The will of the people as to what their real money shall be is supreme. Governments, in presuming to designate what the money of any people shall be, *successfully exercise that power* only when the designation coincides with the genuine will of the people. The money so designated must fit in with all the settled economic habits of the society, of which they are the passing managers.

Unfortunately, we of this day and generation cannot easily recognize this truth, because of the extreme complexity of our economic organization. Apply it to gold, which is certainly the money of the modern civilized world, and it seems *on the surface* not to be true at all. We had occasion to observe in the previous chapter that few individuals ever even see gold coins. Modern men have now become so habituated to using government promises to pay gold that they have come, for the most part, to a curious state of complete unconsciousness that gold is the real money of their nation.

How, then, can it reasonably be stated that it is by the will of the people that gold remains our money? On the contrary, it seems very much the will of an unidentifiable power-wielding group, who underhandedly control the processes of government, and who are, in effect, the world's governors. Henry Ford's diabolic international bankers!

There is something genuinely puzzling here. We have said that gold is the money of most of the world, and that this is because most of the people of the world prefer it and will have no other money; that governments can do nothing about this preference, but merely conform to it in keeping gold as the money of their peoples. Yet—taking individuals by and large over the world by tens of millions—not one in a thousand, probably, would say that he gave a hoot whether gold or silver or any other metal was his money.

In the face of this apparent universal indifference, how can it be maintained that it is *by the final will of the people* that gold is our money?

The elements that confuse us in such a question—and it is far from

291

being academic, for there have been plenty of vehement individuals in recent years who regard gold as an economic anachronism—will appear with some clearness if we follow out a hypothetical set of events.

Suppose in this country, in a future election, we send into Congress a majority of gentlemen who are even more clearly economic morons than some whom we have seen there in recent years. In a burst of inspiration, to acquire "more money" for our needy government, and knowing that the populace is in actuality completely indifferent to gold, let us assume they legislate that hereafter a dollar shall constitute not one thirty-fifth of an ounce of gold, but instead one ounce of pure copper.

Why not? Copper is far more plentiful than gold. It has an ancient tradition as money. There is sound opinion, among some archaeologists, that it was the first metal used as money. Long before the imperial days of Rome, copper—in ingot form—was the common Roman money. It has been the money of many other peoples at different times. As a subsidiary "token money," it has been in the monetary systems of most States down to the present day. It is highly divisible, easily portable, a homogeneous substance. It has, indeed, all the material requisites a money should possess. Accordingly, there might well be some logic in our solons' reasoning: that since nobody really cares about gold, copper might just as well be our money. Since copper is so much more plentiful than gold, they might reason, we can issue an enormously increased number of dollar bills. Instead of keeping gold in our vaults to redeem these paper promises, it would be possible to have much larger stores of copper there. Since it is government and bank promises which are used principally as money, what is the difference if they be promises to give copper, instead of promises to give gold?

What, indeed, would be the difference?

What would happen, in the first place, would be an increase in what we call the "price" of all goods and services. Money is merely the commodity—it happens now to be gold, through long tradition —by which the exchangeable value of all other commodities and all services *is measured*. So much of each thing is exchangeable for so much gold by weight: that is what we call the "price" of any product. Let us say that copper sells at 10 cents a pound. This is merely our shorthand way of saying that *copper exchanges for gold in a ratio of 160 ounces of copper for one thirty-fifth of an ounce of gold*, one dollar. Let us say a certain fountain pen also exchanges for one thirty-fifth of an ounce of gold, one dollar. If then our solons *defined* a dollar as consisting of an ounce of copper, the "price" of the fountain pen would today simply be expressed by the terms of 160 dollars. A pencil now selling for a penny would, with this new copper-dollar, be priced at $1.60.

Let us make an additional assumption, that our law-makers were not wholly moronic, and decreed that all the innumerable half-exchanges uncompleted in this country should not be disturbed by their decision, but should be re-calculated and completed in the present ratio of copper to gold. For example, if a man had agreed to pay a present bill of $350—that is, to give ten ounces of coined gold at a later date—he should be required to give 56,000 of the new copper-dollars, 160 × $350.

The first effect, then, of such a change in our money would be simply an enormous rise in what we call prices. But if *all prices could rise proportionately*, this obviously would be of no great importance. What practical difference would there be, if we gave a retailer, for a fountain pen, a single bill printed with the words "One Hundred and Sixty Dollars" on it, instead of one printed with the words "One Dollar" on it?

Copper at present—it must be realized—exchanges *indirectly through gold*, in well-established ratios of weight or quantity, *with all other commodities and all men's services*. If copper were our money, and not gold, it would merely exchange *directly* for all other commodities and services. *Other things being equal*, it would exchange in the same ratio as at present. The only difference would be, since its ratio of exchange is different from that of gold, that the prices of all commodities and services would have to be *stated* in different and much larger figures. This might very quickly happen, and internally there would be no great trouble at all, caused by changing our money from gold to copper; *if* we had no commercial relations whatsoever with foreign countries which still retained gold as their money; and *if* all prices in the country rose proportionately at the same time!

But there's the rub. These "ifs" constitute an unimaginable condition. Ten thousand economic ties bind us indissolubly to all the rest of the world. An endless stream of goods and individuals enter into, and depart from, our shores; and this is true of every other nation. Even the most backward of them in economic organization, the poorest in wealth, has continual intercourse (though it is but a trickle of business, comparatively) with other persons over its national boundaries. All through the long history of man it has been true that trade knows no boundaries. In the past hundred years this economic intercourse of separate peoples has become more extensive, the economic ties more numerous and inextricable, than ever in the past. The notion that nations may become wholly self-sustaining, the idea of complete economic autarchy that has sprung up in the past twenty years because of the fear of war, is of the most illusory character. At best, as a national policy, it can be practicable only with regard to a few key products and manufactured articles; or, if more universally applied over the entire area of production, only for a comparatively short period of emergency. A few decades of peace in any era would crumble the system at once into desuetude. No people in the world, least of all one such as ourselves, who maintain a high standard of living and are forever engaged in bettering it, can become a modern hermit nation, barring ingress to foreigners and foreign products and egress to our citizens and our own goods.

Accordingly we would continue to trade over our boundaries. What, then, would happen if our basic money were changed from gold to copper, while a large number of the other important peoples of the world had gold as their money?

When we imported raw materials—or when our multitudinous travelers streamed abroad—*they would require gold* to pay for the articles they purchased, and for the good times they enjoyed. Copper would be our money by supposition, gold the foreigners' money. The latter want gold. How are our citizens to obtain it? Only by giving our own money for it. We should be obliged to proffer copper to the gold mining companies, or to those who owned existing stocks of gold. But, outside of our country, copper would be of use only for industrial purposes, not as money. The world's copper, the bulk of it, would accordingly descend in a thousand streams upon our shores, since foreigners would pay for our goods with copper. But, on the other hand, each foreigner in his own country would *accept* copper only up to the point where it would be marketable *there* for industrial purposes. The result would be that the existing world-wide ratio of exchange between copper and gold would change—to the advantage of gold. Each ounce of gold would bring more pounds of copper in exchange.

But all our other goods and services would also be measured in value by copper. In other words, an ounce of gold held by a foreigner would represent a claim, not only upon more of our copper, *but upon more of all our other goods and services.*

There is no need to try to follow here, in the imagination, the economic consequences that could ensue. They would be of the most far-reaching character, and there is not an individual in the land who would escape suffering from them. It is enough, for the particular point to be elucidated, that the deepest disruption of trade, of our present high standard of living, of the occupations of tens of millions of our citizens, would result—if copper were, by governmental action, decreed to be our money, while gold remained the money of the rest of the modern world.

Now, if one analyzes this set of facts—and don't be much bothered if you can't follow them all without a strain on the attention—it is simply to say that there is a basic quality missing from copper as a money, which our legislators would have ignored. It would have all the physical attributes of a money which we identified as being necessary. It does not, however, possess that most necessary of all attributes of a money—universal acceptability in exchanges. *For no people but our own would accept it as money!* Not unless, practi-

295

cally contemporaneous with our own change, a predominating number of other peoples of the world carrying on international exchanges *underwent a like alteration in their money*, could such a change be carried out, without the most deep-going change in the occupations of our citizens and without long-continuing economic disorder.

We can begin, then, to discern the underlying reason why—although most of the individuals in every nation are completely indifferent to gold as their money—no nation can arbitrarily now change its money from gold to something else. *It is because human society is now organized, from an economic point of view, on an international basis.*

Economic relations always have ignored mere boundaries. Today this is truer than it has ever been in the past. We are all, in the modern nations—patriotic and chauvinistic as we may be, politically—an indissoluble part of a world society. *And gold is the prevailing money of this economic world society!* How it has become so and why it remains so is one set of complex historical and psychological phenomena. That it is so is quite another set. And no government, with a supposititious sovereign power over a particular group in this world society, can now change this money arbitrarily. For that change would conflict with the prevailing will of the entire economic society, which knows no territorial boundaries. No more can it do so, without disastrous consequences to itself, than a single community in a given nation can set up and maintain a different money from all the other communities in that nation.

We are in a position here to answer a puzzling question that is often asked: "Why is gold our money?" A more informed question, the foregoing analysis indicates, would be, "Why is gold the whole world's money?"

The question really has two aspects. The reasons this particular *substance* is our money are historical and psychological. Through the processes we examined in the last chapter it has *become* the money of this economic world society; and now the necessities of international trade keep it in that predominance. *There is nothing in*

296

the world salable that cannot be exchanged for gold, and of no other substance is this now true. Silver is the only commodity which even remotely approaches this immediate universal exchangeability. That universal exchangeability in turn—as we saw—makes it the money of each unit nation in the immense earth-wide trading whole.

But there is an *arrière-pensée* in those who ordinarily ask this question. What they frequently have in mind is—not why gold, the substance, is our money, but *why cannot something insubstantial* be money, instead of gold or some other substance?

There are few theoretical questions more difficult to answer satisfactorily, for the reason that the simplest facts about our society must first always be clarified to the questioner. We would be carried far afield if we discussed this moot question of monetary theory here, but one aspect of it is clearly within our present sphere of inquiry. For my own belief is that the confusion about our social mechanism, which prompts this question, can usually be traced back (as so much other trouble can be) to that pernicious mental tendency uncovered in the last chapter: our universal failure to distinguish between promises to pay money and real money. All our lives (my notion is, on this point) we actually *use* insubstantialities as money, mere pieces of paper promising money. How natural it is ultimately, in reasoning that is not too meticulous, to assume that the *substance promised* can *always* be dispensed with, and that therefore a complete insubstantiality may be money; such as a labor certificate, for example, testifying to all and sundry that the holder has done one hour's faithful work.

Let us, for brief illustrative purposes, consider one aspect only of the possible use of labor certificates as money. Those who in theory advocate this, and they are ordinarily the most violent objectors to the use of gold as money, clearly overlook the simplest fact about labor certificates: *that the economic promises of governments would be even more involved with them than with gold.* A labor certificate would merely aver that an hour's honest work had been done—"socially necessary work," I think the Marxian phrase is; for, of course, Marxists are among those who regard gold as an "economic anachronism." Let's leave out of account how it could be determined *what kind of human effort* is the "socially necessary work" an hour of which is to become the unit measuring the value of all goods and all services. Quite aside from such difficulty, which conceivably might be transcended, the mere stark question remains —what good is the certificate, what pragmatic value would such a piece of paper possess, to the holder? A gold certificate likewise certifies, plainly, that so much gold is held by the government. But this mere interesting statement is of no consequence, to the holder of the certificate, unless the gold is given up by the government on presentation of the certificate; *unless, in short, an economic promise of the government is fulfilled.*

Labor certificates would constitute precisely the same sort of economic promise! It could constitute no other kind. *A specified amount of goods would have to be given or guaranteed by the government*, to be relinquished somehow or somewhere for the certificate. Perhaps, instead of gold, the government would promise to give in exchange for the intrinsically worthless piece of paper, an agreed amount of wheat, cotton cloth, milk, what-you-will. But here we are saying that the government *would be measuring the hour's labor by goods*. In other words, at bottom, it would not be the *insubstantiality* (the hour's labor) that constituted the unit of money. The reverse would be true; *a stated quantity of usable and exchangeable things* would be measuring the value of an hour's labor. But this is precisely how our present "promised money" is measured—by an agreed quantity of gold! There would thus be no difference, except that in the case of labor certificates the involvement of the government would perhaps be deeper than with gold.

It is the recognition of this latter phase of all money, I think, which explains the apparently cynical dictum you may have occasionally heard from money analysts: *that gold is the world's money because governments can't be trusted*. This, of course, would be true of any substance other than gold that might have become, or may still become, the world's money. It simply has in mind that *the*

298

present insubstantialities that are used as money (the paper promises of governments and central banks) are still very much "promised money" to the knowing. Until that halcyon day when every government economic promise, without exception, will infallibly be fulfilled, the *knowing* traders—and it is they who, by their actions, lead the vast mass of *unthinking* traders who constitute most of the world's population—prefer to have their real money *a thing which they can see and touch.*

These generalities may all read like cold classical theory, and there are many "managed currency" pundits—not necessarily Marxian—whom I can imagine dubbing it so. It is instructive, therefore, to place it, for comparison, beside the living detail of experience. The short history of money in Soviet Russia provides an excellent opportunity to do so.

Certainly no modern government—and few in all history—has exercised so great a measure of control over the activities of its citizens. Moreover, Marxian theory clearly calls for a money based upon "labor-time." Accordingly, we find that Soviet theorists, in the beginning of the Revolution, believed they could dispense with a "hard money." Indeed, they thought they could dispense with money, in our usual sense, altogether. For a short chaotic period they attempted to build up a system of distribution of goods, based upon ration cards.

But "a government which pays its employees in labor vouchers must provide the relative goods and services *to redeem the vouchers* [italics mine] if not immediately, at any rate within a very short lapse of time, otherwise it will openly default against its employees . . . they would be kept at work only by the alternative of a greater degree of starvation if they refused to work." *

In other words, these most vital deferred exchanges of labor for money *have to be completed as to the second half,* even by a government as ruthless and seemingly all-powerful as the Soviet dictatorship. How could they be completed as to the second half, except by

* *Soviet Money and Finance*, L. E. Hubbard.

the transfer of some goods to be enjoyed? Thus the labor vouchers themselves had to be *measured as to value* by some thing, for which all other things and services in the society could be exchanged.

As this obdurate fact became clear, the Soviet realists, led by Lenin, executed a complete *volte face* in theory, and they did so with little delay. At one of the first important conferences of the Communist Party, after the initial chaos of the forcible Revolution had spent itself—the conference held in December, 1921—it was resolved "that the restoration of a currency based on a metallic cover was the first step toward reconstructing a market."

A metallic cover! This is simply modern financial obscurantism for saying that *a metal is that particular people's money*, as it has been with most nations since prehistoric days; and if any government *promises* are to circulate successfully as money, the metal must be given without fail *in the last half of the deferred exchange*.

The Bolsheviks had destroyed the old Czarist ruble (in ways we shall later examine). This old ruble had been so much gold, by weight. To fit in with the old habit of thought of the society, they wisely called the new money a "ruble"; and then they proceeded to make the new ruble—not a specified amount of labor-time—*but a specified amount of gold;* just like the old ruble, and just like every other important nation in the world, except the Chinese!

Why gold? Here was a supposedly supreme governing power that could certainly have made the money of its people anything. The answer, as our preceding analysis shows, is that money must be a substance in order to measure the value of the goods and services being exchanged; for a government's "promised money" cannot get circulated unless its promises can be and are fulfilled with the transfer of a real form of wealth in the last half of the deferred exchange. Since, then, money must be a substance, it was advantageous for the political managers of Russia that it be gold. For if the Soviet Government wanted to carry on exchanges with all the rest of the world, it was best for it to use the money all the rest of the world uses— gold. To have become a completely closed economy was impossible. Soviet Russia was not so from its first days, and it has become a more and more important part of the whole world economy, through increasing trade, as the years have gone on. On the other hand, had it made its money any other substance than gold, it would have met the same sort of difficulties we analyzed in the preceding pages, where we considered what would happen if the United States, as a nation, changed its money from gold to copper.

Thus, theory was thrown ruthlessly out of the window, upon the realization, by the managers of the Soviet State, of these basic social facts.

The limitations which natural social processes place immutably upon theory have seldom been more clearly demonstrated.

In summary, we can see that what we have really exposed here is a startling fact about the modern world that is seldom realized, though its full consequences are borne unknowingly by all the people of the world. *The sovereignty of individual peoples over their own lives is no longer complete.* It is limited—in this important matter of money, at least—by a supremer will: that of all the people in the trading nations of the world who carry on exchanges of property and service with one another. That modern supreme popular will, of course, is not as yet organized politically. It now makes its power felt in devious and unorganized fashion. But immemorially— the historian at least recognizes!—that has been the way the supreme will of the people, in past smaller segregated societies, has always made itself manifest, and particularly with regard to money. Not officially, with pomp and circumstance, but in subtle, daily, deadly, individual action!

16

The True Relation of Governments to Money and What the Record Shows about Three Thousand Years of Fraud

WE HAVE seen that it is impossible for governments to create money; and that even their theoretical power to designate what the money of their people shall be is greatly limited, since it cannot be exercised arbitrarily. Yet the relation of governments to money remains of the closest character. Governments now hold most of the real money of the world. The gold in the vaults of governments—and of central banks, where it can be seized at any time by governments—amounted to about $24,000,000,000 at the end of 1937; this was about 43,000,000 pounds of gold.* Government and bank promises to pay this gold circulate among the people as "promised money." Since modern governments continue to hold the confidence, for the most part, of their own (occasionally bewildered) citizens, the result is that government control over money seems to be all but supreme in the modern world.

All but! In a mere moment, from a long historical point of view, any government can swiftly be divested of this seeming control—by losing the basic confidence of its citizens. This is an eventuality often dangerously unrecognized, particularly by the important personages in government who are so stupid as to be blinded by their apparent power. There have been plenty of instances of this happening in the past two decades (to say nothing of preceding eras) and they are always highly revealing as to the true relationship that exists between governments and money.

* *Federal Reserve Bulletin*, December, 1937; the figure is as of September 30, 1937.

At bottom that relationship is one of interference by rulers and ruling cliques in the economic activities of their citizens. This interference can be both socially beneficent and harmful. Most often it has been harmful, brutally so, but that is only because of the economic unwisdom of rulers. Again we must go harking back to history, if we want to see the nature of our modern problems with clarity and in perspective.

Originally, the role of the State in the field of money was beneficent to a high degree. *It made possible a limitless increase in the number of exchanges of property*. It gave an enormous impetus to specialization in occupation. Shrouded in the past as this first interference was, it is quite possible to see how it came about, and what its economic consequences were.

In our highly sketchy history of Money two chapters ago, we saw how natural moneys always evolved independently of that form of centralized power, which we conceive of as government. Each family, each roving clan, prehistorically formed a sort of trading unit. Barter ruled, when any exchanges at all took place among these units; and for long eras barter was the method of exchange. The oldest records we have, almost necessarily, are of communities stably organized, with marked specialization of occupation among the people, and with the society pretty well out of the barter stage. A money, we find, *has already developed in it*. But it is always a people's money, a natural money; it is a money in which the ruling clique plays no role. It is cowry shells, or wampum beads, or a cow, a sheep, skins or furs, a knife, a weight of wheat, or any one of the hundreds of things of the types we examined. For untold millennia, our billions of ancestors passed what they considered their money from hand to hand, from ownership to ownership, without the intrusion of their rulers into these separate exchanges; at least, so far as the money was concerned.

As society developed in skills, and metals came to be mined, so necessary in the making of all sorts of new implements, we saw that fixed weights of metal—copper, iron, bronze, silver and gold—superseded other older forms of money, among the more civilized areas

303

of men. Coming down to the earliest records we have, in Egypt, Crete, Babylonia, Assyria, Greece, Rome, we always find iron, copper, bronze, silver and gold. They were passed around, chiefly, in the form of ingots, or bars. So many pounds of iron, copper, bronze, silver, or so many ounces of gold, would be given for whatever was being acquired.

Two things were, obviously, highly important in such exchanges of property. First, reliable scales. Second, certainty as to the purity of the metal being passed in exchange.

The scales were more easily provided than the certainty about quality. They were an early human invention. Representations of them, and of men using them, can be found among the earliest pictures of the Egyptians at least 5,000 years ago. Standard weights also have been found of the greatest antiquity. Every ancient civilization had scales and weights. No one who ever exchanged property could be without them, and of course everybody carried on some exchanges. The natural way to effectuate exchanges was to consider either how many for how many should be given; or how much for how much; that is, the exchanges were governed either by number or by weight. Is this primitive? We still do it. In all the multitudinous exchanges of actual property that go on among men, *weight is the prime consideration* on one side or the other of the exchange —or both! The measure of the money that passes *is always a weight of gold*, and frequently also of the goods. Yet in not one of ten thousand of these transactions do scales ever appear. But that is merely another interesting demonstration of the degree to which men have come to trust one another's honesty. They *assume* that the weight of goods or of money being passed is what it is supposed to be.

Our prehistoric ancestors—yes, and 'way down into historic times —could assume no such thing. Scales were necessary in every exchange, and the fascinating fact to the modern man is that these ancient traders were quite as much, if not more, interested *in weighing the money*, the metal, as the goods.

"We should find it extremely troublesome," says Adam Smith,

"if every time a poor man had occasion to buy or sell a farthing's worth of goods, he was obliged to weigh the farthing." Yet this is precisely what went on in ancient trading, before there was coined money. Scales were principally needed *to weigh the money* which passed on one side of the exchange—since it consisted of nothing but a weight of metal. This continued for long, long centuries. For a good reason, which we shall soon see, it was the money that was always weighed—down to comparatively recent times. Down to the present day, indeed, real money, gold taken in exchanges, is still weighed. But the weighing is no longer done by the common man—which was true of the ancient trader—but solely by banks and by governments.

But if, originally, the *proper amount of metal* being received was an important consideration in an exchange, the purity of the metal being passed was not a whit less important. It could be, and it was, adulterated with baser ingredients. Plainly, uncertainty as to the amount of metal—of gold and silver, in particular—being given or received in an exchange must have constituted a heavy drag and obstacle to ancient exchanges. It would both slow them up, and would make many of them impossible, wherever (and this is important) there was ground for suspicion of the honesty of one of the exchangers.

The original emergence of coined money only dates back, so far as records can be found, to less than three thousand years ago. It originated, the consensus seems to be, in Lydia in Asia Minor. For at least as many thousands of years prior to that, there is no indication—in any of the older civilizations whose dust has been removed for us by archaeologists—of any coined money. Equally interesting is the fact that what may be called the coinage of money almost certainly did not originate with organized communities—that is, with governments. It originated, most probably, with merchants; and most of this was trading with foreigners. These merchants would stamp upon a fixed quantity of copper or bronze or other metal their own seal—*as a guarantee of its quality*. It was exactly like the trademark of an honest production-concern: anyone seeing

305

it knows at once that the quality of the goods is unimpeachable. Many of these ingots have been found. Any trader receiving this ingot, and recognizing the seal, could thus be assured of its quality. He did not have to be assured of its weight, so long as he had a pair of scales.

But ingots and bars—particularly of gold and silver—could only be utilized in large exchanges of property. How about small exchanges, where property of no great value passed? These were effectuated by cuttings from ingots and bars, those small amorphous pieces of metal that have been found so abundantly over the sites of the ancient world. In addition, with gold, silver and electrum, there were "drops" of metal which were allowed to cool. These were, however, *of an even weight*. These "drops" of metal seem almost certainly to have been the antecedents to coined money, and undoubtedly passed from ownership to ownership for several hundred years before coined money appeared.

What finally happened was that, probably first in Lydia—just as they had done with large ingots—merchants began to see an advantage in stamping these small drops of metal with their private seal. The metal thus stamped was first electrum, a mixture of gold and silver. These first coins were, as Sir Arthur Evans says, "simply blobs of metal dumped down on to a rough striated surface—to prevent them from slipping—and allowed to cool, *and rudely stamped on the bossed upper surface before it had cooled.*" [Italics mine.] It was this stamp, this seal, that constituted the guarantee of quality; and it was this simple change—as we shall see—that inaugurated modern civilization, with all its money problems. It was a development "no less momentous, in its sphere than, in another, was the advance made by the printing press on manuscripts." * *For here was the beginning of coined money*, and of the interference of rulers with men's natural moneys.

Gyges, King of Lydia, is often credited with being the first to issue coined money, sometime between 600 and 700 B. C. Whether

* *Cambridge Ancient History, Volume IV: Coinage from Its Origin to the Persian Wars;* by G. F. Hill.

he was or not, he may best be regarded as more a merchant than a king. For like a Medici in later days, he undoubtedly carried on extensive trading operations up and down the coast of Asia Minor and with Greece. These first Lydian coins, whether of Gyges or of other merchants, were at first only electrum. The seal on them turned out to be a reliable guarantee of the weight. But men found, by what tests they could apply, that the amount of gold or silver in them varied greatly. Thus one of the double objects of the seal, to inspire confidence in the *quality* of what was being passed in exchange, was undermined. It was a later king and great merchant of Lydia, Croesus, who guaranteed *both quality and quantity* by issuing, separately, pure gold and pure silver coins. His name has come down to us as almost synonymous with wealth. It is worth while speculating whether his prosperity was not a mere natural result of the integrity he thus manifested. Men found they could carry on exchanges of property with him and not be cheated in what they expected to receive. The gold or silver they received was indeed such, and of the weight his seal guaranteed it to be. Therefore, *the volume of exchanges with him would multiply*, and his wealth with it.

For we can see at once the deep import of this apparently slight change that an honest merchant's stamp upon a piece of precious metal constituted. If the stamp could be relied upon, no scales were necessary. More important, the recipient *could always be sure he was getting* what the other fellow said he was getting. "Before the institution of coined money," writes Adam Smith, "unless they went through this tedious and difficult operation (of weighing and assaying) people must always have been liable to the grossest frauds and impositions, and instead of a pound weight of pure silver, or pure copper, might receive in exchange for their goods an adulterated composition of the coarsest and cheapest materials, which had however in their outward appearance been made to resemble those metals."

Such was the origin of coinage and it remains to this day, unchanged through all the centuries, the essential characteristic of *coined money*. Coinage represents merely a stamp placed upon a fixed quantity of money by a government, guaranteeing to who-ever is concerned—and everybody ought to be, though few are—that the metal is of a stated quality and weight.*

Needless to say, this official stamp upon money, placed there first by merchants and later by rulers, had to be proved by analysis to be what it was guaranteed to be, before it could demonstrate its value as a social invention. Endless weighings, the most careful tests devisable, must have been applied to these original coined moneys—in order to discover whether the issuer really could be relied upon, before they would be accepted without analysis; before, in short, the mere sight of the stamp upon the coin came completely to be relied upon. When, however, this did finally happen, *coined money freed all exchanges, where it was used, from the suspicion of possible dishonesty.*

There is the *raison d'étre* and the true social function of coined money, and of government's relation to money.

As soon as this happened, an enormous expansion of exchanges must thereupon have followed; and with it a more refined specializa-tion of occupation among individuals, and an accelerating develop-ment of all the arts of civilization. It is not mere chance that we wit-ness, at this crucial moment in history, the emergence of the peculiar Greek civilization. For every one of the Greek city-states quickly adopted this social invention of their kinsmen in Asia Minor.

Thus, at the dawn of modern society, we come once more upon our simple loose end of truth. As a relic upon the face of money itself there is stamped the eternal legend that men cannot carry on a successful society without confidence in one another's honesty.

Observe, now, what has happened up to this point, where rulers begin to have a special relationship to money, a relationship which was new in the world. The money of the peoples remained the same. It had not changed. It was still gold and silver and copper and bronze. Instead of being in ingots and bars, however—or *skillings* of them, or blobs of them—the metal was stamped. That was all. A sim-

* This is no longer true of "token" money—that is, subsidiary coins. In this case, the stamp is now merely the evidence of a government's promise to pay real money on demand, as analyzed in Chapter Fourteen.

ple change! Rulers did not decide, out of their will or whim, that a particular metal should be the community's money. Even less did they create the money, bring it into existence. It was the common people, your ancestors and mine, who by their will and desire made their money what it was. The ruler's stamp merely guaranteed that the weight and quality of a given piece of metal was what it was said to be. Again we must point out *that this remains as true today as it was when the first Lydian coin was struck.* The ultimate relationship of the ruler to the money is the same now as it was then.

Unfortunately, this first beneficent interference of the State with money may almost be said to have been its last. A psychological development inevitably occurred, pregnant with the most evil consequences. As long years would pass in a community; as citizens would more and more, by usage and habit, come to have unquestioning confidence in the guarantee of quality and weight represented by the stamp on the money, both rulers and ruled *would fatefully forget what the stamp on the metal represented.* Because their name was on the money, rulers—in particular—would come to think that not the people, but they, created the money. Or, even if they remembered what the stamp really signified socially, the temptation of needy rulers would become too great for their morals. They would succumb to the euphemistic thievery known as "debasing" coins and "clipping" coins.

These practices are so much a matter of the past that few among us today know what they are. Yet they constituted—before rulers discovered the beautiful device of paper money—the chief problems men had with money for at least twenty-five hundred years. The practices were simple enough. As their old coins were received by them in taxes, the rulers would clip a little of the gold or silver from the edges, not enough to interfere with the stamp. Or they would abrade a new gold or silver coin, and acquire a little more pure gold or silver in this fashion; this is called "sweating." With the metal acquired in these two ways, they would mint new coins. Or as new bullion was acquired and minted into coins, *they would put in less gold or silver or copper than before,* of course always attempting to

309

keep the new coin unchanged, in outward appearance, from the old.

All these practices, in a sense, may be counted as forms of counterfeiting *indulged in by the rulers themselves.* Without doubt, rulers learned these neat tricks, for ordinarily they are not very bright, from sharpers who (at any rate, so far as clipping and sweating coins were concerned) found it an easy way to prosper. We who think governments have everything to do with money little realize how frequently in the past adventurous individuals presumed to engage, in whatever way they could, in its manufacture. Counterfeiting today is perilous and occasional. Not so in the past. As recently, for example, as the eighteen-sixties in our country, when bank notes were common as money, at one time, on good authority, there were no fewer than five thousand counterfeit issues circulating, alongside of the genuine bank notes. It must be said that a good many of the bank notes, so far as value was concerned, later proved no better than the counterfeits.

To go back to more ancient days, in this practice of "clipping" and "debasing" coins, no doubt there was often rationalization that blinded the rulers to the essential dishonesty involved. The original purpose of the stamp—that it was a guarantee of quality and weight, a mere economic service to citizens to facilitate exchanges of property—was undoubtedly soon obscured by long usage, in ancient times as well as in our own. Nevertheless, wherever these practices of debasing coins were indulged in by a ruler, the original function of the stamp would speedily reappear in its pristine importance. The clipped or debased coins—by those who were alert, and particularly by those who were engaged in foreign trading—were not so readily accepted as the previous ones that men had found to be honest. The ruler found, sadly, that he had not created more gold or silver, but merely more coins. To those who knew what both his old and new coins were really worth (that is, how much weight of gold or silver or copper was really *in them,* and that could be always discovered by weighing and assaying) he had to give more coins for anything he wanted to obtain. In our shorthand economic terms, we would

310

say that prices rose on him in his own currency. He was only better off during the short period he could keep the fraud secret.

It might be imagined that, with the acquisition of experience, wise rulers would have appeared, clear-eyed enough to see how the society of men really operated, and to realize both the fatuity and the deep-going economic disturbances inherent in such practices. But the annals of money, for at least twenty-five hundred years, constitute a continuous progression in the debasement of coined money by rulers and ruling cliques. The Greek city-states, which were the first extensive users of coined money, were comparatively the most honest in their handling of it. There are a few, but not many, cases of deliberate debasement in their records. When we come to Rome, over the centuries of its rise, domination and decline as a world empire, there was a long saturnalia of recurrent debasement, which never ended, and has not ended today! From the time it was little more than a country Tiber town, almost every ruling clique that came into power, and later almost every Emperor, cheated a little, and then a little more, on its coined money. Money, says H. G. Wells, was then a comparatively new thing in the world—meaning, of course, coined money. The Romans, it seems clear, never really understood the nature of coined money; that is, they never clearly apprehended what the stamp on a coin in actuality represented. Those scholars present at least an arguable case, who attribute the ultimate ruin of this vast empire to the slow but inevitable economic results of this continuous confusion about money.

Following Rome, for two thousand years, the heads of principalities and States, large and small, continued the Roman tradition with coined money. It is a tradition still followed by all governments, though merely hidden under the complexities of our modern existence. At the time of Adam Smith, the English pound had come to represent a third, the Scotch pound a thirty-sixth, and the French one sixty-sixth of their original weights in precious metal. At the moment (something that Adam Smith would have found inconceivable) the weight of the English "pound"—which at the time of

Edward I was a true pound of silver of known fineness—is uncertain. All that is certain is that it will weigh less than it did in 1931. We choose England here—it must be said—as an example, only because its ruling clique is always so self-righteous. But our own beloved land would provide an equally good example. Indeed, debasement of money has been the rule in history, not the exception. *All governments have progressively cheated on coined money since the social invention first came into use.* It is the outstanding historical feature of the invention. The mere fact can be taken as a relic, which fortunately can never be obliterated, of the constitutional dishonesty of rulers.

In other words, for the three thousand years that coinage has been one of the prerogatives of the ruling power, with it—as a corollary—there has gone the royal right to cheat on coins, if cheating could be got away with. There seems to have been hardly a glimmer of understanding as to the true economic significance of the stamp on the coin; although time and time again, endlessly, that significance appeared. The economic agents through whom it was made plain were principally merchants engaging in foreign trade, and money-changers.

These latter have become to the common man, in his ignorance of history, a sort of human harpy. This is principally due, without doubt, to the legendary wrath of Jesus at finding them pursuing their prosaic business in the sacred precincts of the Temple in Jerusalem. It was anger at this defilement of a religious place, surely not at money-changing in itself, which principally aroused him. For almost certainly he, and every citizen of ancient communities, was obliged every now and then to make use of the peculiar economic service provided by these specialists. It was of the most vital character, and its explanation can be found primarily, not in any greed on the part of those who pursued it, but in the fraud and chicanery of rulers—upon whom the money-changers were in reality perpetually checking up.

Money in ancient times was not the easily and thoughtlessly accepted thing it is with us. Coined money—in every ancient trading

312

center—was the only form of money in use. The coins were legion. Every ruler, every little State, issued them; and counterfeiters added liberally to the mess. Moreover, there was no such chauvinism with regard to money as we see today. The moneys of all the principal trading peoples circulated side by side in each cosmopolitan center. The sole question was—*what is in them?* Is the coin good silver, good gold, good copper—and *how much* gold, silver, and copper is in it?

Without doubt every alert person, receiving these coins in exchanges, became to a degree acquainted with the principal coins that were circulating in his neighborhood. Ancient merchants, surely, on the whole, became so experienced, because their good or ill fortune depended upon this knowledge. But for strange coins the money-changer was the specialist who determined in the last analysis what a given coin was worth. He did so by offering locally acceptable coin for it. With the multiplicity of coins, and the justified uncertainty about them, the money-changer thus occupied a crucial position in the economic scheme. He was a conspicuous person in the business world of our ancestors up to within a few hundred years ago. His very presence in the Temple, the heart and center of ancient Jewish life, indicates his economic importance. He was equally evident and important in every other center where foreign trading, to any extent at all, was carried on. Rome, more cosmopolitan even than London and New York today, had its money-changers by the thousand. We see him ever-present in every business center and can trace his career, all down through the Middle Ages until, through his Italian variety, he evolves—into our dignified modern banker! Where, incidentally, he still carries on—as a side-issue, but by no means an unimportant one—his original function of exchanging the money of one nation for that of another. His technique now is merely more devious and more dignified.

Now, without question, among the olden money-changers, cheating was frequent enough, where it could be got away with. But imagine yourself, a freeborn Roman citizen, with a strange coin which had come into your possession, going to a money-changer to learn its real value. He chinks it on the bench before him, bites it if he is

313

not too dignified, weighs it, examines it minutely—and then offers you something far below your expectations! Is he honest, or is he taking advantage of your ignorance? There is no way for you to know, except by trying other money-changers. Yet it is easy to see how, under such circumstances, the reputation of money-changers, as a class, would become of the most dubious color. For they were continuously puncturing dreams of wealth with a little pin-thrust of reality. They were forever revealing to people how they had been duped—no pleasant office at any time, and one not likely to engender good-will. The truth, however, must be that—while fraud no doubt was often engaged in—it could not possibly have been a prevailing practice among money-changers, if for no other reason than because of the intense competition. If you suspected what one money-changer told you about the worth of a coin unknown to you, you simply went on to the next one. Just as today you will see American travelers in Europe hasten to the bank which is giving a minute amount more, in the nation's currency, for a dollar bill. Certainly, it was by no chance, but could only have been by experience of men with them, that finally money-changers became so trusted that they evolved into bankers, with whom men left their all in safe-keeping—rather than trust it on their own premises.

In the meantime, the men of this calling, even the name of which is now so foolishly despised, were performing the most vital economic service to their fellows. Ceaselessly, as part of their day's work, they were engaged in uncovering the fraud and chicanery of rulers, and rendering it (so to speak) impotent.

What the economics student will be delighted to distinguish is that the money-changers, and with them the merchants engaged in foreign trade, were the media through whom Gresham's Law a thousand times was brought into inevitable operation, in a vain attempt to teach rulers a lesson they never learned—that they had to be as honest about coined money, whether their name was on the money or not, as individuals normally are. And here is a striking additional fact to be observed in this connection: Our international banks and our importers and exporters are, of course, the direct economic successors of the old foreign merchants and money-changers. And it is they, who today *are precisely the same economic agents* through whom Gresham's Law operates with regard to modern governments' promises to pay money! It operates through them just as infallibly as it ever did with ancient coined money. They are the modern informal economic representatives, through whom the underlying will and desire of the people of the world, with regard to money, is manifested.

The dilemma of governments, in the face of this stubborn human fact that the multitude of common men, independent of their governors, will determine what their money is to be, and always demand that it shall be an honest money, has forever been a perplexing problem—to the rulers. For it seems almost to be a law of rulership that its needs inevitably expand. They rarely stand still, and even more rarely do they decrease in volume. Rulers are seldom, as Adam Smith puts it, "naturally disposed to the parsimony requisite for accumulation." A greater and greater number of individuals, never fewer, seem to be required for whatever their current purposes are. These myrmidons must be fed, clothed, sheltered and sometimes richly provided for. Since a ruler cannot create real money, this can only be done by the seizure of actual money from citizens, or by the seizure of other forms of wealth which can elsewhere be exchanged for real money. But we have seen that there is always a limit to which citizens will stand for seizure of their wealth.

What course, then, can a ruler follow? He can try war, the seizure of wealth from other communities. A very large part of the bloody past of human history would almost surely find its explanation in this sheer dilemma: that certain rulers found themselves without the means to maintain themselves and their supporters in power, and were obliged forcibly to seize the wealth of nearby weaker communities, because they did not dare risk seizing the needed forms of wealth from their own subjects.

Recourse to war, however, was obviously both dangerous and uncertain. Rulers might end up by having their own wealth, what little there was of it, seized by other rulers. Slowly, over the centuries,

315

perspicacity began to seep even into rulers. They came to discover, and more and more to use, a third recourse. *They began to enter into deferred exchanges with their own subjects and others.* More and more they borrowed the money they dared not seize. In the beginning they borrowed only from the very wealthy, not from the *hoi polloi.* No doubt, in most cases, these transactions took on very much the character of the "forced loans," the "patriotic loans," our present breed of dictators engineer. The lender very often did not dare to refuse to relinquish his property, upon the promise of the ruler to pay back an equivalent sum later, with interest.

This was notably true of monasteries in the Middle Ages. They acquired great wealth, by gifts and peaceful pursuits, and were often obliged—for political reasons—to lend it to seigneurs of high rank, both lay and ecclesiastical. They really bought protection by those forced loans. Likewise the situation of the Jews, in the Middle Ages, was almost wholly governed by this condition. They were marked for prey, as they are in Germany today, because plainly they constituted a small plunderable section of the population, least likely to endanger the rulers' supremacy. Perspicacious Adam Smith, as so often, has a comment illuminating on this matter of the beginning of borrowing by rulers. "The individuals who hoard whatever money they can save, and who conceal their hoard, do so from a distrust of the government, from a fear that if it was known that they had a hoard, and where that hoard was to be found, *they would quickly be plundered.* [Italics mine.] In such a state of things, few people would be able, and nobody would be willing, to lend their money to a government on extraordinary exigencies."

It is worthy of note, in this connection, that these first promises of rulers to pay money never came into use as "promised money." The reasons were two: ordinarily the borrowings were for large sums. But, more important, they were recognized as being too uncertain of completion. The Biblical quotation, "Put not your trust in princes," perhaps indicates how anciently wise men understood that this was a type of deferred exchange very unlikely to be completed. It was coined money alone which for long centuries cir-

316

culated in commerce. "Promised money" was unknown. When it did finally come into existence, it seemed to solve this immemorial problem of rulership—that its needs always expand faster than its resources—which we have identified above.

For "promised money" *was* a form of money governments could create. More and more, as they needed wealth, they could obtain it in deferred exchanges, handing out their own promises to pay money to whoever would accept them. Only one thing they forgot: *that promises of action, to be believed, must be fulfilled.* Since these promises of theirs were specific engagements to turn over real money—gold or silver coins—real money had eventually to be given by them in this deferred exchange, no matter how long the interval to elapse before that unwelcome necessity arrived.

Thus, though they never realized it clearly, rulers were also very much limited in the creation of "promised money." The limit was set *by the extent to which their promises would be believed.* This always turned, as it still does, upon an estimate of their future resources. These are the simple first principles of money that many of our modern governors, after all the lessons of history, have not yet learned.

To understand fully the modern consequences of this peculiar oversight, it will be illuminating first to follow the processes by which "promised money" first came into common use. Only so can we explain many of the most puzzling aspects of modern life, where real money has all but disappeared from common use, and "promised money" is almost the only kind men now employ.

17

How Paper Money Originated from the
Fraud of Rulers

THE perpetual unreliability of rulers, with regard to coined money, had as much as anything else to do with the origin of paper money in Europe. It was a form of protection against dishonest coinage. Ironic enough this is; since later on, with these very forms of "promised money," governments were to demonstrate their constitutional dishonesty on a far grander scale.

Prior to the seventeenth century, when forms of paper money first began to be passed around in parts of Europe, there had been previous sporadic instances of its use.

The Carthaginians, for a time, used a curious device. It is told about in one of the Socratic dialogues.* They took a piece of heavy metal, wrapped it in leather, and sealed it. Needless to say, the value of this unknown material had to be taken on faith. There is no indication how well, nor how long, this device served as a money, nor what promises kept it circulating. It was not copied among the ancient empires.

China—as usual, notable in inventiveness—had used leather "token money" before the birth of Christ. The first instance of this was the use of pieces of white deerskin, a foot square. Soon the emperor (about 100 B. C.) gathered together all the white deer, herded them in his own park, and made it a criminal offence for any subject to have white deer (as it now is a criminal offence for freeborn Ameri-

* *Eryxias*, the dialogue on Wealth.

318

cans to have gold coins). Thus he obtained a monopoly of the current money.

Later, after China invented paper, the perspicacious Far Eastern rulers began circulating promises to pay money, printed on paper, in place of real money, which at the time was principally copper. The Chinese rulers were long centuries ahead of their obtuse Western counterparts in recognizing the usefulness of this device in solving the perennial problem of rulership—how to raise money to pay their expenses. Eight or nine hundred years before European governors even became aware there was such a hopeful possibility as paper money, China had already gone through a number of typical paper money inflations, almost always associated with wars.* One of these, known about in considerable detail, is that initiated by the great Kubla Khan in the thirteenth century.

His use of paper money, incidentally, was one of the phenomena of Eastern rulership that Marco Polo found so enviable. The wide-eyed Marco, like so many of his European descendants, was simply an economic innocent, so far as public finance was concerned; merely purblind to what was going on. The Great Khan and his successors issued notes—forced them, indeed, to a large extent, upon the sections of Eastern Asia they conquered—up to a total value of over two and a quarter billion taels, and ended up by precipitating an inflation all the incidents of which post-war Europeans, in the nineteen-twenties, would have found highly familiar.

After about 1400 the wise Chinese stopped issuing paper money, and did not do so again for over four hundred years, until long after the Western rulers discovered the device and began misusing it, as the Chinese rulers had done almost a thousand years before them!

Though Marco Polo came back with seeming tall tales about paper

---

* Paper money seems first to have been in use around 800 A.D., and was called "flying money." Later it was called "convenient money." It developed, apparently, from certificates of indebtedness handed by the governments to merchants. An interesting chapter on these early Chinese forms of paper money will be found in *The Invention of Printing in China,* by Thomas Francis Carter.

money, and no doubt in other ways it became known that the mysterious Orientals could get away with so strange a device, paper money did not begin to come into use in Western civilization until almost two thousand years after the invention of coinage. Stamped leather tokens were occasionally used by little autocrats. But instances of this kind are comparatively rare. Moreover, the use of such devices was very much localized. They usually represented an emergency measure, and they always quickly ended.

The line of evolution of modern paper money begins in the necessities of mediaeval merchants trading over boundaries, and in the rise of bankers. That is, modern paper money had its real seed in the widening realization among men that *private individuals* could be relied upon to carry out their promises with regard to money. This development was given added impetus—indeed, it was necessitated—by the fact *that rulers could not be so trusted.*

Nobody knew, from one year to the next, how much gold or silver would be contained in a given piece of currency. All that could be known with certainty was that it would be continually debased by clipping and sweating, that it would be counterfeited, and, as frequently as not, that rulers themselves would be the counterfeiters, by issuing new coins with a lower metallic value, made to masquerade, as closely as possible, as the old ones. In some localities annual re-coinages occurred, like our yearly new models of automobiles, except that the coins year by year *became poorer.*

It is highly illuminating to observe that precisely the same situation had come to exist in the early Middle Ages, as had obtained *prior to the existence of coined money* among men, at least fifteen hundred years before. Then men had been obliged to weigh and to assay the quality of the money they received in an exchange. Again they had to do the same. For the ruler's stamp guaranteeing quality and weight, which is the ultimate service governments can provide with regard to money, proved to be a faithless stamp far more often than otherwise. The far-reaching consequence of this was that *no deferred exchanges could be entered into, specifying the delivery of any ruler's coined money as the last half of the exchange.* For the person giving up his wealth in the first half of the exchange could not possibly know how much gold or silver he would get in the last half, when the date of completion arrived.

But healthy processes of social growth go on without rulers, who may obstruct progress by their incompetence and fraudulence—because common men are patient—but cannot forever hinder it. If they obstruct too much, in the end they are steamrollered.

We have seen that from the earliest times trading among peoples over boundaries had gone on; and that, as much as anything else, it was responsible for that specialization of occupation among men, which is the basic condition of an organized society. Against all the disorder and difficulty that fatuous Führers and I Duci could place in its way, for perhaps two thousand years after the invention of coined money, this sturdy and deep-rooted process of international trading never withered. In the face of pirate and prince, and they were indistinguishable, the foreign merchant forever carried on. He might be milched by his ruler, and hampered in a hundred ways. He might even be killed off, as his primitive adventurous ancestor so often was. But soon someone else, of his stubborn ilk, took his place. It was the merchants dealing with one another in other lands—and we must remember, just as in the Greek city-states, that a city a few leagues off was frequently, in the Middle Ages, another land—who principally, *by their needs*, originated our modern forms of "promised money."

The merchant had found that he could rely, in his exchanges, upon others of the same trustworthy kidney as himself. He constantly dealt also with the money-changers, and found that he could trust most of them. All these private individuals, trusting one another, in time found ways of offsetting that fraudulence which was a constitutional defect in governments, manifested particularly in coined money. This trusting of individuals ultimately evolved into banks, *and then into paper money issued by banks.*

One particularly interesting development was that, to a large extent, merchants trading over boundaries came to measure their exchanges by an imaginary money. It was a "money of account." It

321

hypothetically contained so much gold or silver; thus it could be used to measure the value of the questionable coins that were passing in exchanges; but it was itself never minted. In Italy the most useful of these imaginary moneys, mere ideal measures, was called the *scutus marcarum*.

It was a general practice among mediaeval merchants to make their deferred exchanges payable at the time of the fairs, which were so colorful and conspicuous a feature of mediaeval life. Here merchants from different localities, often far afield, would repair, and would pay over the gold or silver specified in the deferred exchanges they had entered into with other merchants. The transactions were usually measured by the *scutus marcarum*.

This significant increase of deferred exchanges among merchants went hand in hand—and to a great extent depended upon—the deferred exchanges the merchants were also entering into with the money-changers. As we saw in the chapters on Banking, the merchants could not keep their gold and silver coins and bullion on their own premises. It was too dangerous. The money-changers had strong vaults. Merchants were continuously dealing with them, anyhow. It was a natural process, as the trustworthiness of individual money-changers was demonstrated time and again, for the merchants to leave their gold and silver with these *campsores*, as they were called. This was particularly advisable because the *campsores* were frequently under the protection of the prince, and many of them had acquired, by purchase or favor, the minting privilege in their little territory.*

Among these local merchants the same situation would prevail as among business men who today deposit in the same bank. One would instruct the money-changer simply to transfer so much gold or silver to the credit of the other merchant. Pretty soon this took place between merchants living in different cities, as well as locally. Merchant Antonio, in Venice, would want to obtain some goods from a merchant in Genoa, and hesitated to carry gold over roads infested

* A good brief account of the beginnings of modern commercial banking can be found in the *Encyclopedia of the Social Sciences*, in an article on Banking by Julius Landmann.

with brigands—and the armed minions of princes. What would he do? He would go to the money-changer, whom he was trusting with his silver and gold, and ask him to facilitate the process. Nothing easier. The money-changer was probably owed gold and silver by a money-changer in Genoa. He would give Antonio a written order on this Genoan money-changer to hand over Genoan coin. He himself would then transfer part of Antonio's money, which he held, to his own store. Antonio would travel to Genoa with a piece of paper, not coins, in his saddle bags; he would present the paper to the Genoan money-changer, get the coin of that realm and obtain his goods. The piece of paper was "a bill of exchange." This was an extremely old instrument *among merchants*, dating back certainly to Greece and perhaps long before. Now, as we see, it began to be used among money-changers, *principally for the benefit of merchants*. It is not in the slightest respect different from those which take place in international commerce today. These bills of exchange among money-changers, by which merchants carried on intercity transactions, were in use at least as early as 1200 A. D. in Italy.* We have said there was nothing easier than this process; but of course it was easy only when business morality had progressed to a point where *the economic promises of everybody involved in the transaction could be utterly trusted.*

The crucial part of this relationship was that clearly the mediaeval money-changer was moulting his feathers to become a modern banker. In the beginning he was not supposed to touch the stores of wealth entrusted to him by the merchant. The *campsores* were originally pure custodians; they charged a fee for the custody of the

* There is some evidence to indicate that bills of exchange among merchants—or something like them—constituted a social invention that may have been in use as early as the days of Hammurabi, in Babylon. They were certainly one of the earliest forms of deferred exchanges, and obviously could never have existed without the same sort of dependability (on the part of those being trusted) as exists today among exporters and importers. That they were also in use to a limited extent in the Greek world, fifteen hundred years later than Hammurabi, is indicated by the activities of the Greek banker, Pasion, one of the most important men of his time, who apparently did a great deal to facilitate Athenian commerce by providing Athenian merchants with bills of exchange on merchants in other cities. The nature of his activities is revealed in some of the speeches of Demosthenes that are preserved.

money. But in time some *campsores* changed this simple relationship. Finding *part* of the money was never asked for, some of them would take chances and lend it out at interest, just as they were doing with their own money. Frequently, like modern American bankers, they were not so wise about the economic promises they themselves were accepting. These half-exchanges would not be completed. Then, if called upon by merchants to deliver in full, the *campsores* could not do so. It is clear enough that disaster among these incipient bankers must have been frequent, for both laws and institutions arose, in the mediaeval Italian cities, to prevent it. In many places, money-changers were prohibited by law from lending to others the money entrusted to them by merchants.

Finally, the municipal authorities—controlled, of course, by merchants—stepped in, and we see the rise of a peculiar municipal bank, entirely different from modern forms of banking. It was purely a bank of deposit; no lending took place. There, indeed, if you were a depositor, you had "money in the bank." Whenever a merchant received coin, he took it to the bank, its true value was there assayed, and he received credit for it in "bank-money." This again was a money that was never minted. For each true ounce of gold or silver delivered the merchant received a piece of paper representing that amount; like our gold certificate. Merchants dealing among themselves passed their goods for this "bank-money." What the institution clearly represented was an economic invention by merchants, by which they could make exchanges on which they could rely, to take the place of the coined money of rulers, on which they could not rely. The first bank of this kind was established in Barcelona in 1401; it was followed soon after by one in Genoa; but not until about two centuries later were the famous banks of this kind in Venice, Milan, Amsterdam and Hamburg established.

Here, of course, was a beginning of modern paper money. Every merchant having money in the bank held but the promise of the bank to give gold of a specified weight and quality on demand. The promise was believed—*because it was invariably kept.* The merchants held the receipt, the evidence of the promise, and these receipts were passed around for goods, and were bought and sold.* But here, we see, the government had an extremely close association with what went on. These banks were municipal banks; and their office certainly was a beneficent one. Just as, in the beginning of coined money, the ruler's stamp on a piece of metal had proved of enormous advantage in facilitating exchanges, so now the government's authority—in communities where the government could be trusted— had eliminated what had proved so troublesome in the merchants' deposit-relations with money-changers. *The money received from the merchants could not be lent out.* Every grain of true gold or silver held by the bank was matched precisely by an amount of bank-money credited on the books of the bank to individual merchants, and matched on the outside by receipts held by merchants. If all the receipts had been presented at the same time for redemption, presumably the holders could have gotten the gold or silver represented. *The receipts were thus like the gold and silver certificates our own government issues.* The system depended completely, it will be seen, on the confidence of the merchants in the municipal bank. For long years, the confidence was certainly justified; and commerce flourished under the system.† But alas, government morals ultimately poisoned this promising growth, as they had previously poisoned the social invention represented by coinage. In the Italian cities very quickly the operations of the municipal banks became involved in lending to the political managers. Also, in the case of perhaps the greatest of the banks, that at Amsterdam, it was ultimately found that the merchants had been deceived in their faith for years; that

* Adam Smith gives an exhaustive and interesting account of the way these municipal banks operated, in *The Wealth of Nations,* Pages 446-455, Modern Library edition.

† The parallel in history between the Renaissance and the rise of Greek civilization is worth speculating about. We see Greek civilization flowering immediately after the invention of coined money, and that social invention—as we analyzed in the preceding chapter—consisted of nothing but the provision of a money that men found to be infallibly honest. Now we see European civilization flowering into the Renaissance with the provision of a different form of money *from which fraud had been eliminated*. In both cases, the origin was with merchants, the function was taken over by governments, and then—after a short period—prostituted by governments.

325

the bank had not been keeping their money inviolate, but had been lending it out the way the money-changers originally had. And to whom? To the municipal government itself! In the case of another famous bank of this kind, that at Hamburg, a subsidiary bank was formed, through which the prohibited lending took place.

This blighting touch of the government, in every economic relation it enters into with its citizens, appears even more clearly in England. The present system of banking and paper money, which is now in world-wide use, really originated in England more than anywhere else, although—as we have seen—the activities of incipient bankers and of foreign merchants on the Continent were a very closely related species. England had no such municipal bank as those we have described. In that tight little isle the merchants of London by long tradition had kept their gold, by privilege of the King, in the Tower. Certainly it was safe there from everybody—except the King! In 1640 Charles I simply seized £130,000 of it, since he thought he could use it to much better advantage than the merchants. To be merely economic in our description of the event, the King's act simply ended this type of deferred exchange in that quarter. What could the merchants do? It was dangerous for them to keep coin and bullion on their own premises. But there was one class of persons in London, reliable where the King was not— the goldsmiths. The merchants began to deposit their money with the goldsmiths. The arrangement was different, in what seems a minor but is really a vital respect, from that which continental merchants had with money-changers. *The goldsmiths were allowed the right to lend out the money at interest!*

In other words, here was the frank and recognized beginning of *that deposit-and-lending system* which obtains in every commercial bank in the world today. There had been sporadic instances of this relationship previously in mercantile history, particularly in ancient Rome, but here it was a recognized part of a commercial system. It was followed soon by another development now universally familiar. The practice arose for those who had money with the goldsmith to write out orders to him to deliver some of it to a third individual.

326

Such was the origin of the bank check, and such it remains to this day. One of the earliest checks of this type is still preserved in the Institute of Banking in London. Here was the beginning of that *transfer of bank promises*, which was analyzed in a previous chapter.

But, then a third highly important development arose. The goldsmiths found, as the money-changers had, that they themselves could issue pieces of paper, promising to pay money, and these would be accepted and passed around for exchanges of wealth. *Goldsmiths' paper promises here were being used in place of real money!*

Before following this momentous development, it is instructive to notice what happened to the goldsmiths—not to forget our theme of a moment ago, of the blighting hand of government. The goldsmiths, in their new economic position, were lending money freely. The scent of any lender will draw a buzzard ruler miles away. The government of England, in its perpetual condition of extremity, borrowed as freely as the goldsmiths would lend. The interest paid was 12 per cent. The security given was taxes—to be collected later. Our tax anticipation warrants! In 1672, King Charles II, having got the goldsmiths' money in the first half of these deferred exchanges, found it inconvenient to complete the second half. *He simply stopped all payments from the Exchequer to the goldsmiths.* Of course the goldsmiths then had to default on their promises to their depositors. Their careers as bankers were ended.* From their ruin, soon afterward, rose the Bank of England; and it is instructive to note that it only acquired its charter by lending money to the government—to pay off its debt! The interest paid was 8 per cent—an indication, remarked upon by Adam Smith, of the low status of faith English merchants then had in their government.

Goldsmiths' notes were bankers' notes. They were the prototypes of the paper money we use today. If bankers could be repositories of the money of individuals—and if their written promises to pay money circulated successfully among citizens—why would not this be true of the government's own promises?

* For a brief account of this early development of modern banking in Great Britain, see *Foreign Banking Systems*, edited by H. Parker Willis and B. H. Beckhart.

If the merchants' *temporary* needs could be financed by the promises of bankers, why could not the government's far greater *perpetual* needs be financed in the same way?

Why not, indeed! As this notion slowly penetrated, rulers and ruling groups used this open sesame to the stored wealth of mankind, and gorged on it like greedy vultures.

The lesson was first widely learned by European rulers and began to be put in practice, in the latter part of the seventeenth and throughout the eighteenth centuries. The shrewder Chinese rulers, as we saw, had learned it centuries before. What was happening, of course, was that *a new form of money—"promised money"—was quickly coming into existence*. It was not, however, regarded as money, any more than today bank deposits (which represent the principal form of modern money, in the sense that they are the immediate media of exchanges) are considered money by most of ourselves. For 2,500 years before, governments had preempted to themselves the right to issue coined money. Now, insidiously and without recognition by either rulers or bankers, this new money—"promised money"—was coming into use. The usurpation happened *only because it was not considered money*. Money even then, as always, was coined money. These printed notes were mere promises to pay coined money; and coined money had to be kept on hand by the banker to fulfill the promises. There was no more reason, originally, for the government to interfere in this particular form of economic promise than in any other deferred exchange between individuals; such, for instance, as the bill of exchange, a very ancient instrument among merchants, out of which the bank check evolved.

But if not money in fact, money in effect bank notes were. And as this slowly became learned, all the possibilities of the system became recognizable to men of alert mind and adventurous nature. It seems almost incredible to us today, but through the eighteenth and the early part of the nineteenth centuries, it was quite within the prerogative of almost every individual to issue what all of us today would call "money." For any man could easily become a banker, *and issue*

328

bank notes. Thousands did. In England, Sir Norman Angell quotes Ellis Powell, "Any person, however impecunious, could start a 'bank' and (down to 1775 at all events) issue notes purporting to be payable on demand. Every grocer, draper, tailor and haberdasher who chose might flood the country with his 'miserable rags.' " * In our own country, the orgy of private banking came later, and—with our characteristic tendency to excess—went to greater lengths. Every man here was a king, and every man had what had previously been a king's right—to issue money. The wholesale manufacture of banks, and the practically unrestrained issue of bank notes, began in this country soon after the founding of the Republic and lasted almost until the end of the Civil War. For example, from 1812 to 1819, says A. Barton Hepburn, the circulating medium "was composed of a relatively small amount of notes of sound banks, an almost equally large amount of counterfeits, and a mass of paper, the value of which could rarely be known from one day to another. The location of many 'banks' was practically unknown, and many of them had failed. *Their notes were nevertheless in use* [italics mine]; others deliberately repudiated their notes, still others pretended falsely to redeem upon demand. Other corporations and tradesmen issued 'currency.' Even barbers and bartenders competed with the banks in this respect. Altogether it appears marvelous that when nearly every citizen regarded it as his constitutional right to issue money, successful trade was possible at all." †

"The banks regarded it as something of a grievance (writes Louis Rasminsky) ‡ when their notes were presented for redemption in specie. In Vermont, a citizen of Boston had to appear before a grand jury for doing this. In order to evade redemption, banks were often set up in unheard-of, out-of-the-way places to which there was little likelihood that their notes would find their way back, once issued. This practice gave rise to the term 'wild-cat' banks. The appellation

* *The Story of Money*, Norman Angell.
† *Ibid.*
‡ Chapter XI of *The Story of Money*—Money in America from Hamilton to the Federal Reserve.

was meant to indicate that the bank had been established in some primitive forest, uninhabitable by all save wild-cats."

It was at this time that the little weekly bulletin we have already referred to, *The Ready Detector*,* came into necessary use, giving a description of every type of note circulating in the country, and of the counterfeits passing for them. By the time of the Civil War, Rasminsky says, there were 7,000 different varieties of bank notes circulating as money, in addition to about 5,000 counterfeit issues. The system was not destroyed till the Civil War, when the federal government taxed the State bank notes out of existence.

Almost, but not quite, coordinate with this adventurous and unrestrained rise of bank notes as money was the use of the same device of paper promises, *issued by governments*. By the beginning of the eighteenth century banknotes were far too prominent in the economic scene to be overlooked by rulers. The speculative furore they engendered, as an easy way of making money, was comparable to the wholesale creation of new corporation securities (also pieces of paper) in the post-War period in this country. As years passed, also, the excesses of private bankers necessitated more and more control by governments; and, of course, the extension of control meant more and more involvement of governments in this system.

As may be expected, at the hands of governments the invention suffered as much abuse as from individuals—if not more. At last the old notion that governments had the power to create money appeared to be borne out by the phenomena. The fact that the piece of paper *was a promise* was forgot as quickly as 2,500 years before it had been forgot that the ruler's stamp on a coin was a mere guarantee of quality. Governments, incredibly, came to think they could extinguish *old promises*—those represented by their National Debt incurred in wars—*by paying them off with new promises*, in the form of paper money.

The first instance of government assumption of this practice of issuing paper promises against metal was in Sweden, in 1694. Certificates were issued against the deposit of copper coins. This very first

* Page 143.

attempt soon ended in disaster, for the same old reason—the unreliability of the ruler. It was soon found that the bank was issuing far more certificates than it had metal on hand. At once, of course, the certificates dropped in value.

But the first great governmental fiasco in this field of promised money was John Law's fantastic scheme, later known as the Mississippi Bubble. Law acquired his power by presenting a highly plausible plan for paying off the French King's debt. This had grown to such an alarming extent that the old promises of the King dropped in value, and his new ones would not be generally accepted. Law succeeded in solving this traditional royal problem, by means of paper money—for a time.

It is highly instructive to mark how governments began using this device. In its natural development—arising, as it did, from the needs of merchants—paper notes were used in the interest of healthy exchanging of goods. That is, the merchants would bring their bills of exchange, bills owing to them by other merchants for the delivery of actual merchandise, and the bank would advance money on these, before they came due. But frequently, instead of taking actual money, the merchants would take goldsmiths' notes to pay money on demand. These they would then distribute to anyone who would accept them. Thus, paper money, originally, was *a mere substitution of bank credit for book credit*. Bank credit was thus a mere facility to trade, just as today loans to business men on promissory notes are such a facility—and of the same type.

The governments never regarded the new device from that point of view. It was of use to them, *to get them out of the trouble in which they were enmeshed*, by reason of their excessive expenditure. Government paper money was first associated, in one way or another, with heavy government debt. It was a mere attempt to relieve them of debt. But since debt itself is nothing but an, as yet, unfulfilled economic promise, what they were merely trying to do was to extinguish old promises by making new ones.

When John Law's bubble was burst, after a speculative fever previously unknown in Europe, it was succeeded in a few years by

331

the so-called South Sea Bubble. This, the record shows, was closely associated with an attempt to pay off the British National Debt. Paper money was not directly involved here, but other government promises were very much so.

Another unforgettable experience with this still-new system of "promised money" was during our Revolutionary War. The war was financed by the issuance of notes by the Continental Congress, giving rise, finally, to the term "not worth a Continental." Over $200,-000,000 worth of them were issued, and finally redeemed at a penny to the dollar.

This, however, was no worse than the individual colonies. Colonial governments were among the earliest to realize the usefulness of the paper device to obtain the money they needed. Massachusetts started it as early as 1693, issuing £7000 in notes to soldiers, who promptly disposed of them generally at a one-third discount.* A perfect comment this is, upon what the soldiers thought of the reliability of the government they were risking their lives for! Farther south the colonies issued paper notes payable in rice and tobacco on demand. By the time of the Revolution all our colonies were well seasoned in this practice of promising money to whoever would accept the promise.

Actually, one of the colonies' deepest grievances against Parliament was a law prohibiting them from making this paper money legal tender. Clear-eyed Adam Smith, who lived at the time, had something to say about this compulsion to accept promises in the last half of a deferred exchange—although he did not use these particular terms. It "was an act of such violent injustice as has scarce perhaps been attempted by the government of any other country which pretended to be free." (United States Supreme Court, please copy!) Throughout the Revolution all the colonies issued paper money in endless bundles. Finally, a state of economic chaos prevailed, which was quite similar to that which occurred in Germany during the inflation of the nineteen-twenties.

"The monetary chaos during this period challenges portrayal,"

* Sumner, *History of American Currency*.

332

writes Sir Norman Angell. "Debtors pursued creditors and forced them to accept payment of their loans, a queer phenomenon indeed. In some states the currency issued by local institutions had depreciated even more than had the Continental notes. In Virginia notes finally passed at the rate of 1,000 to 1 and a person could purchase a tolerably good pair of shoes for $5,000. To buy a dress and a hat for one's wife as well, one must needs have been a millionaire. According to a contemporary account,

> 'Barber shops were papered in fact with the bills, and sailors, on returning from their cruises, being paid off in bundles of this worthless paper money, had suits of clothes made of it and with characteristic lightheartedness turned their loss into frolic by parading through the streets in decayed finery.' " *

The bitter personal experiences that were suffered by our forefathers during this period eventuated in an action, on the part of our Constitution-makers, which few of us today know about. *They denied the right to the federal government to issue paper money!* At the Constitutional Convention a specific motion was made to give the Federal Government the privilege to "emit bills on the credit of the United States." By this they certainly meant the issuance of any form of paper money. *It was overwhelmingly voted down!* Only two persons voted for it. Madison, in reporting the action (again, the Supreme Court, please copy!) states that even if the power had been granted, it would not have meant that Congress had the power to make the notes legal tender! In other words, the dollar-bills which you think of as the most characteristic American money, by any intellectually honest construction of the supreme law of the land, *are unquestionably unconstitutional!*

Whether the Constitution-makers realized the economic significance of what they were doing—in denying the new government the privilege of issuing paper money—is not clear; but there can be no question about their action. That they wished to make impossible the issuance of any form of paper money by the Federal Government is as

* *The Story of Money,* Norman Angell.

333

clear as words can make it to anyone who cares to read the record of the debates.* Its inspiration, without doubt, was the bitter experience, fresh in everybody's memory, with the Continental notes and with other colonial promises to pay money—some of which were finally redeemed, not at the ratio of a penny to a dollar, but a penny to every ten dollars!

In spite of this action of the Constitution-makers, by this time there was no stopping the full functioning of any government in this field. The Founding Fathers were but making, whether they realized it or no, a *beau geste* to the integrity and responsibility of individuals, as compared with governments. They were tilting at a windmill. Within ten years their own decisions were a dead letter. *They had forgotten banks.* If the federal government could not issue notes, banks could. Banks did—both banks chartered by the States, and by the federal government; and the federal and State governments were, of course, completely involved, because they completely controlled the bankers, as they could control any other citizen.

The whole system was too beautifully advantageous to governments not to grow swiftly into one of the most firmly settled traditions of modern rulership. Let us see, clearly, what the system has now become.

First, seize as much as you can of real money—which, in modern times, is gold—from your citizens in taxation. Then acquire as much more as you can in two ways: first, by borrowing on interest-bearing bonds and notes; and second, by issuing paper promises to pay money. You hold the gold in your Treasury. You relinquish bits of it whenever demand is made for fulfillment of one of your promises. By such faithful *piecemeal fulfillment* you forestall any overwhelming demand that all your promises be simultaneously fulfilled, which (if you honored them) would quickly deprive you of the real money you hold. You are safe in this whole course, so long as your own citizens, passing your "promised money" to one another as currency, continue to trust you.

* *Records of the Federal Convention of 1787*, edited by Max Farrand; Vol. II, Pages 308-310.

334

There is, however, a second aspect of the system, a little more involved than this, and more important because more devious; for the great advantages of the system depend largely on the difficulty ordinary citizens have in understanding what goes on. You charter a so-called central bank, *and give it the monopoly of issuing bank notes.* No other banks are allowed to do so. These bank notes, as we saw, are mere promises of the bank to pay real money on demand. The central bank *takes in* gold, but when it is asked for money, on most occasions it does not give out gold, any more than the government does. It gives out its promises to pay gold—these pieces of paper called bank notes. These promises to pay money circulate among the trustful citizens, like gold and silver coin itself. If any citizen comes in and specifically asks for gold, he gets it without question—in normal times. Few do; and thus gold—real money—accumulates *in the vaults of the central bank,* just as it does in your Treasury vaults. But is your central bank an entirely free agent? Oh, no. The bank is your creature. You made it, and you can unmake it. You gave it the power to issue notes and you can take away the power. Moreover, if you wanted the gold in its treasury, you could seize it as easily as Charles I walked off with the merchants' gold in the Tower.* But a modern government is ordinarily compelled to do nothing so stark and crude as this, when it needs money. If it cannot borrow from its citizens, it

* Our own revered government did this in 1933, and it is a highly significant social fact that the precise parallel between its action and the ancient seizure of the coin of private individuals by rulers was nowhere even noticed. On the contrary, it was assumed everywhere that this was one of the "rights" of the Government, associated with the power given to Congress in the Constitution to "coin money and regulate the value thereof." But the gold belonged, not to the Government, but to the Federal Reserve Banks, and the Federal Reserve Banks were not government institutions, but private corporations, the stock of which was owned by the member banks, themselves private corporations. Thus, it was unadulterated *seizure of private property* for the government to require that every ounce of gold be given over to it, in exchange for gold certificates. A reading of the debates in the Constitutional Convention makes it indisputably clear that such an action was an assumption of federal power altogether contrary to what the framers intended by the power, carefully granted, to "coin" money and "regulate" its value. Not only would such seizure of gold from private individuals have been far beyond their notions, but even the issuance of gold certificates would certainly have come under their definition of "bills," the "emission" of which was carefully struck out from among the powers specifically given the federal government.

borrows from its central bank, where most of the gold is; and like a money-lender in ancient days under a strong ruler, *the central bank dares not refuse*. The only difference between now and a thousand years ago is that the central banker gives the government no money. It gives the government, as we saw in Chapter Ten, bank credit—bank credit based on the gold it holds. That is, it gives it a bank-deposit; and the government then transfers those deposits—mere promises—to other persons by means of government checks.

The ancient and primary problem of government—the retention of power by providing sufficient means to support power—*is thus at last solved!* No need for a government to create money for its purposes, when it can borrow all it requires in this hidden fashion.

So, under this system, real money all but disappears from commerce. The promises of governments, and of their creature central banks, take its place. Long years pass, and the trusting of our governments in this respect becomes, one might say, so racially habitual that most of us never even know that our governments are being trusted by us. We use their promises to pay money, and those of their central banks, so universally that we come to think, many of us, that these constitute money more than gold itself does. Yet they constitute, as we have seen in the previous chapter, simple half-exchanges, and nothing more, half-exchanges that must sooner or later be completed!

Now, this acceptance of a promise as money—of a mere deferred exchange which the government or its central bank must complete—is almost the most pernicious social habit that mankind has become inured to. It is a habit in the true sense of the term, *in that it is an act devoid of any conscious mental content*. This is what we meant, principally, by saying that most of the mystery of money will be found in our psychological state; and that the solution of money problems must therefore be sought there. For this is a clear failure to distinguish between a promise and a thing; and it is pernicious because, by remaining *forever unaware of the true relations* between ourselves and our government, we tempt the ruling cliques who manage our affairs also to lose sight of that relationship. Like every ruler in history, they yield to the temptation of rulership—the most improvident expenditure—and with inevitably disastrous consequences, extending everywhere, because of the dependence of all other economic promises upon them.

For, as we showed in Chapter Fourteen, in spite of the fact that all forms of "promised money" are short promises, they are only completed at long indefinite intervals. That is the only reason, indeed, they can serve as money. The promise of the government contained in its laws—or of the central bank—is to complete the exchange; that is, to hand you the gold at your pleasure. But in normal economic weather, there is no occasion nor reason for any citizen to do so, except one. He might have to complete an exchange with some foreigner, and it would be idle to send dollar-bills, which the foreigner could not use. The only thing to do is to send him gold, which is his money. To get the gold, if you were in this situation, you would present your demands upon the government or central bank to complete the deferred exchanges represented by the bills or coins you own. You would not do this, personally. A subsidiary bank would do it for you. But so far as the government or central bank is concerned, the effect would be the same. *It would be put into the position of having to complete some of the deferred exchanges it had entered into.* Aside from this need of making payments to foreigners, and for industrial purposes where gold is needed as a commodity, it is only upon the rarest occasions that governments are asked to complete the half-exchanges represented by their so-called currency.

Incidentally, we surely have our finger here upon the source of the widespread difficulty among men of recognizing paper money and coins as mere economic promises. We do not distinguish the fact that they are mere deferred exchanges, for the perfectly simple reason that, personally, we never *complete* the exchanges! That is, *we actually never have any experience with the second half of the exchange.* Only those who do have occasion to complete such exchanges—that is, bankers and importers and exporters, who deal regularly with foreigners—acquire the daily experience that results in their recognizing that what we principally use as currency are

337

simply economic promises made by our governments or central banks.

But when circumstances are not normal but abnormal, this picture swiftly changes. Then the fatal consequences of this enormous power, which modern rulers have indirectly acquired, begin to appear. For then, by a sort of capillary attraction, this realization—that government and central bank promises to pay money do not really constitute money—spreads through the population like water through the fibers of a cloth. Everybody holding an uncompleted end of a half-exchange with the government or its central bank presents it for completion as fast as he can. What happens? The current political managers are never prepared for such a situation. When these circumstances arise, they have always extended themselves far beyond their ability to carry out their promises. It is general recognition of this fact, indeed, which originates the demand for the wholesale completion of the half-exchanges. The politicians in control always seem to regard the *denouement* as a sort of unfair trick being played upon them; by foreigners, by speculators, or by diabolic rich men. They wrap the flag about themselves, and in defense of home and country do what ruling cliques have done from time immemorial: proceed to cheat their own citizens, and as many foreigners as they can garner into the net, out of the property they dare not seize. They refuse point-blank to complete the half-exchanges represented by their "promised money." They "go off the gold standard."

Since 1914, every important nation in the world has for some period, short or long, taken this course with its citizens. Some of them have done so several times. They wrap the true nature of their acts, like squid, in a cloud of black propaganda; or in misty economic phrases, like this one of "going off the gold standard," the precise significance of which—to their good fortune—is not generally understood by innocent John and Susan Citizen. These latter think, by the term, that a calamity has fallen upon the government, not upon their own simple selves. And, like the good citizens they are, they stand

338

by the government, and suffer in a glow of patriotism; blaming whom the government indicates they should blame!

A clearer understanding among common people is imperative as to what "going off the gold standard" really means. The term has been extraordinarily fruitful of confusion in public thought during the past decade. In particular, many people seem to think—and the very phrase invites the notion—that, at least temporarily, gold *has ceased to be the money* of the country "going off gold." No notion, of course, could be more erroneous. Yet not only the mass of citizens, but a great many publicists who should know better, write and reason as if this were the case. The simple fact, of course, is that *with no exception* gold has remained the real money of every nation that has "gone off gold."

The term means only one thing, which it does not say: that the government refuses *temporarily*—and this temporary nature of the act is all-important—to complete the deferred exchanges it has entered into, represented by its paper money and subsidiary coins.

Does this *temporary* unfulfillment of the government's promise change the real money of the nation, gold? Obviously not. More than ever, it might be said, when a country "goes off gold" *it clings to gold as its money*. The government refuses not only to relinquish what gold it has, but by every means within its power—by threatening its citizens and by cheating foreigners—acquires as much more as possible.

The paradox in this disappears when we examine more precisely what occurs when a country "goes off gold." The government, in effect, says this: "We have unfortunately issued, both our central bank and ourselves, far more promises to pay real money than we have real money on hand. It is a physical impossibility to meet the promises of all of you, if you ask them to be fulfilled at the same time. You citizens are really responsible for this. You allowed us to issue these promises wholesale. You accepted them. Now you turn upon us, unreasonably, and ask us to fulfill them. It cannot be done. We could pay some of you, but not all of you. So, in the interests of

339

all of you, *we will pay none of you*—right now! Later. Let us all wait. Let us wait until most of you forget again that this piece of paper you hold is not real money, but a promise to pay money. When that blissful condition of 'public confidence' returns—then we will indeed pay the smart ones among you who have not forgotten, and 'normalcy' will again reign. After all, this piece of paper is nothing but an evidence of a deferred exchange between us. Now, all we are doing is to require you *to defer the completion of it a little longer.* We cannot complete it now, but you may—you must, indeed —depend upon us to complete it later."

This—and nothing else—is what "going off the gold standard" means. It is most exactly described as *an arbitrary further postponement of an already deferred exchange.*

But such an arbitrary postponement by one party—the government —of a half-exchange (what the diplomatists, amusingly, call "unilateral" action) involves some highly pertinent considerations. Most of the citizens who are on the last half of these exchanges accept such an action like the sheep their ruling cliques consider them. Further deference of a half-exchange, which they personally would never complete anyway, hardly seems unreasonable. So, they go their accustomed economic way, vaguely worrying, but only because of "talk," the true purport of which they do not understand.

There are, however, always some open-eyed ones among them—in particular international bankers, and importers and exporters—who understand quite as much about the true nature of these half-exchanges as government officials. And when a government arbitrarily stops paying out gold, intimating that it will resume meeting its promises later when the demands upon it are not so insistent, a dreadful question raises its thorny head. Will this government ever, in fact, complete these half-exchanges it is now asking everybody to defer to an indefinite future? Even if it does, will it do so on the precise terms specified in its promise, or on some other terms which it finds to its advantage? In short, to get down to hard pan, *how much if any gold* is this government likely in the end to give in exchange for these promises, words written on paper?

340

It is too often assumed that it is profiteers and speculators who bring up this disagreeable question—that it is a mere exercise of financial "smartness," and that the government is quite right in doing what it can to outsmart such harpies. Governments themselves try to give this impression, and they usually succeed in doing so, for the one thing we must grant modern rulers is that they are usually experts in propaganda, when their power is endangered. But put yourself in the position of a foreign banker, or a merchant carrying on international trade, and see what you would do—and what you ought to do, in honesty—with your own creditors in mind. Let us say you have a "deposit" somewhere of $35,000. What do these words mean? They mean ultimately that the United States Treasury has promised to give you 1,000 ounces of gold on demand. Assume that the government suddenly now announces that it is "going off gold." What do these words mean? Simply that no one, for the time being, can get 1,000 ounces of gold for $35,000. Not now, *but when?* And will you get 1,000 ounces? It is very important to you to know. Because, if you are a foreign banker, the amount of gold ultimately obtainable from the government for these promises determines how many units of your own currency you will receive. This affects your ability to meet the demands of your own depositors. And if you are a foreign merchant, the less gold you get the less goods you can obtain, since the exchangeable value of all goods is measured by gold.

It is principally, then, persons who happen to hold the promises of a government, *and who are compelled to get real gold for them,* who ask such an insulting question as: *how much gold* will it ultimately give for its promises, when it says it will suspend giving any?

Unlike the vast mass of citizens, the sad-eyed men who ask this question have cruel, cold and long memories. They know the record. They know how it has gone for several thousand years. "Put not your trust in princes." So far as paper money is concerned, the record shows that when governments "go off gold," they do indeed ultimately go back. In the end they are obliged to, by the economic will of the people, operating in its slow way. After a passage of years, they "resume payment in specie," as it is somewhat speciously referred to. They arrange, that is, finally to complete these half-exchanges they had indefinitely postponed. However, the record also shows that in recent years it has been extraordinary for them to complete these promises *in full*. In fact, it is pretty much now a dominant political theory, that it is somehow an outmoded form of management to give *as much gold* as the original promises specify.

Another useful obscurantism has now been coined for this new form of royal thievery. The governments "devalue" their money. So useful has this word become, in adding to the obfuscation of their victims, that under its protection they nowadays even discuss the thievery for long periods without raising any outcries of alarm, except from a few helpless professors and citizens, who are regarded by the rest as mad mossbacks.

For example, although for a hundred years before March, 1933, our own government promised to give, and its citizens could always receive, 23.22 grains of gold for every dollar-bill presented to the Treasury, in March of 1933 that traditional procedure was suspended. Then in January, 1934, acting upon some economic reasoning, which—as it was outlined in his own public statements—is almost certain to become a classic example in history of muddled economic thinking—President Roosevelt and the representatives of the current ruling cliques in control of Congress, declared that anybody holding a dollar-bill could thereafter receive for it only 13.85 grains of gold, about one thirty-fifth of an ounce. Subsequently, this breach of contract was blessed by a majority of our Supreme Court Justices with some hocus-pocus of legalistic reasoning that surely must have made Lewis Carroll twist in his grave in delight. But so it always goes!— as the historical record shows. On one pretext or another—blessed by the supposed guardians of the law or not—governments will get away with all the forcible seizure of property they dare to, from their citizens and foreigners.

It is because this unchanging dishonesty of governments *is remembered by a few people*, particularly foreigners and those who are obliged to deal with governments, that when one of them "goes off

342

gold," immediately the value of its paper money drops, as compared with real money, gold, and prices in the country rise. How and why does this happen?

Experienced people are compelled to speculate upon a simple question: *How much less gold* will be actually receivable than the government originally promised to give them for its paper? What they fully expect, and what always happens is, that later the government *will call* a smaller amount of gold a "dollar," a "pound," a "franc," or "mark." But what they want—particularly foreign merchants do—is to get *the same amount* of gold for their goods or for their services as formerly. Accordingly, in anticipation of this fraudulent governmental action, prices (in terms of the government-promises) rise. When you say "prices rise," all you are saying is—not that you have to give more gold, but that you have to give more of the paper promises for the things you want. This is because each paper promise itself is ultimately convertible into less gold.

Now, *in between* the date a government "suspends gold payment" and the date it resumes meeting its promises in gold, there is a period of uncertainty. Remember that there is little or no gold in circulation, and none obtainable from the central bank or treasury. The only thing people have is "promised money," and it is this which fluctuates in purchasing power—that is, in its command over other goods and services. This is, principally, because nobody knows how much weight in gold the dollar, the pound, the mark, the franc, will ultimately be said to represent—that is, how much gold *will actually be given* by the government for the piece of paper. Certain publicists seem to think that what determines this fluctuation is some so-called "inherent level of value" in the government "promised money," and that this, principally, is created by the amount of it in existence and the degree of demand for it, particularly on the part of foreigners, who may need it to pay bills with.

This absurd notion is a good example of how some experts can be deceived by their own dialectics. The fluctuations of a currency "off gold" are the clear result, principally, of the changing point of view of

343

many individuals as to the extent to which the government *will ulti-mately cheat* those who trusted its promsies. Precisely *how much gold* will it give for each piece of paper? That is the simple final question. It may fail to give any. Like the German government with its mark in 1923, the promises may prove 100 per cent worthless. Or they may, like the franc in 1923, turn out to be exchangeable for only one-fifth of the gold originally promised. Or, as in our own case in 1934, only about 59 per cent of the gold originally promised will be given.

A good many people have been deceived by some aspects of this obvious set of facts within recent years, among them some gambling ministries. The latter notice, after a first shock of apprehension, that the government's promises to pay gold, the paper currency, continue to circulate, even after the government officially fails to meet the promises. They fail to realize that this is due to two factors: first, because almost all of their citizens are unaware of the difference between promises to pay gold and gold itself, and therefore simply are not conscious that any economic promises are being broken by this action; and second, because those who do know this are uncertain *as to the extent* to which the promise will be unfulfilled.

Whatever the reason, the fact remains—the government finds miraculously—that its promises to pay money *continue to function as money*. After a first violent rise in some prices (principally of goods which are bought from foreigners or sold to them) the exchange value of their promises to pay does not seem to go below a certain point. The purchasing power of the government and central bank promises then does not vary greatly. The paper currency, temporarily "detached" from gold as it is, actually seems to have some value in itself. They find also that, by carrying on some shady transactions—not essentially different from the "wash sales" they send citizens to jail for engaging in, for they are at least *manipulative* sales and purchases—they can keep stable the exchange value of their promises to pay, within certain narrow limits.* They then begin,

* A "wash sale" is buying and selling of a security by the same person or group of persons, where ownership of the property does not actually change; ordinarily the purpose of the transaction is to keep, or raise, the value of the security to a certain figure by the public recording of these wholly fictitious transactions. When governments are "off gold," and their promises to pay begin to fluctuate violently in value (as measured by gold), the Government Treasury busily be-

with that too-frequent tendency of experts to divorce themselves from reality, to theorize learnedly about "managed currency systems," in which gold or any other commodity of value can be wholly dispensed with. The old illusion that governments can in some way actually create money raises its battered head. Possibly modernity has added this new miracle to its many others. They lose sight of the simplest fact: the expectation among informed persons that *some gold* will ultimately be given for the government promises; that is, the anticipation that the promises will at least be *partly* fulfilled. Thus, the residual value, which the government and central bank promises *seem* to possess under these exceptional circumstances, merely represents the average judgment of many informed, and constantly speculating, people as to *how much gold* will finally be given by the government for the promises. This is the solid core, the real value, back of our newly vaunted modern "managed currencies." It is gold, and the expectation of somehow, somewhen, receiving gold.*

The matter can be put this way: when governments suspend payment of gold for their promises the rest of the world (including their own citizens) merely suspends judgment upon them. They continue to be trusted—partly. Let them once make clear, however, that there is no ultimate chance of obtaining from them *some thing of substantial value* for their paper promises; once let it appear that the half

gins buying and selling its own promises to pay gold. The details of these operations are ordinarily kept secret, and there is good reason to suspect that many of them, if the details could be fully known, would be indistinguishable from the activities which the governments themselves punish, as being crooked, when they are indulged in by speculators.

* "No important country will redeem paper money even in gold bars," writes Benjamin M. Anderson, "automatically, and as a matter of right. And yet gold remains the regulator and *such currency stability as there is in the world* [italics mine] is due to indirect linkages between paper currencies and gold. The dollar is fixed in gold at 59.06 per cent of the old gold content, not by the old process of direct redemption in gold coin or of the issue of paper money in exchange for gold coin, but by the policy of the Treasury of receiving newly mined gold and imported gold *at this fixed rate for dollars* [italics mine] and exporting gold when necessary in order to protect the rate. . . . There remains a free gold market in London, and operations by our own stabilization fund and the stabilization funds of other countries in this free gold market and in one another's currencies *hold gold and paper more or less closely together*" [italics mine].—"Gold Stabilization and Prices," *Chase Economic Bulletin*, January 20, 1937.

exchange represented by their "promised money" will never even in part be completed, and their beautiful "managed currency systems" will collapse in the same social and industrial confusion as John Law's bubble currency; as the *assignats* of the French Revolution did; as the Continental notes of our own Revolution; as the ill-fated notes of the Confederacy; as the mark in Germany; the ruble in Russia; and in countless other cases—since the days of Kubla Khan—where ruling cliques deceived themselves into believing that the promises of governments to pay money are the same as real money. *Promises to pay money are no different from any other promises.* They do not change their nature because they involve gold, and become something other than what they are—mere words. And—to repeat our refrain—*promises to be believed must be fulfilled.*

We give our governments long grace in this respect—so long that, unfortunately, we confirm both them and ourselves in tragic fallacies about the relations which exist between us. But ultimately the simple nature of that relationship re-emerges. We relinquish our money to them for their promises, solely because we expect the promises to be fulfilled. *Somehow, somewhen, they must be proved by performance.* If they do not, our faith ends, and we will trust them no more than we would a proven crook. This is what finally makes a paper money worthless, when it becomes so. For what is a worthless paper money but the promises of a government that not even the least stupid of its citizens will believe? Yet at one time everybody in the community completely believed the promise, so much so that everybody freely and thoughtlessly relinquished his property, or performed work, for it.

18

How All the Considerations Which Affect
Other Economic Promises Govern
Modern Money as Well

BY a circuitous and perhaps wearisome route—and yet the travel may be worth it, if the simple truth be finally grasped—we ultimately come *upon the same familiar set of facts*, with regard to modern money, which we have seen operating in all other fields of human action.

The psychological factors involved in the half-exchanges represented by "promised money" are precisely the same *as in all other* deferred exchanges.

They are obscured to us because only on the rarest occasions do we directly and personally experience them. Somebody, however, relinquishes his property to, or performs labor for, the government. He receives not gold, but a promise to pay gold whenever he asks for it. He accepts this promise, evidenced by a piece of paper, because of his belief that it will be fulfilled. The promise is not made to a specific individual, but to anybody. Not only the first recipient of it, but everybody else believes that it will be fulfilled and is willing to exchange genuine wealth for the piece of paper. And what proves to be back of this belief, what is the explanation of it? *Performance only!* Time and time again, under normal circumstances, anybody who does go to the proper government official and asks to have these deferred exchanges completed, finds that they are completed by the delivery of gold. This record of infallibility may not be marred by

347

a single lapse; *and it is not marred*. This invariable completion of half-exchanges, over a long period of years, so lulls apprehension that only for industrial purposes, and for the benefit of foreigners, to whom gold must be delivered, are any demands at all made for the completion of these deferred exchanges. But once let this record of infallible performance *be broken* and the whole structure, supported by faith, collapses when the faith proves to have been deceived.

Just as past performance is a crucial element in these exchanges, so the other element that explains all deferred exchanges—*sufficiency of resources to complete them*—is present here, and always acting in full force.

The ability of any supreme government to fulfill its promises might seem to be an academic question, since in theory it can seize all the wealth of all its citizens. In practice, however—as we have already seen—this power is very much limited. Moreover—in extremities—there have been cases where governments' promises, as represented by their paper money, have exceeded the wealth of all their citizens, if all of it were seized.

It is easy to see what factors are taken into account by the initiate, in estimating a government's ability to complete the half-exchanges represented by its paper money. There are two controlling factors, which must be compared with each other:

(a) The *magnitude in volume* of all the obligations the government has to meet. These consist not only of its paper money and its subsidiary metallic currency, but also of its interest-bearing bonds, and of the deferred exchanges with employees and suppliers, which it must continuously enter into, in order to carry on its functions. These must all be added together, and compared with

(b) an estimate of the extent to which citizens will allow their property to be seized in taxation, to meet this total volume of economic promises.

Many people think a third factor is highly important: namely, *the actual amount of gold* the government has on hand, as compared with its promises to pay gold. While this, of course, plays a large role when a government is in a crisis and is being called upon to pay out

348

gold in undue amount, it is not nearly so crucial as the ratio between the government's total current obligations and its total income.

When the obligations of a government become recklessly huge, and when at the same time its income from taxes and other seizures fails to total as much as its current outlays, the red flag flies for the initiate. We say, then, that its "budget is out of balance." A great deal has been heard of this term in recent years, and the ordinary citizen realizes vaguely it is something dangerous and reprehensible in government management. But precisely why, he does not know, and in recent years he has been inclined to say, What of it?

Its chief importance lies in the fact that it is apparent, from the continued discrepancy between its outgo and income of claims to real wealth, that the government has managed to reach that not easily determinable point where its citizens will not allow themselves to be more imposed upon. It *could* seize more of their claims to wealth; it could seize their all. But it dares not. What is the significance of this? Merely that the principal reliance for the completion of all the government promises *is the seizable wealth of its citizens*. The citizens are, though temporarily unconscious of it, the guarantors. The obligations are theirs. If they balk at more taxes, *they balk at ultimate completion of the exchanges*. There is only one "out" for a government in such a situation. If it cannot seize sufficient wealth from its citizens to meet its current expenses, it must *use* less wealth in its own maintenance. That is, it must cut expenses. *But the expenditures of governments seldom decrease; they almost invariably increase.*

It is at this point that those whose business it is to watch such matters begin to doubt the ultimate ability of the government to complete the half-exchanges represented by its "promised money" and bonds. Gresham's Law then begins to operate with this "promised money" just as surely as, for twenty-five hundred years, it has so often operated with coined money. Whenever these knowing persons receive any of this "promised money" in an exchange, they get rid of it quickly. They much prefer gold and they get gold—or some other tangible form of wealth *that can surely be exchanged for gold*

349

—while the getting is good. Slowly this point of view spreads, and the realization of the government's true situation becomes more widely recognized. As a result, instead of a trickle of demand upon it for gold, an increasing volume of its promises to pay are presented to it for completion.

It is at this point that the amount of gold in the government's treasury is important. It must meet every demand, like a bank experiencing a "run." One failure to do so would arouse the consciousness of every holder of its promises to the situation; and most of them are still unconscious of it. If they were waked up by the trumpet call of a single refusal to complete, a Niagara of demands would descend upon it, and sweep away all the gold it has. If it has much, it may indeed finally avert the flood. If it has little, and continues to overspend, just before the Niagara is ready to break, it saves what little store of gold it has by "going off the gold standard." That is, it suspends—*it still further postpones*—the deferred exchanges represented by its paper money.

But does "going off gold" increase its resources in any way? Certainly not, except perhaps indirectly, by giving its exporters certain advantages over those of other nations, which at the time have not "gone off gold." As these particular citizens prosper,* the volume of taxes seizable from them may slightly increase. This is, however, a problematic, a slow, and an insignificant addition to the government's resources. Those who are estimating its ultimate ability to complete

* The modern apologetics for altering the gold-content of a currency (observe that this is always a decrease, never an increase) always include prominently this contention that certain groups within the country will be benefited by being able to undersell foreign competitors. This, indeed, is usually true for a period. A false "prosperity" is likely to ensue, its benefits arising principally from the fact that other groups, in other lands, are being damaged. The ultimate economic result of "going off gold"—invariably followed, nowadays, by changing the gold content of the currency—is one of those polemic fields where economists are in most bitter dispute, even if modern statesmen are not so much so. Keeping, according to the intention of this inquiry, as close to indisputability as possible, this question cannot be discussed here. The only proper point to be made, for the purposes of our own study, is that these particular apologetics, obviously, always constitute an afterthought. Beneficial or not to their citizens, no government ever goes off gold, and then later alters its currency, *until it cannot keep its own promises with regard to gold*. That is, the action is represented as being beneficial to citizens *only when* it is necessary to get the ruling cliques out of trouble they have previously gotten themselves into.

its promises pay very little attention to it. If the government's budget continues out of balance; if it allows its expenditures to increase, instead of cutting them; if it continues to show the same reluctance to seize the wealth of its citizens, but on the contrary weakly borrows from them, thus still further increasing the volume of its outstanding promises—clearer and ever clearer does it become that it will never fully complete the half-exchanges represented by its bonds and "promised money."

The final crisis arises when this situation becomes so self-evident that the government *can no longer borrow from its own citizens.* The same verdict then falls ruthlessly upon it as upon the sorriest trickster who is expert at handing out I O U's, until he is discovered. Once people recognize that it will never complete past exchanges in full, no one will relinquish ownership of property to it *in any new deferred exchange.* It cannot sell its bonds. The end thereupon swiftly comes in catastrophe. In a panic, it prints more "promised money," palming it off on whoever will accept it—and that is, principally, its own employees and suppliers, who have no alternative but to accept it. These promises mount in total to sums of gold out of all relation to the amounts it can ever hope, in the wildest imagining of anyone, to seize from its citizens.

For example, when the German Government had ceased running its printing presses toward the end of 1923, the amount of marks it promised totaled 496,507,425,000,000,000,000.* This is 496 million million million. One mark at that time was defined as about 5½ grains of pure gold. The total amount of gold, therefore, that the German Government promised to pay in these issued promises was about six million million million ounces. The total amount of gold in all the central banks in the world at the time was only a tiny portion of this. Actually, the German Government had promised to pay about *fifteen billion times as much gold as there was in the banks of the whole world at the moment!*

This, of course, is an extreme example, but it is not unique. The Communist Party in Russia, when the old regime was successfully

* J. W. Angell, *The Recovery of Germany,* Appendix.

overthrown, deliberately went through a like process. "According to some versions of the early Soviet economic policy, the original idea was to continue printing currency until Soviet notes possessed absolutely no value, and thus allow money to achieve a sort of suicide." * Before letting it expire, however, the record shows very clearly that Lenin used it methodically to acquire wheat from the stupid moujiks before they woke up to what was going on. It seems that about 2 thousand million million rubles were printed.† The wildness of the promising is indicated by the fact that in 1924, the government announced it would redeem its promises—at the rate of 50,000,000,000 paper rubles for one gold ruble.

Such a fantastic and conscienceless geometric multiplication of promises, as these of Germany and Russia—passed off on those who were either compelled to accept them or who were ignorant enough to do so—at least serves as a simple and beautiful illustration of the role which *ability to pay* plays in this field of deferred exchanges represented by "promised-money." Obviously, there must be some rational relation between the sums of gold a government promises to pay in these half-exchanges, and the proportion of that wealth of the country that citizens may reasonably be expected to allow themselves to be despoiled of, without revolt. When that relation becomes questionable; and, indeed, fantastically absurd, as in these cases cited above, the government's promises become unbelievable—and as money, recognizably worthless.

In the past decade our newspapers have been full to bursting with discussion of such governmental acts, and their consequences; and yet it may not be amiss to point out what precisely they signify in events, and the somewhat entertaining process which is always pursued.

What the actions amount to, in their ultimate effect, is of course *a total or partial cancellation*, by the government, of the old deferred exchanges it has entered into. The unfortunate *final holders* of the promises become the actual payers of the government debt. This is

* *Soviet Money and Finance*, L. E. Hubbard.
† *Foreign Banking Systems*, edited by Willis and Beckhart.

always well understood by those who advocate the procedure as a governmental policy. Holding little or none of the promises themselves, they are actually blind enough to think that those who do hold them are rich men, and that this is a smart way to utilize the property of the wealthy in order to extinguish the government's debt. The procedure does indeed extinguish the government debt, but seldom at the expense of rich men, who are (ordinarily) precisely the ones who know what is going on and have long since stowed themselves in the storm-cellar. Whether they are aware of it or not, they have long since been following the precepts of Gresham's Law. The extinguishment of debt takes place at the expense of the little fellow, who is uninformed and has thus far been undisturbed in his happy-go-lucky confidence in his government. For, of course, these government promises are economic promises. Chiefly banks, insurance companies and like institutions—and only minimally, rich men—hold the promises. *These institutions cannot protect themselves from the acts of governments.* Millions of small people are trusting their promises, and the completion of these promises rest upon those of the government.

Accordingly, *a complete readjustment of all promissory relations* has to occur throughout the entire society, when a government is compelled, by its own previous excesses, to wipe out any part of its economic promises, upon which all others are resting. This readjustment in the ownership of property takes place, not only in direct loss of a fixed amount of gold by those who *at the moment* hold the promises represented by the paper-bills. That is disturbing enough! But it occurs to a greater extent through the medium of prices. We can see this best when we examine the actual process by which the eventual result is consummated.

The process is one which, it to be hoped anyway, must give somebody in an extra-terrestrial world a little amusement. For, certainly, it is too disturbing to be amusing to those who are involved in it—and everybody is! The whole affair is carried on simply by legally *changing the meaning of a word in the dictionary.*

For example, on March 6, 1933, the definition of the word "dollar" was that it constituted 23.22 grains of gold. On January 30, 1934, through the delegation of the power to President Roosevelt, the definition of the word "dollar" became 13.85 grains, one thirty-fifth of an ounce of gold.

Now, imagine an old fellow by the name of John Van Winkle who had been living somewhere in Maine or Vermont, and who held promises of our government totaling $3,500. He goes to the Secretary of the Treasury, and says:

"Give me gold for this paper; I want to go abroad, where they tell me the barbarians will accept only gold."

The Secretary gives him one hundred ounces.

"You're short-changing me," says John. "Here, in my almanac, the law says the word 'dollar' means 23.22 grains. Also it says that you are obliged by law to give that much to me for each dollar bill, without any question. Come across with 169 ounces. That's what I cal'late your written promise clearly was."

"Oh, no," says the Secretary, "you're looking in the wrong almanac. The new up-to-date almanac says the word 'dollar' means one thirty-fifth of an ounce of gold. That's what I'm giving you. And, like it or not, you must go by the new almanac."

It is by this simple, brazen and fraudulent changing of the meaning of an important word—changing it to their own advantage and leaving the injured no recourse but to accept the new meaning—that practically every government in the world, in the last two decades, has wiped out all or a great part of the half-exchanges it has entered into.

An amusing variation of this process took place in Germany. There, before the War, the mark by definition was 5.53 grains of gold. Then, in 1923, when its promises totaled almost 500 million million million marks, the word "mark" was expunged from the German dictionary, except as an archaism. A new unit of currency was created, called the *reichsmark*. But the definition of this was *also* 5.53 grains of gold, just the same as the old mark. Two things like to a third are like each other: one of the first principles of logic.

Imagine, then, Hans going into some august presence, with a note

354

saying the German Treasury owed him one thousand marks. "Give me 5,530 grains of gold," he demands. "Here it so promises."

"Let's see what is written," says the Presence. "Ah! marks. Marks no longer exist—don't you know that? We now have no marks in the Treasury."

"Oh, yes, I've been told that," says Hans, "but in the old legal dictionary it says marks are 5.53 grains of gold, and in the new dictionary it says the reichsmark is also 5.53 grains of an ounce of gold. So give me reichsmarks. It's all the same to me."

"Dummkopf!" shouts the Presence. "Can't you see this paper reads marks, not reichsmarks. I can't give you marks. The State says they no longer exist. And why should I give you reichsmarks, when they were not promised to you in this paper? If they were promised here, I would give them to you! We keep our promises—to the very letter. And, if you ever say to the contrary, beware!"

To such sorry verbal tricks do our modern States descend—to cancel the deferred exchanges they have entered into. How much more honest, in their outright robbery, were the two Charleses of England! For all the world, this modern process is like the cold-blooded cheating of little children.

But, of course, these verbal gymnastics are of the most dangerous character. By changing the dictionary meaning of dollar, pound, mark, franc and similar words—true enough, the government can put itself in a position where it has to deliver much less gold in its own economic promises.

Unfortunately, *its economic promises are not the only ones*. We have seen, in this entire study, how all the processes of modern life are carried on by deferred exchanges. In all but the tiniest portion of these, *it is money which is promised in the last half of the exchange!* Not only the government's deferred exchanges, but all others specify that dollars, or pounds or marks or francs, shall pass in the last half of the exchange. Now, of course, if the meaning of the word dollar, for example—the statement as to how much gold it is—is changed for the government, *it is changed for everybody else!*

What happens now? Everybody who is under the misfortune of

355

being on the last half of any exchange has to accept a smaller amount of gold—because the definition of the word "dollar" has been changed by the government. Of course, everybody goes by the new definition. The State by *force majeure* compels everybody to do so! Even if, foreseeing such a possibility, the word "dollar" is not wholly relied upon in the promise, but a definite weight of gold is specified, the State—through its judicial officers—says that the new meaning of the word, "dollar," must hold. That, almost incredibly, is what happened in this country.* Only a mind steeped in legalism could thus torture the clear meaning of words. Posterity—let us hope, more clear-eyed than ourselves—will know what to think of the five Supreme Court judges, guardians of the sacred law, who so coolly winked at this brazen fraud.

The deep disturbance to all the multitudinous transactions that go on in modern life, which arises from this compulsory change in the meaning of a crucial word, cannot be followed here. It affects directly, of course, all *long* economic promises. Persons who are on the last half of these are obvious sufferers, since the money they receive in the last half of the exchange turns out to be of far less value, sometimes of no value. But, of course, through them—through the diminution of their resources—this economic disturbance spreads in endless waves that cannot be followed, throughout the entire population.

To illustrate merely the character of what goes on, an extreme example may be given. At the beginning of the War, long-term promises based on landed property in Germany totaled 40,000,000,000 marks, about $10,000,000,000. It represented about one-sixth of all the property in Germany. This was the amount of wealth, in other

* Because our government went "off gold" during the Civil War, it became the practice to specify in long promises that the second half of the exchange should be completed in gold coin of "the present standard of weight and fineness." In the famous "gold clause decisions," early in 1935, a Supreme Court majority held that citizens could not protect themselves, in this straightforward fashion, against the fraudulence of the government. This was clearly the ultimate purport of these decisions, which as a precedent will certainly plague our children for generations to come. For it now sets up, as a sacred doctrine, what had been the pernicious practice of rulers: that these, the most crucial of all economic promises, need not be kept by the promisor, and mere expediency—not necessity—may, if the government wishes, be considered the guide.

words, which individuals had relinquished to others, in mortgages and similar long promises based on land and buildings. When the mark was finally "stabilized"—another beautiful modern euphemism! —at a ratio of one trillion marks to one gold mark, what were these long promises worth? A trillion is a million million. These long-term promises, forty billion marks of them, were thus exchangeable for about one of our pennies! * To this extent was the ownership of wealth forcibly transferred in Germany from some individuals to others.

What this amounts to is: if the State can complete its deferred exchanges with mere words, it cannot prevent everybody else *from doing the same thing with the same words!* In extinguishing its own long promises in this fashion, it is extinguishing all other long promises in the nation.

When the fraud is not complete, *but partial*, the extinguishment of the debt is not so clear. It is unclear, however, only because the mere words confuse people. What happens is that the promise is completed in *the proper number* of dollars—or pounds or marks or francs or rubles—that were originally specified in the transaction. But since the word "dollar"—for example—now means *a smaller amount of gold* than before, the recipient gets less gold. But actually—as we saw—in either case he gets no gold at all. He gets pieces of paper called "dollar bills"—or some other kind of bills—and he gets precisely the number specified in the documents. These pieces of paper, however, since they are exchangeable for less gold *are exchangeable for less goods*.

For we must realize that when we talk about the price of every one of the tens of thousands of articles and commodities that men handle, what we are saying merely is—*how much gold it will exchange for*. Where gold is the money, the value of everything else is stated in terms of gold. That statement is what we call its "price." This comparison with gold *is just as true of the pieces of paper called "dollar bills"* as it is of anything else. They are worth exactly, no

* *Foreign Banking Systems*, edited by Willis and Beckhart; Chapter VIII, on the German banking system, by Paul Quittner.

357

more nor less, than the amount of gold they can be exchanged for. Now, the amount of gold that will be accepted, or given, for any product or service is one thing the government has no control over. It can, for example, change the meaning of the word "dollar," saying that it is fourteen grains of gold, instead of twenty-three grains, but it cannot compel a foreigner (shall we say?) to accept fourteen grains of gold for ten pounds of rubber, when formerly he was getting twenty-three grains of gold for that amount of rubber. What the foreigner will say, quite sensibly, is: "Change the meaning of the word 'dollar' all you please. I want the same amount of gold as before. If the new meaning of the word 'dollar' is fourteen grains, in order to give me the same amount of gold as before you will have to give me $1.69, for ten pounds of rubber."

In other words, the price of rubber rises in terms of the paper money. *No more gold* is given than before, under these circumstances; but, because of the new definition, *higher figures in dollars have to be used to designate the same amount of gold.*

Now, the movement of prices—of the ratio of exchange with gold, which every product and every form of labor has—is an extremely complex study. These ratios change endlessly. All sort of factors—principally the relation between the demand for and the supply of the product—govern the changes. For our own purposes here, all that need be pointed out is that when a government changes the definition of words like "dollar," "pound," "mark," "franc"—making them represent less gold than before—sooner or later the change shows up *in the stated prices* of all products and services. These changes in price—that is, the statement of their exchange value in terms of gold—happen immediately in some cases; very soon in others; fitfully and slowly in still others; and by processes which often seem in no way related to the change in definition of the currency. But, no matter how hidden and intricate the process of change, the careful economist can ultimately trace it back to the change in definition, whenever the latter event takes place.

Come back now to the man who happens to be on the last half of a long economic promise, when a government—for its own purposes—changes the meaning of the most important economic word in each nation's dictionary. He gets the same amount of dollars, or pounds, or francs, or marks, when the exchange is completed. But he gets less goods, *because the price of everything has risen.*

In short, *the State is an ineradicable part of our economic world.* It does not exist in an economic vacuum. Far from it. It cannot confine its acts to its own half-exchanges, for in a thousand devious ways *they are intermeshed with all other economic promises.*

When it follows a procedure, then, with regard to its promised money, such as we have analyzed, social and economic disturbances of the most widespread character are inevitable.

The fact that there is no State in the world that has not taken such action in the past two decades has lulled us all into an incredible complacency in the face of this portentous phenomenon. Rulers have always been a distrusted breed to common men, but is open fraud henceforth to be an accepted ingredient in the ethics of our governors? The widespread acceptance of this new State-philosophy, with regard to money, must be taken into account as a modern economic fact of the first importance.

For it must be evident, to any person of reflective mind who has read his newspaper for ten years, that not only have States involved their populations in the disturbances caused by repudiation of their promises; but that apologetics for the action are always forthcoming from the most honorable gentlemen! We see the current political managers in every important nation of the world—and so-called leaders of opinion with them—coolly discussing these fraudulent actions as questions of national policy. They publicly debate, in short, whether it is advantageous, or perhaps not so much so, or when and how it may be more so, for the government to perpetrate a barefaced fraud upon those who have trusted its promises.

Aside from the ethics involved, what an extraordinary revelation this is of the economic intelligence of those who have most to do with managing the affairs of men today!

As I say, these remarks are presented, not as political, but as economic comment. The notion that economics deals with things, and

359

not with the states of mind of men, is as absurd as it is dangerous. States of mind dictate the actions of men, and it is the actions of men that are the study of economics. Accordingly, the conception of public morals that is displayed by those key individuals who—by shrewd managing or by gulling of their fellowmen—run the affairs of great masses of people, is of inestimable economic importance.

No one who lived through the World War will ever forget the conclusion which slowly, over the four years, became fixed among an ever greater and greater number of common men and women: that this wholesale mad slaughter, this vast misery endured by tens of millions of simple, likable, well-meaning people, had its ultimate origin in the senseless pride of opinion and the stupidity of ruling cliques in the warring nations; that stubborn and unintelligent "old men," as they were sometimes referred to by those in the front lines, were to blame for leading their peoples into this *cul de sac* of tragedy. This universal opinion of the common citizen, at the time, about who were responsible for the War, was undoubtedly right.

It would be just as right, it seems to me, if it held the post-War ruling group responsible, in their economic unintelligence, for all the widespread social misery that has been so marked in the two decades since the World War ended.

Events of the kind that have occurred in these twenty years are no more inevitable than the World War was inevitable. The political managers, of one or another of the nations, can always be found, by the analytic and unimpassioned economist, to be at the bottom of any troublesome situation. Particularly is this true where the trouble has to do, directly or undirectly, with money.

It seems inescapably to be the fact—even from the survey we have made here—that all the troubles modern men have with money arise from the fact that governments have the close association with money that they do. After three thousand years of such association, there is, of course, no changing this. It is now an inevitability of modern society. In such a complex world as ours, some supreme body must indeed be responsible for the money, which measures the value and thus facilitates the exchanges, of all products and all labor. The whole body of a people, which is really the State, can now be the only guarantor of the weight and quality of its real money—whether gold, silver, or anything else. But to say that this relationship of the State with money is now a necessary one is not to say that it need be a fraudulent one. *But such, unfortunately, is the bald economic fact.* The records are clear on the point that, with rare exceptions throughout history, it has always been so, and all our modern experiences show that it still is. Rulers' promises with regard to money are not now, nor have they ever been, inviolable.

But modern rulers now have a greater power over money than ever any ruler had in the past. For now, through the growth of the promise-system, that has been unfolded in these pages, practically all the real money of the world—by which the multitudinous exchanges of men are carried on and measured—are owned and held by the governments. *Never before this era has this been true.* In the past, rulers had very little of the real money. Citizens carrying on their business held almost all of it. Now common citizens have nothing but the rulers' promises. The rulers hold practically all the real money.

There is a startling modern phenomenon for the political philosopher to sit long, like a Buddha, and ponder over.

For, unfortunately, it must be considered in connection with another no less startling fact. It seems almost a certainty that those who enter into half-exchanges with governments—if they allow enough time to elapse—will find themselves, in the end, either wholly or partly cheated out of their property. Apologists for each State will always find a reason for this, which can be argued on both sides. But while the argument goes on, there stands the hard, sad record. Yet money is the lifeblood of modern society; and since "promised money" has universally replaced real money in common use, it becomes true, in the last analysis, that *upon the economic reliability of our governments all the other active processes of modern civilization now rest.* The social disturbances that ensue from this faith, which we continue to bestow, with a blind fatuity, upon our governments

361

are endless. They are a principal component, without any question, of most of the social, economic and political "problems" that make our time so perplexing.

The whole record makes pertinent a simple summary observation. Men, as we have seen, in their individual relationships are pretty decent and reliable animals. It does seem, however, that behind the bulwark of power, if they can acquire it, they feel that they can be scoundrels with impunity. Government, it might be said, is the one area of human activity that constitutes the last real stronghold of scoundrelism in human nature.

19

Who Owns What Today? How Modern Ownership of Wealth Differs from That of All Our Ancestors

W HAT today do we mean by the words *wealth* and *ownership of wealth*?

One conception of wealth would include, no doubt, everything, both material and incorporeal, that contributes to human well-being. In this sense, the health of an individual and his strength—that is, his very ability to work upon the raw materials of Nature he finds about him—are forms of wealth. Frequently, in reasoning about the wealth of a nation, the labor power, the acquired skills, even that indefinite quality described as the "character" of its citizens, are included as forms of wealth. Sometimes one comes upon elaborate estimates, in which an attempt is made to measure these incorporeal elements by gold, and, where they are not fully utilized, to count the results as "losses" of wealth. A little far-fetched, it seems.

Another more limited conception of wealth is to eliminate the incorporeal and confine the meaning to the *material things* which contribute to human well-being. This latter is a more useful conception of wealth, in that at least it enables us to distinguish more clearly what we mean by its *ownership*.

For one pragmatic characteristic of wealth, thus delimited in meaning, is *that it is owned*. This indeed is certainly one of the basic and indisputable facts about human affairs. The ownership of wealth, for the greater part, is by individuals and families. To some extent,

363

it is by groups large and small. To an increasing extent, it is by the entire community itself.

What we mean, pragmatically, by ownership of any form of wealth is that he whom we call the owner has the right—without molestation or interference by others—*to dispose of the thing owned at his will and pleasure*. He can consume it or use it himself. He can destroy it, if he wills. He can give it to others, so that they then have the full disposition of it. Or he can allow others temporarily to enjoy its use. And none may say him nay in these royal decisions. Such is the ultimate pragmatic criterion of ownership of any form of property; and—it will be observed—it is, in an important sense, negative. It involves, quite clearly, the notion that *others may not interfere* with the owner in his free disposition and enjoyment of the form of wealth which is owned.

Now, some obvious considerations present themselves here. This use of any form of wealth without interference from others is, clearly, no "natural" right of a human being. Interference plainly can arise, and all through history—down to the turbulent present—it has. The so-called right—the assumption to full unmolested use and enjoyment—is only available because of the recognition of it, the acquiescence in it, by others. It is thus, so to speak, a social right only. Plainly it includes, not only the owner, but everybody else, in its purview. It is one of those deep-lying agreements, taken for granted and unanalyzed, which have come to constitute through long eons the *mores* of human society. The full conception of ownership not only involves this ordinarily unperceived participation of others, but in modern times another more observable delimitation: the owner is not wholly free to dispose of the thing owned at his will and pleasure. In using it up or enjoying it, if he either harms other individuals, *or interferes with their ownership of other wealth* by his action, the community will step in to restrain him. In other words, ownership of wealth must now be peaceful and uninterfering use and disposition.

For meticulous thinking, it must be observed that these considerations are quite as true of what we call *the common ownership* of

364

wealth as of individual ownership of it. Frequently, idealists have confused themselves into reasoning that there was a special quality about the "common" possession of forms of wealth, which made the ownership different from separate and individual ownership. The truth is that all through the long history of man *common or group ownership* of wealth and *individual ownership* have existed side by side. Possibly, in the dim past, common ownership was more predominantly the condition; but as soon as forms of wealth became more abundant, individual ownership became by far the predominant state of affairs.

Nevertheless, common or group ownership *has never been extinguished among men*. Far from it. We can still find, in Africa and Australia, groups of men in a primitive status of civilization who share, without thought or quarrel, a great many of the things which we ourselves would consider personal belongings. In a pastoral state of civilization, when men lived chiefly in tribes, no doubt the larger part of their possessions was considered common property, to be used up or enjoyed by anyone in the tribe who so pleased, *but under definitely understood customs*. Then and later, as men became settled as tillers of the soil, land was almost always owned in common. No individual of the group could preempt a favored spot for himself and be allowed the undisputed privilege of enjoying it. In the early extensive civilizations, the religious mentors of the community, always organized themselves in strong and well-defined groups, and owned property in common. This remains today the form of ownership of property by the priests in men's communities. The world-wide Catholic Church provides a striking example of common ownership of wealth to an extent that rivals the owned wealth of most States. Also, the custom of common or group ownership still survives, extremely virile as an institution, in the modern harmonious family. The individual units in it, usually, share freely the larger part of the forms of wealth they own.

Is it not clear that our pragmatic criterion of property, when applied to common ownership, remains as valid as it is of individual ownership? When land was owned in common, for instance, it was

365

the *single group* of persons who regarded themselves as having the sole and undisputed right to its use and disposition. If any individual among them—or if any outside group—sought to divest them of possession, they would strive to retain it with all the power they could muster. *Unselfishness did not extend beyond the group.* There was no such thing as an altruistic notion that the enjoyment of wealth should be shared, as of right, with every animal bearing the face and figure of a human. So, likewise, this sense of possession—almost amounting to instinct—is quite as virile in the primitive community, where food and many seemingly personal belongings may be used and enjoyed without quarrel or question by anybody—*in the group!* No one outside the group would be accorded the privilege, except in a manifestation of friendliness; any more than the belongings of a modern family would be considered by its individuals at the free disposal of any outsider who desired to use and enjoy them.

The essential difference is plain, then, between common and individual ownership of wealth: simply many persons, instead of one, *confirm themselves in their own minds* as the ultimate disposers of the wealth; and that assumed right, it is clear enough, rests finally upon the combined force they can exercise to prevent others from using and enjoying the wealth which, as a group, they say they "own."

Common or group ownership of wealth is often confused, by those who reason carelessly, with State ownership of wealth; or, as it is often referred to, *public property.* There are not a few who seem to think, either that this is something new and socially salutary in the affairs of men, or that it means going back to what they regard as a more "natural," a more ideal, form of social structure. Examined realistically, from an evolutionary viewpoint, State ownership appears to be far more an extension of *the ownership of wealth by rulers* than a reappearance, or recrudescence, of early forms of common or group ownership.

Theoretically, it is now true, ownership of State wealth vests in all the people. But this notion, as we saw in examining taxation in Chapter Thirteen, is a mere rationalization of a hoary historical proc-

366

ess, by which individual rulers, by superior force, seized possession of what wealth they could acquire from their own subjects and from outside groups. In the present day, only as a people, under rigidly prescribed rules and by complex processes, may the final disposition of State-owned wealth be determined. No single one of those whom we vaguely conceive of as "owning it in common" may exercise his individual will and pleasure in using it up, disposing of it or enjoying it, which is the pragmatic criterion of ownership.

The sharp distinction which should be made between this and genuine common ownership is no mere matter of quibbling. Food owned in common by a primitive group may, for example, be eaten by anyone in the group. Each unit of the group—*at his pleasure if he keeps within prescribed custom*—may use up or enjoy the group wealth. But let any modern member of a community attempt to acquire and use for his benefit a tiny bit of the gold, for instance, which theoretically he "owns in common" with all his fellow-citizens, and see what happens to him. Or let him, free and full citizen that he is, forage for food, when he is hungry, in some army cantonment. He "owns" it, does he not, in common with all his fellow-citizens? If, in innocent logic, he tried it in Russia, supposed paradise of common ownership, he would be shot to death. The word "ownership" here means precisely nothing in practice, *so far as the individual who "owns" it in common with others is concerned.* This wealth is State-owned. Its real owners, today as always, are those who know the intricate stops by which the modern organ of Power is played. These wielders of power can and do *determine the use and disposition of the wealth,* which must be the final criterion of ownership. Through their actions, the people—who theoretically "own" it—*can divest themselves of ownership* to these forms of wealth, in favor of individuals and special groups; and they do, continuously.

The sense of possession seems instinctive and ineradicable in men. Particularly when the form of wealth has been created by one's own labor, it appears to become identified with one's personality. "What is mine is dear to me," said Plautus, "as his own is dear to every

367

man." The very word, *property*—cold and lifeless to us now—comes from a word meaning "myself," and has all the dearness and warmth of that identification with personality. Yet, curiously, we find persons, otherwise apparently intelligent, who will reason themselves into the notion that *ownership of property in itself* is the source of all our economic difficulties—particularly, ownership of wealth by individuals; and that if ownership of wealth, as an institution, could be somehow extinguished, an earthly Paradise would at once be upon us.

It is instructive in this connection to observe that those stubborn, but in some respects realistic, theorists about human society—the Communist Party in Russia—still regard this deep-seated and hoary instinct of individual ownership of wealth as an inevitable part of, and support to, their own social structure. In respect merely to ownership of wealth, the basic difference a so-called communist State represents, as a change from the past, *is a further extension of State ownership of wealth*—that is, of ruler ownership. This is true in Russia, both in practice and in theory. But this extension of State ownership of wealth, it must be seen, is a development that has slowly been going forward in human affairs for untold centuries. It is a development, incidentally, fully as apparent among those peoples whom communists regard, and who regard themselves, as most confirmedly "capitalistic."

State ownership of wealth—as a mere extension of ruler ownership, which it is—is ancient, both in principle and in practice. It has existed, coincident with individual ownership and group ownership of property, as far back as there are historical records. Any further extension of it, particularly to the degree that obtains in Russia, *since it means an increased interference of power-wielders in the economic processes* by which men keep themselves alive, obviously has consequences of the most far-reaching nature. More so today than ever is this true, when our world society has become so cooperative in occupation and interdependent upon promises. But all the more reason, this, for seeing the development for what it is, and not

368

to allow it to mislead us as to the true nature of the ownership of wealth.

The simplest truth about wealth is that it must be owned. Who has the unmolested disposition of the wealth, be it individual or group, and be the group small or numerous, is the pragmatic owner. This has been true since men came down out of trees, and by no person, with a grain of realism in his observation, can any probable future form of society be envisioned where wealth will not continue to be owned—by individuals, by groups, and by the State itself.

The real question the rational theorist has to deal with is not change or abolition of ownership of property *as a human custom and institution*. That represents pure chimera. He must concern himself, really, with *changes in the processes by which new wealth is produced and ownership of it acquired* by those who will own it, whether they be individuals, groups, or the entire people.

Our present business is not with the question of suggested changes in these processes by which new wealth is produced and acquired— a question which extended government ownership of wealth so sharply raises. The economics student should be concerned first, in proper humility, with what actually takes place in human affairs. Only when he is certain, if he ever can be, as to the correspondence of his observation with actuality, may he safely theorize as to what changes may be possible or advisable. It is not a bad principle, in short, to be sure of our physiology before we attempt surgery.

At the moment, accordingly, it is most profitable to attempt to see, as clearly as possible, *to what extent* individuals, groups, and even States, really own any forms of wealth today—under the pragmatic criterion of ownership that has been set forth.

Now, the remarkable fact is—as we have already intimated—that, within the last few centuries, there has been a radical change among men in the conditions surrounding the ownership of wealth. It is a social change that has been little observed and commented upon, except by almost hermit savants. Certainly, it is not commonly appreciated by the multitudes of individuals who are most nearly affected by it. The vast extension of half-exchanges among men has been wholly responsible for this development.

The curious phenomenon is that everybody today conceives of himself *as owning a great deal more wealth than in actuality he does;* and States themselves may be included in this statement.

Shakespeare described the prevailing status of affairs, as he did so many times, in a quick phrase: "His means are in supposition," says Shylock, of Antonio. *The means of all of us are in supposition.*

Your present wealth, as you regard it, should be—for unconfused observation and reasoning—divided into two categories.

First, there are those things which you may be said truly to own, in that you can dispose of them in any way that suits your fancy.

In the second category, there would be the forms of wealth which you may own, and no doubt in the future will, *if* a large number of persons, corporations and States fulfill promises that have been made to you, directly or indirectly.

Nothing in this second category, plainly, is wealth. It consists of promises only—words, words, and more words. It might be called, if you please, "When-As-And-If Wealth." If those upon whom you are relying justify the reliance by some future action, then indeed the promises *may eventuate* in tangible forms of wealth, which you may use and enjoy to the exclusion of everybody else.

Nevertheless, you may not blink the fact that the promises *may not be fulfilled!* Indeed, insofar as they consist of promises of a State, if you wait long enough—as we have seen—there is more than an even chance, in the present condition of State integrity, that ultimately you will find yourself cheated out of all, or a good part, of the enjoyable possessions you expect to receive.

The most cursory examination reveals the fact that, with most individuals in modern society, this second category of "When-As-And-If Wealth" constitutes *by far the larger proportion* of the wealth they think they own. This is true of everybody except the poorest individuals, who own very little real wealth. But they also own no promises! This is to say that persons nowadays who count themselves wealthy—whether moderately or greatly—are comparatively poor in real possessions, and rich only in holding promises.

It is well enough to assent to this as a sort of amusing anomaly. But it may prove salutary—in accentuating the deep significance in your life of promises, about which you are so blandly unaware—to sit down and take a careful inventory of your worldly possessions. You will soon learn how poor, not how wealthy you are, should unknown men, upon whom you are relying to be honest, prove to be otherwise. Only by leaving the cold and pallid general, and getting within the warm aura of one's own experience, is it possible to appreciate, in their full force, the actual relations we have with other persons; and, therefore, the present nature of our society.

If for no other reason than entertainment it may be well for you, for once, to be fully realistic as to the status of your wealth. Sit down, then, and set forth a statement of your assets, dividing them into the two categories mentioned above.

Possibly you own the home in which you live. In 1930 about fourteen million families in the United States did, out of an estimated thirty million families, roughly speaking. But stop! Do you own it free and clear? If you do, under our definition of ownership, you are in a position, unhindered, to do what you please with it. You can give it to someone else, if you feel generous. You can rent its use to someone else. You can alter it in any way you feel inclined to. You can burn or pull it down, if you are eccentric, and want a home in every respect different. *Your home may, however, be mortgaged.* If such is the case, no matter how small the loan you have obtained by putting it up as forfeit, your ownership in it is very much limited by rights which you have relinquished to the mortgage-holder. Search out and read through the mortgage agreement. Quickly you will find that there are a great many things you cannot do with your home which you could do, were it owned by you free and clear. In other words, if your home is mortgaged, your ownership of it *is a highly conditional ownership.* It rests completely upon acts which you yourself have engaged to perform in the future—namely, to complete specified half-exchanges on definite dates. No doubt you fully intend to perform these acts. Also, your present means may

371

be ample to enable you to perform them. But surely, after the past ten years, you are now aware how fickle economic circumstance is. And if those recollections do not suffice, it may be salutary for you to read a little American history, where swift changes in the value of real estate have been as responsible as anything for the color of events. The most important act which so conditions your owner-ship—payment of the principal of the loan—is long distant. You may not, in the end, be able to perform it. No; to be properly realistic, if your home is mortgaged, it cannot be put down in the first list of wealth you really own. The fact alone that you have been obliged to borrow upon it raises the question, no matter how slight it may be, whether your means will indeed be ample enough—in the end—to enable you to complete this deferred exchange you have entered into.

But also to be realistic—you may well argue—it would be fair to put into this section of your inventory a sum of dollars, represent-ing what you call your "equity" in the home. This would be the difference between what you think the home would bring in dollars, if it were sold, and the sum of money you owe on the mortgage. But if you were compelled to sell it, how can you know how many dollars the home would bring? How even may you be sure it can be sold? Conditions change radically, as they did in 1929. All home-owners then found that their so-called equities were far smaller than they had anticipated, and in millions of cases did not exist at all. Your so-called equity depends merely *upon a different set of conditions*, in which not you, but others, are principally involved. It is, plainly, nothing but an expectation, a hope—one of the events to be hatched with others from bawdy Circumstance. But we are seeking items of real wealth for this first branch of our inventory; not possibilities, nor even probabilities. Under our definition of true ownership, we must leave out your home from this list, if it is mortgaged, no matter how small the mortgage is.

Better to start with what is in it. No doubt you own most of that. Of course, there may be in it a piano, a radio, an automobile, an oil-burner, a refrigerator, a set of books, a vacuum-sweeper—or some

372

other form of what the economists call "household capital"—which you are paying for in instalments under a contract which has a "repossession clause." No such item, of course, may be put upon the list. It clearly does not belong to you until the deferred exchange has been completed. But let us assume you do own, free and clear, all your household mechanical genii. You may then add to your list of these—your clothes; the rugs and carpets on your floors; the furniture throughout the home; the pictures on the walls; some jewelry, no doubt; bedclothes and table linen; crockery and silverware; a few household tools; some books, let us hope. Nor must you forget to write down whatever consumable food you have at the moment. Add to the list all you possibly can: some unmortgaged land, if you are fortunate.

Now read over the list. If some cold analyst were to ask you, in surprise, "Is this all the wealth you own in the world?"—to be intellectually honest, you would be obliged to answer, "It is."

Everything else on your list of assets would have to be included in the second category—the forms of wealth you *may* own in the near or distant future. But only if promises upon which you are relying are faithfully performed!

The dollar bills in your pocket are promises of the State to give you a specified weight of gold. The last eight years have indicated how much of that gold, if any, you may ultimately receive.

The "money in the bank," of which you have a record in a little notebook, is not owned by you; *it is the bank's money*. What you have are mere banker's promises.

The equity in your insurance policy, upon which you have been paying for years, consists also, obviously, of nothing but promises from similarly unknown individuals.

A few bonds, which you say you own—of a railroad, a power company, an industrial corporation, or a county, a foreign government, or your own government—all of them, clearly, are forms of "When-As-And-If Wealth," dependent upon the faithful fulfillment of promises. A mortgage or two you may hold, upon a piece of farmland or a home, are, of course, in the same category.

How about those Stock Certificates which you have been acquiring painfully for years? As we have seen in Chapter Twelve, no single shareholder has a vestige of control over the disposition of the wealth owned by his corporation. The treasured piece of paper, with your name upon it, entitles you only to a specified share of the distributed earnings of the enterprise, *if there should be any*. Or to a specified share of the total property, should the enterprise cease to function, and *if anything is left* to be divided amongst the shareholders. Both of these are very large ifs.

Paradoxically, it appears from this survey, the wealthier a man is in the present day, the smaller is the proportion of real wealth which he owns. He may become ever richer and richer—yes, but only in promises. What "richer and richer" means, pragmatically, is that *more and more numerous become the individuals* who engage to give him wealth in the future. More and more, in other words, does he in actuality *give his wealth away in deferred exchanges*, putting it completely beyond his own control into that of others, upon whose ability and honesty he must rely. In the meantime, his actual possessions—the forms of wealth he can see, use, enjoy and dispose of at his will—increase in no such ratio. Far from it!

It is a highly significant social fact, that today—so far as the ownership of enjoyable and usable things is concerned—there is comparatively little difference between any moderately well-to-do family in the United States, with a total so-called wealth of $40,000 or $50,000, and our present-day Croesuses. How much more can the multimillionaire own? No doubt a far more palatial home; perhaps several homes. A number of automobiles, instead of one or two. A slightly greater variety of clothes, perhaps. More jewelry. Old masterpieces of painting that have a present rarity value, instead of new ones that may attain a fictitious value. Perhaps a yacht, instead of a motor boat or canoe. The difference is noticeable, yes; but quite trivial when it is compared with the differences in "When-As-And-If Wealth" between the moderately well-to-do man and the millionaire.

In what, then, lie the modern advantages of being rich? It is obvi-

374

ous that the rich man, if he will, can both do more and obtain wider satisfactions. Among these is the power to enlist the service and labor of a larger number of persons. This, immemorially, has been the principal advantage of being rich. It is an economic power. Nevertheless, it must be noted that in the modern world this greater field of action, this increased economic power, arises only from the fact *that promises themselves are commonly exchangeable;* because men, as this whole volume has indicated, freely exchange both their actual property and their labor, for promises later to be performed.

Now, since the greater part of ownership of wealth today consists of nothing but promises, the power that goes with aggregations of modern "wealth" *rests finally upon the simple fact that men can be relied upon to be honest in their relations with one another.*

How utterly different is this state of affairs from the olden past! When men were rich in ancient times, indeed up to within a few hundred years, they were rich—*in things!* It may be illuminating to examine the difference more precisely.

Job, says the Bible, was "greatest of all the men of the East. His substance was 7,000 sheep and 3,000 camels and 500 yoke of oxen and 500 she-asses, and a very great household." "And Abram went up out of Egypt, he and his wife and all that he had . . . and Abram was very rich in cattle, in silver, and in gold." Later, his eldest servant, "that ruled over all he had," is sent by him to acquire a wife for his son Isaac, and gives to Rebecca's parents a slightly more detailed statement of his financial condition. "And he said, I am Abraham's servant. And the Lord has blessed my master greatly; and he is become great: and he hath given him flocks, and herds, and silver, and gold, and menservants, and maidservants [all these, of course, are slaves—Ed.], and camels and asses."

The Bible is replete with descriptions of wealth like this, counted in material things. Never a mention of promised wealth.

This is equally true of Homer. Almost on every page one finds evidence of what was regarded as wealth by the "steel-helmeted warriors." For example, when Achilles announces that he will fight no more but will return home, because his meed of honor, the fair

375

Briseis, has been seized from him by Agamemnon: "On the third day I should reach deep-soiled Phthia," he says. "There are my great possessions that I left when I came hither to my hurt; and yet more gold and ruddy bronze shall I bring from hence, and fair-girdled women and grey iron, all at least that were mine by lot." Slaves and metal—gold and ruddy bronze and grey iron—*this* was the wealth he was taking home to add to his "great possessions."

It is illuminating, also, to observe what Agamemnon offers, through emissaries, to make him change his mind. "Fool was I, I myself deny it not," he admits to his assembled chieftains. "But seeing that I was a fool in that I yielded to my sorry passion, I will make amends and give a recompense beyond telling. In the midst of you all I will name the excellent gifts; seven tripods untouched of fire, and ten talents of gold and twenty gleaming caldrons, and twelve stalwart horses, winners in the race that have taken prizes by their speed. . . . And seven women will I give, skilled in excellent handiwork, Lesbians whom I chose me from the spoils that day he himself took stablished Lesbos, surpassing womankind in beauty. These will I give him, and with them shall be she whom erst I took from him, even the daughter of Brises; moreover I will swear a great oath that never I went up into her bed. . . . All these *things* [italics mine] shall be set straightway before him."

Perhaps three thousand years later, the extraordinary Schliemann discovered the Treasury of Atreus, deep under a grass-covered sunny Grecian hillside; and a portion of the wealth of Agamemnon which Homer describes—or that of his fathers—can be seen today in the museums, as the *tangible things* it then consisted of. And a bare portion of those spoils of Troy, of which he offered a boatload to Achilles, were unearthed by the same Schliemann. "When it was later counted, weighed, measured and entered, the treasure was found to include two gold diadems, one consisting of ninety chains, 12,271 rings, 4,066 almost heart-shaped plaques, and 16 idols. In addition there were 24 gold necklaces, eardrops, buttons, needles, prisms, 8,700 gold articles in all, also a large golden goblet, weighing

376

601 grams, a gold bottle and also other goblets, one made of electrum and one of silver." * What, of course, had been discovered, was principally the wealth that was in the form of gold. What other innumerable forms of wealth there were in Priam's stores—all tangible—who now can conjecture? But its nature is clear enough. It consisted, entirely, of things.

Not far distant from Troy, in a later age, Croesus became the symbol of riches for all time. What form did his wealth take? No doubt it consisted, in considerable part, of gold, silver, and electrum, for Lydia was one of the few regions, in the days of antiquity, where these precious metals were mined. Herodotus intimates how much gold and silver Croesus owned. He tells the tale of Alcmaeon, an Athenian, who was invited by Croesus to help himself to all the wealth he could personally take away. Going into one of the store-rooms, he filled large oversized boots with gold, sprinkled gold dust liberally upon his hair, filled the capacious folds of a cloak, and then staggered forth to Croesus' amusement—and with the gold, Herodotus says, founded one of the wealthiest families of the time. He was an ancestor of Pericles! But, of course, gold and silver must have been but a tithe of Croesus' wealth. In great stores it must have been kept, closely guarded: oils, wines, grains and other foods in superabundance; metals of every character then known; jewelry, utensils and vessels in an endless variety; great stores of fabrics, and the wherewithal to make them; armor and spears and javelins in enormous quantity; oxen, cows and sheep by the thousands; slaves too, menservants and maidservants, by the thousands; and ships by the hundred. The wealth of Croesus was *in corporeal things*, material and living. It could be seen, handled, counted, measured, weighed, enjoyed. So all ancient wealth was!

In his novel, *Salammbo*, Flaubert gives an unforgettable picture of what ownership of wealth meant in ancient times. The father of Hannibal, Hamilcar Barca, comes back to Carthage from Spain, "this man who made legions tremble," and takes account with his stew-

* *Schliemann*, by Emil Ludwig.

377

ards of what is left to him, after his treacherous colleagues have allowed the thousands of mercenary Barbarians to sack his wealth in a Dionysian feast.

"The door of the emporium was opened, and he entered a vast round hall from which long passages leading to other halls branched off like the spokes of a wheel. . . . As he perceived the accumulation of his riches, he became calm; his thoughts, which were attracted by the vistas in the passages, wandered to the other halls that were full of still rarer treasures. Bronze plates, silver ingots and iron bars alternated with pigs of tin brought from the Casterides over the Dark Sea; gems from the country of the blacks were running over their bags of palm bark; and gold dust heaped in leathern bottles was insensibly creeping out through the worn-out seams. Delicate filaments drawn from marine plants hung amid flax from Egypt, Greece, Taprobane and Judea; madrepores bristled like large bushes at the foot of the walls; and an indefinable odor—the exhalations from perfumes, leather, spices, and ostrich feathers, the latter tied in great bunches at the very top of the vault—floated through the air. . . ."

In another apartment, carefully concealed, "were large gold shields and monster close-necked silver vases, of extravagant shape and unfitted for use. With his torch he lit a miner's lamp which was fastened to the idol's cap, and green, yellow, blue, violet, wine-coloured, and blood-coloured fires suddenly illuminated the wall. It was filled with gems. . . . There were callaides shot away from the mountains with slings, carbuncles formed by the urine of the lynx, glossopetrae which had fallen from the moon, tyanos, diamonds, sandastra, beryls, with the three kinds of rubies, the four kinds of sapphires, and the twelve kinds of emeralds. They gleamed like splashes of milk, blue icicles and silver dust and shed their light in sheets, rays and stars. . . . The fires from the stones and the flames from the lamp were mirrored in the great golden shields. Hamilcar stood smiling with folded arms, and was less delighted by the sight of his riches than by the consciousness of their possession. They were inaccessible, exhaustless, infinite."

378

As a contrast, I had the experience recently of being shown an auditor's analysis of the wealth of a modern millionaire who had just died. It had been prepared for inheritance tax purposes, and was thus beautifully minute in detail. It consisted of comparatively meager personal possessions, valued at about $2,500; and a home, unmortgaged, valued at $89,000. These were all the *things* this modern Hamilcar really owned. Yet, of course, if during his lifetime, he had not invested in promises (it would be better said, divested himself of property) but had acquired actual wealth, it would have been heaped in piles of treasure a hundred times greater in quantity, and infinitely more varied than Hamilcar's. What a description a Flaubert could have given of it!

The rest of his so-called wealth, which measured by dollars came close to two million, consisted of about sixty thousand dollars in so-called cash—this was nothing but bank's promises, of course. There were about forty thousand dollars in loans to friends—the promises of individuals. There were about seven hundred thousand dollars in "bonds"—corporation, municipal and State promises. The balance was in stock certificates, shares in a vast variety of modern enterprises. All promises!

What a deep-going historical change in the ways of men is telescoped in such a contrast!

Now, this difference in *the way in which wealth is owned* has, obviously, the most far-reaching social consequences. Formerly, the owner of wealth was concerned principally with its guarding and safekeeping. It was hidden when it could not be certainly protected. When it came to accumulate in quantity, the owner of it was under the necessity of spending his most vital thought and energy in providing adequate force *to prevent its being seized from him*, as Hamilcar Barca was. Thus the whole detailed structure of society, for long centuries, was determined by this necessity. It might go far, indeed, to explain both the rise and the actions of rulers. For the force primarily provided for the protection of wealth *could just as easily be utilized to seize that of others*.

But nowadays, the owner of wealth gives only the most cursory

379

thought to its physical protection. He takes this largely for granted, except from the rare criminal. He is concerned principally about the honesty and ability of persons who have made promises to him. Most of our rich men and our modern experts in wealth—our bankers and brokers and investment medicos—are at bottom nothing but cold and experienced appraisers of the honesty and ability of individuals and groups. They might well be called "promise-appraisers." They are concerned with, and principally deal with, the relations between men, and only distantly with things, about which in reality they care little and see less. On the other hand the industrialist, the enterpriser, concerns himself principally with things, and only secondarily with relationships.

Perhaps we should not pass too hurriedly the view opened up here, as to the way in which *the mere form in which wealth is owned* principally determines the nature of the current society. Adam Smith, as usual, has some acute observations on this point. There are few more fascinating passages in *The Wealth of Nations* than his exposition of how the growth of cities—and the gradual increase in manufactured articles—ended in a complete metamorphosis of the way of life of men of wealth, and consequently of everybody else. One of the sights of London for all visitors is still Westminster Hall, but few of those who stand in amazement at its proportions have any notion of its deep social significance. "Ah!" I heard an American exclaim when he first saw it, "here at last is a room big enough for an outdoor man to live in!" It was *the dining hall* of William Rufus, son of the Conqueror, "and might frequently, perhaps," says Adam Smith, "not be too large for his company." Hundreds upon hundreds of individuals dined there daily, as a matter of routine. But was this a mere monarch's show? Is it to be taken primarily as a form of ancient ostentation? It is best understood—indeed, it can only be understood—as a social phenomenon necessitated by the way in which wealth was owned, not only seven hundred years ago in England, but for several thousand years prior to that. The forms of wealth produced then *had to be consumed because they could not be*

380

exchanged; and that basic fact conditioned the manner of life of the entire society.

"In a country which has neither foreign commerce, nor any of the finer manufacturers, a great proprietor," explains Adam Smith,* "having nothing for which he can exchange the greater part of the produce of his lands which is over and above the maintenance of the cultivators, consumes the whole in rustic hospitality at home. If this surplus produce is sufficient to maintain a hundred or a thousand men, *he can make use of it in no other way* [italics mine] than by maintaining a hundred or a thousand men. He is at all times, therefore, surrounded with a multitude of retainers and dependants, who having no equivalent to give in return for their maintenance, but being fed entirely by his bounty, must obey him, for the same reason that soldiers must obey the prince who pays them. Before the extension of commerce and manufactures in Europe, the hospitality of the rich and the great, from the sovereigns down to the smallest baron, exceeded everything which in the present times we can easily form a notion of. . . . It was reckoned a piece of magnificence in Thomas Becket, that he strowed the floor of his hall with clean hay or rushes in season, in order that the knights and squires, who could not get seats, might not spoil their fine clothes when they sat down on the floor to eat their dinner. The great earl of Warwick is said to have entertained every day at his different manors, thirty thousand people; and though the number here may have been exaggerated, it must however have been very great to admit of such exaggeration. . . . Upon the authority which the great proprietors necessarily had in such a state of things over their tenants and retainers, was founded the power of the ancient barons."

He goes on to expose how the system was slowly undermined, and in the end utterly collapsed, when new forms of manufactured wealth came into existence, for which the barons *could exchange their surplus produce* and get things they really wanted. To pick up one of our former themes, here again we see at work the leaven

* *The Wealth of Nations,* Page 385, Modern Library edition.

of the international merchant, determining by his activities the basic forms which the society finally assumes.

Adam Smith utilizes this change in the available forms of wealth to explain the ultimate overthow of the feudal system. But it points up, equally well, the complete metamorphosis that has occurred in what is modernly considered wealth. All the instances he gives illustrate how wealthy men, in ancient times, owned a superabundance of things—and few, if any, promises. *The reverse now is true.* Society in this respect has advanced far beyond its condition in Adam Smith's day. For nothing so obvious as the present state of affairs would have escaped his trenchant analysis. The wealthiest men today own few more real possessions than the rest of us. Instead of a superabundance of *things*, they now hold a superabundance of *promises* of other men.

Some highly pertinent considerations, with regard to this phenomenon, must be examined, to avoid confusion of thought.

The forms of wealth which we have identified as being truly owned—those which were in the first category of your inventory—consist largely, although far from entirely, of what today we call "personal possessions." But there is a great deal more wealth than that in the world. How about all the factories of the world; the business buildings of every sort; the machinery of unimaginable variety; the quite incalculable stores of finished goods; the materials of every conceivable character, raw and partly processed, in our warehouses or being worked upon in the countless factories dotted over the world? How about land itself, with all its rich resources? Who owns all this wealth, which is plainly the greater part of the present wealth of mankind, if—as our analysis seems to indicate—individuals, rich and poor, really own little more than their personal possessions and homes, everything else, which they think they own, being mere "When-As-And-If-Wealth"?

Leaving out land for the moment—for it requires a little special examination—so far as all the other forms of wealth are concerned, it is true that they are occasionally owned, free and clear of conditions, by individuals. The greater portion of them, however, are owned by

382

individuals *who are engaged in business*, or by corporations; or by units of governments—including, of course, the supreme government itself. But are we exact in saying that it is "owned," under the pragmatic definition of ownership by which we must guide ourselves? Is this ownership free and unhampered, or is it conditional ownership of some sort—like your home, if it is mortgaged?

As a practical matter of economics—under both law and custom—with rare exceptions *it is highly conditional ownership.*

This may best be seen by taking, as an example, a small corporation. It is engaged, let us assume, in manufacturing a simple machine of some sort. Let us analyze its financial statement, dividing its assets into the two categories of Real Wealth, and what we have called "When-As-And-If Wealth."

The first list would include, no doubt, a building; complicated machinery to fabricate the contraption it is marketing; some unsold stock on hand, of the contraption itself; and, finally, a fairly large amount of the various materials going into its manufacture. We cannot put into this category what the corporation euphemistically calls its "cash on hand and in bank," nor its "notes and accounts receivable." These are obviously forms of "When-As-And-If Wealth." They represent economic promises, which the corporation is expecting banks and other business firms or individuals to complete.

On the other side of its statement are what the auditors call its "liabilities." Let us say, first, it has issued bonds, the proceeds from which were used to erect its structure and acquire its machinery. Also, let us assume, it has borrowed money from a bank to carry on its current operations. In addition, there will be found in its records a long list of "accounts payable." These latter constitute largely what it owes for the raw materials, out of which its product is made.

Now, all these deferred exchanges, in which it is being trusted, the corporation fully intends to complete. It must, indeed, complete them in order to remain in existence. But how can it complete them? It must rely chiefly, for doing so, upon exchanging the items on our List Number One, its "owned" property, for money. This easily exchangeable wealth consists principally, at any moment, of its stock of finished goods. That stock—by the firm's intention—*is pledged*, it may be said, to be used for the benefit of those to whom it has promised money in deferred exchanges.

Moreover, whether such is its intention or not, if it appears unlikely that it will complete every one of these deferred exchanges, those who are on the last half of the exchanges may call in the State to compel it to do so. The State can step in, seize the whole property—auction it to the highest bidder for what it will bring, and distribute the money, not to the shareholders of the corporation who, we loosely say, "own" it as a group, but to their creditors.

Plainly, under such circumstances, the real wealth the corporation "owns" is *conditionally owned*. The ownership is provisional *upon the continued completion of its own deferred exchanges*. It is far from being free to dispose of the property in any way its autocrats determine, which is the final criterion of ownership.

This simple example is universally applicable. Every individual and every group of individuals, carrying on an economic enterprise, is in precisely this status. He or they own nothing outright, in the sense that a man owns his clothes and can hand them to a beggar if he chooses; or owns a home free and clear, and can set fire to it to enjoy the spectacle, like a little Nero, if he has the mind to. It is not wealth owned as Abraham's and Hamilcar Barca's was; and as wealth was owned by all our billions of forefathers.

A good way to appreciate the extreme degree to which all such modern ownership of wealth is conditioned by economic promises is to reflect upon the details of the bankruptcy laws that exist in every civilized community. When a man has made a promise to deliver wealth in the future in a deferred exchange, and fails to do so, the State steps in to compel him to do so. Whatever he has is seized and distributed proportionately among those who hold the promises. Now, it may thoughtlessly be assumed that *up to the moment* this interference of the State is invoked, he owns everything in his possession—in the pragmatic sense we have used, of being able to dispose of it in any way he pleases. Not at all! If there is the slightest evidence available that he has not exercised a normal concern about the execution of all his economic promises, he gets into trouble. If he has favored one creditor more than another, the State will seize *from that man* the amount the debtor has paid and redistribute it properly, and the promisor may go to jail for fraud. The same thing may happen if the promisor makes a present of the property to someone, or hides part of it. Almost certainly, in these cases, he will go to jail for fraud. Fraud? Was it not his property, his fully owned wealth, at that moment? Could he not do what he pleased with it? Most certainly he could not. Accordingly, it cannot reasonably be said to be "owned" by him. *The wealth is under pledge.* He himself, in one sense, has been made trustee of it for the benefit of those to whom he has made promises. But he cannot dispose of it with full freedom, any more than a trustee can dispose of wealth placed in his possession. The conditions are merely not so stringent as in the case of a trustee, but there they are, and can be disregarded only at his peril. In Great Britain, France, and many other countries—particularly in Latin America—there are criminal penalties imposed, even when it is found that a man, who owes other people money, fails to complete the promises because of gambling, or excessive expenditures—or even for not keeping books of account! This property, which he nominally owns, is very much conditionally owned. *The condition is that he completes his economic promises.*

This state of affairs, as to the ownership of wealth, holds true through the entire fabric of society. Very little real wealth is owned outright. The ownership of wealth by any enterprise or individual who makes economic promises is conditional entirely upon the completion of all the deferred exchanges they have at the moment entered into.

The hard substance of the matter seems to be, when we X-ray that vast mass of transactions by means of which human society keeps in operation, that by far the greater part of the existing wealth of mankind is not, in a true sense, owned by any individuals or groups at any moment. *It is forever in a state of pledge.* It has been put up at forfeit, both in actuality and informally by custom, in the completion of deferred exchanges. Its true ownership remains suspended.

It cannot be said to be fully owned by him who has temporary title to it, until he has completed all his economic promises. Yet at the same time it is certainly not owned by his creditors, who own, if anything, nothing but his promise. Who ultimately will own this vast and incomprehensible mass of property being held in forfeit *is contingent entirely upon events*. These events, when you look at them, turn out to consist of nothing but the fulfillment or non-fulfillment of economic promises.

How about the owner of *unmortgaged* land? He surely owns something of value, and certainly nothing so incorporeal as a promise. With regard to land, we must observe that a great part of the valuable land in civilized nations—particularly that containing mineral resources and urban land—is owned by persons or groups who are engaged in economic enterprise. Therefore, when its owners have entered into deferred exchanges, it is quite as much under pledge as other forms of wealth. Let us consider, however, the unmortgaged land of an individual who has no debt of any kind—a fairly rare bird in modern society. If he owns and uses it himself, he can be said truly to own it outright and unconditionally, as much as he does his personal possessions. If however, he does not use the land himself, *it is worthless to him*, unless he relies upon promises. As soon as he rents the land for use by others, he becomes no less dependent upon the promises of others than the man who own bonds or any other form of deferred exchange. He simply has the promise of his tenant to pay money, or to give him a physical share of the crop. If the tenant fails to do so, what recourse has he other than that which every other holder of a promise has? He may call in the State to evict the tenant forcibly from the premises, and to compel him to complete the exchange, if there is any wherewithal by means of which this may be done. But, after having used this recourse, what can he do—to acquire any wealth from the land—except to rely upon a new tenant's promises, if he cannot use the land himself? While he is a true owner, he can receive no vestige of value from the ownership except by the route of fulfilled promises, or by expenditure of his own labor. For this reason, most land ownership and building

386

ownership—*where the owner himself does not use the land or struc-ture*—for all practical purposes, is in the same category as other forms of "When-As-And-If Wealth." *It only results in wealth if promises are fulfilled.*

By this removal of the encrustations which, through thoughtless-ness and habit, have become deposited upon the picture of human society, at least some of the true line and color of the genuine original is revealed.

It is a picture of men living largely upon promises.

If we look at our world with open eyes, we see literally hundreds of millions of men daily giving up to others all the energy that is in them, physical and mental, upon the promise of receiving money.

We see this skill and labor producing forms of tangible wealth in an unimaginable variety, and then those who own this real wealth giving it away to others—for promises.

We see the goods carried to every market of the world, and those who perform this service of distribution receiving again—promises from those who benefit by it.

All but a fraction of the hundreds of millions of us, when we ac-quire by our hard labor any real money—that is, gold or silver coin—give it by roundabout processes to the State; we receive in exchange —promises, in the form of paper or poorer metal.

We take these promises to pay money, and relinquish them with-out thought to banks and insurance companies—receiving promises in exchange.

The banks and insurance companies in turn, as speedily as they can, give these promises to pay money to economic enterprises and governmental units—again receiving nothing but promises.

So, in a ceaseless cycle, it goes on, this interchange of real wealth for promises; of promises for other promises; until, as we have now seen, our very conception of wealth has been utterly altered from what it has been in all past history. Today men own, principally, not real forms of wealth, but promises of other men to transfer wealth to them.

387

But this universal circulation of real wealth for promises is only the surface of the picture. Let us not be blindered by a metaphor, in referring to what happens as a "picture." These promises, with comparatively few exceptions, are performed. Real wealth does finally pass in these countless deferred exchanges. The half-exchange is completed, the promise is wiped out and canceled. Faithful fulfillment is necessary, as we have seen, to the continuous operation of the system. Otherwise the promises, in the first place, will never be believed. But what we observe—when we stop taking for granted the common processes of living—is that as old promises by the hundreds of millions daily are completed, new ones by the hundreds of millions take their place. No matter how misanthropic or cynical we count ourselves, no one of us may ever escape participation in this vast round of faith. Everlastingly, each one of us trusts, and is being trusted utterly, by others. The whole is a vast and intricate interdependence of men upon one another's honesty and ability. Like the force of gravitation in our cosmogony of universes, it is simple human reliability which holds the society of men together, and makes it run as it now does.

This earth-wide interdependence of men upon one another's reliability has never been accorded the amount of attention, by economists and social theorists, that has been given to the interdependence of men upon one another's labor. Yet it is clear that the two must be inseparably linked, if we are to see straight in threading through the maze of human relations.

Now, the diversification of human effort, in the production and distribution of goods, is one large indisputable fact about human society which economists of every school of thought recognize. This is how men, at long last, have come to live. They now know no other way. They are born and trained from infanthood into this way of life. It is as much the environment to which they must adapt themselves as Nature itself. Change, if any, is likely to come—as it always has—in the direction of *still more minute diversification* of physical labor and thought.

But why has it remained so long unnoticed that, inseparable from

388

this large phenomenon, there is another process equally indisputable, *equally extensive in its operation and perhaps even more basic* —namely, that this superfine diversification of human effort has both evolved out of, and is maintained by, the interdependence of men upon one another's promises?

Every aspect of the system finds its final basis and explanation in the simple fact that men can now be relied upon, as a general rule, to do what they say they will do. In most cases! Not, as yet, invariably.

If simple honesty and reliability is the bedrock of the system, insofar as it operates successfully, is it not possible that we may find an explanation of the troubles that beset us, when they do, in its reverse—in dishonesty and unreliability?

There is at least a great deal of light to be found here—enough, at any rate to delineate the true nature of quite a few of the economic problems which confront and ordinarily puzzle the common citizen.

20

How the Volume of Promises Made by Men Both Measure

and Determine the Well-being of Society: The

Heart of the Mystery of Business Cycles

THE loose end of truth with which we began this inquiry has led a long distance. It could be followed profitably in many other directions. There is, indeed, very little that happens in human affairs, of an economic character, that cannot to a very great degree be illuminated by asking these few simple questions:

What economic promises are involved in the situation?

Who did the promising and therefore has to do the performing?

Who relinquished his property in the first half of the exchange?

How many people will be affected, and in what way, if the promise is completed?

How many, and in what way, if it is partially or totally incompleted?

Finally, what *other* economic promises are vitally related—so far as completion or incompletion goes—to those which are under immediate consideration?

But to follow our loose end of truth, wherever it leads, would make an encyclopedia of this volume. The restricted intention of our effort will be remembered: to set forth for that inquiring citizen, young or old, who finds himself bewildered by our complex world, a few economic phenomena that are fundamental and indisputable, and which being so, it is necessary to bear in mind, in order to be always clear in understanding and thus avoid mistakes in our necessary attempts at changing the society.

There is, however, one additional large fact, suggested but not examined, that is clearly within this category of indisputability. To clarify its relation to other facts, perhaps first it is advisable to summarize, briefly, a few of the phenomena, so far disclosed, which no reasonable person would dispute.

First, we saw that forms of wealth in the modern world *must be owned*, either by individuals, groups of individuals, or by the whole State; ownership meaning, pragmatically, the right to unmolested use and disposition.

Second, we saw that the occupations in which men engage are now infinitely specialized; and that this is the outstanding characteristic of the modern social environment, as distinct both from the ancient and from the natural one. Every child born into the world now instantly begins to adjust himself to this highly specialized modern social environment.

Third, because of this ownership of forms of wealth and this specialization of effort, men can only keep one another alive and fairly happy by exchanging their goods and their labor.

Fourth, of these exchanges that go on, a small proportion are immediately completed; they are mere swaps. But *in most of the exchanges the second half is deferred*. That is, a lapse of time occurs before the person who first gives up one form of wealth gets the other form of wealth he expects in the last half of the exchange.

Fifth, because of this lapse of time, almost all the endless exchanging that takes place *involves promises*. But promises cannot be believed, unless they are infallibly performed. Therefore, the ultimate reliance of this present universal system of deferred exchanges rests upon two things: first, the honesty of the promisors; and second, an accurate estimate of the resources they will have when the second half of the exchange has to be completed. The high importance of this second consideration was revealed in the difference between short and long promises.

Sixth, these economic promises, *so far as fulfillment is concerned*,

391

are interdependent. By an almost inconceivably intricate honey-combing of promises, the ultimate performance of every promise is affected—sometimes slightly, sometimes wholly—*by the completion of others.*

All these statements will accord with everyone's observation and everyone's experience. No school of thought can dispute them. Therefore, all schools of economic thought can at least begin with these phenomena as a basis of reasoning—in contemplating social change.

I need hardly point out there are probably many other phenomena, in the strictly economic sphere of human affairs, about which every school of economic reasoning might agree. For the purposes of this particular inquiry—to help men understand broadly the precise role of promises in human affairs—these are sufficient. Not, however, unless there be added one more indisputable fact, indissolubly related with these.

In a human society now organized according to the description given, the degree of well-being of all its members in theory would be, and in fact is, *determined principally by the volume of exchanges, of property and of labor, which goes on within it.*

Certainly there is nothing difficult to understand about this simple large fact. Bring it within your own experience and you see at once how true it is. If you are a merchant with a stock of goods on your shelves and cannot exchange them—for money—you are in a pretty bad pass. If you are a laborer and cannot exchange your work for money—which you are compelled to do by the very nature of our society—you are perhaps in an even worse pass. What is true of these tiny parts is true of the whole. What is true of a single merchant, a single manufacturer, a single laborer, is true of all the hundreds of millions of us. *The total volume of exchanges that goes on in our society* is both the explanation and the measure of the degree of well-being which the society enjoys.

The attentive reader will perhaps have been aware of this theme being sounded—in preparation for development, so to speak—

throughout this entire inquiry. It was sounded wherever we called attention to certain kinds of exchanges which, because of the current absence of means of one of the parties—like instalment contracts and seasonal credit extended to farmers—*could not take place at all* unless the last half was deferred to a later date. It has been even more clearly suggested, time and again, whenever it was pointed out that all deferred exchanges take place *only* because of the virtual certainty that they will be completed. Whenever any question arises as to this fact, *they simply are not entered into:* that is, the total volume of exchanges is thereby diminished!

I do not think there is any single fact more important for men to recognize, with all its implications, than this simple one—*that their individual well-being, as well as that of the whole society, is determined by the volume of exchanges going on in the whole society.*

Not to recognize this basic fact, and then to theorize in any way about social change, is as futile as anything that can be conceived of —and dangerous.

The well-being of mankind is, of course, the concern of every social philosophy, of the classical economist and communist, as well as of the cracker-barrel commentator. To ascertain how best it may be served is the spring of all economic analysis. All theorists unite in setting it up as the be-all and end-all of their speculations; and then they proceed to a bitter battle—even to the death of millions, if necessary—as to the means by which they can bring this common glorious end to fruition. The irony in this is accentuated by the further fact, which an examination soon discloses, that seldom do these embittered doctrinaires analyze, except in the haziest fashion, the precise nature of the end they seek to serve.

What, it may sensibly be asked, do we have in mind when we talk, as we all so glibly do, about the "well-being" of society?

In the first place, it is most important to observe that the conception cannot be of a static condition. The well-being of mankind, whatever it may be, is a changing condition of human affairs. In the past it has had, at different times and places, wide degrees; and when

393

we consider the state of well-being of the discrete individuals in our present society, most obviously it still has very wide degrees. The conception of well-being, clearly, is of something relative—eternally relative. It is relative to what has been, relative to what we observe currently as being practicable and possible.

Elementary enough this is, but it is far from unimportant to be always sharply aware of it. For we have had our respected thinkers and still have, who visualize future states of society, economic Arcadies, in which a complete contentment and happiness shall be the lot of all. What we now call poverty will be non-existent, and whatever any man thinks he needs he shall forthwith have. It is not only the hasty communist, but also plenty of modern capitalists, in whose sclerotic ideas of the world this notion is inherent.

Now, these are all clearly conceptions of society in a condition of well-being—or comparative ill-being, as one may want to consider it —which is static. Were any such condition possible, it is quite safe to venture, if human beings retain the least of their present instincts and habits, it would be found, by those who had to suffer it, as deadly-dull as a heaven. No doubt the living conditions our descendants will enjoy five hundred, or even a hundred years from now, would be counted Utopia by most of us who are now alive; just as our present condition of general ill-being—as most of us would now fairly call it—would nevertheless have been counted Utopia by the greater number of our ancestors equidistant in the past. But it is fairly safe to predict that our descendants themselves will count their standard of living, whatever it may be, no Utopia. Many of them will envy us, as some of us now envy our forebears, for living conditions *of the past* which seem far more pleasant and more bearable. The Golden Age will then be in the past, to a great many people, as it is to some of us and as it has always been in the estimation of a certain kind of person. At the same time, equal horizons of possible change, if not vaster ones, will then beckon men onward, as they now do. The very substance of human life, in all its eons, has been change.

When we begin to look critically into the conception of "the well-

394

being of society," *the degree of contentment* diffused throughout the population seems hardly to be a helpful criterion. Man obviously is a highly adaptable animal. Absence of molestation in the ways to which he has become accustomed—molestation proceeding either from Nature or from other men—is a matrix that will breed contentment in any living conditions under which he finds himself. There have always been, there still are, literally hundreds of millions of individuals, who, *if let alone*, though possessing little, are beautifully content and happy in their condition. Yet that condition would be considered, by those better-off, as one of the greatest hardship and trouble, a very low state of well-being by present accepted standards, unclear as these are.

It is by comparing what men have and enjoy *with what they can have and enjoy*—quite irrespective of the contentment or discontent of the possessors—that we measure the well-being of an individual, a homogeneous community, a whole nation. This hazy and distant goal—the well-being of society, which is the concern of all social theory—seems to be a somewhat unclear, but definite enough notion, of making available to *ever more and more individuals* the vast variety of goods, satisfactions and enjoyments, which it is seen that the current society can produce, for it is already providing them to a few within the population: more and better things to eat; a greater variety of and more comfortable and pleasing things to wear; homes of greater convenience and of more beauty, in which to live; a wider diversification of pleasures and more leisure in which to pursue them; a hundred new services not previously available to everybody; and always, of course, more freedom from molestation in our ways of life, which is the *sine qua non* of contentment and is what we ultimately mean by "security."

To improve the well-being of a whole community *is an averaging upward* throughout the population of the goods and satisfactions which the current civilization can provide. When the degree of general well-being is lowered it is an *averaging downward* for the entire population of the sum of goods and satisfactions currently obtainable.

395

Even the most superficial acquaintance with history indicates that the trend of this averaging, over the centuries, has been upward. The commonest citizens, in the more organized nations of the world, now enjoy thoughtlessly—almost as of right—goods and conveniences that were not only rare, but even non-existent in the past. Within the past one hundred and fifty years, particularly, the averaging upward of well-being has gone forward at a geometric pace, and within the past fifty years, it has been noticeable, so to speak, to the naked eye.

For about the past two decades, interestingly enough, statisticians have attempted to measure this material progress. What this measurement shows, as to the United States, is illuminating. The available data by which the measurement has been made have been sadly incomplete. They consist, for the most part, of production figures of a great many commodities, raw, finished, and partly finished, and some figures covering the physical distribution of goods. These have been computed into what have been called "total production indexes"; the word "total," however, being very much of a misnomer, for the indexes are far from being inclusive. The period covered was of course determined by the availability of the data. The two "total production indexes" which seem to have the least questionable elements for economists cover a period of somewhat more than sixty years, up to 1930.* One of these analyses showed that the average increase in the total volume of goods produced was 3.7 per cent per year during this period, the other 3.8 per cent per year. In the meantime, our population increased at the rate of 1.9 per cent a year. During this period statistical economists have identified no fewer than sixteen so-called cycles.

Significant as these figures are, they are far from telling the whole story of the material progress that has taken place in this country well within the memory of those now living. One of the most searching studies of trends in production in the United States has been made under the auspices of the National Bureau of Economic Re-

* One of these is known as the Day-Persons index, compiled by Warren M. Persons and E. E. Day. Its detail will be found in *Forecasting Business,* by Warren M. Persons. The other is known as the Warren and Pearson index. Its detail will be found in *Physical Volume of Production in the U. S.,* Memoir 144, Cornell University Agricultural Experiment Station.

search, by Dr. Arthur F. Burns. The conclusion he states about the figures above, as a measure of our economic growth, is this: "The indexes probably understate the average rate of advance in the physical volume of total production. . . . The increase of total physical production *has almost certainly been greater* [italics mine]—quite possibly, a good deal greater." *

While all the reasons for this pregnant conclusion cannot, with proper fairness to Dr. Burns, be adequately presented here, some are important enough at least to be indicated. First, the indexes include only economic activities that have been going on steadily since 1870, or a few years later. This was necessarily so, or otherwise the rate of growth *over the full period* could not be measured. This results in what Dr. Burns calls "a downward growth bias." His own exhaustive analysis of separate industries shows that almost invariably they grow more slowly, if at all, in their later years. This would naturally be expected. In their early years they tend to grow fastest, and then—unless some radical change occurs—their *rate of growth* from year to year becomes lower. Accordingly, practically all separate production records included in these total production indexes would show a "downward growth bias." But in the meantime, many of the newer industries—merely because they were not old enough and figures for the whole period studied were not available—were for the most part excluded from the series represented in these total production indexes. The measurements of growth do not cover, for instance, such common things in our present life as production of radios, motion pictures, aircraft, all the newer chemical industries, many electrical appliances, and all the thousand other new goods which have radically transformed our lives within the past half century. As Dr. Burns puts it, "The index becomes progressively anachronistic, for the new industries which are not covered are generally in the vanguard of industrial advance."†

Moreover, as he points out, the measures are quantitative, and indicate nothing about the enormous improvements *in quality of product*

* *Production Trends in the U. S. since 1870*, Arthur F. Burns.
† *Ibid.*, Page 258.

which have also taken place within the period. Finally, these total production indexes hardly include at all measurements of increase in "service occupations." Yet it is manifest that one of the striking characteristics of the period covered has been the multiplication of service activities of all kinds. Not only have the number of persons in the ancient service occupations—like those of doctor, lawyer, priest, barber, domestic, teacher—increased enormously. Coincident with this has been the creation and extension of a fascinating variety of new service occupations, never dreamed of by our fathers.

Finally—and this point is properly, of course, not covered by Dr. Burns, since it has little to do with production-growth, although it clearly has a great deal to do with the well-being of society—the indexes reveal nothing of *the progressively shorter working day*, and increased leisure, which has accompanied this geometric increase in the production of goods.

Accordingly, we unspecialized laymen may accept it as a pretty well-established fact that the 3.75 per cent annual improvement, shown by certain indexes in our total production of goods, merely suffices, as Dr. Burns very conservatively puts it, "*to indicate the lower limits* [italics mine] of the average year-by-year progress."

Let us spend no time pluming ourselves upon it. It is of some satisfaction, but it is not the whole picture, by any means, and with it we must contemplate some aspects of human affairs that will deflate our egoism, if we could only take their lesson properly to heart, as much as this steady proved material progress would inflate it. This trend upward in what we conceive of as the well-being of mankind is clear enough, but it must be remembered that our progress, as measured by "production," does not proceed in a straight line upward. It goes up and down—with the trend upward! That is, downs in the general well-being of the race—and of any nation—alternate with the ups. Every now and then the downs go so low and cause such trouble— as in the past nine years, for example—that if there is a Zeus with an auricular capacity in some portion of the universe, the howls of humankind, with its new powers of noise-making, must seem loud to him, indeed.

398

In short, the current state of well-being of human society is not only far from being fixed and static. It also does not necessarily change in one direction, that of improvement.

Now, the dictum which we are engaged in examining is that the factor which really determines these ups and downs in the well-being of society *is a change in the total volume of exchanges of property and labor which take place among our two billion fellow-beings.* What induces these changes in the total volume of exchanges, when they do occur, is the present chief mystery of economics. But at least it is of prime importance—for a clear understanding of human affairs and for unconfused reasoning about them—to be forever aware of this indissoluble relation *between the total volume of exchanges going on in our society and the degree of well-being enjoyed by the members of the society*, at any given moment.

This tie can be both amply and simply demonstrated. But first, it must be admitted, we are on ground here that might be debated. Superficially, it would seem to be a truer statement to make that the degree of well-being of all of us is determined, not by changes in the total volume of exchanges which we engage in, but much more by changes in *the volume of physical goods produced*. Goods—aside from personal services—are what we all enjoy. If they are available in greater abundance, general well-being, by so much, is more widely diffused. But if, for some reasons that are now hidden in the social mechanism, the production of goods is lessened, by so much the general well-being of the race seems to suffer. This is true enough; but it is a sort of myopic representation of the whole truth.

It is clear that those enterprises which have to do with production turn out goods *solely to be exchanged*, and not to be used and enjoyed by the producer. Goods are produced modernly for no other reason. If the enterprisers think they cannot soon or late be exchanged, they simply are not produced! If the enterpriser makes a mistake and produces more than can be exchanged, what happens? The mere excess production in no way benefits either the producer (if he cannot consume it) or anybody else. It contributes in not the slightest fashion to the well-being of anybody in the society, *unless*

399

it can either be consumed by the producer or unless it can be exchanged. If it cannot be consumed by the producer or exchanged, it rots away or is destroyed. More often it is a hindrance, rather than a help, to social well-being.

It is the possibility of exchange, then, which governs the modern production of goods at all times. The exchangeability of any kind of goods is, in a sense, the thermostat which effectually controls the volume of its production. If anyone wishes to believe that changes in the physical volume of goods produced (together with changes in the volume of services rendered) determine the current condition and well-being of society, he may rationally do so; but only if he recognizes a more fundamental fact: namely, that this is only true because the volume of actual and anticipated exchanges very closely *and continuously* controls the volume of goods which are produced. In other words, it is exchanges of goods and service we should concentrate our attention upon, and not their production.

This is only true, it should be seen, of a society like our present one, with its highly specialized diversification of occupation. It would not be true of other types of economy. It was not true, for instance, of those communities in the past, which, by circumstance, were almost totally closed to trade. It was not true of the manor system in the Middle Ages, nor of American society in the early period of our history, where each family produced almost everything it needed. In such cases, indeed, the well-being of the whole group was principally determined and measured by the total physical volume of goods which was produced, and not by the total volume of exchanges. Adam Smith's comment, which we quoted, on the necessity of hospitality of great landed proprietors of the past, is but one aspect of this wider truth. It has been predominantly within the past two hundred years, with the infinite refinements in specialized labor and the all but complete decline of family production for use, that the total volume of exchanges taking place has become so closely tied up, as it now is, with the current well-being of all of us.

That tie, it was stated above, could be amply demonstrated in common experience. The proposition has an unnecessary tinge of abstraction to those not accustomed to think in economic terms, and after all it is a pretty inclusive concept for the imagination to embrace. For all the activities of the two billion members of the human race are included in it, and the conditions under which they live, changing over periods of time.

But if the mere words "total volume of business" are substituted for the words "total volume of exchanges," the essential truth of the proposition at once comes more within everybody's common experience and is beautifully verified by it. The trouble is, of course, that we never think in terms of exchanges. We are blandly unaware that what we daily engage in are exchanges. What we talk about, commonly and universally, is "business."

But what do we mean by "business"? If ever there was a shorthand word in common use, completely obliterating to apprehension the actualities of daily existence, it is this one. Its original meaning, of course, is the state of being busy. If it now meant only that, it would be a little curious to ask a man, "How is your business progressing?" We might as sensibly inquire, "How is your laziness getting along?" Or, "How was happiness last week, Bill?" The word plainly has come to refer, not to the state of being busy, but to the activities which we are busy in performing. But what are these activities? What are we all so busy and so engrossed in doing? *We are all busy in carrying on exchanges*—of labor for money, goods for money, money for money. These are the human activities the word "business" modernly means.

Now, it must be observed here—supplementing our analysis above —that in this common use, the word never refers to the production of goods, *but only to their exchange!* No matter how busily engaged a manufacturer may be in fabricating goods, he does not say his "business" is good or poor, without reference to *the exchanges* he has just made, or those he is expecting to enter into. His true criterion of "business" is, not how much he is manufacturing, but his orders on hand which he is engaged in filling, or those which he has just completed; that is, exchanges of his goods for money. If he is completely unintelligent, he can, indeed, keep his plant running full tilt making unordered goods, for which no immediate exchanges are anticipated. Even so, if he were asked while doing so, "How's business?" his sour reply would probably be, "There is no business." Meaning, of course, he is making no exchanges of the goods he is so busy in fabricating. Or take the farmer. It is not the volume of crops he grows—he knows only too well—that makes his "business" good or poor. It is the volume of them he can exchange, and for how much money.

The word "business," then, clearly has exchanges as almost its sole, certainly its principal, criterion. Indeed, the common and the ultimate measure of benefit from our activities is universally obtained *by measuring our exchanges*, and by nothing else. The total "amount of business" which any production enterprise carries on is measured—in its books of account—neither by the amount of certain kinds of goods which it buys, nor by the amount of finished goods that it manufactures. *The amount of business it does is measured solely by its sales—that is, by its exchanges.* So of distributors. They do not measure their "business" by the dollar value of the goods they buy; nor by the dollar value of the goods they have on hand over any period. They measure it solely by what they sell—again, exchanges only.

It is within everyone's experience that when the "business" of any enterprise is poor—in other words, *when the volume of its exchanges is low*—the well-being of all those who are tied up in its fortunes is adversely affected. It may, for a time, have enough resources to continue without any effect upon the lives of those associated in it. But not for long! Soon or late, if the volume of exchanges remains low, a more or less large number of the individuals connected with it suffer in their well-being. Conversely, when the "business" of an enterprise is improving—that is, when its exchanges *are increasing* in volume—the average well-being of all those associated in it is bettered. Or if this is not so, at least *more people* are brought within the range of its benefits. In either case the well-being of society is raised by so much.

Quite obviously, what is true of any single enterprise is true of the sum total of all the enterprises which go on within any nation; and of that still larger total, which embraces the activities of all the two billion inhabitants of the earth. All these people, within the associated civilized areas of human society, are more or less directly involved in an economic enterprise of some kind. There are, literally, millions of these separate economic enterprises—individual and group enterprises. Some of them affect but a handful of persons. Others bind together within their fortunes hundreds of thousands of individuals. Every single one of these enterprises, tiny and huge, is carrying on exchanges of goods for money, service for money, or money for money. It *calls* this exchanging its "business." The well-being of those associated in it, obviously, varies with and is determined by the volume of its exchanges—that is, by the amount of "business" it succeeds in carrying on.

It almost becomes a truism, then, to say that the welfare of the whole society varies with and is determined by the volume of exchanges—that is, of business—that goes on within it. Quite so; but it is no less important for being a truism. Only very clever people may be contemptuous of truisms; and one cannot be clever, one must unfortunately be very solemn in this matter of seeing, without confusion, how this mad world of our goes 'round. The interesting fact seems to be, with regard to this particular truism, that it is of the sort which is immediately apparent to anyone who looks in its direction. But, *commonly it is almost totally unrecognized*, except among a comparatively small group, consisting almost entirely of economists and a few informed bankers and business men. Indeed, even among economists and social theorists it has not been many decades that there has been any focusing of attention upon this indissoluble tie between the total volume of exchanges and the well-being of society. Moreover, it is clear enough that even now comparatively few social theorists have grasped the full implications of this pregnant relationship. Often hypnotized by their own doctrines, they look elsewhere than in this obvious direction for the secret of what really governs the well-being of mankind.

Yet, fortunately, the supreme importance of this relationship has been widening in recognition during recent years. Men now attempt

403

to measure the changing volume of exchanges which currently go on within the whole society. The origin and purpose of this measurement was primarily for guidance in business operations, rather than for guidance in social analysis. But this mere wind of chance, if it is ill, has blown great good. The measurement appears now, in every financial journal periodically (sometimes weekly, sometimes monthly) under the form of what is called an "index to business activity." This is ordinarily a chart, with supporting figures, which astute financiers and industrialists are supposed to watch with a hawk's eye in its every gyration; which often little business men and petty speculators, and some of our political boll-weevils, follow with a sort of gossipy interest, but seldom with any understanding; and which the vast balance of us do not even know exists.

Different "business indexes" vary in their composition; that is, in what they include in measuring. Almost all of them include freight-car loadings. These are measurements of goods being shipped by carloads. The goods were ordered from manufacturers and will have to be paid for. Accordingly, their changing volume from week to week will give some inkling as to the changing volume of manufacturers' exchanges.

Most of the indexes now also include electrical power production. Since electric power is heavily used in manufacturing goods, and its use would diminish in any plant which had few orders, it is clear that the *total electric power produced and used* gives a roundabout indication of the *total volume of exchanges* manufacturers of goods are entering into.

Total bank loans, changing from week to week, measure directly the volume of exchanges business men are having with banks. But also, like electric power production, they throw an *indirect* light upon the present and intended business activity of hundreds of thousands of business men. For a business man only borrows for one of two reasons: because heavy orders are already on hand which must be financed—that is, the exchanges of his enterprise are definitely increasing; or because he sees a more than reasonable chance of spend-

404

ing the money in such a way that his sales—that is, his exchanges—will be measurably increased in the near future.

All together, there are a score or more items, used in one index or another, to provide clues as to this changing volume of exchanges among men. For instance, total production of key products, like pig-iron, steel, cotton-cloth, bituminous coal, lumber; new capital issues (that is, the seeking of money for new enterprises or the expansion of old ones); contracts for building, both residential and business, which measure exchanges in a very wide field; and, in some cases, the changing prices of key products.

Incomplete as they are, the revelations of the business index are decidedly hazy on the main point: namely, *total volume of exchanges*. Yet the upshot is that they do answer roughly, for the sum of all enterprises within the nation, what each enterprise can answer for itself: "How's business?" That is, do the exchanges, which are going on *among all the people*, seem to be increasing or decreasing in volume?

The indexes are of some practical value to those who are already tied up in a long promise, or who may be anticipating getting involved in one. For they are at least reliable in disclosing the *trend* of change. It may be that, within the inner sanctums of very large enterprises, the Napoleons of industry and finance are really influenced in their actions by the business indexes they are presumed to watch so closely. But generally, in the business world, it is doubtful that any current revelation of these "general business indexes" strongly influences business decisions one way or the other. Its revelations are both too generalized and too uncertain to be of current practical use by those who are deep in the details of their own enterprises. Improved and perfected—as they could be, with some help from our politicians—and it is conceivable that the business indexes could be of enormous value to those who are engaged in short-term half-exchanges, as almost all economic enterprises are.

But though the business index may be of questionable practical use, the data of which it is composed are of inordinate value to, and hold unending fascination for, the speculative social student. For they supply statistically, and beyond any possibility of dispute, an enormous mass of evidence about the fluctuations from week to week, month to month, and year to year, in the total volume of all exchanges. The various statistical series, of which the business indexes are composed, all serve to reveal the most momentous and most mysterious of present-day social phenomena: *that the total volume of exchanges among men goes up and down, over periods of time, in a fairly regular rhythm;* in short, that our society as it is now constituted, is cursed with that set of phenomena which we know by the name of "business cycles."

There are few alert-minded persons who now have not become cognizant of the fact that there are such things as business cycles, and almost nobody who is not now aware, by name, of one phase of the business cycle, depression. I was delighted recently when a common gardener, a transplanted foreigner, a skilled and conscientious man whom I respect highly, confided to me while digging away among his plants: "This here depression, you know, it caused me a lot of trouble." Yes, the world of men has become conscious enough of the business cycle, in one phase of it, its nadir.

But so it has been for at least a century and a half. It appears that in every third or fourth cycle, the up-and-down gyrations are severe. The depression phase of the cycle (which men notice more, for they always are more alive to trouble) is manifested as an economic visitation. Misery, anxiety, despair, hunger, struggle, revolution, death—flood as from dark clouds upon humankind. The world as we know it seems to be breaking up. Every settled way, so dear to us, seems as if it may be undermined. Unable to comprehend what has happened, we chatter privately and chaffer publicly, with all the means modernity makes possible. In a land of really advanced intelligence, like Germany, we turn upon the Jews as scapegoats and hold them responsible for all the trouble. Elsewhere, like those ancients and African savages, who according to Frazer in *The Golden Bough* frequently killed the king when it did not rain, we consider our current power-wielders to be the culprits. They are promptly thrown out and the new ones, in genuine fear of us, proceed to actions which seldom help and much more often stamp us deeper in the mire. All the public howling, all the action, has one object in view—to scramble back out of the current trouble into a condition of life which we remember as being more pleasant, and which we often refer to as the "normal."

But that is one of the important things we commonly do not understand about the business cycle: *there is no happy and pleasant normal.* The normal course of economic events, if we use the word in its proper sense—as what is usual, what ordinarily obtains—*is precisely this constant change* from scarcity to comparative abundance —and back again! The "normal" includes these periods of widespread misery and social disturbance, alternating every few years with a period of relative ease, quiet and less misery, which we call "prosperity." Now these rhythmical oscillations between what used to be called "hard times" and "good times" constitute the most important discovery of modern economics; and, at the same time, its most perplexing mystery.

In general, this is what the discovery consists of: Economists, by means of exhaustive statistical records, by business annals and other reliable means, have ascertained that the volume of exchanges among men fluctuates in wide arcs, so to speak; that these changes in volume *recur* at fairly regular intervals, and finally that each cycle of change invariably goes through stages that are like those of every other. Beginning at the high point of the volume (one can begin anywhere) there is "prosperity," sometimes referred to as "the boom," where the volume of exchanges is going on at a feverish pace. This is ended—although not by any means always—by a "crisis," at which point the increasing volume stops dead in a business "panic." There follows "recession," a diminution in the volume of exchanges, which becomes progressively less and less. This leads into the period of "depression," during which the volume of exchanges is at its lowest point and—in the severe and strongly marked cycle—remains at that general level for a more or less prolonged period, while loss of wealth plagues those who owned it, and despair spreads like a poison throughout that part of the population which has nothing to live

407

upon but its labor. But slowly, now, an increasing volume of exchanges begins to take place. When it does we enter into the phase of "revival" or "recovery." The volume of exchanges, during this phase of the cycle, becomes increasingly greater and greater. Soon we are in the full bloom again of "prosperity." Finally, at its peak, we either stop dead once more at a crisis, or slip slowly down, *as a new cycle recurs.*

For almost a century and a half now—at the least—society has been suffering these regularly recurrent changes in its total volume of exchanges. Economists have collected sufficient data to identify clear business cycles, with each well-marked phase following upon another in the order described, as far back as 1790. The further back we go, of course, the more meager become the data. There are some economists who think business cycles may be discerned in the days of Greece and Rome. It is not impossible, particularly as to Rome, since society there, in its constitution, was in some respects not greatly different from ours. But there is not enough information available to identify, scientifically, what we know as business cycles before 1790. We may, of course, guess at their previous occurrence. There were economic crises, about which there are clear historical records, for fully three thousand years back. There were also many long periods of general wretchedness which can be identified in history, and other periods which were clearly marked by greater economic activity and by a more widespread well-being. But whether these changes occurred with the *rhythmical sequence* which characterize the modern business cycle, there is simply not enough evidence to show to satisfy the modern economist, with some scientific caution in his training. Both the crises, whenever they occurred, and the long periods of wretchedness—which we would now call "depression"—may have been due wholly to non-economic causes: to pestilences, or to wars and those other accidents, which the inanities of rulers might at any time produce.

It is the *seemingly inevitable recurrence* of these alternations in the volume of exchanges which economic students find significant. For they point to an economic—as distinct from a non-economic—cause

408

APPROXIMATE DURATION OF BUSINESS CYCLES IN CHRONOLOGICAL SEQUENCE

(White inset figures indicate approximate duration in years)

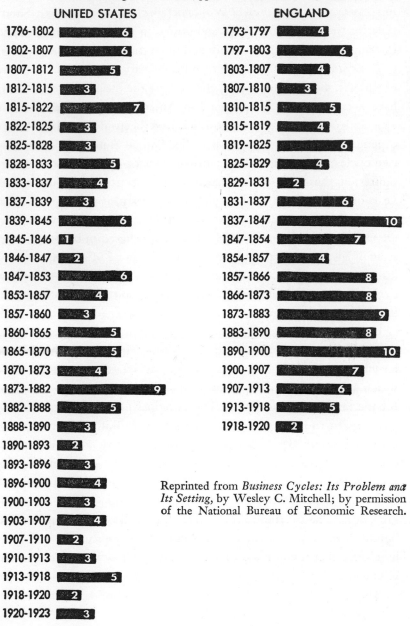

UNITED STATES		ENGLAND	
1796-1802	6	1793-1797	4
1802-1807	6	1797-1803	6
1807-1812	5	1803-1807	4
1812-1815	3	1807-1810	3
1815-1822	7	1810-1815	5
1822-1825	3	1815-1819	4
1825-1828	3	1819-1825	6
1828-1833	5	1825-1829	4
1833-1837	4	1829-1831	2
1837-1839	3	1831-1837	6
1839-1845	6	1837-1847	10
1845-1846	1	1847-1854	7
1846-1847	2	1854-1857	4
1847-1853	6	1857-1866	8
1853-1857	4	1866-1873	8
1857-1860	3	1873-1883	9
1860-1865	5	1883-1890	8
1865-1870	5	1890-1900	10
1870-1873	4	1900-1907	7
1873-1882	9	1907-1913	6
1882-1888	5	1913-1918	5
1888-1890	3	1918-1920	2
1890-1893	2		
1893-1896	3		
1896-1900	4		
1900-1903	3		
1903-1907	4		
1907-1910	2		
1910-1913	3		
1913-1918	5		
1918-1920	2		
1920-1923	3		

Reprinted from *Business Cycles: Its Problem and Its Setting*, by Wesley C. Mitchell; by permission of the National Bureau of Economic Research.

or group of causes. They point to some factor or factors continuously, and not factitiously, operating. That is, it seems inescapable, from the very regularity of the movements, that there is something *in the nature of our present economic mechanism* which is responsible for these momentous ups and downs in the total volume of our exchanges, which so profoundly and universally affect us all.

The data disclose this rhythm and regularity beyond the question of a doubt. The accompanying charts show the business cycles which have been conclusively identified in American experience between 1796 and 1923, and like cycles which have been identified in British experience between 1793 and 1920. The United States has had thirty-two cycles in the period, Great Britain twenty-two. The white inset figures, at the right of each bar, state the approximate duration in years of each cycle. This duration varies greatly, as will be seen. The cycles longest in duration are those that have been most severe; they are usually, also, the ones which have been ushered in by a crisis, instead of by a more gradual recession in the volume of activity. American cycles have had *an average duration* of about four years, British cycles about seven years since 1837. There is no telling, of course—at the time—how long any cycle will take in running its course.

The layman, in examining and in cogitating over these charts, should be careful not to allow them (as charts may do) to deaden his imagination. Economic charts are simply devices to picture concepts which are otherwise difficult to grasp. They are mere springboards for the informed imagination. The principal point to bear in mind, with regard to these charts, is that there were not thirty-two well-marked, discrete experiences (so to speak); but that what took place over this 127-year period in the United States and Great Britain (and needless to say, like charts could be supplied for other modern nations) *was a continuous up-and-down movement in the volume of exchanges*. The rhythm in the process then will be apparent; and its significance. For this cannot have occurred by chance, nor will it be by chance that it continues to occur, as it surely will for a long time to come.

410

It hardly seems necessary to point out the momentousness to the human race of the problem this remarkable set of phenomena presents. All the other problems that confront us can be considered minor to this one great problem—and part of it. The problem of persistent comparative poverty among men is obviously involved in it. The problem of involuntary technological unemployment is but one aspect of it. The so-called paradox of "want in the midst of potential plenty"—about which we have heard so much in recent years from new-fangled economists—is less the paradox it seems than an unclear, and often a somewhat peevish paraphrase, of this larger and more sharply outlined problem. The questions raised by the ever-increasing economic activity of governments are also inextricably tied up in this one over-all problem.

The challenge to the intelligence and ingenuity of mankind is clear. Why do these recurrent and rhythmical changes in the volume of exchanges take place among the two billion inhabitants of the earth? What is it, in the present constitution of human society, that causes them? Can the causes first be discovered, and then controlled, *so that the recessions do not occur,* and so that the long upward trend—which has so definitely been established as existing—is not punctuated every few years regularly, by periods of readjustment, in which sometimes tens of millions of persons are involved? When men have solved this problem of the business cycle—and who dare say it cannot be solved?—it is a safe prophecy to make that most of the slings and arrows of outrageous fortune that now harass us will be bad dreams in a human past. No doubt we shall then have other evils we shall count as great, but at least they will not be those of human degradation and despair, arising from the fact that men are blocked—they know not how—from exchanging what they own, or the work they can do, for what they need to keep themselves decently alive.

In an inquiry like this, we cannot ourselves engage in solution, but only in an attempt to understand the nature and some phases of this problem. It is helpful to such understanding to be aware that the

411

problem of the business cycle can be narrowed down to one seemingly not so vast. Moreover, the narrowing down has some advantage (to the non-specialist, at any rate) in that it indicates *the direction* at which efforts toward solution may finally be successful.

It is important, first, always to be aware that what we really mean by the words "business cycle," is *recurrent and rhythmical alternations in the total volume of exchanges.* The words refer primarily to a change *in exchanges,* and only secondarily to a change in production.

Now, the inquiry we ourselves have been making can contribute at least a few glimmers of insight into the problem, when it is presented in this form. The disclosures of this whole study make apparent— and it is surely beyond question from the commonest observation —that in the modern world by far the greater part of the exchanges which take place among men *are deferred exchanges.* Immediately completed exchanges are a very minor portion of the total volume.

It follows, then, that when this crucial volume of exchanges—with which our well-being is so closely bound up—increases or diminishes, *it is principally deferred exchanges which thus change in volume.*

Let us get down to hard pan, and illustrate this with figures. They may be in themselves dry as a bone, dismal as Carlyle thought all economics was. But not when they are taken all together to demonstrate a broad social fact. For that reason, even the most unmathematical student can find some interest in these few figures.

The sales of all corporate enterprises in the United States in 1929 were over $118,000,000,000; by 1932 they had decreased to a little over $53,000,000,000. Almost all of these sales can be identified as deferred exchanges.*

The sales of all retail stores in 1929 totaled over $49,000,000,000. In 1933 this had decreased to a little over $25,000,000,000.† Roughly, perhaps *about half* of these were deferred exchanges.

Wages and salaries in the United States in 1929 totaled about

* *U. S. Statistical Abstract, 1936,* Page 186.
† *Ibid.,* Page 790.

$51,500,000,000. By 1932 this had decreased to about $31,000,-000,000.* These were the vital deferred exchanges of labor for money.

The depositing of money with banks in 141 principal cities dropped from about $935,000,000,000 during the full year 1929 to about one-third of that mammoth total during 1932—$322,000,000,-000.† These, too, were all short deferred exchanges.

Outstanding loans made by banks for industrial and other enterprises stood at about $40,500,000,000 on June 30, 1930. Five years later, on the same date in 1935, these vital deferred exchanges stood at something short of $20,500,000,000; they had been almost cut in half.‡

In 1929, the new money entrusted to corporate enterprises and governmental units in long promises (including stock subscriptions) was over $11,500,000,000 in the year. In 1933 it had declined to less than one-tenth this sum; it was a little over $1,000,000,000.**

The number of stock certificates that changed hands on the New York Stock Exchange was over 1,100,000,000 shares during 1929. During 1932, it was 425,000,000 shares; †† and the average price per share had dropped from around $89 a share to around $26.

New loans on real estate are not totaled for the country. But an indirect measure of the diminution in deferred exchanges in this particular field is shown by the construction industry, which depends so much on the long economic promises called mortgages. For 1929 income produced by the construction industry stood at about $3,250,-000,000. By 1933 this had dropped over 80 per cent—to about $600,-000,000.‡‡

Our merchandise trade with foreigners, consisting entirely of deferred exchanges, totaled about $48,000,000,000 in the five years prior to and including 1929. For the succeeding five years this had

* *Ibid.*, Page 274.
† *Ibid.*, Page 269.
‡ *Ibid.*, Page 244.
** *Ibid.*, Page 293.
†† *Ibid.*, Page 289.
‡‡ *Ibid.*, Page 274.

diminished to about $23,000,000,000; it was more than cut in half.*

So on, wherever one cares to look into the records.

In short, wherever we examine *into the detail of the diminution in volume* that took place in the recession and depression phases of the past great cycle, we can identify the exchanges that were lessened as consisting almost entirely of deferred exchanges.

It must not, of course, be overlooked by the reader that this decrease in the activity was accompanied by a great drop in what we call "prices." In other words, the differences cited above, for mere illustrative purposes, *are always measured by money.* The drop in prices that accompanied the decrease in volume would greatly exaggerate, in some cases, the differences in volume that would appear from the mere figures. Nevertheless, the marked alternation in volume is manifest enough.

Well, what of this? Whatever significance it may have, the fact at least indicates that it may be profitable to pay some particular attention to *the relation of deferred exchanges to business cycles.*

If the "business cycle" is the name we give to alternations in the volume of exchanges, may it not be illuminating to concentrate our scrutiny *on the regions where the alternations occur?*

Of course, it may well be held, this point of view may simply be beating the devil around a bush. Indisputable enough it is, anyone will agree, that most of the exchanges that go on among men are deferred in their completion. If by the first two stages of the business cycle, recession and depression, we mean a lessening in the total volume of exchanges, then naturally that lessening would show up in the measurement of deferred exchanges between two periods, inasmuch as, nowadays, almost all exchanges are deferred in their completion.

But this surface explanation may be a mite too large for hasty swallowing. No scientific mind would cavalierly dismiss the possibility that perhaps *the actual deferrence of the exchanges*—perhaps

* *Ibid.,* Page 429.

414

the very eventuality of fulfillment or non-fulfillment of the economic promises—may have a great deal to do with the phenomenon of change itself.

Aside from this—for our own inquiry—there is a practical advantage toward full understanding of our society in carrying on an investigation, from this approach, into business cycles. For, after this book-length analysis of half-exchanges, we ought to know a little something about them. It should not be difficult to distinguish, with some clarity, what it is that discourages and blocks them, *and thus decreases the volume of them* most perceptibly, and, on the contrary, what it is that encourages and increases their volume.

Since "business cycles" themselves are nothing but *changes in the volume of exchanges*, and since almost all of these exchanges are deferred exchanges, by applying what we have ourselves discovered about what increases and decreases deferred exchanges, we may be able to dispel a little of the mystery, at any rate, which surrounds this crucial human problem of the business cycle.

21

The Processes by Which the Completion and Incompletion of Economic Promises Bring About the Rhythmic Phases of the Business Cycle

THIS whole study has demonstrated that by far the principal factor operating to diminish the volume of deferred exchanges is *incompletion of them.* Closely associated with it, and having the same effect, is *fear of incompletion.*

When any economic promise turns out actually to be incompleted, the total volume of exchanges is diminished in three directions.

First, the particular stream of business—that is, of exchanging—that may have been flowing for a long time between the promising and the promised person dries up at once. For example, you will not, as a business man, send goods to anyone who already owes you money and does not pay it.

Second, the person who first relinquishes his property is, by so much, poorer when an economic promise made to him is definitely unfulfilled. This may lessen his personal exchanges for consumable goods. Or, if he is engaged in an economic enterprise, it may have a far more important effect. In the latter case, he has in turn made many promises to complete half-exchanges. His loss may now be so great that he may be compelled, against all the bent of his integrity, to inform those who trusted him *that he must also default on his promises.* Thereupon, their half-exchanges with him cease forthwith; that is, the total volume of exchanges is diminished additionally from this direction.

416

Third, even if the loser does not now default on his *old* deferred exchanges, the volume of *new* deferred exchanges he enters into is almost certain to be diminished, unless the sum involved is quite insubstantial. For every prudent enterpriser cuts the volume of his attempted transactions to the cloth of his certain resources. If he himself is not prudent enough to do this, those who trust him, by their caution, compel him to. If he has sustained a substantial loss by reason of the failure of somebody else's promise to him, although his remaining available resources may enable him to complete *all his old promises*, and thus save his enterprise from extinction, prudent conduct of his enterprise compels him to reduce the volume of the *new economic promises* he makes. That is, he buys as little as he can on credit; and, as much as he can, he reduces his employment of labor.

Thus, every time a deferred exchange is actually incompleted it results *in reducing the total volume of exchanges* in not one, but in many radiating directions.

Fear of incompletion has the same effect as *actual* incompletion of economic promises. When one person learns that some other, whom he has trusted in a deferred exchange, has had his resources so depleted that he will be unlikely to complete the *old* promise, he at once ceases to trust that man as freely in *new* deferred exchanges.

If it is one enterprise trusting another on "book credit," orders received are not accepted.

If it is a bank trusting an enterpriser on a loan, the loan is not "extended" on the due date; it is closed out.

If it is a depositor trusting a bank, he makes no new deposits, but on the contrary extinguishes the old promises as fast as he can by "withdrawing his deposit."

So on, everywhere. Anticipation of the incompletion of deferred exchanges, as well as the actual event, slows down exchanges; and frequently is active in sooner bringing about what it foresees.

But fear of incompletion of deferred exchanges also acts in an *indirect* way to diminish the total volume of economic activity: *through the medium of prices and profits.*

417

This effect is a trifle devious, but it is an extremely important one for the student to trace.

First, we must keep in mind that there are two considerations that animate everybody in entering into a deferred exchange: the honesty of the promisor, *and the sufficiency of his resources*. Let us concentrate attention now solely upon the latter.

The ultimate resources of any economic enterprise depend upon three obvious things: (a) the price at which it sells its products; (b) how much of its product it sells—that is, *the volume of exchanges it can succeed in entering into;* and (c) whether it gains or loses money as a result of this exchanging—that is, upon its profit or loss.

Is it not obvious that its *sufficiency of resources*, which are so necessary to enable it to perform its economic promises, can be vitally affected by any one or all three of these factors?

Apply the criteria to the business you yourself are engaged in, or one you know something about.

If the prices you get for your product drop, although the number of the exchanges remains the same, your total available resources soon diminish, provided your current expenses remain unchanged.

On the other hand, your prices may remain unchanged, *but the number of your exchanges lessen*. In this case, you say your "total sales drop," and this, too, soon diminishes your total resources if your expenses remain the same.

Finally, if as the result of the relation between your sales and prices and your expenses, you end up with less money at the end of the year, you say you make no "profit." In this case, also, most certainly *your total available resources* are less than they might have been.

Now, whenever *total resources are diminished* because of any one of these factors—a change in price, a change in the volume of exchanging, or a change in profit—the ability of the enterprise to perform its economic promises *becomes justifiably more suspect*.

With smaller resources how can it be as reliable in completing the same volume of economic promises as in the past? Accordingly, those who had formerly been trusting it in deferred exchanges, are inclined to do less trusting, less exchanging, with it.

Moreover, here again, if the contraction in volume of exchanging does not originate with the watchful trustors in such a case, it is certain to originate with the promisor, *if he is prudently conducting his enterprise.* The first instinct of the economic enterpriser, who sees his resources being depleted, is to enter into fewer deferred exchanges himself. Why? *So that he can infallibly complete those he does enter into.* The fear of incompletion of new promises influences his actions quite as much as it does those of anyone who trusts him.

Now, these two great keys—the actual incompletion of economic promises and fear of incompletion of them—will be found to open a good many gates in that perplexing maze of events that constitute the business cycle.

Let us employ them, not so much with the notion that they constitute *the* cause, or even that they are the *major* causes of business cycles. The concept of causation here, as in many matters where human life and action are involved, may contribute less to understanding than it does to confusion. What we see as cause may often be analyzed as the effect of other causes, and we are pretty soon in a round of hen-and-egg reasoning. It is better to employ these keys rather with the notion of illuminating the course which business cycles take—to see merely *what happens during them.*

This illumination can at best be partial. For if we were able to describe, with an unquestionable accuracy, the full detail of events which occur during any business cycle, we would be in a position fully to understand these mysterious phenomena, and might soon be on our way to solving the problem of how to control them. But that is just the point: the call upon the imagination here seems to be beyond human capacity. The interrelations of almost countless enterprises are so involved; the exchanges of goods for money, labor for money, money for money, are so multitudinous and so diverse in character; *the interdependent promising is so complex,* that a clearly delineated mental image of the whole—as it takes place over a given period—is of an order of magnitude quite beyond human powers. More so is this true, because this immense complex of relations and events is not a static whole. It is a living whole. *It changes in all its parts at every moment.*

But even if it were within our mental capacity to envisage this whole volume of exchanging and promising, in its detail as it goes on, we are actually not provided with the information to re-create a fully accurate picture. The whole volume of transactions that goes on among the two billion inhabitants of the earth—and even more so, the unique psychological background of each transaction—is knowable to us only in quite fragmentary aspects. Yet it is *as a whole* we must consider this entire volume of transactions, if we want fully to understand business cycles.

Under the circumstances, the economist is obliged to resort to piecemeal imaginings about this whole volume of transactions. It is this necessitous piecemeal imagining, incidentally, which surely accounts for the multiplicity of theories among economists about the business cycle. Each is one of the proverbial blind men feeling and describing, usually with a pretty fair accuracy, a portion of this enormous elephant. Of course, piecemeal imagining is not to be decried as a method of ascertaining truth. It is pointed out here, as the method economists must at present use in acquiring full comprehension about human society, simply that we may be aware of what we are doing; and as a warning to students, if one is needed, as to the necessary limitations of economic insight at this time. Yet the fact is that men have made their great advances, in every field of knowledge, by this very method of piecing together, here a little and there a little more, of fact which they found they could always corroborate by experience.

In applying these particular keys, then, with which we are provided—the way in which incompletion of exchanges, and fear of incompletion, *changes the total volume* of exchanges—it will be understood that we are, in a sense, merely sketching a pattern of what, on the whole, happens during a typical business cycle.

That it is necessarily only a partial description of what happens will be apparent to anybody, even with a short memory. For other distinguishable phenomena can be discerned which also occur during the business cycle, in addition to that diminution of economic promises, which is the plainest feature of it. Many prices, for example, fall and rise. The initiation of new enterprises increases and decreases. There are increases and decreases in the number of "business failures." There are marked changes in the physical production of goods, and more particularly of that type called capital-goods, which are not consumed at all, but are utilized solely in producing goods which are consumed. What is called "overproduction" of some goods at one period, and "underproduction" at other periods, is manifest. Profits diminish and increase. The amount of "promised money," created through loans of banks and governments and being passed from ownership to ownership in place of real money, changes by enormous sums. Employment also notoriously varies, to the distress of millions. With these latter variations, the means—the "purchasing power," it has been newly called—of vast masses of persons to obtain consumable goods alters. Finally, there are mass psychological phenomena, a wide-spreading optimism among enterprisers, succeeded by waves of fear and pessimism.

Business cycles may be described, and have been by different economists, with any one of these clearly observable phenomena (and others also) as the factor principally utilized to give meaning and order to the events, and to trace the sequence of them.* I employ for this purpose that diminution of total exchanges, which results

* The most exhaustive research into business cycles has been conducted, for a period of sixteen years now, by the National Bureau of Economic Research, under the directorship of Wesley C. Mitchell. The first results of that study were published in 1927 in the form of a book by Professor Mitchell, *Business Cycles: The Problem and Its Setting.* The first chapter of that book sets forth an invaluable summary of the various theories that have been advanced as to the nature and causes of business cycles. For most of the factual matter about business cycles contained in this and the preceding chapter, I must acknowledge my complete indebtedness to Professor Mitchell's work and to other publications of the National Bureau of Economic Research. As to the theory advanced in this chapter—the particular view of business cycles that is taken—I must warn laymen that there is no specific authority for it in Professor Mitchell's work. It is merely my interpretation of the revelations this painstaking scientific study of the National Bureau provides; one more theory to be added to the many others that have been advanced, and of no value unless it proves in the end—like any scientific theory—to give an explanation of the phenomena that is always verifiable by experience, and is all-inclusive in its elucidation of the phenomena. Dr. Mitchell's own conclusions from the studies of the National Bureau are still to be published.

from actual and feared incompletion of economic promises, for one reason. I believe it provides *both a deeper and a more comprehensive insight* into the facts. All the phenomena distinguished above, as being noticeably present in every business cycle, are of course interrelated. But each one of them can be shown, by analysis, to be particularly closely related to the completion and incompletion of economic promises. In short, by using this as our key, it seems that we may be able to obtain *a more inclusive picture* of the realities of the business cycle. Yet, the economics student must beware, it remains a fallible human picture we are attempting, by this principal means, to sketch out. Art is, of course, forever a matter of selection and emphasis to assist in the representation of actuality; and in economics, as in every science, more than laymen commonly recognize, Art in this rather wide sense has its place.

The first strokes in this ever-changing panorama of human activity may be splashed in at that point of the business cycle where the total volume of exchanges begins to lessen. What makes it lessen? What have economic promises to do with the lessening?

To envision this comprehensively, we should be sure to leave out no area of human activity where deferred exchanges commonly go on in great volume. Fortunately, we have already seen what these main areas are.

First, there are the economic promises that governments enter into. They are of two kinds. First, the short promises represented by its paper money and "token money." Second, the long promises represented by bonds and certificates of one kind and another. All of the latter pay interest, and are commonly referred to as "government debt."

Second, there are the economic promises that fiscal institutions like banks, insurance companies, and building and loan companies, enter into. These run into as many staggering billions of dollars as the promises of governments. Some are short, some are long. We do not need to identify them again, nor demonstrate how necessarily the promises are interdependent upon one another.

The third great economic area in which we have seen economic promises completely prevailing is among the hundreds of thousands of enterprises engaged in producing and distributing goods. This is called "book credit." Book credit is made up entirely of short promises. In magnitude of volume, over any given period, it is quite comparable to the economic promises in which governments and fiscal institutions are involved.

An equally enormous volume of promises centers around land and buildings. There are both short and long promises in this area, and both are measured by billions. The short ones we include in the conception of rent. The long ones we call mortgages.

A fifth large area, in which economic promises go on in an enormous magnitude, is that of corporate enterprise. We find here those billions of half-exchanges called corporation bonds. These are always long promises. Closely allied to them—although they are not economic promises—are purchases of shares in corporate enterprises. Here the property has been relinquished by the original owner with no promise of return. It is a fully completed exchange, not a deferred one. Yet, as we have seen, there are involved even more faith and trust in other persons than in a deferred exchange.

A sixth enormous area, in which deferred exchanges necessarily take place, is in employment. These promises are very short, and are usually fully completed. But that is no reason (quite the contrary) for ignoring them as deferred exchanges. They add up currently to quite as many billions as in any of the other areas where economic promises prevail. Their total volume (as we shall soon see) is very injuriously affected by the actual and feared incompletion of promises in other fields. Thus affected, they turn around (so to speak) and diminish or increase the volume of exchanges in other directions.

This is true, likewise, of the seventh large field where deferred exchanges play a notable role—in the retail market, where the goods produced and transported for consumption are finally presented to the millions who will consume them. As we observed, in Chapter Four, this is the one great area of human activity where deferred exchanges do not wholly prevail. On the contrary, immediate swaps

423

of goods for money predominate here. Yet the volume of promising that goes on here is far from unimportant. It is represented, of course, by the goods which are sold under the sobriquet of "consumer credit." This includes both charge accounts and instalment purchases.

Now, there is a simple plan we may follow as an aid to comprehension of what takes place in the course of the business cycle. We can isolate in our imagination a sample enterprise, in each one of these large fields of human activity, and see how the actual or feared incompletion of economic promises decreases its own total volume of exchanges. At the same time, we can watch how it does something else: *how it decreases the number of exchanges entered into by all the enterprises which deal with it,* and all the individuals engaged in it. We could then later attempt to replace the units into that inextricable living relation they all have with one another. By this piecemeal imagining, we could approach an accurate picture of what happens through the various stages of the business cycle.

But to do this, one after the other, with each of the seven areas we have identified—where economic promising goes on in enormous volumes—would be a lengthy procedure. It might have an advantage in being exhaustive, but it would also, certainly, be exhausting to the reader. And surely it is unnecessary, in an inquiry such as this. What would certainly be disclosed is that what happens in one area happens in all, under like circumstances. We have shown abundantly that the considerations are the same with all types of economic promises; *and they result in like events.* It may be sufficient, then, for purposes of illustration, merely to show what occurs to economic promises in two or three of these areas during the course of the recession and depression phases of the business cycle.

First, let us take a sample unit very easily followed—the incompletion of that type of economic promise represented by employment. Incompletion here seldom occurs, but where it does its effect in diminishing the volume of exchanges is very easily discerned.

424

Assume, for example, a large corporation with a payroll of $500,-000 a month. Purely for purposes of illustration, let us assume also that it pays its employees only once a month. Suddenly, like a bolt from the blue, on the last day of the month, it announces that it is bankrupt, closes down, and includes within its liabilities the unpaid month's wages of $500,000. This would be considered by the workers as rather a dirty business trick upon them. But in essence it is no dirtier—if that is the word for it—than the treatment being accorded all the other parties to whom it had made economic promises, and which it now announces it is unable to complete. Ignoring whatever ethics there may be in the matter, our question is, *How does this mere event of incompletion*—of the promises to the workmen alone —affect the total volume of exchanges in the nation?

Obviously, the exchanges of money for labor that have been going on *between the corporation and the wage-earners* would end at once. No wage-earner, with the certainty that the exchange will not be completed by the delivery of money, will contribute his work to this particular corporate enterprise in a deferred exchange, unless it is reorganized under more responsible auspices. All the workers involved must, accordingly, seek other enterprises with which they can exchange their labor for money. Until all those previously employed are re-employed, the total volume of exchanges of labor for money —as to this one group of men, clearly—is diminished. This, however, is only one quarter in which the diminution of volume of exchanges takes place.

The workers, under our hypothesis, are immediately poorer by $500,000. This was the amount of money promised, and which they did not receive. Now, of course, currently in the retail market, they have been accustomed to exchange their wages for goods to be consumed, pleasures to be enjoyed, and services that were needed by them. The loss of $500,000 means that they must immediately *diminish these purchases in the local market* almost up to the total of this sum.

Let us ignore the effect of this upon the community's servicers— the doctors, dentists, bootblacks, manicurists, barbers, and so forth.

For these are put, by this circumstance, in the same type of situation as the workmen thrown out of a job. Let us merely follow what happens to the retail merchants. Exchanges with *their* customers are lessening. The stock of goods they have on hand is being consumed less rapidly. Accordingly, *they enter into fewer exchanges with their suppliers.* They may even be obliged to cut down on their own employees, thus further reducing the volume of exchanges *of labor for money* going on in the community. In any event, the volume of exchanges, *which their suppliers enjoy,* is quite plainly diminished, with an effect in each case on *their* laborers. There is involved, likewise, a decrease in the services of trucks and railroads bringing consumable goods into the community.

All this damage—and we have sketched but part of it—would not be confined to the mere diminution in volume caused by the loss of the original $500,000 of promises not completed by the corporation. No doubt most of the workmen have a small cache of wealth to draw upon. In those cases where it is a small one, it is soon used up. But both where this happens, and where it does not, all of the persons involved very definitely "economize." That is, they are far less free in entering into the exchanges they have long been accustomed to. Their "standard of living," as it is called, definitely lowers. They buy fewer goods, and demand fewer services of those who have specialized in service occupations. This lessened tempo of exchanging *is progressive with every individual in the group,* until he succeeds again in regularly exchanging his own labor for money. The total effect, as measured by money, goes far beyond the $500,000 originally lost by the workers.

There is still another direction where we can observe consequences sprouting quickly, like overnight weeds. We have said the workmen were obliged to repair each to his little cache of wealth. Where is it? It is in the banks. It consists, really, of bank promises to the workingmen. These are brought to a close—and no compensating new ones take their place! But when a bank's deposits decrease, *it must turn around and decrease its loans to business enterprises.* What that means, in the way of further diminution of exchanges, we must later

426

see. In the meantime, it is apparent—even from this quick and sketchy survey—that the original incompletion of an economic promise, represented by employment, markedly and inevitably decreases the volume of exchanges elsewhere.

Take book credit. This practice among men—of giving away goods and services to others upon the mere strength of promises—is measured each year by literally tens of billions of dollars. When a single one of these promises is incompleted, what happens *to the total volume of exchanges* in the nation; and why does it happen?

For purposes of example, let us take a factory making an essential part of an automobile, and—to make the case flagrant—we shall assume that a substantial portion of its output has been taken by one automobile company. Over a period of several months it has shipped $500,000 worth of goods to this automobile company "on credit." Suddenly, it is apprised of the fact that this chief customer has become hopelessly bankrupt, and that instead of receiving $500,000 within a few months, the best it can hope for is to receive $50,000 at the end of some long legal palavering. This, of course, would be a simple incompletion of an economic promise. How precisely does it diminish the total volume of exchanges carried on in every direction (a) by our enterprise; (b) by other enterprises which deal with it, and by all the individuals associated with it; and, therefore, (c) the total in the nation?

First, all exchanging ends at once, of course, with the defaulting customer. Unless these exchanges of goods for money *can be replaced* by similar exchanges with other customers, the volume of outside exchanges the factory carries on is clearly lowered by so much. We say, simply, that its sales drop. We mean by these words that its exchanges of goods for money decrease. This, in turn, means obviously that fewer workmen are needed in the factory. They are discharged. If then we wanted to shadow the discharged laborers, like economic Hawkshaws, we would find each one in turn diminishing his individual exchanges in the retail market and with servicers, with all the radiating consequences we followed a moment ago.

But in addition to decreasing the employment of labor, the company must at once lower its purchases of raw material for the product it manufactures. These purchases, of course, are deferred exchanges with suppliers. These firms find their volume of exchanges lessened. In turn they may have to discharge some workmen and decrease purchases of *their* raw materials. The service of carriers, also, is diminished; and of such economic units as suppliers of electric power; and even of telephone and telegraphic communication, and the sale of postage stamps, all of which are *less used* because of this series of developments.

All this, however, may be but a beginning of the resulting diminution of exchanges; and comparatively fortunate everybody will be if it ends there, and slowly the factory begins elsewhere to regain its so-called lost business. But the consequences *only end here* if the enterprise possesses such ample resources that a loss of $500,000 does not cripple it. Its financial condition, however, may easily be such that it must itself at once cease operating. In other words, at this point *the fear of incompletion of economic promises* begins to operate to diminish exchanges. How and why does this happen?

Purely for purposes of simple illustration, let us assume the enterprise is none too wealthy, but has been operating on a thin cushion of net resources. Its financial condition might be, roughly, something like this: It owns $100,000, consisting of deposits in a bank; there were also $500,000 of "accounts receivable" from the defaulting automobile company; $300,000 more of "accounts receivable" from other customers; and $300,000 worth of goods, finished and partly finished—its inventory. All these would be its "quick assets." They total $1,200,000.

Against these "quick assets" of $1,200,000, it owes (let us assume) $200,000 on a promissory note to the very bank in which it has $100,-000 deposits, and $300,000 in "accounts payable" to its suppliers of raw materials. These are its "quick liabilities"—that is, they constitute the promises which, within a short period, it will have to complete.

So long as it could safely rely upon $500,000 due from the now defaulting customer, this ratio between what the factory soon expected to pay out was nothing much to worry about, although its quick resources could be ampler for safety. The relation, under the hypothesis, is $1,200,000 soon to be paid in, and only $500,000 soon to be paid out.

But with the news that $500,000 is for the most part lost, this picture radically changes. All the factory may now really count upon is $100,000 from its bank deposits, and $300,000 from its other accounts receivable. True, this may be expanded by the fortunate sale of a good part of its $300,000 inventory. But then again it may not be, and probably will not soon be, since the defaulting automobile company was its chief customer. All that is really sure, under this hypothesis, is $400,000 to come in. But even more certain, as having to be paid out, is the $200,000 bank loan and the $300,000 accounts payable. What happens under these circumstances?

The *fear of incompletion*, on the part of the creditors, becomes acute; and it is certainly justified. Let us assume the bank loan comes due ten days after the news of the $500,000 default. Would the bank "renew" the loan of $200,000? It is highly unlikely. It has its own economic promises to fulfill with depositors and can take no such risk of loss. Whatever money the factory had on deposit with it, on the due date of the loan, would be applied mercilessly to the reduction of the loan. But by thus compelling the factory to utilize its deposits to pay the bank loan, the bank would be stripping it of all available so-called cash. Yet it needs cash to fulfill its other economic promises. What are these? First, there are the continuing deferred exchanges with its employees, for labor. These it must never fail to complete. If it does not meet these—the most vital of all economic promises—it must close down at once. In addition, it still has $300,000 of accounts payable to meet. Unless it does, its suppliers—who also, of course, soon know all about its troubles and who are animated by the same fear of incompletion as the bank—will not continue to supply it with raw materials. It has been stripped by the bank of ready cash, and must rely on incoming money from its other accounts receivable, which must be eked out here, there, and everywhere to meet its obligations. There is no need to examine any further into what probably would occur, and how. The company might be able, by selling a good part of its $300,000 inventory, at sacrifice prices, to raise money enough to stave off disaster. If it does this—through lowered prices—it may easily start a new line of serious consequences, *to other concerns*, tending to diminution of the volume of exchanges. But almost inevitably—unless by good fortune it acquires some new and additional quick resources which will enable it to meet all its old promises and any reasonable amount of new ones it may have to enter into—the enterprise will be forced to suspend operations.

That is, the fear of incompletion, *justified because of depleted resources*, will bring about actual incompletion.

Not part, but all of its continuing volume of exchanges would then be subtracted from the total volume in the nation. All of its employees, instead of a portion, would be affected. And all of its purchases of raw materials, instead of a portion, would be subtracted from the exchanges it had formerly entered into with suppliers. Far afield the consequences would go.

This set of circumstances has been deliberately imagined, showing fear of incompletion arising from the fact that a large part of an enterprise's resources has been wiped out at once—by bankruptcy. Frequently enough this happens. But more often the trouble arrives not quite so dramatically.

Resources can be depleted by the fact that the enterprise *must accept lowered prices* for what it has to sell, at a time when it cannot proportionately reduce its expenses. Resources can also be depleted by mere lessening in demand. That is, the number of exchanges an enterprise can enter into simply decrease—for any number of reasons that can be imagined; the best one, for illustrative purposes, being that the period is the recessive one in a business cycle.

Lowered prices with the same volume of exchanges—or lowered volume of exchanges with the same prices as formerly—both result at once in depleted resources. Depleted resources—if the depletion is progressive—means an ever-mounting fear that economic promises

430

will be incompleted, *unless they too are reduced in volume*. Reduced they are, accordingly, both by the prudent enterpriser who is affected, and through less extensive credit by cautious trustors.

This reduction then proceeds to have the same radiating consequences, toward diminution of volume, which we have seen appearing more dramatically in our previous illustration of a bankruptcy.

Let us have one last illustration. What is true of book credit is certainly true of bank credit. Bank credit constitutes the most sensitive of all economic promises to the effects which arise from actual or feared incompletion. Their explosion-point, so to speak, is very low. The deferred exchanges of a bank, of course, are distinguished by the incoming and outgoing money. On the one side are its deposits, the economic promises *made by the bank* to complete deferred exchanges. On the other side are its loans and investments, the economic promises *made to the bank* by individuals and enterprises and governments.

It need hardly be pointed out how, when a bank fails to complete its own most vital promises—that is, to give money to its depositors on demand—the volume of exchanges is diminished in a thousand directions. These bank promises—as we abundantly demonstrated in Chapter Nine—constitute the very money being used by all those who trusted the bank. It is what is being accepted and given for goods and services. Now the bank closes, and it is not available. It is non-existent. By our hypothesis, it is a form of "When-As-And-If Wealth" which in the event proved illusory. All those who thought they owned real wealth are now poorer for this loss, and must necessarily enter into fewer exchanges as consumers.

So far as individuals are affected, this would principally diminish their exchanges in the local markets, for consumable goods, and with servicers. But worse in its consequences than this is the fact *that bank deposits of economic enterprises are far larger than those of individuals*. Each enterprise, far more than individuals, has constant economic promises it must complete. Because of the loss of this—ordinarily the most reliable of all resources—most of these enterprises

431

would find great difficulty in completing their old promises. They would therefore all be obliged to curtail their new promises, because of the loss of these ready resources.

Moreover, here again *the fear of incompletion* enters the engagement with a supporting barrage of trouble. Every other concern, dealing with those which had lost money in the bank failure, would see that their resources were depleted. They would, therefore, be more cautious in extending credit. Many of the concerns with money in the failed bank, accordingly, might soon be obliged to default on their old promises, and to suspend operations completely. Whether they suspend entirely, or *merely lower* their volume of exchanges to accord with the new condition of their resources, the further radiating consequences, which we have examined—*always toward diminution of volume*—would ensue in each case.

This, however, is only half the story. When a bank closes its cashier's window where the promises go out, it must also close the president's door where the promises come in. It must collect the loans—that is, extinguish the promises—made to it by business enterprises. That is what liquidation of a bank largely means. Now, this bank-credit was actually being used as money. Recall our analysis in Chapter Nine. The bank credit was being given and accepted for goods and services. When the loan must be repaid by the borrowers and no new one takes its place, so much bank-promise money *is wiped out of existence!* All those enterprises which had formerly been using it, as part of their available resources, *have those quick resources lessened* by the amount of the loan, in each case. With lessened resources they must, in prudence, enter into fewer exchanges.

No less clear is the diminution of volume which results—when the other main type of deferred exchanges of banks is incompleted; that is, when promises *made to the bank* are unfulfilled: that is, when its loans are unpaid.

What, precisely, happens when a concern, which has borrowed $50,000 from a bank, fails to pay it when the note comes due?

First, all lending to the borrower at once ends, not only on the part of the bank which has been deceived, but on the part of all other banks. Almost all "book credit" to the defaulting borrower would likewise end. He becomes, in a sense, an economic pariah. For none but the most careless of business men would send goods to, or perform services for, an enterprise which had failed to carry out an economic promise to a bank, a record not easily hidden.

But, again, this single line of consequence would be multiplied in other directions. Because of the incompletion of the exchange, the bank has lost $50,000. Let us assume, that is, it can recover nothing by throwing the borrower into bankruptcy and having his assets divided up. By losing this loan of $50,000, it must now *decrease other loans* by this or larger amounts. For safety's sake! In short, because A has failed to complete his economic promise to the bank, B, C, D, and E must have their loans in whole or in part decreased.

But when their bank deposits are lessened, *the wherewithal to complete their own promises is lessened;* they are compelled thereby to lessen the volume of new deferred exchanges they can enter into. The extent to which the bank is obliged to "contract" its loans depends upon how great the loss is that it sustains, as compared with its total quick resources. What is now operating here, it must be observed, is *fear of incompletion,* on the part of the bank, of its own promises.

If the loss is really substantial, this fear of incompletion extends beyond the bank's own doors. Some forehanded large depositor (not infrequently this may be a friend of one of the bank's own directors, who has been tipped off) takes quick advantage of his knowledge to end his deferred exchanges with the bank. That is, he "withdraws his deposits." The result, of course, is additionally to decrease the quick resources of the bank. This compels it further to contract its loans to enterprisers as they come due. The final result may well be a panic "run" upon the bank, where everybody becomes imbued with the fear of incompletion, and tries to end an economic promise, in anticipation of incompletion. Under these circumstances, unless the bank's resources have been managed with the greatest caution, it will probably have to close its doors, fail to complete *all* its promises, and extinguish bank credit by winding up all its loans—with the calami-

433

tous and widespread consequences, *in diminution of volume in every direction*, that we have already examined.

It begins to be possible, after this piecemeal consideration in a few fields—to identify the effect, upon total volume of activity, of actual or feared incompletion of deferred exchanges; to see, *in a general pattern*, what happens throughout each business cycle; and, at the same time, to form a valid notion of why one business cycle breeds the next.

These separate economic areas we have examined are, of course, not segregated in actuality as we have segregated them in imagination. *The interdependence of promises extends in every direction one examines, without break.* Every one of the countless units of enterprise is linked back and forth by continuous promises with many other enterprises. Each one has the same inextricable relation with one or more banks, the banks in turn with governments, and the government back again (through money and its long-term debt) with all banks, insurance companies, enterprises, and individuals. The whole might be compared to a living body, and the blood coursing through it, keeping it alive and in action, consists of promises. Prick your body at any point, and your blood at once makes its appearance. Do it with the economic enterprise, no matter how tiny, with which you happen to be most closely associated, and you find it flooded with promises, as the tiniest bit of flesh with blood. The society is a vast living whole. Its tissues—its individuals and its enterprises—have become indissolubly united. None can live of itself, isolated. Each part of it is connected by an endless series of relationships with every other part, and is more or less affected by what affects every other part. The relationship—when we look beneath appearances and cease to be confused by the thoughtless acceptance of words—we see to be merely one of endless exchanges of property and labor. But almost all of these exchanges are deferred in their completion. Promises intervene. And what really supports this living whole, and keeps it going, *is the unifying fact that the promises are fulfilled*. When they are *not fulfilled* in any large volume, or when

434

it is feared that they may not be, this cannot help but disturb the processes by which the whole society operates. The disturbance may be measured by the diminution of the total volume of exchanges which ensues.

The business cycle, as we have seen, is merely the inclusive descriptive term we give to *the alternate increase and lessening in the total volume of exchanges going on among men.* But with the view opened up here, would it not be more illuminating to regard the business cycle as *alternations in the volume of promising* going on among men?

With what insight we may have gained from our piecemeal imagining in different fields—of the effect of actual or feared incompletion of economic promises—let us try to follow, roughly, the course of these changes in volume.

Economists are pretty well agreed,* in the first place, that the beginning of the lessening of volume *is at least associated* with a situation where a large mass of economic promises, in a sector of the society where many enterprises and individuals are closely related, are either actually incompleted, or have been proceeding on such a scale that fear of eventual incompletion, *as to a large portion of them,* is justifiable in any person of caution and experience. How and why this dangerous extension of deferred exchanges occurs we can later come back to examine, as the full cycle unrolls. We merely begin at this point. It is the overhanging break of the wave at the top point of that stage of the cycle, the extremely active exchanging that is going on, which we describe by the word "prosperity."

If it is *actual* incompletion of promises on a large scale that occurs, the drop from this high point ordinarily begins with what economists call a "commercial crisis." Far from happening invariably, this only occurs on the average with every third or fourth cycle. If it is mere suspicion of possible incompletion that begins the slowing-down

* The justification for this statement, I think, will be found by an examination of the many theories about business cycles summarized by Professor Mitchell in the first chapter of *Business Cycles: The Problem and Its Setting.*

process, this stage of recession in the cycle is more likely to set in gradually, without that excited and sudden contraction of activity, which is financial panic. The onset of a recession, as a matter of fact, is ordinarily seldom noticed by business men.

Now, the chief task of the student of *any single cycle* is to identify the particular mass of economic promises which were either actually incompleted, or of which there was justifiable fear of incompletion on an extensive scale, and from which the ever-accelerating process of diminution received its first strong impulsion.

For purposes of illustration, let us examine the last phases of the great cycle through which we recently passed. The downgrade from the peak in volume began in 1929, but it began earlier than is commonly believed. Most persons date the beginning of the depression in the past cycle from the notorious collapse of stock-market values in this country in October of that year. Actually the recession from the high point in the volume of exchanges, as to the United States, had begun in 1928 in the construction industry; by June of 1929 it was well marked in a majority of industries.* Careful economists now give June, 1929, as the month showing the peak of the cycle preceding the greatest depression in history.

Precisely why the diminution of volume began with the construction industry, lacking complete information about our society as we do, must still be a matter of speculation. One fact may be observed, however: the industry is one in which long-time promises play a major role. Little construction goes on without lending upon mortgages. There had been a great boom in construction in this country following the War. With it there had been an enormous extension of

* "The contraction began in the construction industry. Total construction contracts declined after February, 1928. This decline is due to the drop in residential building, beginning on that date. Orders for passenger train cars and shipments of apples followed within six months. Late that year contracts for industrial buildings and the production of oak flooring, inner tubes and solid tires, turned downward. Portland cement began to decline in January, 1929, and five series in February, including passenger automobiles. Thereafter the recession spread rapidly over the industrial field. By the end of the year all but fourteen of the series in Table 4 [73 different business activities were included.—Ed.] had joined the procession."—*Production during the American Business Cycle of 1927–33*, by Wesley C. Mitchell and Arthur F. Burns, National Bureau of Economic Research.

436

lending on real estate, particularly urban real estate, on the part of banks, insurance companies, building and loan associations, and wealthy individuals. One reliable estimate shows that loans upon urban real estate *had increased by eighteen billion dollars* between 1921 and 1931.* Quite an increase; and none too healthy a situation! It is that very extension of economic promises, in mass, ordinarily associated with the beginning of a recession. The promises represented by this vast increase could obviously never be completed in full, *unless rents remained at the high level they had attained.*

Nevertheless—to those who have good recollections and others who care to look up the records—it could not have been fear of incompletion that stopped the flow of money into mortgage loans, and therefore slowed down the construction industry. All through 1928, and during the first six months of 1929—at the very time the construction industry was declining—we were rising to the height of the boom, and there was no general expectation that rents would drop. On the contrary, we were supposed, even by economists respected at the time, to be in a "New Era"; and one statesman may go down as famous in history for predicting that we had, at the time, finally abolished poverty in this favored and glorious land-of-the-free.

Dangerous as the urban mortgage situation later proved to be, some other explanation than fear of incompletion of these particular economic promises must be advanced for the general decline in the construction industry during 1928 and 1929—a decline which either spread, or at least became manifest, in a large number of activities from June, 1929, onward. One explanation—with at least partial plausibility in it—is that this vast extension of economic promises, ordinarily supporting the construction industry, *was coincident with* an equally vast extension of economic promises in other areas of activity, some of which were more attractive; and notably that which centered in the stock market. Appreciation in values was proceeding, by 1928, much faster in corporate shares than in real estate. It was far more attractive to risk money in the stock market than in long-

* *Internal Debts in the United States,* Evans Clark.

term loans on buildings. This enormous flow of capital into the stock market, beginning in 1928, *may have depleted* the usual flow of money which ordinarily streams into loans to support building.

At any rate, one conclusion is certainly supportable. Whatever began the decline in the construction industry in 1928, by the time this decline had spread to other industries—which happened by June of 1929—the recession, which then began to be generally manifest, would have been far less severe than it was, had it not been that it was very decidedly *associated with* an enormous extension of economic promises in the stock market; and in other areas of activity— as we shall see. But, in particular, very quickly in the stock market, the actual incompletion of promises, and the fear of incompletion, played their role.

The prices of shares had risen to heights never before reached, and trading in 1929 was proceeding on an unprecedented scale. Not only our own citizens were involved, but moneyed persons abroad transferred their funds, by the hundreds of millions, to our shores. Notoriously, almost everybody of high and low income was "in the market," exchanging corporate shares for money and money for corporate shares. Teachers, policemen, barbers, even bootblacks on the street, were blithely, in excited good humor, buying and selling shares.

It has been the rather unclear assumption, in some quarters, that it was this mere gambling on the part of inexperienced persons, who could be fleeced, which constituted the dangerous feature of this market. But this is not probing deep enough. What does it matter whether gamblers win or lose on their expectations, if they have ample possessions with which to settle their gambling transactions? If ownership really passes, what one loses the other gains. The trouble in our stock market of 1929 was that the several millions of gamblers, most of them, were doing their gambling *with other people's money*. Only the tiniest portion of the enormous volume of corporate shares being bought at the time were bought outright, paid for by the owners in full, and put away in safe-deposit boxes and bureau drawers.

Why was this? It was because the millions of owners actually did not have enough money to pay for them in full. They had borrowed money from the brokers to buy the shares "on margin"—putting up, that is, a very small portion of the purchase price themselves. The brokers, to finance their own lending, had borrowed the money "on call" from the banks. On September 30, 1929, the amount of money lent to brokers by banks was over $8,500,000,000.* This was aside from other billions lent by the banks to individuals direct, upon the securities being traded upon the stock market.

The collapse in the stock market which occurred in October, 1929, can better be understood *as a collapse of promises* than as a collapse in prices. For the latter was incidental to the first. The prices of shares never would have collapsed, certainly not to the degree they did, if the promises which sustained them could have been fulfilled. What clearly happened was that in mid-1929 a few astute persons, aware that a cyclical industrial recession was even then in process, began to see that a very large portion of these extensive promises would never be completed. The resources to complete most of them, on the part of the owners, were simply not there. There was only one possibility of the owners being able to complete them: *if the values of shares went ever higher and higher, and never lower.* What chance was there of this, with an industrial decline already making itself apparent? It was clear enough what this situation involved: the ultimate selling of the shares, in order to raise the resources to complete this enormous mass of promises. The astute ones, then, knowing that if their analysis of the situation was accurate, the recognition of it would soon spread, sold everything speculative in value at the high prices then available; and stopped buying. What animated them at bottom, it will thus be seen, was fear of incompletion of economic promises. Soon enough the recognition of this basic uncertainty in the situation did spread. As it did, more persons sought to divest themselves of the speculative values, while the exchanging could be done at a high price. Suddenly it appeared that there were many more sellers than buyers of shares in the market, and the fat was in the fire.

* *U. S. Statistical Abstract*, 1936, Page 289.

439

The first real pressure put upon this enormous volume of promises, which was supporting the high value of corporate shares, revealed how slender were the actual resources behind them. As the price of each security dropped, the broker called upon the owner for "more margin." That is, he merely announced to the borrower that he himself *would lend less money upon it*. Most of these persons, not having additional resources to put up, ordered the brokers to sell the securities, and cover the loan in that way. This increased the avalanche of selling, forcing prices still lower. Those who did not so instruct the broker found their securities sold anyway. For the broker, under any circumstances, was going to cover his own borrowings from the bank. Remember, they stood at the enormous total of $8,500,000,000 at the time. Under the rights accorded him, the broker could sell the security, before he himself sustained any loss upon it.

The student will observe that there can be identified here a precipitate and *an enormous diminution in economic promises*—in loans. First, on the part of brokers to customers, and then on the part of banks to brokers. This diminution can be measured. Between September 30, 1929, and December 31, 1930, loans of banks to brokers decreased by over $6,600,000,000; between that date and June, 1932, they decreased over $1,600,000,000 more. They finally stood at only $244,000,000. Altogether, in this short period, *almost the entire amount of these $8,500,000,000 loans of banks to brokers were wiped out*. There was approximately the same drop, accordingly, in loans of brokers to their customers.

Violent price changes in the shares of corporate enterprises are ordinarily to be regarded more as a consequence of recession than as influential in contributing to decreased economic activity. They have much more to do with the ownership of wealth—and with absentee ownership, under modern conditions—than with economic enterprise. They less affect than they are affected by industrial changes. But this particular *debacle* in 1929, extremely violent as it was, greatly contributed to the diminution in the total volume of exchanges that had already begun several months before.

440

This was so, because of the literally hundreds of thousands of individuals who were involved. Counting their "When-As-And-If Wealth" as real wealth, they had all felt themselves rich and getting richer. Now they found themselves in actuality even poorer than when they had gone into the market. They were all obliged, even if it were not their inclination, to be economical, instead of lavish in expenditure, to decrease their exchanges in the retail market. Industries and services which were in the category of "luxuries" almost immediately recorded this diminution in the volume of exchanges.

Aside from this, there were few business men who had not been "in the market." Many of them found their total resources seriously affected by the drop in corporate values. Frequently enough, personal resources and the resources of economic enterprises are almost one and the same thing. *The depletion of one depletes the other*. Accordingly, after 1929, a very large number of enterprisers unquestionably were obliged to be far more prudent in the new economic promises they made.

Along these two routes, principally, the consequences of the 1929 stock market *debacle* traveled, to diminish the total volume of exchanges. It has been accepted, commonly, as signalizing the onset of the great depression. But, as we have seen, it was merely a dramatic accentuation of a recession in industrial activity that had begun months before.

As it happened, however, it was particularly damaging in its effect for still another reason. The extreme vulnerability of the mass of promises underlying corporate ownership at this period *coincided with other weaknesses*, no less vulnerable, in our economic structure; and by weakness is meant, simply and primarily, that *vast masses of certain types of economic promises existed*, which at the time were highly speculative as to ultimate completion.

There were at least four additional weak areas that can now be identified, besides that of marginal trading on the stock market, which was merely the first one to collapse in widespread non-fulfillment.

One of these four we have already pointed out, the enormous extension of lending on urban real estate which had gone on in the preceding years. The lending itself had already slowed down, affecting all the industries directly and indirectly connected with construction. But the mass of loans was itself still undiminished, for they are long-term promises. They could all be completed in full, *only if rents remained high*. But rents would remain high only if economic activity continued in high volume. This distended urban mortgage debt in 1930 stood at about $37,000,000,000. On top of it was a mortgage loan total of about $9,000,000,000 on farms.* This latter was another mass of economic promises which could never be completed in full, unless farm income from crops remained at least as high as it was, and as to some crops, even went higher.

All these long promises based on real estate were particularly dangerous because of the high proportion of them that were held by banks. As we saw in Chapter Eight, the interrelation of these long promises and the banks' short ones contributed in large part to the epidemic of bank failures.

A second large area in which there had been an undue distention of a great mass of deferred exchanges was in lending to corporations and governments, particularly foreign ones. For a number of years prior to this event there had been an incautious and enormous lending to foreigners, such as this country had never before seen. The War made us think—financial tyros that we were—that we could, without preparation, take the traditional place of Great Britain in being long-time bankers to the world. The inordinate lending that took place was carried on under the auspices of our investment bankers, whose judgment was innocently trusted by citizens who thought that they were specialists who could be relied upon. Actually most of them were commercial bankers, who should have stuck to their simple knitting (at which, even so, they were none too skillful) of short-term economic promises, instead of forming, as many of them did, so-called investment-affiliates, and proceeding to meddle in long-term promises, in which, as the event proved, they were sadly injudicious and inexperienced.

* *Long-Term Debts in the U. S.*, Page 6.

442

As a result of their activity, between 1919 and 1930, close to $7,-000,000,000 was lent by Americans to foreign governments and industries. In addition, during this period, these investment bankers peddled and placed throughout the country no less than $58,000,000,-000* of loans to, and stocks of, American corporate enterprises.

Just as in the case of that vast mass of money lent by brokers to marginal owners of stocks, it began to be realized that a great portion of these long promises—more particularly, but not solely, among those that had been made abroad—*could never be fulfilled*. This fear of incompletion played its inevitable role. Those who owned the evidences of these deferred exchanges—the pieces of paper called "bonds"—began even before the stock market panic to try to get rid of them to less suspicious persons. The usual series of events followed. Their exchangeable value was thus undermined. Their prices dropped. Their owners found their resources depleted by so much. Fear of incompletion of their own economic promises made them curtail their activity to the new measure of their resources—in the case of banks, to restrict loans. All these effects, as we have seen, radiate diminution of economic activity.

A third weakness in the then state of affairs was that our banks themselves were in none too safe a condition to complete their economic promises. Their deposits on December 31, 1929, were about $55,000,000,000.† These were all particularly vulnerable economic promises, because completion of them could be called for at any moment. But a great many of the banks had *an undue amount of their resources* tied up in the very long-term economic promises that were most questionable and which we have been identifying: (a) loans on mortgages, both farm and urban, and (b) so-called investments in corporate enterprises (really loans, that were ordinarily easily marketable). The actual incompletion of these long promises, if held in large amounts, would break any bank. On the other hand, *fear of incompletion* of them, which soon spread, would result in lowering their values, so that the bank's available resources would be lessened.

* *U. S. Statistical Abstract, 1936,* Page 292.
† *Ibid.,* Page 241.

In either case, the condition of a very large number of American banks was clearly unsafe. How unsafe it was soon appeared when the banks began to pop. In the five years, prior to and including 1929, 684 banks closed on the average *in each year*. But in the one year of 1930, 1,352 closed their doors; in 1931, 2,294; in 1932, 1,456.* All these closings—with their heavily contributory influence toward the diminution of the total volume of exchanges—were due solely to the fact that the long promises these banks had counted upon for full completion could only in part be completed, or were wholly incompleted. Accordingly, these banks were unable fully to fulfill their own economic promises to their depositors.

A final dangerous weakness, seemingly more remote, but no less potent for being indirect, in its influence on economic activities in this country, lay in the volume of *existing government debt throughout the world*. For, of course, we are but part of a larger economic whole. Our own national debt had, by 1929, been decreased by some $10,500,000,000 from its high point in August, 1919. But the borrowings of our subsidiary government units (it will be remembered, there are about 180,000 of them) had increased from 1913 by the sum of over $15,000,000,000, rising to a total of something over $19,635,000,000 by 1932.† More important than this, the government debt of other nations than our own had increased in volume, while ours was decreasing up to 1932. What the total government debt was for the whole world it would require quite a study to ascertain, and for our present purposes it is unnecessary. For, notoriously these central and most vital of all economic promises—even more so than those of banks—were very much in question as to fulfillment. How justifiable the doubt was became clear when, during the next seven years, every government in the world, including our own, took advantage of the depression to default on a great portion of its obligations, through debasement of its money. "Everybody's doing it," was, in simple essence, their principal justification for this action. "If we do not, we place our citizens at a disadvantage with those of other nations." Take the rationalization for what it may be worth. Its

* *U. S. Statistical Abstract, 1936,* Page 252.
† *Long-Term Debts in the U. S., 1936,* Page 31.

444

validity will be assayed differently, according to which nation one is prejudicially considering, and according to one's economic philosophy. The core of fact, in any case, remains: that *all the economic promises of governments outstanding in 1929* were partially canceled during the next seven years, and a great portion of them wholly canceled—with all the effect toward diminution in the total volume of exchanges, which we examined in our hypothetical illustrations earlier.

The example provided, then, by the last great cycle, substantiates in abundance the observation that has been made: that the beginning of recession in each cycle is at least *associated with—if it does not start from—an enormous extension of economic promises* in one or more large sectors of the economy; an immense mass of promises which are justifiably suspect, so far as fulfillment goes.

What then, in general, is the sequence of events in each cycle? What plausible pattern, if any, can be drawn to describe and explain every cycle?

When we take any one cycle, as we have pointed out, we have only the most fragmentary data of the events themselves, and even of the sequence in which they occur. The events themselves, of course, are multitudinous, and in a proper picture, there is no slightest one that can be ignored as to its effect. No housewife buying one loaf of bread fewer during a week, and thus making a bakery somewhere produce less; no economic enterprise discharging an office boy, in order to lessen expenses and thus enable it more easily to complete its deferred exchanges; no tiny grocery store going into bankruptcy, and thus lessening the available resources of a wholesaler or manufacturer above him; no farmer failing to pay a tiny interest payment, and thus lessening the value of the mortgage a bank or insurance company owns; no insignificant country bank closing its doors, making it necessary for individuals to lessen their purchases and for economic enterprises either to default on their own old promises, or to enter into fewer new ones with employees and suppliers—no seemingly unimportant event of this kind may be ignored.

445

Each one of such mites as these adds to the total of that subtraction from volume, which constitutes the first stage of the business cycle. But all such events, in their inconceivable multiplicity, and in the precise economic effect each one has *somewhere*, are lost forever in unrecorded oblivion. Only the barest few are recorded and show up finally, as a result, in some cold statistic. Nevertheless, with such few facts as are recorded, and with "general knowledge" of what takes place, we are now in a position, with a fair degree of verisimilitude, to outline *the pattern of events* in every cycle, and show how the incompletion, and fear of incompletion, of economic promises are the principal factors in making that pattern what it is.

We see, first, that the society is in a stage where the promises to complete half-exchanges have distended enormously. Either slowly or suddenly the distention ends. This is because of the realization that here, there and everywhere, among this vast mass of promises, many cannot be fully kept. The diminution in the total volume of exchanges begins at this point. Once started, any extensive actual or feared incompletion of exchanges spreads its radiating consequences, *all of them tending to further diminution in every direction!* Individuals are poorer in resources, because of their loss from the incompletion of a promise, and carry on fewer exchanges in the consumers' market. Carriers have less demand made upon them for the movement of goods. Producers have less demand for the fabrication of goods. Those economic promises, which we call employment, wane; and a strongly accentuating influence toward diminution then operates from this quarter. Enterprises in increasing numbers begin to go bankrupt, failing to meet their promises to other enterprises and banks. These other enterprises, with their resources depleted, must in prudence curtail their *new* promises. Prices tend to fall, because of lessened demand. Or if the prices of some commodities do not fall, at least the demand for them diminishes. In either case, the profits, *and therefore the resources,* of every enterprise are diminished. Because of depleted resources from this cause, *every enterprise must curtail its new promises.* Banks likewise, with their resources dimin-

446

ished, must contract their loans, in order to protect themselves on their own promises. This diminishment of "bank money," by billions of dollars, compels all but the richest firms to be less active in enterprise. Because of the actual or feared incompletion of long-term loans—upon land and buildings, and to corporations and governments—the ability of banks to complete their promises becomes suspect. Here, there and everywhere—in a country like our own, where banking is so incautious—banks close. This intensifies the ever-accelerating trend to diminution. And occasionally, in some cycles, the most crucial of all economic promises become suspect as to completion—those of governments—and something approaching paralysis of the body politic occurs. There can be little doubt that the past depression, which has been far the most distressing in the recorded history of business cycles, became so *because the promises of every government in the world were involved.* None was free from question; and all of them, as it turned out, were wholly or partially incompleted.

As to the entire process in these first two stages of the cycle—recession and depression—it seems clear enough what on the whole it consists of. It is a slowing down, in every field of economic activity, *of the making of new economic promises.* This is due to a clear and connected set of reasons.

The originating cause seems to be that old promises, on a wide scale, are either being actually incompleted, or become justifiably doubtful as to completion. The actual and feared incompletion of old promises depletes resources either directly through loss, or indirectly—through drops in prices and the lowered volume of exchanges. *Resources with which to complete promises then decrease.* This means, on one side, that the prudent enterpriser enters into a lower volume of *new* promises, and on the other side that trustors are more careful in entering into new deferred exchanges with those who have lowered resources. Short economic promises—that is, book-credit and bank-credit—contract down to what is completely certain of fulfillment. Long economic promises—loans on real estate, to corporate enterprises and governmental units—are even more invidi-

447

ously affected. For in such times owners of property are more fearful as to the completion of promises in the long-distant future, which they cannot foresee, than in the near future. But whether it is a long promise that is *not made* for fear of final incompletion; or a short one that is *not made* because of insufficiency of resources; or even if it is an immediately completed exchange in the market that is *not undertaken,* because of the necessity of economizing—it is apparent that the trend toward diminution in the volume of exchanges cannot be segregated nor stopped. It must extend. It extends because the warp and woof of our economic relations consist of these promises to complete deferred exchanges; and the completion or incompletion of any one of them inevitably affects all the other promises that are more or less intimately linked to it.

This, then, is the general pattern of the process by which diminution in the total volume of exchanges takes place and continues in the first and second phases of each business cycle—those termed by the economists recession and depression.

Two pertinent questions at once arise. First, what determines *the length of the period* during which these two clearly associated phases last? Second, in what way does the matter of completion or incompletion of promises bring this spiral of lowering volume to an end? What makes the volume begin to increase again—as it unquestionably does, in every business cycle?

The length of the period of the recession and depression is chiefly determined, without question, by the extensiveness to which the mass of promises *that are subject to likely incompletion* has gone in the preceding phase of increase, which is termed prosperity. Perhaps a more quickly understandable way of stating this is: that it depends upon the volume of *justifiably questionable debt* in the society.

What can always be observed as happening is that, when the diminution in volume of exchanges once begins, it keeps on proceeding *until the larger part of the old promises that are in question are settled one way or the other*. Either they are completed, or they are not. Either the debt which is in doubt is canceled, and the loss to the trusting person becomes established as a fact; or it is not.

448

Now, obviously, as the volume of exchanges decreases, this is accompanied by *a growing depletion of resources* of practically all enterprises. Few economic enterprises, in such years, increase their total resources. This is due not only to loss arising from the incompletion of old promises, but also to the fact that actually less tangible wealth is being produced in the society, under the diminished activity. Moreover, the exchangeability of most old forms of wealth is lessened. In short, prices and values drop, *since less exchanging is going on.* The owners of tangible forms of property who are compelled, because it is an excess, to get rid of it, must offer more of it for a given quantity of real money. The pressure is forever to exchange, exchange, exchange! Get rid of what you do not need for what you do! Under this pressure, the natural thing is to offer more of what you own, in order to induce exchanging on the part of others.

But this very drop in prices and values lessens the available resources of the person who owns the property. His smaller available total of resources then throws into question *any old or new promises* he may have to complete. Thus, as the diminution in volume of exchanges proceeds, through both the drop in prices and volume of business, *new areas of economic promises progressively come within the field of doubt.* As these new questionable promises develop, they too must be settled one way or the other—by completion, or by acknowledged incompletion.

The stages of recession and depression in each cycle last *until this necessary answer is given* to the greater part of all the economic promises which are in question. They must be cleared up! Often the word "liquidation" is applied to this process. It means final settlement, throughout the society, of the question of ownership. Trusting must remain at a lower ebb, until this multitudinous detail of doubt is settled one way or the other; until two things become fairly manifest: *who owns what,* and whether the property which individuals and enterprises own *is ample enough* to enable them certainly to complete all the promises they have entered into in the past, and those they may engage to complete in the future.

449

Time elapses, necessarily, for this process of *adjustment in promissory relations,* and in the ownership of property. Eventually, over the greater part of economic activity where it has been in question, this doubt as to the infallible completion of deferred exchanges *is* dispelled. When this point is reached—business men, in general, are seldom aware it has been reached, but only learn of it afterward—we are in the next phase of the business cycle, which is termed revival or recovery. Now, what basic explanation is there of this reversal? Why does not the volume of exchanges continue to go ever lower and lower? Why does the process of diminution change to an increase in volume?

It is because, even under the most widespread and deep-going economic disturbances, men still find that they can trust one another implicitly. It has been obvious, even from this bare sketch, that the actual and feared incompletion of economic promises—which ushers in and then progressively accentuates recession and depression—is due not to dishonesty, but to the failure of the other vital element in every deferred exchange—namely, sufficiency of resources to complete it. It is almost wholly *doubt as to available resources* which makes men question the probable completion of old promises and the possible completion of new ones.

Now, the phases of recession and depression, while they last, represent in a large degree a readjustment in the ownership of property *due to old promises!* This is what the settlement and non-settlement of debt consists of.

Toward the end, then, of these two disturbing phases of the cycle, it has become ever clearer who owns what, and to what extent each person and enterprise can be relied upon, *so far as resources go.* The customary trusting, consequently, can proceed more freely, once this shadow over sufficiency of resources is removed from any quarter. The salient fact for the economics student to observe is *that trusting itself never ends.* Far from it! Even in the depths of the worst depression it goes on in enormous volume. It must go on. It is the very breath of life of modern society. It is simply more meticulously careful during the recession and depression phases of the cycle. This more

450

sensitive watchfulness is directed, with an Argus eye, *at the available resources* of every person and enterprise seeking to enter into a deferred exchange. But real forms of wealth are not wiped out, and new real wealth continues to be produced, even if this happens in lower volume. It is owned. Exchanges of it for other forms of wealth and for services go on still in enormous volume—even in such a cataclysmic drop in activity as we saw in the past cycle, undoubtedly the worst on record. These exchanges continue to be, for the most part, deferred exchanges. They are still explained only by the integrity of the promisor and the sufficiency of his resources.

In other words, the basic trustworthiness of men is like a solid continent, upon which a high tidal wave of doubt can advance, and inundate the populous shores in a sweep of destruction. But when it gets to the high rock, it is stopped, held—and slowly recedes. Once the question of sufficiency of resources is, *on the whole,* cleared up; once the necessary readjustments in the ownership of property have for the most part been made; once—above all—it appears that, as a result of these two developments, the total volume of exchanges has ceased to decrease, and that therefore the drop in prices (which so threatens total resources) has ended, then trusting begins to increase. For a simple reason: *it is again more widely justified.*

And now the very reverse of the previous processes tending to diminution of volume can take place. It does. Economic promises increase here and there, where they were not recently entered into; then they slowly accelerate. This happens because each new deferred exchange, increasing the volume of activity as it does, becomes a center of influence *now tending to increase* the volume of all exchanges. For example, the extension of book credit by an enterpriser to a new customer—or to an old one, who has been worthy of less credit a month before—means an increase of activity, *both of the firm which gives the credit and of the one which receives it.* It can be measured by more employment and more purchases of raw material on the part of the former, and additional goods to sell on the part of the latter, and more employment there.

More employment, in both cases, means more exchanging in the

451

retail market. This, in turn, means more call upon other suppliers for goods. Each responsible producer, meeting his promises infallibly as they come due, now becomes a *radiating center of increasing volume*. Then the increasing volume of exchanges makes both old and new forms of wealth more easily exchangeable. More people now want them, and also people have more wealth to exchange for them. There is no longer need for any necessitous sacrifice of ownership, in order to provide means to complete old promises. With this development, another crucial change occurs, tending now to increase the volume of exchanges.

Since values and prices, instead of tending to fall, tend to remain firm or to rise, and since at the same time the number of exchanges of each enterprise increases, the available resources of individuals and enterprises increase. *This makes deferred exchanges all the safer to enter into!* So the very increase in the volume of exchanges breeds additional increase. Bank loans soon rise, for enterprisers are both more active and the resources of their enterprises are in a better condition to justify loans. This means that bank deposits increase by the amount of bank loans extended. But modern bank deposits, we saw, *are as much money* as government paper money. Their increased use tends further to swell the volume of exchanges on the part of whoever commands them.

Finally, after the recovery is fairly under way, the fear of entering into *the crucial long promises* begins justifiably to be dispelled. Those large-scale corporate enterprises—in which a great deal of old wealth and labor must be sunk before new forms of wealth and satisfaction are obtainable—begin again to be trusted. This, notoriously, includes the construction industry, and others grouped in a large category called "capital goods" industries.

The tempo of exchanging accelerates, as promising increases, practically everywhere. More and more of it goes on. There is more and more employment; and more and more satisfactions, goods, and services are demanded by, and are available to, the population. We have seen that the long-time trend of exchanges has long been upward, at the rate at least of 3¾ per cent a year. All the proportional advance,

452

then, that may have been lost in the preceding two low phases of the cycle, is made up now in the years of revival. We move fast from that phase into the full bloom of prosperity. The volume of exchanges now—of money for labor, money for goods, and money for money—soon goes to a higher peak than ever.

What, now, makes the volume *begin to decrease*, as at the lowest point of the depression it began to increase?

This accelerating volume of exchanges—it will once again be seen —consists almost entirely of an increase in deferred exchanges; that is, of economic promises. If these half-exchanges *could always be completed* by those who promise to do so, it is doubtful that there would ever be a recession. But, invariably, the promising on the one side and the trusting on the other, go to an extreme *in one or more important areas of the economy*, where a large number of individuals and enterprises are involved in close promissory interrelations. It is rarely that this too-extensive trusting takes place in book credit —that is, in the reliance of the productive and distributive enterprises upon one another. More often it is in the field of bank credit. Bankers, for instance, enter into long-term exchanges with land and building owners. In the United States extensive real-estate speculation, financed by bank credit, has been one of the notorious causal phenomena of business cycles. Sometimes it is an unwise extension of long-time lending to corporate enterprises—like railroads. Or it may be too extensive trusting of individuals, who are speculating in the values of corporate enterprises, as in 1929. Or it may be governments which have been trusted, by banks and individuals, far beyond their ability to complete their economic promises. In the various cycles that have occurred since the World War, without any question the inability of certain governments fully to carry out their deferred exchanges, was always a major factor in the recession.

In any case, this too-extensive trusting, in one or more important areas of the economy, seems inevitably to be found in the later portion of that phase of the business cycle we call "prosperity." It is certainly associated with, even if it does not initiate, that change in volume which we call "recession." This change happens because the interrelation of promises, in this one questionable large field, with all other sectors of the economy, *makes it impossible to segregate the damage.* Once any large body of promises is actually incompleted, or it becomes evident that eventually they will be incompleted, other promises are inevitably affected. If this occurs to such a degree that the total volume of exchanges is lowered—*affecting prices and profits and thus available resources everywhere*—like a line of standing cards, economic promise after economic promise becomes involved, and the whole process, which we have reviewed, begins over again.

This, then, broadly sketched, is the pattern of the business cycle, outlined from the point of view of the completion and incompletion of economic promises. It is a pattern, almost certainly, broadly true. That is, it explains, *in great part*, the actualities which constitute business cycles. Nevertheless, our warning must be remembered: that as a picture it is inevitable that over-emphasis is part of the representation; as it would be—in the present state of our fragmentary knowledge—with any description of the business cycle. For the full actuality, if it ever proves possible to envision it, correction in detail would almost certainly be necessary.

That correction any inquiring student will abundantly find in other theories as to the principal factor, influencing events throughout each cycle; and later, in additional information which economic research will in time surely contribute to the material now available for the moving picture that has here been so flickeringly run off.

But for the narrow purpose of our own study, the pattern described here is sufficient enough. That purpose—to repeat—is to set forth, for the unspecializing student of economics, some at least of the principal phenomena about society which are indisputable, so that in any attempt to comprehend the whole he shall be unconfused. And this representation—of the outstanding role that actual and feared incompletion of economic promises plays in the sequence of events of business cycles—is quite indisputable. The commonest experience confirms it, and by reference to all available records it can be traced everywhere in the events.

454

A point to be observed is that this pattern is complete enough not to leave unexplained any of the other principal economic phenomena which have been identified, by different economists, in different phases of each cycle.

It includes an explanation, for instance, of the rise and fall of prices and values; these are due, principally, to changes in the volume of activity, involving (in the case of falling prices) the necessity of sacrifice in order to acquire means to complete old economic promises. It includes an explanation of the enormous changes in the volume of employment that take place, and therefore the development of that apparent vacuum of "purchasing power" in the retail market, by which some theorists account for the recession and depression phases of the cycle. It likewise explains the similar vacuum of "purchasing power" which seems to be evident at certain periods, as between enterprises. It explains the apparent "overproduction" of certain types of goods, at some periods of the cycle, and the apparent "underproduction" of them at another period of it. It explains the changes in the volume of "promised money" issued by banks, which in turn have so crucial an effect on both the volume of exchanging and on the prices of goods. It explains the increase and decrease of profits, since they depend entirely upon changes in volume and in prices. Through the possibility of future profitmaking, it explains the vital changes that take place in the initiation of new enterprises. It provides a rational explanation, also, of the very marked changes that take place in the production of so-called capital goods, as compared with lesser changes in the production of consumption goods. For the production of so-called capital goods is very intimately linked with long promises, and these are much more in question during certain phases of the cycle than short ones. Here too, it would throw some needed light on the variants of the "over-saving" theory, by which the onset of crisis and depression has come recently to be explained in some quarters.

However, it must be observed that while the actual and feared incompletion of economic promises throws a searchlight on all these other phenomena of business cycles, the reverse also is true. Each one

455

of these phenomena, it might be held, has a great deal to do with the completion or incompletion of economic promises—and throws some light on how completion or incompletion comes about.

In short, we must return to the point made: that the account which is finally given of business cycles, the picture which finally emerges, is largely determined by one's emphasis and angle of vision. But it is fair to ask: From what direction, if we look at all the phenomena of business cycles which are at present verifiable, do we understand most clearly what happens in the course of them?

I myself do not doubt that the detail of events throughout each cycle is elucidated, both most fully and most simply, by showing how indissolubly they are related to the completion and incompletion of economic promises. This picture, in other words, is *the most inclusive one* it now seems possible to provide.

It is a particularly advantageous viewpoint for this whole inquiry which we have undertaken into the present nature of human society. For it disentangles still further, in the maze of human relations, that simple loose end of truth with which long ago we started. It imparts *some additional unification* to those phenomena of human society, which can fairly be put in the category of indisputability.

We have seen everywhere how men, in the forms to which our society has evolved, have succeeded in making it as productive as it is, *and in keeping it so,* because of the reliance they can have upon the promises they make to one another. It is this which makes human society run successfully, when it does. In theory, it should fit into that set of facts that the ills society suffers might in great part arise from the fact that the promises are often incompleted. In short, our greatest economic evils might be attributed to a breakdown—now and then, and here and there—in this promise-system. In the foregoing analysis, ignoring this theory and taking a direct view of experience alone, we now see that this seems to be the case. All the facts seem to support this unifying theory.

22

Some Necessary Aspects of an Ideal Society, and

What Must First Be Done To

Bring It About

THIS inquiry we have been engaged upon might be likened to a great running river. Once get launched upon it, and one can be carried on endlessly, with a fresh vista of truth appearing at every turn. We must put into port somewhere. A natural place to anchor is to consider whether there is any practical application of the particular truths about society that seem to have been uncovered.

We are squarely in the area here of politics and social reform. We are at that juncture which long ago in this inquiry we were careful to distinguish: where what we are considering is not the processes by which men live, which is the first office of economic study, but how these processes either could or should be altered.

To venture into this region certainly means straying off that basic Roman road of indisputability which has been so comparatively easy to travel. It would be mad to plunge deeply into such thickets so late in this inquiry, and after all it is not part of the restricted business we originally set for ourselves. But even here, if we follow cautiously, for a short distance—merely where our original loose end of truth seems to lead—we can acquire a pretty good notion of *the general direction* in which human society might both profitably and practicably be changed.

Perhaps a helpful thing would be to compare this particular picture of our world, which in broad outline we have obtained, with one which might be considered an ideal. If we then reverse the usual question and ask, What's wrong with the real picture?—as compared with the ideal set up—we may be helped somewhat in answering the other more practical question, What most needs to be done, *what general courses of action seem most necessary*, in order to make our poor world a better one?

Of course, it is a pretty large order to try to conceive of an ideal human society. But a good many persons have not been feazed by the difficulty; and if any good theoretical purpose is to be served by the attempt, we may not shrink from it.

My own admittedly undetailed notion of what an ideal *economic* world would constitute—I stress the word, economic—would have two principal features: First, it would be one where *all economic promises, especially those of States, would be almost invariably fulfilled.* Second, it would be one where every adult would be able to exchange his labor, whatever form it took, for physical goods and incorporeal satisfactions sufficient to keep him, and those necessarily dependent upon him, in a condition of material well-being which it would be reasonable for him to be ambitious to obtain.

Such a supposititious world would not be equalitarian, so far as possessions go. For it is obvious that men would want *different* satisfactions, and that some would want *more* satisfactions than others; and by supposition—through exchanging sufficient of their labor—would find it reasonably possible to obtain what they desire.

There would be no business cycles—no great alternations in general well-being—in such an ideal economic world, because the invariable fulfillment of economic promises would remove the principal cause of them.

There would be no unemployment in it, save voluntary unemployment. Nor would there be insecurity, for by supposition every adult at any time would be able to exchange his labor for whatever goods he could reasonably demand.

There would at least be no *economic* need for wars, since by supposition a condition of shared abundance would internationally prevail.

There would be no poverty, such as we know it, for again by supposition there would be a superabundance of goods available at prices so low that everyone, by doing whatever work he could, could meet more than the barest needs of food and shelter. Poverty, such as there might be, would only be comparative. The average standard of living, quite obviously, would be very much higher than that of today. It would be comparable—shall we say?—to that of the well-to-do man of the present, who—we may as well recognize—does, indeed, now pretty much live in this happy economic state described.

Here at least is one sketch of an ideal economic world; and for the purpose of acquiring clearer notions about our real world, there are several observations that can safely be made about it.

In the first place, it must be accounted *far less visionary* than it seems. For it can be demonstrated that, *partially*, all the conditions set forth now prevail; and also that in the one respect, where it seems most visionary, it is not at all so. I refer to the *superabundance of goods* of every character at very low prices. This is a recognized potentiality of society, in this present day and moment. Mankind, without any question, has solved the problem of the production of enjoyable goods in sufficient abundance so that all the world—*if we could but learn how to do it*—could exist as comfortably as the more fortunate ones among us do today. This almost incredible consummation of science has never been true before, and it is what makes our age perhaps the most crucial one in all history.

This momentous fact is now one of the commonplaces of modern economic observation. All wideawake economic theory has become impregnated with it—and incidentally has been upset by it. For a maddening state of affairs seems to exist. We see this clear and easily attainable potentiality before us, but something, we know not what, lies in the way of its consummation. There the beckoning potentiality stands. It is no mere will-o'-the-wisp—we know it is not. It is so true and rosy a prospect that all manner of hasty doctrines are advanced—and some tried, no matter at what cost—to reach this seemingly near goal; including the strange notion that men must be fashioned into physical and intellectual robots, if any state of society is to be attained where material abundance is the normal condition, and not scarcity. What this notion amounts to is that mankind must be herded into a state of abundance through sheer force. *We must be made over into some other sort of animal*, to be rendered worthy of this new kind of world. It seems unnecessary, not to say a little unpleasant.

Most of the confusion of doctrine around this point arises, I myself believe, from simple unrecognition of the fact that the problem presented by this new state of affairs, which modern science poses, *is wholly one of exchanges*. Production of goods does not precede, it follows upon exchanging. We saw indisputably, two chapters ago, that exchanges constitute the thermostat which completely governs production.

The central problem, then, is not to see what blocks *production* in the modern world. It is clear enough that it is the inability to exchange that blocks production. The problem to concentrate upon is what blocks exchanging among men!

Here, then, must be the chief consideration of everyone who is at all concerned about the general human welfare. The first thing to be done, in any thoroughgoing and rational reform of our present society, *is to identify—beyond dispute—those factors and those conditions which encourage on one side, and which block on the other, exchanges of property and labor among men.*

This, it seems to me, is the prime problem which our own and coming generations of men will have to solve. It is the principal study they must engage in. In it are comprehended almost all the other problems, fallacious and genuine, which beset men in carrying on their affairs. It is a problem that will only be solved, of course, by the devoted labor of a breed of men, who will have infinite patience in the collection of fact and great imaginative capacity in envisioning it; who, in the humility and integrity which science imposes, will have no other guide but the ascertainment of truth; and who, like ancient saints concerned with sin, will seek to cleanse themselves of every vestige of that self-interest and environmental influence which not

460

only shape opinion, but, quite as subtly, direct inquiry. It will only be solved, in short, by economists who can be true scientists, and not partisans, conscious or unconscious.

That this is indeed the first rational direction for any effort aimed at reform of our society, we need only recall—in the last two chapters—the demonstrated dependence of the welfare of great communities of people—and therefore of human society entire—upon the volume of exchanges which go on. The two are inseparable. They are almost, in a sense, two views from different angles of the same aspect of human affairs. As the volume of exchanges that go on increases, the welfare of men, in the community where this takes place, is bettered. The standard of living, as we expressed it, is leveled upward. As the volume of exchanges that occur lessens, the reverse happens: the welfare of men suffers. There is no shadow of doubt about this. An analysis of comparative poverty, wherever in the modern world it exists, could only result in *an identification of the condition* with the simple fact that few, and sometimes no, exchanges are taking place among those who suffer the poverty. On the other hand, an analysis of comparative wealth would also finally result in an identification of that condition with the fact, that in this happier quarter, exchanges are going forward with extreme activity.

What more simple and more sensible conclusion can follow from this observation than the one we have drawn: that the principal task humankind can set itself—with its economists in the van—is to identify with complete certainty what it is that blocks exchanging among men, and then, as humanely as possible to those who may chance to be affected, remove these great blocks to a more orderly human progress, as they become identified to the satisfaction of all intelligent men.

First, or finally, this needs to be done; for in a society that lives by exchanging *progress can only mean removing the blocks to exchanging.*

But can such research and identification be regarded as part of a program of social reform? In the widest sense, and in the long run, of course it is one. For several things seem fairly clear in connection with it.

In the first place, economic inquiry only haphazardly takes this direction at present. If inquiry inspired by this particular approach were deliberate and organized, there are few scientific "digs"—in my own belief—that could uncover truths more precious to the human race.

In the second place, political policy (which is the mere representation, in action, of the common economic notions then current) takes this direction not even haphazardly. On the contrary, its chief guiding principle, more often than not, is to take a precisely opposite direction. The thoughtless *blocking of exchanges*, in the supposed interest of a predominating group or groups within the population, is still, as it has always been, the immemorial device of amoral and unintelligent rulers to bulwark themselves in their transitory power.

In the third place, such a general program of research would necessarily point to many particular necessities of social change, and unquestionably some very radical ones. For the mere discovery of a set of actions, or of a complex of erroneous ideas, that was blocking exchanges among men—a discovery which all informed and intelligent men might well agree upon as being unquestionable—would be far from being the same thing as its removal. To extirpate it from the path of progress would call, in almost any case one might conceive, for a widespread readjustment of relations among men, and for social engineering and social invention of the most intelligent character.

This whole book has provided a demonstration of what I myself believe constitutes the principal block to exchanging among men—*the actual incompletion and feared incompletion of economic promises.* It need hardly be observed that this is far from being the only way the total volume of exchanges among men becomes blocked and lessened. No economist worth his salt could fail to find many groups of associated phenomena that definitely have that effect.

Because of the light that may be thrown on this entire matter of social change, it may be advisable to consider two comparatively simple cases of blocking—one having to do with government, the other

462

with industry—and observe something about the nature of the difficulties that immediately arise.

For example, it is perfectly apparent that the restrictions which modern governments place upon international commerce—upon swapping over boundaries, which often must be marked artifically to make men even aware of them—represent a blocking of exchanges. A tariff, the simplest measure of this sort, is deliberate blocking; and a practice, of course, hoary with age. Let us not go into the involved reasons which are always advanced for this willful interference with what might be considered the normal processes of worldwide economic evolution. They always consist of rationalities, with *the supposed good* of the persons chiefly affected as the animating principle; and, of course, the large majority of those affected are persuaded by the rationalization, or else, it is safe to infer, the acquiescence of hundreds of millions of persons in this sort of procedure would not be as universal as it is. But, of course, the reasons advanced, and unintelligent acquiescence in them by those affected, do not make the procedure other than what it is: a diminution in the total volume of exchanges. The very purpose of every tariff is *to block exchanges with the foreigner*—by raising his prices. The domestic producer then raises his own prices to that level. But raising prices is almost another term *for diminishing the number of exchanges that can take place.* It would be a strange thing if a full and completely disinterested analysis ever showed this result to be to the best good, even of the particular group supposed to be benefited, when the lessening of exchanges is so damaging to human welfare under every other circumstance. It may, of course, be to *the temporary good* of a few people, in that it saves them, usually, from some immediate disagreeable readjustment in their activities.

Let us set forth the second example, before examining this first one for what lessons there may be in it. We saw, in Chapter Twelve, how great a proportion of the economic activities of men—particularly in production—are now carried on by those informal little republics called corporations. There is one outstanding feature of these entities that we did not remark upon, when we examined their deferred

463

exchanges, simply because there was then no occasion to do so. When they become an important part of their industry *they tend to become monopolies*.

By this, economists mean that they have a degree of control over the goods they produce or distribute, so that irrespective of the need or the circumstances of the consumers of the product, they can demand what they please in exchange for it—up to that bearable point on the part of the consumers, where otherwise they will be forced to do without the product. In other words, corporations—particularly large ones—are often such self-sufficing economic entities that, far more than individual enterprisers, they can keep their prices at a high level. Now, this growing *rigidity of prices* is a phenomenon that has been remarked upon, by many thoughtful economists, as one of the most significant features of modern society. It seems clearly to be associated with—if it is not an outcome of—the increasing role that corporate enterprise has come to play in modern economic life.

But what does *rigidity of price* really mean, when it is analyzed? It means, primarily, that if the owner of the product cannot get what he wants in exchange for it, *he refuses to enter into exchanges at all*. Corporations frequently are rich enough to reduce their total volume of exchanges by an enormous proportion, without going out of existence—without suffering, in other words, as an individual would. What really happens is that a great proportion of the individuals connected with the corporation, through employment, do the suffering, but not the corporation itself. In other words, the corporation is ordinarily in a less precarious economic position than the individual enterpriser is.

Now, of course, this pointbank refusal to exchange, on the part of the owner of goods or of money, is his privilege, in the kind of world we live in. What reasoning animates him in such a position is not so clear as it is sometimes assumed to be. I myself am convinced it is not merely an inordinate greed for all the profit the traffic can bear. The position arises in most cases, I believe, from a singular inability on the part of enterprisers to recognize that large profits arise far more often *from the volume of exchanges entered into* than from

464

high prices. But business men, on the whole, much prefer to depend for their profits upon high prices and a low volume of exchanges. It seems safer. Lowering a price ordinarily is almost the last action an enterpriser contemplates and he does so always with deep misgiving, under compulsion. All his effort is to keep his prices up. He seldom voluntarily lowers them; he seldom tries to increase his profits by making possible, through lowered prices, a larger volume of exchanges. As an economic theory, he may agree blandly that lowering prices might indeed greatly increase his exchanges, and therefore his profits. But it is only the most daring and adventurous of enterprisers who follow this procedure as a business policy. The great mass of enterprisers unquestionably take the opposite view. Whether or not this is the explanation—a growing, an unnecessary and a dangerous rigidity of prices is certainly an outstanding characteristic of our modern economic life.

What is its result? If a producer or distributor will not sell, except at his own price—even though he could make the price lower in each exchange, and garner more profit by having more exchanges—*is he not, by the action, lessening the volume of exchanges that takes place?* There can be no possible doubt of it. For obviously the consumers of his product would do more exchanging with him—would be able to do more exchanging—if he lowered the price for his product.

This firm fixation of prices by large corporate enterprises—for they chiefly are the culprits in this respect—is certainly one of the large and hidden blocks that occur, affecting the total volume of society's exchanges.

Here, then, are two fair samples of the ways in which the total volume of exchanges among men gets blocked, and enormously diminished. There is not much need, I imagine, for any organized new research to establish beyond dispute that these *are* blocks. It is almost certain that present opinion among economists would be strongly preponderant that both these examples represent undesirable and injurious social situations. The best that might be advanced

465

for them would be of an apologetic character: that they seem necessary, almost inevitable, in the kind of world we live in. But this is no logical position to assume, when the very thing we are considering is *how* the present forms of society may be fashioned into something better for everybody. What, manifestly, is bad about these two particular complexes of affairs is—like every other blocking of exchanges —that they are injurious to the welfare *of the entire society*. They stand, monolithic human institutions, in the way to improvement in that welfare.

But how are they to be removed?

I have chosen these two cases as illustrations because they so clearly pose an outstanding difficulty to anyone who wants to theorize, other than irresponsibly, about social change. These two clearly injurious human institutions—the blocking of commerce over boundary lines by governments, and the rigidity of prices that arises from unwise policies of corporations which tend to be monopolistic—can neither of them be changed, so it almost appears, by anything short of a revolution in men's affairs.

This would also be true of a good many other examples of blocking of exchanges that might be cited.

Now, revolution—as a method of social change—is not something the economics student need shrink from speculating about. On the contrary. The trouble is that the activities that are ordinarily meant, by those who think they are advocates of revolution, are far from representing a reform of social processes directed by intelligence. What goes by the name of "revolution" is more often an explosive reaction against abuse, which finally has become unbearable, than a cool and clear-eyed effort at social change. Revolutions have been occurring among men since the days of Greece—*vide* Thucydides, for one of the most illuminating and incisive accounts of them ever penned.* The sane economist does not fear revolution in itself. He would not shrink from it, if he ever thought it much more than futile

* I refer to his account of the manner in which the Corcyrean revolution spread throughout the cities of Greece. The parallels to occurrences within the past two decades are of the most striking character. See Pages 189 to 191, *The Complete Writings of Thucydides*, Modern Library edition.

466

and superficial, in its final effects. His attitude is rather one of distrust than fear—and with good reason. No student of all the so-called revolutions that have occurred among men—I mean by revolution, forcible social change taking place over a comparatively short period—can ever find, when he is unimpassioned, any vital difference in the conduct of men's affairs *after such revolutions* from what it had been before. After all the boiling up has simmered down, he finds that *economic unintelligence continues to govern the affairs of men*—and in much the same way. It is simply directed, after revolutions, to trying to benefit *other people* than before. The sanest economists, in a sense, are far more radical than the so-called revolutionaries. The changes they would like to see, and hope to bring to pass, are changes that would be so certainly effectual in improving the condition of the entire society that they would indeed become lasting, since they would be basic.

But here we are, with our two examples. How are we going to bring about deliberate change in situations like these without compulsion or violence? Governments, for instance, do not impose restrictions upon beneficial exchanges out of sheer wilfulness to cause trouble. The governments merely always represent—they are, indeed, *nothing but*—predominating groups within the population. It is the *supposed advantage of these special groups* that is the animating principle of the action. Can it be conceived that such groups in every nation—unless their predominance be overthrown, or unless they become convinced that the action is not really to their ultimate advantage—will relinquish the position of advantage they think they have obtained?

Considering our first example—the blocking of international trade —to anyone with a grain of realism in him, nothing seems more illusory than international free trade, or anything but the slowest approach to it in our present world. The readjustments it would make necessary, in the occupations and the way of life, of tens of millions of people, are inconceivably vast, and the resistances set up to these readjustments would everywhere be of the stubbornest character.

This is equally true of our second example. How can the dangerous *rigidity of price,* which so clearly prevents an abundance of goods from flowing where it otherwise would—how precisely can it be altered? Must the stronger power of the State be utilized to control and set prices? And what guarantee can there be—what even is the most remote possibility—that prices would then be made less rigid, that they would tend to drop freely rather than to remain the same, or to rise?

To any person with the least knowledge of history, or with the least clarity of observation as to what is going on under his nose—no matter where in the world he lives—what prospect can there be of responsible, let alone intelligent handling, on the part of governments, of so vital a thing as the prices of goods and services?

For let us be aware of what we are saying. When we speak of governments controlling prices, we mean nothing else than *that they completely control the necessary exchanges of all their citizens,* and therefore the standard of living and the nature of the activity of everyone within the population. This is the essential change that has happened in our day in Russia. There is a clear trend in that direction, also, in the other present authoritarian States. But is this a new thing in the world? Fiddlesticks! Read the Code of Hammurabi and see how 4,000 years ago, a well-meaning individual despot—instead of a well-meaning group—completely controlled the economic activities of the people, *through setting the prices at which they had to exchange their goods and labor.* In our own day, in every case so far, what the informed economist would expect has occurred. The rigidity of the price system is intensified, not broken. Prices have risen, not fallen.* The flow of exchanges is not more freed, *it is more blocked!* Rulership has now changed only its coat, not its nature.

* This would not be disputed as to Germany and Italy, where fairly accurate factual data as to price changes are available. It might be disputed by some as to Russia, because of the conflicting accounts of journalists, none too experienced in the analysis of price changes, and because of the really revolutionary change from government price-fixing and consumer-rationing to a comparatively free market in the past three years. Thus the certain price increases might be laid merely to an ideological change. Ideological or not, the final fact of price-rises remains. A reliable notion as to changes in the internal purchasing power of the ruble between 1913 and 1935, over goods in the retail market, will be found in the Appendix to Mr. Hubbard's book, *Soviet Money and Finance.*

Aside from the tyranny involved—for, of course, such a close control over all the aspects of common life could not exist except with a terrified, subdued, or completely ignorant population, which has no glimmer of understanding of how its life is hiddenly controlled through prices—it may be advisable for freer peoples to wait, for perhaps fifty years, to see what the economic outcome of such experiments really is. They must wait to see whether there is more of an increase in the volume of exchanges than occurs where the government is not so completely involved in the economic system. They must wait to see, in short, whether government can succeed in changing—not human nature—*but its own nature*, and become any more reliable and intelligent in economic matters than rulers have ever been in all history. The informed historian and economist may certainly be pardoned for remaining—at the moment—a little skeptical about this.

But is the citizen who tries to be intelligent about social change to be thus completely deadlocked? Is there nothing that seems both rational and practicable to be done about such matters? Must we allow what we call "evolution"—a mere chance and anarchic struggle between special interests—finally perhaps to shape our world into something better? Is this the only way to get rid of such clear injuries to the whole society, as the two we have just identified—examples of many others!

To adopt such a view is a defeatist refusal to accept the inherent challenge in the situation, a defeatism that will appeal to nobody, except those who are old and tired mentally. It is a counsel of despair that runs against the deepest human instinct. Rather revolution, which, with its alarums and excitements and undoubted sufferings, at least holds some possibilities of human benefit. Rather this than a sour and chapfallen do-nothingism. This instinctive reaction—that *something* must be tried to change a world where abundance for all seems so near—must indeed be an element, if it is not the yeast, in the revolutionary spirit that is so marked a characteristic among young people of our age. "We must do something! We *will* do something," the young cry. "What can we do?"

469

Well, to be unemotional about it, the challenge really is to social invention in all such examples as we have considered—where the injury sustained by society is clear-cut, but where resistance to any change would be of the stubbornest kind. Pending some future social inventors, some statesmen of more character, ingenuity and intelligence than the sorry figures we ourselves have seen in our lifetimes, at least one general direction of fruitful effort can be observed. It is a long and difficult, but a not irrational program, and not impractical.

The nature of the effort is suggested by a little closer examination of what really prevails in such situations. It is always a case of *group-interests predominating over the interests of the larger society*. Inside each nation, easily identifiable groups are able to subordinate the certain advantages of the entire population to their own supposed advantage. Then, in the international sphere, each people—a small part of the entire world society—in the same way subordinates the interest of the entire race to its own.

But how can this predominance of groups, large and small—and how can this successful subordination, by each nation, of the larger society of which it is a part—take place and continue, when it is to the disadvantage of the larger society? To be more specific—as an example, how can a tariff on bread ever be acquiesced in, as it has been, by those who have to pay the extra price of it? The answer is obvious. Those most concerned do not know what is happening! They are totally unaware of the injury being done them, *or of the greater benefit to be obtained by a different course of action*.

Pure economic error and ignorance can be the only ultimate explanation—both on the part of populations and their governors—for a state of affairs where their welfare is undermined *by a lessening of exchanges*, which they not only acquiesce in, but often originate.

We arrive, then, *by conclusion*, at the same practical and necessary course of action that was outlined in the very first pages of this study. It is an unexciting program, but one that can, in the end, be deadly in its effectuality. What men can do is to strive—with at least as much effort as they put into other educational enterprise—to raise the standard of economic literacy among men; to teach every man

470

and woman, so that they cannot mistake it, *nor be misled by politicians*, how their acts contribute to or injure one another's welfare.

Of course, we must observe here, as we did in our Introduction, that no realistic person can have any illusion as to the difficulties to be met in such a program of universal economic education. But to have a population thoroughly enlightened on economic matters, as it is enlightened in other respects, is a sure way—even if it is a long way—to remove the greatest blocks from human progress. For the truth clearly is *that the blocks are ultimately explainable, more than anything else, by economic ignorance and error*, both on the part of rulers and ruled.

Nor may this prove to be so long and hopeless a process as we may anticipate. For example, it seems utterly mad at this moment to imagine that nations will ever agree to abandon restrictions upon any foreign commerce which they consider deleterious to groups within their own borders. There is no national prerogative more widely practiced, nor more firmly rooted in tradition, than the imposition of a tariff on imports. Yet not much more than a hundred years ago there was another economic doctrine, just as firmly rooted as this. It was the governing consideration in all international commerce: namely, that it was injurious for nations to allow gold to be exported. All industry and commerce had to adjust itself, and for several centuries was largely influenced, by this particular erroneous notion. It is dead as alchemy now. Perhaps, at not so distant an age, tariffs and other restrictions on international commerce may go the same way. Almost surely they will, if a quietus is finally put upon another absurd economic notion that has an enormous influence upon events: that there can ever again, with our society evolved to the forms it now has, be any economic gain in war that cannot be obtained, more certainly and at far less cost, by peace.

At least, then, we can observe two general courses of practicable action to take—to make our world a better one. One follows upon the other, if we reflect upon it. It is clear enough that no more beneficial thing could be done than to identify—exhaustively, carefully

471

and certainly—every complex of human relations and ideas that blocks exchanging of goods and labor among men. But when this can be revealed to the satisfaction of every rational person, what is to be done about it? The most useful thing to be done about it is to see that at least a working majority of the citizens born into the world comprehend this full truth, or at least the better part of it.

One may be charged with undue optimism in conceiving that this can ever come to pass—with the sort of abysmal economic ignorance that at present prevails among men. But not with reasoning that, should it come to pass, our most puzzling economic problems would then be more swiftly on the way to solution than by any other course.

Economic ideas completely govern all our actions now—we should be thoroughly aware of that! They determine almost every action we take, and certainly the material conditions under which we live. The trouble, clearly enough, is that these present governing economic ideas are mostly erroneous ideas! They prevail, only because the great masses of men are so uninformed about their society that they cannot recognize the error. If they did recognize it, would they stand for it? Would they ever allow the advantage of all to be subordinated to the advantage of a few? It seems mere common sense that, just as the most honest economic research is indispensable, so that men may not be *misguided* in any effort they may make to change their world, so the most widespread economic education is indispensable, in order that stupid obstructions may not successfully be raised to social action, which the discovery of any truth may clearly call for.

To the reflective person, this must finally appeal as not merely the swiftest—it would be slow enough!—but as perhaps the *only* practicable way to alter the most basic abuses in our society.

For the supreme economic power in our society is that of the State. How is the State to be changed *in its nature*, how is the rulership of great masses of people to be made both reliable and intelligent, except through those who are ruled. Let us make no mistake about the modern State. We are too much inclined here to drop into

472

our besetting vice of being blinded by mere words. We conceive too often of the State as being a separate supreme entity of some sort, antagonistic to us as individuals. But we—all of us together—are the State. Its preponderant ideas are *our* ideas. Its manifest economic stupidity is ours. Its tyranny, where that exists, is ours. What we all suffer from governments, we suffer from ourselves.

One of the certainly indisputable revelations of this study has been the utter unreliability of the State in the performance of economic promises. Yet, as we have also seen, our entire economic system—with its inconceivably intricate interrelations of promises—rests finally upon these clay promises of States. Now, if anyone thinks that in a future society, ideal or not, *economic promises will play any lesser role than they do now*, he is reasoning about some illusory fairyland. It is impossible to conceive a condition of society where the promises of men, and utter reliance upon them, *does not remain as basic as it now is*. But compare the ideal world we set up in our imagination—where all economic promises are fulfilled, *including those of States*—with the present real world. No need to point out, certainly after all our analysis, what is wrong with the real picture in this respect! How, in heaven's name, is this ingrained unreliability of States—so deeply disturbing a factor in our present economic system—to be transformed into the reverse—invariable reliability? It is something that seems hopeless to contemplate. *But if it is vain, then a perfect economic system is vain;* "capitalist" and "communist" alike may as well begin their speculations from that point!

But at least one thing is certain: that if this degraded status of State-morality is ever to be raised, again the only route by which this is possible is that of economic education of all the people. They, in the final analysis, are the State. Their actions as individuals have become almost unexceptionable. Their actions, as groups, can only become so, when as individuals they are far more aware of responsibility for their group-actions than they now are.

We can go further in this direction of analysis, and by direct reference to some of the detailed revelations of this study can see that the practical course suggested here, of universal economic education,

473

might not be so hopeless as it may at first seem, even in changing the ingrained unreliability of States.

How do States come, it is a pertinent question to ask, to break their economic promises? They certainly do so ruthlessly when they have to, but even so—it can be observed—there is always some hesitation in the action, because the current managers who are responsible always well understand that widespread readjustment in ownership of property will result and that this may endanger the power they hold. Why, then, do States break their promises? For the same reason that any enterprisers must leave an economic promise unfulfilled—because they simply do not have, and cannot acquire, *available resources to fulfill their promises*. This simply means, of course, that their promises have been far too great in volume to be fulfilled. But then we saw, in Chapter Thirteen, that this only happens because citizens—in whose name the promises are made, and who must ultimately fulfill them—are completely unaware of the nature of what is going on. Well! Here we are right back again to that condition of general economic illiteracy that prevails in the population. There it is—in the background of this problem, as of all others.

It does not seem too wildly illusory, that a preponderant part of the population in every State should be thoroughly informed at all times of the volume of economic promises being made in their name; that they should recognize that they or their children will have to fulfill the promises; that if they are unfulfilled, the greatest social disorder, distress and readjustment will result; and that therefore the current managers of the State should be checkreined at all times in this matter of making economic promises. All this amounts to saying is: that the financial management of States might well be kept *as cautious and reasonable as that of any well-conducted economic enterprise*. It would almost certainly be so conducted, if the majority in the population were fully aware of the inevitable consequences to themselves, when it is otherwise conducted.

It would seem, from this, that if economic enlightenment were more general, there would be less need to try for the apparently hopeless end of changing the ethics of States. Almost as good an economic purpose could be served if general enlightenment in such matters reached a point where States *would never be allowed by their citizens* to make a volume of promises that was finally unfulfillable.

In short, this particular problem would be almost as well solved, if it never became *necessary* for States to be as dishonest as it is in their nature to be!

The problem is almost the same—and the nature of the remedy that indicates itself is not greatly different—with other types of economic promises than those of States. The latter are key promises, certainly, but they are far from being the only type of economic promises that are unfulfilled, and certainly not the only type where fear of unfulfillment does its damage.

Our ideal world—to repeat once more—would be one where practically all economic promises would be fulfilled. Were such a state ever attainable, there seems hardly any doubt, from our analysis, that a quietus would then be put upon the most disturbing problem that at present afflicts human society—the business cycle. But as we review, in recollection, all that we have examined about deferred exchanges, why do economic promises of individuals turn out to be unfulfilled, when this occurs?

We saw abundantly—time and again—the two reliances upon which fulfillment depended: honesty on one side, and sufficiency of resources on the other. So far as honesty is concerned—aside from States—there was only one general area of economic activity where it was anything but almost infallibly reliable: that was in the field of corporate enterprise, and only to a partial extent there. Everywhere else, where unfulfillment of an economic promise occurs, it is almost invariably due to *insufficiency of resources* at the moment the deferred exchange had to be completed.

This is saying, it seems clear, that where individuals most go wrong, in this respect, is in estimating what the future may be. Every economic promise, obviously, deals with the future. Let us come back —in order to understand our real world more sharply—to the consideration of our ideal world. If all economic promises, in this ideal world, are to be fulfilled, it would mean that men would never *over-*

475

estimate what their available resources would be at any given future moment? Is this so unattainable a consummation in the real world? The truth of the matter is *that a very large portion* of all present economic enterprises are currently as well managed as this! They meet all promises unfailingly, and they can only do so, manifestly, by keeping the volume of their promises prudently within both their present and their future likely resources.

But we saw that the onset of the recession period in every business cycle is certainly associated with—if it is not principally caused by—a great magnification of promises in one or more important economic areas, to the point where they are very unlikely to be fulfillable when the deadline-day of performance comes. The promisors have made utterly erroneous calculations about their available resources at a future given moment. The damage from unfulfillment spreads, and is difficult to be confined, because of the interrelation of all promises.

What general course of remedy is suggested by this set of facts other than *education in economic enterprise?* Men cannot be forced, nor legislated, into caution and intelligent calculation, any more than into honesty. At the same time, the intelligent conduct of economic enterprise is not an art that descends upon one like a fairy blessing at birth. There are no esoteric mysteries about the conduct of business; it can be grasped by the most ordinary intelligence. Yet it must be learned by apprenticeship and experience; and it would be a fatal oversight not to observe that simple economic ignorance operates here, in each tiny field, and very potently when the effects of the ignorance *are all totaled together,* just as much as it does in respect to more widespread economic promises. For example, remember the trouble that almost every little banker in the United States caused, from 1914 onward, by relying upon long promises to meet short ones.

Where it is not resources, but honesty itself that fails, what general course of remedy is suggested? We saw that, aside from States, the only economic field where dishonesty is at all a modern problem is, to some extent, in the realm of corporate enterprise. We saw, too, in Chapter Twelve, the probable explanation of the more frequent dishonesty in this area. It is because those who are faithless here are in a position to keep their actions hidden, and do not suffer either social or economic injury from their scoundrelism. A few of these high-placed bandits in jail, and the disbarring of a few of the shrewd lawyers who guide them in their plundering, would clear up this economic swamp in short order. Both of these events would be perfectly possible under honest and impartial administration of the present law we have. It is an undoubted fact that these social criminals could be identified, and their practices wiped out, with not much more difficulty than the far lesser fry of plunderers whom the officers of the law, in this country, now concentrate upon. The truth seems to be that, whenever these high-placed robbers do happen to be brought to judgment, they come before soft-hearted men of their own ilk. The open and ruthless disclosure of their manifestations of faithlessness, in simple terms so that all the world could understand it, if it did not send them to jail, would at least send them into social coventry; so that henceforth, instead of continuing to be respected, they would become the scorned social pariahs they ought to be.

This is the only remedy for faithlessness in these high places, just as where dishonesty is less devious. That it works is shown clearly in Great Britain, where corporate practice is just as complex as in the United States, but where entirely different corporate standards of ethics prevail. Justice there does not allow corporation lawyers to render it blind. It is at least as open-eyed as the big thieves; and any discoverable faithlessness in these high quarters means jail almost as certainly as the sorriest pilfering does. As a result, there is no greater proportion of dishonesty manifested in corporate enterprise in Great Britain than in other areas of economic activity among that people. The phenomenon is most noticeable, among the great nations, in the United States, and it seems to be a reflection, more than anything else, of the low standards of justice dispensed in our country. It would almost be the most easily reformed of our undesirable economic situations. For it can be changed whenever our guardians of the sacred law merely remember their oaths and become honest-

477

minded enough to deal with these malefactors as they are now able to. Some of them, on the contrary, so forget their oaths—for all lawyers, of course, are officers of the courts—that they advise the big thieves *as to how to evade the law*. It is hard to see what difference there is between the millionaire corporation lawyers, who counsel their clients as to how deviously and safely to plunder in High Finance, and the shysters who are hired by gangsters to keep them out of jail. Except that the shysters seem a little less loathsome, in that they put up no hypocritical front.

We have been trying to see what practical action society *as a whole* can take to make itself operate more beneficially, to the advantage of all its members. If we consider this question from the point of view of the individual, it takes on more of an ethical color. The young person, particularly—eager to play his part in this difficult but adventurous new world—tends more to exclaim, "What can I myself do about this whole great affair? That is what I want to know. Not what society as a whole finds it must do."

There is one aspect about the position of the individual that it is almost too easy to overlook. We are all of us inclined, in our humility, to think that any part in this great human adventure, of refashioning our world, must be beyond our aspiration. We may be spectators cheering on those few, who with all their might are playing the game, helping them as we can with our moral support. But not for us is there to be the honor of mixing actively in this high struggle.

Well, there is a solemn fact that every citizen, no matter how humble he is, nor how ignorant he may count himself, may be inspired to contemplate. It has been the whole theme of this study that it is the reliability of men which accounts, above all things, for the very form our present society has taken, for the smooth processes by which it continues to go forward, and for whatever good we can identify in our civilization. Nothing could be more unseeing than to apprehend this notion sketchily, as a mere cold abstraction. As we pointed out in the first sentence of this inquiry, when we study economics, we are really studying the actions of about two billion hu-

478

man beings, and we must think of them, difficult as it may be, not *en masse*, but as two billion individuals.

It is *you*, in short, who manifest this reliability that makes our world go 'round. The record we have shown, of practical infallibility in the performance of promises, is *your* record—with that of millions of unassuming people like you. This integrity is second nature to you now. You are not even aware of it. But there the clear fact stands! Take your due for it, and be proud.

In short, every time you make a tiny economic promise, and eventually fulfill it, you can have some satisfaction in the fact that you are actively—not passively—assisting in making our economic system *work successfully*. When you make promises you cannot fulfill, by this tiny bit you slow down these intricate wheels of human progress.

In short, no man in the modern world, however lowly, can *escape participation* in this adventure of making the society work successfully. Your actions, whether for good or ill, weigh as much as the next man's in the final count. You can be happily aware that in this one respect, of continuously demonstrating your dependability, you are playing your part every day in this great social drama being run off in Time, and playing it well—as the records set forth in this book conclusively show.

But the study shows clearly enough, also, in what respect you are probably playing your role execrably in this drama.

While it may be true you are making the world run as well as it does by being honest, you are just as certainly keeping it from running as well as it can, by your complacent ignorance.

If, as an individual, you care to identify what you can do to make the world run better, almost everything we have disclosed in this study points the way sharply enough. Your shortcomings, unless you are an exceptional individual, *stand out as the principal factors in its failure*, just as your dependability appears to be the chief factor in its success.

No need to be specific about these shortcomings; they can be summed up in one statement: like a little lizard motionless in the sun, you are content to rest in a state of almost complete unaware-

479

ness of the actualities of the larger world you live in. You let habit blind you as to what goes on. You have hardly a glimmer of the certain truth that your own economic benefit may best be served in every way by considering the economic benefit of everybody. Because of this lack, you think only—and work only all your life—for what appears to be your own trivial little economic benefit. By this thoroughgoing economic unintelligence, you intensify all the ancient elements of anarchy in our society. You are too often inclined to blame your rulers for this. Blame yourself! Your rulers in these days are truly your servants, no longer your masters. They become your masters only by gulling you—false servants that so often they are! But if you can be gulled, who is most to blame—you or they?

If, as an individual, you really have some concern about the best way to change our present world to a better one, not a bad principle to follow is to identify the enemy. It should not be true, but unfortunately it is, that your immediate enemies remain, *as they have always been*, your rulers—your government. At all times, it is a wise thing to suspect both their intellectual honesty and their intelligence in economic matters. Nothing can be lost, everything can be gained, by doing so. Make them prove themselves in these respects —and be utterly ruthless in your judgment! When they seem most plausible, in *your* particular interests, it is not a bad course to *suspect their economic intelligence the most*. They are, in these days, the managers of a highly complex world. You have placed them in this management, and you acquiesce in it. But, unfortunately, they give not the slightest indication of being any more capable in handling the affairs of masses of men than rulers have been through all history.

But how can you judge them, as their every act and word should be judged, without fair standards? You must know how the society operates, as well and better than they do, to judge them properly.

Here then is a simple general formula of action which, if it may not be the best one, is good enough for anybody to follow, in whatever station of life he may be. You must make an untiring effort to understand the economics of this world in which you live, and neither be content nor discouraged until, in honesty, you can feel that your

480

comprehension is not too unclear. This mere effort at fuller understanding, carried on by all intelligent citizens, and guided by the
unsparing intellectual honesty of the scientific spirit, would soon
enough have its beneficial consequences.

For we can end this whole study with the observation of a simple
truth: it is not error as such, but principally complacence in error,
which has forever bedeviled the common life of men, and always
will, while we allow it to prevail.

INDEX

A

Activity, human, ix ff., xvii, 14
Agricultural land, value, 99
Agricultural products, effect of World War upon prices of, 99; used as money, 264
American Bank Failures, C. D. Bremer, 134 n
American Telephone and Telegraph Company, 198
Amsterdam, bank, 324, 325
Angell, Sir Norman, 329; quoted, 332
Animals, used as money, 261 ff.; products, 263
Antonio and Shylock, 203
Armies, economic, 198, 200
As Goes Michigan, A. Pound, 131 n
Assets and liabilities, ratio, 126 n
Associations, ancient and mediaeval, 201
Assuan, trading in, 46
Austria, debt, 250
Automobile factory, effect of incompleted promises upon, 427
Automobiles, lower-priced, x ff.; sold on instalments, 65

B

Babylon, 139
Bacon, Nicholas, 182
Baldridge, Cyrus Leroy, 94 n
Bank account, 148
Bank checks, 147 ff., 327
Bank credit, 151 ff., 331, 431 ff.; lent to borrowers, 151, 404; allied to government credit, 153, 336; central

bankers, control of, 180 n; lent for stock market trading, 439, 440
Bank Credit, C. A. Phillips, 137, 146 n
Bank deposits, 282, 336, 413, 443; short-term promises, 124, 128, 166; increased by amount of loan, 145 ff., 154, 169; subject to check, 149; sources, 150; created by banks own action, 150, 153; as deferred exchanges, 152; decrease in, 154, 155, 157; time-deposits, 190
Bank failures, 35, 120 ff., 130, 134, 431 ff., 444
Bank holiday, 121, 131
Bank-money, 324
Bank notes, history, 328 ff.
Bank of England, 327
Bank of United States, 130
Bankers, 122, 134, 135, 172, 214 ff., 442
Banking Act, 216
Banking laws, 135; and customs, 143
Bankruptcy, laws, 244, 384; far-reaching effects, 427
Bar money, 266, 306
Barter, 259
Banks and banking, rural banks closed, 101, 130; mortgage holders, 108, 111; focal point of interdependent promises, 115 ff.; panic run, 120, 130; American and European, 122; ratio of assets to liabilities, 126 n; investments, 128 ff., 245; Canadian, 130; bond sales, 133, 215 ff.; weakness, 134; promises used as money, 138 ff., 147; origin in Europe, 139; mediaeval, 139; free of Federal Reserve control, 163; ignorance about central banks, 164; as defense for in-

483

Commercial crisis, 435

Commercial loan, 123 ff.

Commercial structures, mortgages on, 103

Commodities, exchange of, 259; used as money, 261 ff.

Common ownership of wealth, 364, 367

Completed exchange, 5 ff., 43, 384

Compulsion, 69 ff., 240, 241, 244; social, 70; economic, 71; by the State, 71, 89, 384; fear of, 82 ff.

Confidence a factor in exchange, 6 ff.

Congress, monetary acts, 101 n

Constitutional Convention, influence of land-speculators, 105

Constitution industry, 112 ff., 436

Consumer, promises, 55 ff.; credit, 424

Consumers' goods, 37 ff., 43

Continental notes, 290 n, 332

Contract, Roscoe Pound, 71

Control, revulsion against, 90; of corporate enterprise, 219

Copper money, 273, 292

Corporation bonds, 229

Corporation lawyers, 220 n, 223, 478

Corporations, as employers, 16; promises to banks, 128, 132; defined, 196, 208; nature and activities, 197 ff.; in U. S.: business enterprises, 200; history, 201 ff.; mortgages, 209 ff., 219; capital stock, 210, 218, 221; honesty and ability, 212; ownership by, 217; control of, 219; dishonesty, 219, 476; controllers and owners, 220; wealth, 383; financial statistics, 412 f.; incompletion of exchanges, and business cycle, 425 ff.; loans to, 442; monopolistic tendencies, 463; price rigidity, 464

Counterfeiting, 310

Cover, John G., 36

Credit, 6 ff., 10, 55; book credit, 59, 423, 427; *see also* Bank credit

Criminals, social, 477

Crises, economic, 407, 408, 435

Croesus, 307, 377

Currency manipulation, 251, 272, 350 n, 354; *see also* Money

D

Debased money, 289, 309 ff.

Debt, and credit, 6 ff.; losses from bad, 34; slavery, 92 ff.; imprisonment, 94 n; sabbatical cancellation, 97; liability for, 206 ff; *see also* Government debt

Default, on corporation bonds, 219; governments in, 249, 444

Deflation of long-term assets, 134

Deferred exchange, 6 ff., 12 ff., 21, 43, 85 ff.; labor for money, 18; dependability in, 54; consumer promises, 55 ff.; instalment purchasing, 64; compulsion by State, 71, 89, 384; in antiquity, 72; rent, 73 ff.; miscalculation of resources, 87 f., 101; secured loan, 127; bonds, 128; kinds, 152; reserves, 160; in insurance, 183; as basis of modern enterprises, 201, 209; of government, 225 ff.; of gold for gold, 276; rhythmic change in volume, 406, 410; diminution in U. S. after 1929, 412; and business cycles, 416 ff.; fear of incompletion, 416 ff., 462; areas of activity, 422

Democracy, xxi, 238

Demosthenes, 182

Department stores, 56

Deposit-and-lending system, 142, 326

Deposit-banking, 64

Depression, xvi, 396; effect on labor, 102; mortgages, 113; purchasing power, 156; on bank loans, 157; on insurance companies, 187; responsibility of bankers, 215; a phase of business cycle: effects, 406; effect on exchanges, 412; length of, 448; *see also* Busines cycles

Detroit, automobile factory x, 16; banks closed, 131

Devaluation of money, 251, 342

Dictatorships, and property, 238; prices, 468

Dishonesty, as cause of bankruptcy, 36; corporate, 219, 476

Dismal science, ix, xiv

Dispossession of tenant, 84

485

payments in specie resumed, 341; exchange value of, and price movements, 357; exporting of, 471

Gold certificates, 176, 278, 279

"Gold clause decisions," 356 n

Gold Standard Act, 275, 276

Golden Bough, The, Sir J. G. Frazer, 406

Goldsmiths, 140, 326 f.

Government, compulsion by, 71, 82 ff., 89, 384; control of economic relationship, 140 n; banking and, 142, 330; is the people, 227, 233, 289, 467, 472; confused with State, 234; primary function, 235; power of taxation, 236 ff.; reliability, 240, 241, 248 ff., 472; relation to money, 251, 255, 287, 288, 302 ff., 315, 318 ff., 333; going off gold standard, 338 ff.; resume payments in specie, 341; crisis following inability to borrow, 351; ownership of wealth, 366 ff.; predepression loans to, 442; restrictions upon commerce, 463, 467, 471; control of prices, 468

Government bonds, 170, 225, 227, 232, 239

Government credit, allied to bank credit, 154

Government debt, 226, 231 n, 242 ff., 444; World War, 225, 249; of dictatorships, 238, 250; resources for payment of, 245, 474; defaulting nations, 249, 444; extinguishment of, 352

Government promises, 225 ff.; to banks, 128, 132; reasons for, 232 ff.; completion by compulsion, 240, 241, 244; identification of money with, 255 ff., 271 ff.; earliest paper, 330 ff.; factors governing ability to complete, 348; cancellation, 352

Great Britain, 94 n, 201 ff., 223, 249, 250, 251, 311, 326, 409, 410, 477

Greece, 139, 182, 197, 201 n, 202, 206, 323 n, 446; money, 263, 264, 308, 311, 325 n

Greek Commonwealth, Alfred Zimmern, 46 n

Greenbacks, 278, 279

Gresham, Sir Thomas, 289

Gresham's Law, 289, 290 n, 291, 315, 349, 353

Group enterprises, 200 ff.

Group ownership of wealth, 365, 367

Gyges, King, 306

H

Habit-forming, 30 n

Haiti, marketplace, 49

Hamburg, bank, 324, 326

Hamilcar Barca, 377

Hammurabi, 76, 95, 139, 323 n, 468

Handicraftsmen, first, 47

Henry, Patrick, 105

Hepburn, A. P., 329

Herodotus, 377

High finance, 196

History determined by trade, 44

Holland, enterprises, 208

Home capital, 58

Home Owners Loan Corporation, 109 n, 110

Home ownership, 371

Homer, 263, 265, 375

Honesty, 33, 69 ff., 80, 87, 89, 241, 478

Household capital, 373

Hudson Vehicular Tunnel, 230 n

Hughes, Charles Evans, 185

Human race, 42, 44, 69, 70; activities, ix ff., 12, 25, 33, 111

I

Ideal society, 457 ff., 466, 470 ff.

Ideas, economic, 472

Illiteracy, economic, xx, xxii ff. 470 ff.

Imagination, x ff.

Indexes, business, 397, 404 ff., 412

India, trade, 206

Indians, money, 264, 266 n, 267

Individuals, relationship with State, 233; rights of, 235; fulfillment of promises by, 247; participation in economic system, 478

Industry, relation with mortgage loans, 112

Inflation, 171, 319

Performance, past, 32
Phillips, Chester Arthur, **137**
Pirates, 205
Plautus, quoted, 367
Political managers, 360
Polo, Marco, 319
Pound, Arthur, 131 n
Pound, Roscoe, 71
Pound, weight in metal, **311**
Poverty, end of, 459
Powell, Ellis, 329
Prices, ratio of exchange with gold, 357; rise in, 343; lowered, 430; corporate, drop in, 440; effect of tariffs upon, 463; rigidity, 464; control by governments, 468
Priests, group ownership, 365
Producers, 50, 52
Production, 24, 33; excess, 43, 399, 459; machine, 53; part of deferred exchange in, 152; trends, 396 ff.; control by exchanges, 460
Production goods, 37 ff., 41
Professional services, 21
Profits, prices, and volume of exchanges, 464
"Promised money," 316; origin, 321, 328 ff.
Promises, and performance, 9 ff., 19, 23; role in production, 24 ff.; consumers, 55 ff.; over-extension, 60; compulsions behind, 69 ff.; short and long, 85 ff., 129; interdependence of, 86, 121, 123, 133, 162, 181, 229, 252; psychology of, 89 ff., 104; dependence of activity upon, 113; fulfillment lies in custom, 117; made to and by banks, 123, 129; "on demand" exchanges, 124; performance and non-performance, 135 ff.; used as money, 138 ff., 147, 255 ff., 271 ff.; 336; for promises, 152; of individuals and governments, 159 ff.; of central bank, 175; government, 177, 225; insurance companies, 182 ff.; importance of honesty, 240, 241; available resources, 240, 245; completion by compulsion, 240, 241, 244; connection between U. S. money system,

282; the final resource of rulers, 316; factors involved in promised money and deferred exchanges, 347 ff.; cancellation of government debt, 352; appraisal of ability to complete, 380; well-being of society determined by volume of, 390 ff.; and business cycles, 406 ff., 416 ff.; areas of activity, 422; liquidation, 449; in ideal society, 458 ff.
Promissary note, 167
Property, 258, 368; attitude of rulers toward, 236; ownership, 363 ff.; public, 366; *see also* Wealth
Prosperity, 407, 408, 435, 453
Public opinion, xx
Purchase and sale transactions, 3 ff.
Purchasing power, 58, 156, 157

Q

Quick assets and liabilities, 428

R

Railroads, 198, 200
Raminsky, Louis, 329, 330
Rating, 31
Ready Detector, The, 146, 330
Real estate, 105, 108 ff., 130; *see also* Mortgages
Recession in business cycle, 407, 435, 448, 453
Record of sales, 33
Records, xiv
Recovery, business, 408, 450
Rediscounting, 167
Reflation, monetary, 251
Regulated Companies, 206
Reichsmark, 354
Relinquishment of property, 26 ff.
Renaissance, money, 325 n
Rent, 69 ff., 103, 152, 437, 442
Reorganization committees, 220 n
Repossession clause, 373
Representative money, 284
Republics, economic, 197
Research, economic, 461
Reserve Banks and the Money Market,

T

Tariffs, 463, 471
Taxation, 236 ff., 245, 349
Tenant and landlord, 75 ff., 81, 84
Territory, opened, 106
Thucydides, 466
Time-deposits, 144 n, 190, 191
Time-lapse in promises, 85
Tobacco as money, 264
Token money, 284, 308 n, 318, 320
Trade and trading, 37 ff., 413; Jews in international, 141; history, 201 ff.; restrictions upon, 463, 467, 471
Translations from the Chinese, Christopher Morley, 272
Transport, 53
Treasury notes, 225
Troy, wealth, 265, 376
Truth, xxii, 3 ff.

U

Underwriting bonds, 214
United States, Department of Commerce, Retail Credit Survey, 65, 67; Government takes over mortgages, 109; gold certificates, 176; no control over insurance, 189; corporations and their business, 200, 216, 217, 219; valuation of wealth in, 217; debt, 226, 444; war loans, 249, 250; currency manipulation, 251; right to issue paper money, 333; financial statistics, 1929-35, 412
Utensils as money, 262, 264

V

Via Saleria, 46
Voting rights, 218
Voyages, speculative, 202, 205 ff.

W

Wages and salaries, 12 ff., 412, 425
Wampum beads, 267
Warfare, economic and military, xvi, 458, 471; seizure of wealth, 315; *see also* World War
Wash sales, 344
Washington, George, 105
Wealth, created by labor, 17 n; forms of, 37; custodianship, 193; hoarding, 141; represented by bonds, 229
Wealth, ownership of, 363 ff.; by corporations, 217; common or group, 364, 367; by States, 366; change in conditions surrounding, 369; effect of promise system, 370; true vs. conditional ownership, 370, 382; by individuals, 370; by millionaires, 374, 379; in ancient times, 375, 380; protection, 379; forms in which owned: effects, 380; compulsion of payment, 384; dependence upon promises, 387, 388
Wealth of Nations, Adam Smith, 380
Weights and scales, 304
Well-being of society, 390 ff.; upward trend, 396 ff.
Wells, H. G., 10 n, 311
Wild-cat banks, 329
"Will of the people," 234, 288
Work, Wealth and Happiness of Mankind, H. G. Wells, 10 n
World War, aftermath, xvi; and agricultural prices, 99; money outlay, 225; national debts, 225, 249; origin, 360

Z

Zelie, Mademoiselle, 259
Zimmern, Alfred, 46 n